WRITING RESEARCH
PAPERS ACROSS
THE CURRICULUM

WRITING RESEARCH PAPERS ACROSS THE CURRICULUM

THIRD EDITION

Susan M. Hubbuch

Lewis and Clark College

Harcourt Brace College Publishers

Fort Worth Philadelphia San Diego New York Orlando Austin San Antonio
Toronto Montreal London Sydney Tokyo

Publisher	Ted Buchholz
Acquisitions Editor	Michael Rosenberg
Developmental Editor	Christine Caperton
Senior Project Editor	Charlie Dierker
Production Manager	Annette Dudley Wiggins
Art & Design Supervisor	Vicki McAlindon Horton
Text and Cover Design	Candice Swanson

Library of Congress Cataloging-in-Publication Data

Hubbuch, Susan M.
    Writing research papers across the curriculum / Susan M. Hubbuch.
—3rd ed.
      p. cm.
    Includes index.
    1. Report writing.   2. Research.   3. English language—Rhetoric.
4. Interdisciplinary approach in education.   I. Title.
LB2369.H83   1982
808'.02—dc20   91–20256
                                            CIP

ISBN: 0–03–054978–7

Address for Editorial Correspondence
Harcourt Brace College Publishers, 301 Commerce Street, Suite 3700,
Fort Worth, TX 76102

Address for Orders
Harcourt Brace & Company, 6277 Sea Harbor Drive, Orlando, FL 32887
1-800-782-4479, or 1-800-443-0001 (in Florida)

Printed in the United States of America

3   4   5   016   9   8   7   6   5   4   3

Cover Photo   Lamont Library, Harvard University; © Image Bank/Steve Dunwell

P R E F A C E

To My Student Readers

Since I pictured myself talking directly to you throughout this text as I take you, step by step, through the process of doing a research paper, here I need add only a few words about the way this book is set up.

It is very important for you to begin where I do, with the first two sections, because there I explain what a research paper is and show you how to set up your Researcher's Notebook. After that, it may occasionally be necessary for you to consult parts of this book in a different order from the one in which they are printed because different research projects have different requirements. But don't worry. The cross references and the table of contents should make it very easy for you to find exactly what you need when you need it. As you will discover, the term "research paper" can mean different things to different instructors. Thus in Section 5, I explain three basics types of research papers—primary research reports, reviews of the literature, and critical papers. Similarly, since instructors in different departments prefer different methods of documenting sources, I explain the basics of five modes of documentation. But I have tucked this mechanical information out of your way in appendixes at the end of the book; once you decide which form of documentation is appropriate for your paper (and I give you lots of help in making this decision) you can use a particular appendix as a mini style manual.

The most important thing to me is that you feel secure and confident every step of the way and, to give you the confidence you need, I explain each step in the process and give you a variety of strategies to use to accomplish each step. Because my suggestions and strategies come from years of working with students, I know they work, but you may not be totally convinced until you see them work for you. At first you may distrust some of my advice or find some of the strategies awkward. It is difficult to do things in a new way, especially when you are under the pressure of deadlines and grades. And you may not fully experience the benefits of my suggestions until you've used them in several research projects. It is for this reason that I've designed this guide so that you can use it while you are doing a paper for art history and use it again next year when you are doing a paper for economics. Instead of thinking about this book as a text to sell immediately at the end of the semester, I'd suggest you look upon it as a reference book to keep on a shelf with your dictionary and other handbooks.

To Teachers

There are multiple paradoxes involved in writing a guide for doing research papers, not the least of which is the anomalous position of "research paper" in the universe of discourse. Once it moves beyond the composition curriculum, "a research paper" becomes a discipline-specific mode of discourse, governed by the aims and conventions of that discipline or field. Thus it is very difficult, in one book, to prepare a student to write a meaningful analysis of a Shakespearean play using the interpretations of critics and a primary data study of the cost-effectiveness of a metropolitan transit system. My aim in this book has simply been to alert students to the existence of different kinds of research papers, with attendant differences in conventions, format, and documentation systems. Similarly, in a world of exponential increases in available information and day-by-day advances in computer technology, it is impossible to give students full and current information about all possible sources of information, or even all of the means of gaining access to such information.

These are some of the reasons that I have abandoned the approach of traditional textbooks on research papers, with their preoccupation with the mechanical and technical aspects of the task. But I have a more important reason for putting the emphasis on the researcher's experience of the research/writing process, a reason only partially inspired by the popularity of the "process" approach in the field of composition. The major impetus for this book came from, and its approach continues to be inspired by, my years of experience in working directly with students who are doing research papers for a variety of courses in various disciplines. These experiences have shown me that most of the problems we find in the final drafts of research papers have their roots in students' common (mis)conception of what a research paper is, which can be characterized as a bastardized encyclopedia article or review of the literature, or an attempt to let the teacher see that they have "looked into" (but not necessarily read and digested) a set number of books and articles on a topic. Thus my goal has been to change students' whole perception of the process, to turn them (in my language) from passive sponges into active detectives, so that they experience the intellectual challenges and satisfactions of true researching/writing. This objective underlies everything in this text, from the opening two sections, to the multiple strategies I offer, to the tone I have adopted of offering explanations along with suggestions rather than taking the directive "do this" stance. Thus I consider the most important elements of this text—both introduced in Section 2—to be the Researcher's Notebook and the strategy of giving direction to the process with a research question and a working hypothesis or thesis, open to modification as evidence is gathered.

I consider this text a self-contained guide that students can use on their own to take them through the process. But since the world of "research papers" is so large and because the experience of every researcher can vary so much, I have assumed that teachers would be available to offer necessary assistance. I have assumed that teachers would be available to give students the benefit of their knowledge, for example, about reference materials and specific sources that both space and my own ignorance prevent me from covering. Similarly, the appendixes are nothing more than introductions to four common documentation styles; they do not pretend to do more. There is no substitute for a style manual, and I believe a student's initiation into the research/writing process ought to include becoming aware that style manuals exist and using the appropriate manual for the task at hand. *Writing Research Papers Across the Curriculum* attempts to send this message to students. But I rely on teachers in disciplines whose styles I haven't covered to guide students to the appropriate manuals, and teachers in disciplines whose styles I do introduce to help their students use the proper manual to locate forms for those sources I have not had space to include.

In addition to forms for documenting sources, style manuals also cover matters related to the appearance of the manuscript itself—appropriate margins, modes of pagination, indentation and spacing of specific units of the text, layout for title pages, and the like. Given the focus of *Writing Research Papers Across the Curriculum*, I have limited my discussions of conventional styles to forms for documentation only. In Appendix F, subsection B, I make my own suggestions for manuscript form, but I urge students here and in Appendixes A through E to check with instructors on points that fall into the category of manuscript format. In preparing students to write research papers across the curriculum, teachers should be sure students know that recommendations for manuscript form can vary from style manual to style manual and, for this reason, instructors in various departments may well have differing expectations regarding the appearance of the final text.

On the other hand, manuscript and documentation forms are a small part of the larger picture. While it is important for students to recognize that there are standardized means of acknowledging sources and to use a standard form, I am far more concerned about the way students are stunted in their intellectual growth by continuing to write research papers that are little more than ill-digested regurgitations of what they have read. It is far easier to show students how to fix a reference list than it is to enable them to develop their own ideas by analyzing and synthesizing the work of others.

Thus the most important role I have envisioned for teachers is that of assisting students in the process of digesting material and crystallizing their thinking about their research question. In this process, there is only so much that printed words can do. There is no substitute for the responses of another human being, acting as a sounding board or partner in a brainstorming session, offering meaningful reader response to a draft, operating as a touchstone that the student can use to measure his or her actual progress toward a meaningful paper, and providing reassurances or those suggestions that only a specific draft can occasion.

Teachers who have used *Writing Research Papers Across the Curriculum* in the past will notice changes in this edition designed to refine and clarify further the aims and approaches that have characterized this text from its first publication. To enhance the usefulness of the sample papers as illustrative of ways actual authors put various conventions and principles into practice, I have augmented annotations of Elizabeth Cookson's "The Forgotten Women" and added comparable marginal notes to the other three papers. Since the Researcher's Notebook plays such a critical role in my conception of the research/writing process, I have elaborated in Section 2 on its purposes and have given more detailed descriptions of the four divisions. Section 5, "Writing Your Paper," has been subjected to rather radical surgery. Following a new introduction that addresses the issue of genres, the overview of the writing process consolidates strategies applicable to all types of papers; maps of the territory and abstracts/first drafts are now discussed here as strategies for working from whole to part, and emphasis is placed on writing for readers. These revisions and others in the first five sections are my continuing efforts to help students break free of formulaic concepts of research papers so that they can experience researching and writing as the intellectually exciting and challenging adventures they ought to be.

Many people have contributed directly and indirectly to the development of this text; to all of them I wish to express my gratitude for their time, energy, and encouragement. Recognition, first of all, must be given to the students I have worked with in the Lewis and Clark Writing Center. I want to give a special thanks to Jen Welsh, Sarah Jo Chaplen, and Karen McCracken, who have not only generously allowed me to reprint their papers, but who expended much of their own time in carefully revising their work. So many of my colleagues on the faculty and staff of Lewis and Clark have contributed to the development of this book over the years that space prevents my acknowledging them all by name, but I want to express my special appreciation to Jean Ward for her help with parts of this edition. I am grateful to the following colleagues for helpful review of the manuscript: Karen L. Abele, Northern Illinois University; Cora Agatucci, Central Oregon Community College; Arthur B. Coffin, Montana State University; Casey Gilson, Broward Community College—North Campus; Meredith J. Jones, Andrews University; and Nancy J. Mote, DeVry Institute of Technology. Finally, without the faith, attention, and efforts of the staff of Harcourt Brace Jovanovich, a third edition would not have appeared.

S.M.H.

CONTENTS

SECTION 3

Finding The Evidence   42

SECTION 4

Reading Critically and Taking Notes   84

S E C T I O N   5

Writing Your Paper   115

SECTION 6

How to and How Not to Incorporate Your Evidence into Your Paper   161

SECTION 7

Documenting Your Sources   193

Humanities Systems: The MLA Style   202

APPENDIX B
Humanities Systems: The Chicago Style 224

APPENDIX C

Scientific Systems: The APA Style   253

APPENDIX D

Scientific Systems: The Chicago Author-Date Style   272

APPENDIX   E

Scientific Systems: The Numbered Reference List Form

APPENDIX   F

The Final Manuscript of Your Paper

Four Sample Research Papers   305

WRITING RESEARCH PAPERS ACROSS THE CURRICULUM

S E C T I O N 1

What Is a Research Paper?

To many students, there is nothing more discouraging—or even frightening—than the words "you are required to do a research paper for this course." "Research paper" often conjures up a depressing picture of hours of frustration and mindless busywork. Not knowing where to begin or what to do, many students spend weeks fretting—and procrastinating. Finally, a few weeks before the paper is due, they drag themselves to the library, flip through the card catalogue, and copy an endless number of sentences from a few books. Back in their rooms, surrounded by an imposing pile of notes, they struggle to find a way to string *all* this information into some sort of paper that "flows."

- Have I just described some experiences you have had?
- Are you confused about how to go about doing a research paper?
- Are you discouraged by the grades you have gotten on research papers in the past?
- Are you tired of doing research papers that have not given you a sense of real personal accomplishment?

If your answer to any of these questions is yes, you should find this guide helpful. I have written it for anyone who feels frightened, confused, discouraged, or frustrated by research paper assignments.

A. How to Use This Guide

There is no magic formula for doing research and writing a paper using the research you have done. No two research projects that you do will be exactly alike. The subjects you investigate will vary, the purpose of the research will vary, the way you analyze your evidence will vary. The study you do of red-eyed fruit flies for your biology class will be different from the study you do of F. Scott Fitzgerald's novels for your literature class; the study you do of group communication processes for your communications class will be different from the study you do of seventeenth-century Dutch portraiture for your art history class.

My purpose in writing this guide is to help you develop a clear sense of direction and purpose when you set out to do a research project, regardless of the subject matter and the field in which you are working. If you do not feel that you know what you are doing, if you do not feel that you are in control of the whole research process, you will feel frustrated, discouraged, "lost." I want to allay your anxieties, to help you cut down *unnecessary* expenditures of time and energy, *unnecessary* frustration.

This section of the guide is devoted to an explanation of the general purpose and nature of research projects. *Don't* skip over it. If you want to have a clear sense of direction, a sense of control, you must understand what you are doing when you do a research project. I emphasize the word *research* here because the secret of an effective research *paper* is the *research process* that precedes it. The preparation you do at the beginning of the process can make all the difference between a paper that is really yours and a dull, pointless regurgitation of a few books and articles you find in the library. So you mustn't skip over this section of the guide, and you mustn't skip Section 2. But you should stop at the end of Section 2 and apply the techniques and suggestions I have laid out for you, using the actual research project you are doing for a class. Do not read over other sections in this guide until you are ready to begin those parts of your research project. Doing a research paper is a rather complex operation. But the one thing I want to avoid is having you become overwhelmed by the project. Instead of having you give up because the process is too complex, I want you to have a sense of control throughout the whole process so that you can eventually produce a paper that gives you a real sense of personal accomplishment. So I am using a problem-solving approach. Instead of tackling the major problem (writing a good research paper) in its entirety, we will break that major problem down into parts and tackle each part. This book is not a book *about* research papers; it is a *guide* to the *research process*.

My focus in this book is on you, the researcher, and what you should be doing at various points in the research process. Any technical information I have introduced (using the library, documentation forms) I have tried to introduce in ways that allow you to use the information when and where you need it. I have not tried to write a style manual. There are many style manuals and writing handbooks on the market that you can use in addition to this book if you need them.

B. *Overview: What Is a Research Paper?*

During the past few years I have worked with hundreds of students as they were doing research projects for history, communications, economics, biology, art history—for classes in almost every department on campus. One of the biggest problems that many of these students face is their notion of what research and research papers are; their notions are very distorted and inaccurate.

Let's get things straight. A research paper is *not*

- a mindless regurgitation of everything you have read about a subject;
- the reiteration of an argument you have found in a book or article, with a few other sources thrown in here and there to show your teacher that you "covered" the subject.

A researcher is *not* a passive sponge. As a researcher, you are not going to the library to absorb countless pieces of information that you will, when you write your paper, regurgitate for your instructor. If all you were supposed to do as a researcher was to reproduce what you read, wouldn't it be much easier to photocopy sections from the books and articles you read, staple them together, and give them to your instructor?

Actually, *you* are the most important element in your research paper. Your job is not simply to absorb information; your job is to digest information, to think about it, to determine what this information means *to you*. The paper you eventually write will focus on the thinking you have done about your subject.

A research paper is a report that an individual presents to others about the conclusions he or she has reached after investigating a subject and carefully assessing the information he or she has gathered.

If you are wondering what a research paper looks like, you need go no farther than the books and articles you will be reading on your topic. One secret to your success in doing your own research project is your recognition that books and articles are not records of "truth" or "facts." Fields such as history, economics, biology are not static bodies of knowledge in which everything to be known is known or in which everything that is considered to be known remains unquestioned. Quite the contrary. History, economics, biology, and other disciplines are best defined as groups of people working together to discover more about the object of their mutual interest, to explain the puzzles and problems that arise as they search for understanding. Historians, economists, biologists construct and reconstruct what they "know." Because members of a discipline work together, they spend a great deal of time talking to each other—exchanging information, telling each other about things they've uncovered, sharing their theories and views of a particular phenomenon, trying to convince each other that one way of interpreting certain evidence is superior to other interpretations. And a very common means they use to carry on these lively dialogues is to write books and articles for each other, the very books and articles you'll be reading. These published texts are really segments in a conversation that is still going on right now.

When an instructor asks you to do a research paper, he or she is inviting you to join one of the conversations in progress in his or her field. You shouldn't be intimidated by this fact. Your instructor realizes that there is a difference between you and experts in a field. Experts become experts through years of investigating and thinking about their subjects, through years of listening to and talking with their peers face to face, and by reading and writing. They have a sense of confidence that you may not feel right now. But this does not mean you have nothing to say. When an instructor asks you to do a research project, he or she is inviting you to experience what it feels like to be a professional. Doing a research project not only gives you the chance to learn about the problems the experts are puzzling over, but in doing a research project properly *you will be doing the very same thing* the experts do. Even if you aren't planning to major in the field in which you are taking a course, in doing a research paper you'll find out what the discipline is by thinking the way members of that field think. Doing a research paper properly allows you to strengthen the same skills that an expert uses when she sets out to investigate a subject. A research paper, then, is an invitation to sharpen your ability to think critically.

C. *Learning, Thinking, and Research Papers*

Since the seventeenth century, in Western culture the word "thinking" has become synonymous with the acts of observing, questioning, investigating, analyzing, and synthesizing. The scientific method has moved beyond the natural sciences into the study of human beings and society (thus the birth of the fields of psychology, political science, sociology, economics, communications). In the humanities—as you will become aware when you take courses in literature, history, philosophy—the emphasis is also on observing, questioning, investigating, analyzing, and synthesizing. This is what critical thinking means.

Critical thinking—*your* critical thinking—lies at the heart of any research project.

Thus, when you set out to research, you are setting up a process that involves

- asking questions;
- gathering as much information as possible on the subject in an effort to find answers to those questions;
- carefully and systematically judging the meaning of the information gathered, so you feel confident that the answer you have developed is a reasonable one.

D. *The Evidence*

A contractor cannot build a house without lumber, nails, pipes, electrical wiring—the physical materials of a building. You cannot develop an idea, a conception of the world, without concrete facts about the world. Depending upon the type of research project you are doing, the evidence you gather about your subject may be *primary* or *secondary*.

1. Primary Research Projects

In a primary research project a researcher sets out to gather his or her facts or evidence by going directly to the source itself. Thus, a chemist or nuclear physicist sets up an experiment in the lab to see exactly what happens when chemicals are mixed or when the atom is split. The archeologist goes directly to the place where people of an older civilization lived and begins to dig. The historian goes to the papers written by a great general or statesman or to the records kept by civil or church authorities. A philosopher wants to see the notebooks or letters of the philosopher he or she is studying. A businessperson carefully checks the annual reports of a company—and may even want to prowl around the factory and offices to observe their operations.

2. Secondary Research Projects

When doing a secondary research project, researchers concentrate on the conversations the experts are having about the work they've done. These researchers read others' research papers—published as books and articles and housed in libraries so that they are accessible to all—in order to educate themselves about the problems, proposed solutions, points of view that people in the field are talking about. In these books and articles the researchers find the conclusions (theories, hypotheses) others have developed, the investigations they've done, the facts or evidence they've discovered and used.

Experienced researchers do a combination of primary and secondary research. Because they want their own work to be a meaningful contribution to the common enterprise they are engaged in with their peers, they carefully study the work that their peers publish. For example, psychologists who want to test their own theories about short-term memory by setting up an experiment (a primary research project) will carefully study the experiments that other psychologists have developed. The researchers will carefully examine the experiment themselves (the precise mode of testing; the number of the subjects; the identity of the subjects in terms relevant to the study, for example, gender, age, educational level, and so on), as well as the data that were collected and the way in which the data were measured. The researchers are thinking critically when they read the work of other experts. When you look at the work others have done, you, too, must always think critically. What type of facts is the author using? Where did these facts come from? Are you aware of facts that the author didn't use? How does the author interpret the facts? What is the author's argument? Is this argument reasonable?

To make these decisions, the researchers are also gathering facts directly from the source and putting them together in a way that makes sense to them. Thus researchers also use *primary sources,* either by setting up their own studies or experiments, or by doing their own careful study of the object of their research, such as the novels of F. Scott Fitzgerald or the writings of Voltaire or congressional debates on a particular bill.

3. Classifying Evidence

The evidence you uncover can be classified in one of three categories:[1]

a. Facts

Facts are pieces of information that can be objectively observed and measured, like

- the size and chemical composition of rocks found on the moon;
- the standardized test scores of specific students at a specific school in a given year;
- the number of images related to the sun in Shakespeare's *Richard II*.

b. Inferences

Inferences are statements "about the unknown made on the basis of the known."[2]

A conclusion drawn by an expert—for example, a statement that "busing increases the academic performance of minority students"—is an inference. The researcher cannot have studied the academic records of *every* minority student who has ever been bused to another school. His or her statement—about *all* bused minority students—is based on a study of *some* minority students who were bused. His or her conclusion is *not* a statement of truth; it is a *hypothesis* that may or may not be valid. Similarly, a statement like "Richard's fall and the usurpation of Bolingbroke emphasize between them the necessity of the political qualities for the successful exercise of kingship" is also an inference.[3] Observing certain elements of Shakespeare's *Richard II*, the critic Derek Traversi has reached this conclusion about the meaning of Shakespeare's play. It is not a statement about *the* meaning of the play, since the play contains many features that can be interpreted in a variety of ways, depending upon the point of view of a particular critic.

---

[1] I am using the categories of S. I. Hayakawa as they are set out in *Language in Thought and Action,* 4th ed. (New York: Harcourt Brace Jovanovich, 1978), 33–38.

[2] Hayakawa, *Language in Thought and Action,* 35.

[3] Derek Traversi, "The Historical Pattern From *Richard II* to *Henry V,*" in *Shakespeare, the Histories: A Collection of Critical Essays,* ed. Eugene M. Waith, Twentieth-Century Views (Englewood Cliffs, N.J.: Prentice-Hall, 1965), 105.

Traversi's statement is his inference of the meaning of a variety of elements he has observed in the play.

c. Judgments

Judgments are, in Hayakawa's words, "expressions of the writer's approval or disapproval of the occurrences, persons, or objects he is describing."[4]

Statements like "Busing harms students" or "*Daniel Deronda* is George Eliot's weakest novel" are judgments. They are statements about the writer's personal feelings about a subject.

Making inferences and judgments is the natural function of a human mind. Facts in and of themselves are meaningless. What difference does it make that the temperature outside is 23°F or that there are forty references to the sun in *Richard II*? Such facts simply "are" until a human mind operates on them and makes some type of meaning out of them. Reacting to the thermometer that reads 23°F, one person may say, "It's cold out there; I'd better wear my hat and gloves." Another person may say, "Perfect skiing weather." The fact—the temperature of the air—has been interpreted by each of these people to "mean" something according to the mental sets and needs of these two people.

Researchers gather facts to test, to reassess their inferences about a subject. Researchers also carefully examine the inferences and judgments of others to determine for themselves whether these inferences or hypotheses about the world seem reasonable.

E. Evaluating Evidence

Researchers and writers use numerous ways to put facts together to create meaning. In academic circles, a field is called a *discipline* to alert us to the fact that, in a field, material is studied in a systematic, "disciplined" fashion. If our goal is eventually to discover some truths about our world, about human beings, about societies and cultures, we need to avoid, as best we can, our own biases and prejudices, the idiosyncrasies of our own minds. Thus, we look for some systematic, objective way to assess and examine facts. Based upon their goals, the objects of their investigation, and their histories, various disciplines work out their own procedures for testing theories and assessing evidence. The pure and applied sciences, for example, prefer empirical modes of testing, modes that rely on mathematical models and/or

[4] Hayakawa, *Language in Thought and Action*, 37.

the use of instruments. The humanities, on the other hand, analyze texts and ideas by applying certain standards of logic or interpretation. As you make your way through the college curriculum, you'll be introduced to those specific methods generally accepted in particular fields.

In developing your research project, you will have to select some systematic method of analyzing the evidence you gather. Otherwise, you may end up simply *rationalizing* or *justifying* one of your opinions. Justification and rationalization are the antithesis of the whole purpose of research, which is actually to open one of your inferences or judgments to objective testing.

Whether you are doing a primary research project (setting up an experiment or study) or a secondary research project (in which you will be relying heavily on the work already done by experts in a field), you will still be working the way experts work. You are obliged to gather as much evidence as possible about your subject, and you are obliged to use a method of testing or assessing the evidence that is considered appropriate to the field in which you are working. In short, in doing your research project, you will constantly be using your brain—questioning, searching, weighing, assessing, drawing inferences of your own, and critically examining the inferences of others.

F. Summary

By this point, it should be obvious that you cannot see a researcher as a passive sponge, mindlessly soaking up the ideas and facts set forth by others. In reality, research demands constant mental alertness and a critical frame of mind. The work of a researcher resembles that of a detective. Researchers set out to find a solution to an intellectual puzzle or mystery. Like good detectives, they are always asking questions, always alert to the possibility that the smallest piece of information may be a central clue. They look in the most unlikely places for evidence, always trying to put clues together toward a satisfactory solution. Their work is not easy. They do run into dead ends. Clues are not handed to them on a silver platter. Researchers are constantly arranging and rearranging evidence until it falls into some meaningful pattern.

So before you begin a research project, you must think of yourself as a **detective.** The mystery is not going to solve itself. *You* must find and develop a solution.

There is, however, one major difference between you and Sherlock Holmes. Sherlock Holmes usually comes up with *the correct* solution to the mystery. But it is unlikely that you—or any researcher—will find *the* correct solution. As Milton says of truth, "Yet it is not impossible that she may have more shapes than one."

Your quest is not for *the* solution, *the* final truth. Your quest is for *a* solution, *an* answer that the evidence points to. Your evidence is going to point the way to your conclusion. The individual who seeks only the evidence that supports his or her original assumption and disregards the rest is not a researcher but a rationalizer, an ostrich burying his or her head further into the sand.

Now that you understand the major purpose and aims of a researcher, where do you begin?

SECTION 2

Where Do I Begin?

A. *Some Opening Remarks . . .*

Most students think that the first step in a research project is to run to the library. If this is the first thing you normally do, perhaps you remember that once you get there you usually wander about for hours trying to figure out where to start.

The successful research project begins at home. The smart researcher begins with himself or herself.

I must stop here to interject a warning that you have probably heard so many times that you are sick of hearing it. But I must repeat it:

You must begin your research project early.

The researcher needs *time to research.* Your search for facts and evidence will lead you into dead ends and into highways and byways that you cannot predict when you begin. You must give yourself plenty of time to find everything you need.

The researcher needs *time to think.* As you gather your evidence, you must think about it. You must mull over what you have discovered, push the facts this way and that, decide what further evidence you need. You will constantly be formulating ideas and discarding them.

One weekend is certainly not enough time; nor is one week, or even two. This is my advice:

- Set up a work schedule for yourself, working backward from the date on which the paper must be given to your instructor. In subsection I at the end of this section you will find a handy work sheet on which you can record these deadlines:

- ○ due date.
- ○ date on which final, polished draft will be done. I'd suggest one to three days before the due date, depending upon the time needed to type and proofread the final typed copy. If you are having someone else type your final paper, you must be realistic about typists' schedules, and you need to allow enough time for you to proofread the typed copy *and* take it back to the typist for corrections. If you are typing the final copy yourself, be realistic about your typing skills and speed, and leave yourself sufficient time to proofread and correct the typed copy. If you are doing your drafts on a word processor, your schedule won't be quite so tight, but you need to leave sufficient time to proofread the final version carefully and make any necessary corrections.
- ○ date on which your first rough draft will be finished. This date is dependent upon the length and complexity of your paper and the amount of work you have to do for your other classes between this point and the due date. I'd suggest a date no later than two to two-and-a-half weeks before the due date, and you should allow yourself more time if the paper is going to be longer than ten pages.
- ○ date to begin your first rough draft. This date is also the target date for having the major part of your research completed; for those of you doing primary research projects, this is the date on which you will have all the necessary results and data from your study or experiment in your hands. I'd suggest no later than three weeks before the paper is due, perhaps earlier if your paper is more than ten pages.
- ○ date to begin work on the research project: when the assignment is given!

- ● Once you have set the deadlines above and developed your research strategies, you will be able to—and should—set deadlines for yourself for intermediate steps in the process. If you are doing a secondary research project, you should set deadlines for such things as gathering your first list of sources from indexes and bibliographies, having certain books and articles read, doing interviews, and the like. If you are doing a primary research project, it is crucial for you to set a number of deadlines: when your research design will be complete; when you will put together your apparatus or find your subjects or pass out your questionnaires; when you will run the experiment or study itself; and so on.

- Plan to devote an hour or two *every day* to this project. If you follow the steps laid out in the first four sections of this book, working on this project in small units of time won't be that difficult.

If you space your work out over weeks and even months, rather than trying to cram it into a concentrated period of time, you allow your brain to do its work—and your brain is the secret to a good research project.

Before you begin to gather evidence, there are three major decisions you need to make:

- You must decide *which idea* (working hypothesis/thesis) you are going to test.

- You must decide *how* you are going to test that hypothesis/thesis.

- You must develop a research strategy, a plan of action for finding your facts and evidence.

B. Step 1: The Researcher's Notebook

The first thing you need to do when you begin a research project is to buy a notebook that will be your Researcher's Notebook for this research project. Your Researcher's Notebook is probably the most important part of your research project. In it you will keep an ongoing record of what you need to do; more importantly, in it you will keep an ongoing record of your thinking about your topic as you do your investigation.

Consider this Notebook a strategy designed to help you write a successful paper. Nothing about the Researcher's Notebook is set in stone. Divide it up the way I suggest, or create your own divisions. What's important is that you understand the purposes it serves. The first purpose—more obvious in my first two divisions—is comparable to the function of those planner/organizer notebooks so popular today. It's a central place to direct and plan your investigation. The Researcher's Notebook's second purpose—and its more important one—is found in the last two divisions. It is a journal of what is happening in your mind as you examine your evidence.

1. The **Sources section** is simply a place *to keep a list* of books, articles, and other sources that have the potential for providing the evidence you need. Here you will write out complete citations for the books, journal articles, documents, and newspaper stories you find in indexes, abstracts, on-line computer searches (you'll learn more about reference materials when you get to Section 3). If you decide to do interviews, this is a good place to jot down the names, addresses, and phone

numbers of people you want to interview; you should also note the dates of the interviews. You need to keep a record of full bibliographic information for promising books and articles because you won't always have time to locate them when you come across information about them. Keeping a list of sources in one place makes it less likely that you will forget about, or misplace essential information about, a book or article or document you want to look at. When you are ready to locate these sources, you will be assured you have all the information you'll need to do so. The Sources section is just a labor-saving device; it will save you unnecessary frustration, too.

2. The **Research Strategy section** contains *lists of things to do.* You may want to subdivide it into several sections. The first page of the Research Strategy division of your Notebook would be a good place to record your various deadlines (see 2.I). Another subdivision should be devoted to writing out the research questions suggested by your working hypothesis/thesis and various places to check in your quest to answer them (see 2.F). There are any number of ways you could lay out this subdivision: questions on the left-hand page, places to look for answers straight across on the right-hand page; questions separated by lines left blank so that you can fill in places to look for answers; questions in one color of ink, places to look for answers in another.

You should probably reserve another part of this division for a miscellaneous ongoing list of things you need to do. These are the types of items that might appear on such a list:

- ○ See if Reed College has a copy of Browning's book.
- ○ Make a list of books to request on interlibrary loan—and put in those requests!!!!
- ○ Ask Prof. Smith for names of people I could talk to at the Boys and Girls Society.
- ○ Find a color reproduction of *Afternoon on Grande Jatte*—check shadows.
- ○ Find out about Bahai—some encyclopedia of religion?
- ○ Read Wilson's book NOW!!!

3. In the **Reading section** you will *freewrite*[1] about the reading you are doing *as* you look at various books and articles. Please note that you will *not* be recording the evidence itself in your Researcher's Notebook.

---

[1] Freewriting is a means of talking to yourself on paper, a means of recording what is happening in your mind as you are mulling over an idea. Freewriting is a very loose, unstructured mode of writing. When you freewrite, use abbreviations that you are comfortable with, and don't worry about correctness (grammar, spelling, sentence structure); all you need to worry about is putting down enough on paper so that you know what the words mean.

Your evidence or data will be recorded on notecards or computer printout sheets—some means that make the evidence or data easy to review and manipulate (see Section 4.A). In the Reading section of your Notebook you will be writing about *your reactions* to the conclusions of other experts and the ways in which they have reached their conclusions. Here you will be asking, and answering, questions like What do I think of this author's work? What are his/her conclusions? What methods did he/she use to test these conclusions? How does this study compare to others? What facts did this expert use? Am I aware of facts that this author didn't use? Do I fully understand the argument a particular author is making? You'll find samples of such entries when you reach Section 4, "Reading Critically and Taking Notes."

4. The **Working Hypothesis/Thesis section** of your Notebook is the most vital one. The rest of this book is premised on the assumption not only that you will keep this journal of your thinking but also that your work in this section—and in the Reading section—is your assurance that your own thinking will remain the core of this whole project. It is in this section that you should use the strategies laid out in the next three steps of the process. Once you have a working hypothesis/thesis and start testing it, you should return to this part of your Notebook every few days, writing to yourself about what you are thinking at each stage about the accuracy of your working hypothesis/thesis, about whether it is the "right" answer to your initial research question. If your research project is going to change direction, it is here that you will make that discovery and here that you will decide which new direction to take. If you decide that your original thesis is not "right," it is here that you will rewrite it to fit your current thinking. In this section of your Notebook you should talk to yourself, honestly and specifically, about whatever comes to your mind when you focus on the puzzle or mystery you've decided to "solve." Jot down any ideas related to your topic that pop into your mind. Write down any questions floating around in your head, no matter how silly or farfetched they may seem. Talk to yourself about confusions you are experiencing and tell yourself what you need to do to clear up these confusions. Use this section of your Notebook to carefully fit parts of the puzzle together.

    There are no real rules for a journal of one's thinking—except that, when you write here, you need to be thinking. It would be a good idea frequently to devote a whole entry to your answers to these questions: What picture is emerging from the evidence I already have? How does it compare with my original hypothesis/thesis? What areas of the emerging picture are still fuzzy for me? What information do I need to make them clearer? Should I revise my working hypothesis/thesis? What *should* it say?

Here's a sample of what an entry made several weeks into the research process could look like:

I came into this project convinced that an open classroom was the best environment for kids' learning. Now I'm not so sure. Ramirez, Wilhelm, and Kim all stress how important it is for children to have structure. So—what's the story? A completely free environment in which kids do what they feel like doing when they feel like doing it or a version of military school? There has got to be something in the middle. OK, let's start with structure. What does that mean? If I am understanding what I've been reading, these experts are saying that children need . . . what? (1) a sense of what is appropriate and inappropriate behavior, (2) they need to know what kinds of tasks they are expected to do and when they should hand them in, (3) they need to know how to go about doing these tasks. Do students need to sit in rows of desks facing the teacher, never talking unless asked a question by the teacher, to have these kinds of structure? NO. Children talking to each other doesn't have to be classified as inappropriate behavior. In fact, Hashimoto and DeMartino both say that kids learn best when they work in groups. But they do need to be told HOW to work in groups. There's the structure. I'm cooking. Let's go on with this.

I cannot emphasize too much how important it is for you to *use* your Researcher's Notebook constantly throughout the research process. If you want to break the "passive sponge" syndrome and take control of your research process, you must keep a *written* record of what is happening in your head. If you do not jot down ideas that pop into your head, you forget them. If you try to work out a complex idea in your head, you may soon become confused and overwhelmed. Write out these ideas; putting them down on paper will give you the chance to look at them and decide what is right and what is wrong. I've seen too many students get so befuddled by trying to work out their ideas just in their heads that they give up all hope of ever sorting out what they really think. Don't let this happen to you.

If you continually write in your Researcher's Notebook *as* you do your research, you will find that you are actually doing the important groundwork for your final paper. You are discovering what *you* want to say about your subject. When the time comes to start drafting your final paper, you will realize that an important part of the writing process has already occurred.

Once you have purchased your Researcher's Notebook, you are ready to set up your research project.

C. Step 2: Deciding on the Research Question/Assumption That You Are Going to Test

As you take various courses in college, you will find that the conditions set up for your research projects will vary. In some classes your professors will give you a list of possible areas of investigation. In other classes the professor will outline the type of investigation you should undertake; she may, for example, tell you that your task is to design and carry out a study in which you observe some specific way in which people use nonverbal communication, or she may instruct you to focus on the connection between the rituals of a particular culture and the underlying values of that culture. In other classes the instructor will leave it up to you to choose both the area of investigation and the method of testing your hypothesis/thesis.

In some classes you will feel comfortable selecting a topic for your research because you are familiar with the material. In other classes you may be very ill equipped to choose a topic because you know very little about the course material.

In the next few pages I will provide some strategies for selecting your area of investigation because, as you may well have discovered firsthand, selecting a topic is a critically important part of the research process; it can make all the difference in the quality of the paper you eventually write. But you cannot afford to spend weeks making the decision; every minute you waste flitting from one possible topic to another is a minute you could have spent researching.

One way to take some of the fear and anxiety out of the need to commit yourself to a topic is to see your topic as a "point of departure" rather than an "end point." Many students are in the habit of selecting a topic on the basis of their perception of the amount of information available about the subject. Their thinking goes something like this: "I have to write a ten-page paper. Ten pages is a lot of pages to be filled. I'll write about computers because I know that there are lots of books and articles in the library on computers." Let's consider the basic problem with this line of reasoning. The student who is thinking this way is really saying to herself: "If I had to write a ten-page research paper for this class *today*, I would have a very difficult time filling up ten pages because I do not know much about the material." But every researcher feels this way. If I had to write my conclusions about a subject *before* I researched the subject, before I thought carefully about the subject, I would have a difficult time filling up ten pages. What students often forget is that between the time they choose a topic and the time they write the final paper, they will have gathered quite a bit of evidence about the topic, regardless of what the topic is, and they will have generated all kinds of ideas about the subject. If you do your research properly, more likely than not, when it comes time to write your paper, you will wish that you had more than ten pages to discuss your conclusions. All of us experience the anxiety of "how can I write this paper?" when we begin a research project. The best antidote is to get on with the actual business of selecting your topic and using a more reasonable criterion for making that choice.

Because you are committing yourself to spending a great deal of your time and energy on the research process, you should be thinking in these terms: What do I want to know more about? What am I personally interested in investigating in some depth? What subject is important enough to me that I need to spend time and energy learning more about it?

Regardless of the form a research assignment takes, you will use this criterion for selecting your area of research:

Choose a subject in which you have some type of *personal investment.*

If you want to produce a research paper that gives you a sense of personal satisfaction, you must begin the research process by selecting a subject/topic that has some *personal meaning or importance to you.* You must select a subject/topic that *you* want to know more about.

If at this point you respond that nothing really grabs your interest or that you are too ignorant of the material to know what might interest you, here are some strategies you can use to overcome these obstacles. Do not put it off. Get out your Researcher's Notebook and start writing out your answers to these questions in the Working Hypothesis/Thesis section:

- Think about the reasons you had for taking this class:
  - What did I expect to learn in this course?
  - What did I assume the textbook or the teacher would say about the material?
  - What questions do I have now about the material?
  - What do I look forward to learning about?
  - Have any issues been raised in class that I want to pursue further?

- Have I had any contact with this subject before?
  - Is the subject related to material I've studied in other classes?

○ Have I read about this material in magazines or newspapers? What have I learned?

○ Have I heard anything about the subject on the radio or TV? What have I heard?

○ Has this subject come up in conversations I've had with others? What was said?

● Is the material in this course related *in any way* to subjects I already know quite a bit about? Don't neglect the obvious. If you are interested in rock music, and one subject covered in your course is baroque music, research in baroque music would deepen your understanding of music in general.

● Take out your textbook, your course syllabus, and, if your instructor has provided one, the list of topics for this paper. Look them over.

○ What particular subjects attract me?

○ What have I enjoyed learning about, or what do I look forward to learning about?

● If, in the course you are taking, you are dealing directly with primary materials—art objects, pieces of music, poems and novels, or the writings of people important in the field (Darwin's *Origin of Species*, Machiavelli's *The Prince*)—go directly to these primary sources. Acquaint yourself with them.

○ Do any of these works catch my interest?

○ Would I like to see more paintings by one particular artist? Would I like to read more poems by one of the poets? Would I like to read one of the primary sources, like Darwin's *Origin*, more carefully than class time will allow?

Do not simply look over these questions. If you expect to find a topic for your research paper that truly interests you, you must write out your answers to these questions. The questions are here to give you a place to start exploring, to discover that area of the course's subject matter that you want to pursue further on your own. At this point it does not matter if you feel you don't know much about the subject that interests you. The important issue here is choosing an area of investigation about which you have some personal need or desire to increase your knowledge. Without that personal involvement, the research process is probably going to be a dreadfully boring process that you will hate and resent. Without that personal involvement, you will never feel the curiosity and thirst for knowledge that drives the experienced researcher forward.

D. Step 3: Formulating Your Research Question/Assumption

Once you zero in on a subject or area that you want to know more about, the next step is stating your topic. Perhaps you are used to expressing research topics in simple phrases like "the causes of the Civil War" or "sun imagery in *Richard II*" or "the importance of nonverbal behavior in communication." Perhaps you've already discovered that such phrases aren't very helpful in giving you a clear sense of direction in your research. They map out an area in which you can gather information, but they don't express *your* personal involvement or interest in the material.

From now on out, therefore, I will not talk about "topics"; instead, I will talk about research questions, assumptions, working hypotheses/theses. These terms refer to full grammatical statements (complete sentences and questions), and you will be expressing your area of interest in these full grammatical statements.

The *research question* is the specific question you have about your material; the *assumption* is your answer to that question, the answer you assume is the answer you will find *before* you begin your research. In Step 4 in this section we will refine your assumption into a *working hypothesis/thesis,* a statement of your assumption that can be tested. It doesn't matter if you are fairly certain that your assumption is not correct. You will be turning it into a question anyway.

In the Working Hypothesis/Thesis section of your Researcher's Notebook, write out your assumption and your research question. If you have more than one assumption, or more than one question, write them all out.

Here are some examples of research questions and assumptions:

Assumption	Research question
In the winter I take lots of vitamin C because I've been told that vitamin C helps you fight off colds and flu.	Do large doses of vitamin C help the body fight off colds and flu? Is there any scientific evidence that vitamin C in large quantities actually counteracts viruses or bacterial infection?
In class we've talked about differences between males and females. From listening to my brother and his male friends and comparing	Is there a difference in the ways males and females talk? Do they use different vocabularies? Do they talk about different things?

Assumption

their talks with the conversations I have with my girlfriends, I'd say there is even a difference in the ways males and females talk.

When I drive to and from school, I notice that houses in some of the rundown parts of town are being fixed up. There must be a reason that people are sinking good money into these dumps.

I've seen a lot of Western movies on TV; I love them. We haven't talked much about cowboys, Indians, and the Cavalry in this U.S. history class, but I wonder if cowboys and Indians were really like the cowboys and Indians in these movies. I'd guess the movies aren't very accurate.

Yesterday in our international law class we got onto the topic of environmental issues that cross nation-state boundaries: industries in one country dumping pollutants into rivers that another country uses for drinking water; acid rain (U.S.-Canada); global warming. Evidently there is no international organization that has the power to establish, and enforce, international environmental policies. There ought to be!

Research question

Why are people spending money to fix up these old houses? Are they living in them? Are people fixing up old houses only in Portland, or is this happening elsewhere? What are the economics of this kind of urban renewal? Are there tax incentives? Are governments (local, federal) providing financial help?

Are Western movies accurate? Do they portray the way things actually were in the Wild West?

Why isn't there an international organization to establish and enforce environmental policies? Aren't environmental problems considered important enough? Does it have to do with issues of national sovereignty?

Assumption	*Research question*
I've been disgusted by what I've read about Warren G. Harding in our U.S. Politics class. He was a terrible president.	Why do I say that Warren G. Harding was a terrible president?
Lots of adults are turned off by rock music; they say it's just noise. As far as I'm concerned, rock music is *music*. The Beatles are as good as Beethoven.	Is rock music, music? Were the Beatles good composers? Could they be compared to Beethoven?
My prof says that Dickens' novels were published sections at a time over many months, in magazines. That's probably why they are *so* long. I wonder if he wrote the whole novel first, or if he was still composing it after sections were published. If he wrote in sections, I wonder how he kept the plots and characters straight. I'd imagine that an author who writes a novel as it is being published writes differently from an author who writes a whole novel, then publishes it.	How did Dickens write his novels? The whole novel at once, or as it was being published? Did anybody else publish novels in magazines? Why? If Dickens wrote his novels as they were being published in parts, did he write differently from an author who composes the whole novel first, then publishes it?
Most diet foods and drinks now use a new artificial sweetener. They say it's safer than saccharine. Now that I've had some chemistry courses, I wonder if I could understand what these artificial sweeteners actually are and why they are sweet. I'd like to know why aspartame is safer than saccharine.	What is the chemical compound called saccharine? What is the chemical makeup of aspartame? How are they different? Why is this new compound safer than saccharine? How do chemists go about developing artificial products like these sweeteners? What problems do they run into? Will all the new information we now have about DNA and RNA help scientists to make artificial products like these?

In doing a research project for some classes, you may find that it is easy to come up with a list of assumptions/research questions that you'd like to pursue. But in other courses you may find that your sense of your ignorance of the subject matter stops you cold. You may find yourself saying, "How can I write my assumptions about what I will find when I know almost nothing about this material?" "Maybe I'd like to investigate the Crusades, but I'd be starting from scratch. I don't even know what the Crusades were." "I've heard this term *behaviorism* a few times, but what is it?" "Black holes sound intriguing. What are they?"

In those cases in which you find that your knowledge of a subject is so meager that all you can say is, "I'd like to know more about X, but what is X?" you will have to do some basic preliminary reading before you can formulate your assumption and research question.

There are two strategies you can use to find an assumption/research question in a subject about which you feel very ignorant:

- If you find yourself saying, "I'd like to know more about X, but what is X?" begin to educate yourself by reading material that is meant to be an introduction to the topic:

  ○ read about X in your course textbook or any textbook that introduces the subject.
  ○ read about X in a book that is designed to be an introduction to X. Ask a librarian to help you, or browse in the bookstore. Read the author's preface to find out whether the book is intended for novices.
  ○ read about X in an encyclopedia. A specialized encyclopedia or dictionary may be more helpful than a general encyclopedia (see sections 3.F.1 and 3.F.4).

- Browse in the library. Go to the section of the library where recent issues of magazines, journals, and newspapers are displayed. In articles in these periodicals the experts are talking about what they consider the most interesting research questions and areas of investigation in their fields. Look for articles on issues or subjects you are studying in your course. You may want to look specifically for periodicals in the field that are authoritative but accessible (see section 3.E). As you browse, you are looking for articles you want to read because they interest you. The article may suggest a research question you'd like to use as your research question, or the subject matter of the article could be a subject you'd like to investigate further.

But don't turn into a passive sponge now. Even as you are doing this preliminary reading, read critically. In your Researcher's Notebook, record questions that pop into your head. Write down assumptions that you are making about what you will find as you read further. Be particularly alert to any associations you find yourself making between this material and knowledge you already have.

Once you have your research question/assumption, you are ready for the next step, which is to refine your assumption into a working hypothesis/thesis.

E. Step 4: Formulating Your Working Hypothesis/Thesis

Remember that the whole research process—the activities you will be engaged in during the coming weeks—is a process of *testing* assumptions that you are making now. You are not committing yourself to proving your initial assumptions correct. Indeed, your attitude toward your current thinking should be quite the opposite. Instead of saying to yourself, "I already have the right answer," your stance needs to be, "How valid are my present views?"

Testing ideas—opening them up to systematic, objective analysis—is the key to research. In fact, the readers of your final paper will not be judging your work simply on the conclusion you finally draw. They will be far more concerned about the way you drew that conclusion; they will be far more interested in your testing procedures and the way you analyzed your evidence. As they read your paper, these are the questions they will be asking:

- Is this researcher actually testing the hypothesis he said he was testing?
- Does this researcher's final conclusion rest upon legitimate, relevant data?
- Do I consider the reasoning in this paper to be logical, valid?
- Has this researcher found and considered all the important evidence?

You are beginning this research project with assumptions you are making to assure yourself that your own thinking will be the heart of the process. If you don't start with your assumptions, you don't really have anything to critically analyze, assess, and examine. Your assumptions give you something concrete to test. At this stage you are going to turn your initial assumptions into one considered statement that answers your initial research question. Think of this working hypothesis/thesis as a means to an end, not the end itself. It will act as a touchstone, giving you a model of *one* way to make sense of your subject. If you phrase it properly, it will tell you the type of data/evidence you need to look for, and it will suggest a means you can use to assess and analyze the evidence you find. As you gather and assess the evidence, it is very possible that you will decide that your initial assumptions were not valid, but the working hypothesis/thesis will have led you to other, more informed and thus valid, ways of fitting the parts of the puzzle together into a meaningful picture.

The following three strategies will help you turn your assumptions into a working hypothesis/thesis. So take out your Researcher's Notebook, open it to the Working Hypothesis/Thesis section, and follow the procedures outlined in the next three steps.

1. Strategy 1: Discovering Your Assumptions about Your Area of Investigation

If you have stated an assumption that you have made about your subject (and you should already have written out such an assumption, even if you think it is probably wrong), you do have some ideas about the subject. You may know that your ideas are very general. You may know that your ideas are probably wrong. You may know that you don't have any sound reasons for assuming what you have assumed. The issue here is not the correctness or validity of your ideas. The point is that you yourself must be aware of the thoughts and feelings you have about your subject or thoughts and feelings that have influenced your thinking about your subject. Whether you are aware of these thoughts and feelings or not, they will influence your research and the way you look at your evidence. You will have more control of the research process if you put these thoughts and feelings down on paper, where you can take a long, hard look at them.

I personally believe that it is impossible for human beings to be entirely objective, but there are gradations on the subjective/objective scale. We can strive to be objective, an effort that, to me, means opening ourselves to ways of looking at a subject that are not the ways we have been used to looking at a subject. In my own experiences as a student and researcher, I have found that one important step toward objectivity is having as clear a picture as possible of what my present point of view is. I need to know my *basic* assumptions and attitudes toward my subject. I need to know what I *want* to find when I research. Pulling these assumptions out of myself is not easy, because they feel as much a part of me as the color of my eyes or my name.

To make yourself aware of your basic assumptions and attitudes toward your subject, do some freewriting. For this technique to work, you must be as honest with yourself as you can be. Try to put on paper things that seem so obvious that you feel they don't need to be said. As you do this freewriting in your Researcher's Notebook, be as personal, as concrete, and as specific as possible.

- Go back to your original reasons for selecting your assumption/research question. Why did you choose this assumption or question? What train of thought led you to this assumption?

- What associations do you have in your head when you think about your assumption? Do *not* throw out ideas just because they don't seem related. Write down *everything* that pops into your mind.

- When you write down a statement, force yourself to question that statement. Ask yourself, "What do I mean by that?" "Why do I say that?" "How did I arrive at that idea?"

Here are three examples of freewriting in which writers explore assumptions and attitudes they have about their subjects.

As I start this investigation of child care programs offered by businesses, I have to admit that I am very biased. I believe very strongly that women have a *right* to demand that companies provide such programs. To pretend that I'm totally objective just isn't going to work—but I have to come up with some kind of assumption that can at least be tested. Probably the first thing I'd better do is find out why I believe that women have a right to child care. OK. Let's start with the fact that more and more women are working. And let's assume that women will continue to have children. So—somebody has to take care of the kids! Who? Grandma? Househusbands? Baby sitters? Day care? I assume that most women are paying someone to look after their children. So where do businesses come in? Well, the businesses hire these women; they can't just turn around and say "Having kids is your problem—we pay you—you can use your salary to pay for child care." Hmmm, why do I say that businesses can't say "It's not our problem"? I'll bet that's the attitude of a lot of companies. But it is my opinion that businesses ought not to be able to say that . . . here we go. Child care is a national problem . . . a general social problem . . . businesses have to take responsibility, become involved . . .

For this bio class I decided to look into the whole spotted owl/old-growth timber controversy because it's making headlines right now. Of course, in class we've been talking about how important ecosystems are and how important it is to save species. So I tend to take the side of the conservationists. Let's see. I could just investigate why old-growth timber/spotted owls are ecologically important, but I don't think that's what I really want to do. And it doesn't get at the headlines. What about the other side? Mill workers and loggers. A different group from the greedy developers that environmentalists are usually fighting. This isn't a question of building expensive houses in the spotted owl's habitat. If the old-growth forests are off-limits, the people who are affected aren't fat cats, but the guys who log and work at the mills. Mills close; loggers and mill workers are laid off. So they collect unemployment and welfare—tax money—but they aren't paying taxes themselves. And we're talking about whole towns that are going to be affected. Ha. Maybe a good way to go about this investigation is to look into the economics of conservation. Environmentalism costs! Now that sounds interesting. Maybe I could start with the assumption that the old-growth timber/spotted owl controversy points to the important economic dimension of environmentalism. What I'd need to look at is how this decision is going to affect the economy of the Pacific Northwest.

So I'm assuming that Saturday morning cartoons teach kids to be violent. Why do I think that? In class we've already talked about how much TV kids watch. And we read those articles about how children can't always distinguish between the program and the ad & how ads that look like cartoons are a great way to persuade kids that they have to buy this cereal and that toy. So what does this have to do with violence? It's been a while since I've watched Saturday morning cartoons (!) but I remember a lot of violence—some character ends up holding a bomb that goes off in his or her face, somebody is thrown off a cliff, or somebody else is run over by a truck and flattened out. And wasn't my nephew going on the other day about some killer-robot program he loves to watch? At any rate, he's talked Joanie into buying him all sorts of toy soldiers and guns and stuff I'll bet he's seen on TV. What does all of this add up to? Kids are affected by what they see on TV. If they have to have cereal and toys they see advertised, why wouldn't they also copy the behavior of characters on TV too? And if cartoon characters go around trying to destroy each other, then I'd assume that kids will learn to go around trying to destroy each other. What I really want to get at—and maybe cartoons aren't the best way—is the idea we talked about in my sociology class last semester: how violent Americans are & how physical violence is the only way too many people know how to resolve conflicts. Yes, that's really where I'm coming from. I'm assuming that TV, since we watch so much of it, reinforces this idea—and kids, because they are so impressionable, learn this way of resolving conflict from TV. That sounds right. But now that I've gotten this far, I realize that what I really have in my head aren't TV programs but movies. Maybe what I'm really thinking about is how violence in *movies* affects kids.

Even if it seems to lead you off the track of your specific research question/assumption, this exploration of your personal thoughts and feelings about your area of investigation will help you in two important ways:

- You will know what your emotional reactions to your subject matter are, and you'll begin to see that some of your personal values and judgments have influenced the assumption you've made, even if you don't seem to have any personal feelings about your research assumption/question. Once you are aware of your own point of view, you are in a better position to open that point of view to critical analysis: Do I have any concrete, specific, logical reasons for my feelings and attitudes? Are they based on facts and evidence? Am I going to be able to look at this issue objectively?

- You may discover that the research question/assumption you started with is not really the research question/assumption you want to work with. As you freewrite, you may discover the real assumption you want to test. Do not worry about how narrow or specific the question seems. Look for the question/assumption that you want to pursue further.

2. Strategy 2: Turning Judgmental Statements into Inferences

If you remember my discussion of facts, inferences, and judgments in Section 1, you'll remember that a judgmental statement is a statement about a person's approval or disapproval of something. Judgmental statements don't lend themselves very easily to testing. Here are judgmental statements:

Socialism is the best form of government for Kenya.
Abortion is wrong.
The Industrial Revolution hurt the common worker.
Urban sprawl should be stopped in our metropolitan areas.
The Beatles were a great rock group.
Warren G. Harding was a terrible president.
You should take lots of vitamin C.

You can begin to turn such judgmental statements into inferences, into statements that lend themselves to testing, by underlining judgmental or evaluative words or phrases and then writing down what these judgmental or evaluative words mean to you.

Judgmental Statement

Socialism is the best form of government for Kenya.

When I say "best," I mean:

Socialism will allow Kenya to become more economically independent.

or

If the government takes over the industry in Kenya, the industry will become more efficient.

or

If the government takes over all industry in Kenya, the government can assure each worker a living wage.

Judgmental Statement

Warren G. Harding was a <u>terrible</u> president.

When I say "terrible," I mean:

Warren G. Harding exhibited few leadership qualities, qualities that all presidents are expected to have.

or

Warren G. Harding put together an administration of men who were irresponsible and corrupt.

or

The way Warren G. Harding was chosen as the Republican candidate in 1920 shows the weaknesses of the nominating process.

Judgmental Statement

You <u>should take</u> lots of vitamin C.

When I say "should take," I mean:

Vitamin C is a necessary component of a healthy diet.

or

Large doses of vitamin C allow the body to resist colds and flu.

Judgmental Statement

The Beatles were a <u>great</u> rock group.

When I say "great," I mean:

The Beatles were a well-known, commercially successful rock group.

or

The Beatles composed very sophisticated music.

or

In the history of popular music, the Beatles formed a bridge between rock 'n' roll and acid rock.

Judgmental Statement

Genetic engineering must be curtailed.

When I say "must be curtailed," I mean:

According to my personal Christian beliefs, genetic engineering is immoral because it is wrong to alter life as God has created it.

or

Because manipulation of DNA could produce mutant microorganisms that are dangerous to human beings, genetic engineering should be controlled in two ways: regulations should be developed for the kinds of buildings in which gene splicing could go on, and regulations should also be developed for the kinds of gene splicing that is allowed.

or

At a time when money for scientific research is so limited, the money that is available should go into research that has immediate practical application, like the search for a cure for cancer.

Judgmental Statement

Urban sprawl should be stopped in our metropolitan areas.

When I say "should be stopped," I mean:

The flight of the middle class to bedroom communities, leaving the poor and disadvantaged in the inner cities, is segregating metropolitan areas, economically and racially.

or

The uncontrolled building of homes and industrial parks on the edges of cities is ecologically unsound; the environment is being destroyed.

or

To form a real community, people must live in areas where shops, work places, churches, homes, places for cultural and other leisure activities are close together.

When you underline and explain the judgmental words in your own assumptions, you may come up with two or three statements, as I have done. Notice that each of these statements is a separate assumption with its own focal point and direction. In the last example, the first statement points to a study that will focus on the socioeconomic status of inhabitants of the inner city and suburbs. The second statement focuses on the effects of suburbs on the natural environment. The third statement reflects an interest in the concept of "community." Obviously, each statement would point me in a different research direction. If you come up with several statements, you should give some thought to whether you want to pursue all these lines of inquiry. Each of the statements in the last example would be broad enough for a research project.

3. Strategy 3: Defining Your Terms

Defining key terms in your statement is yet another means you can use to turn your assumption into a working hypothesis/thesis. Like the other two strategies, defining your terms is a way to clarify your idea for yourself.

In defining your terms, do not, at first, use a dictionary. What you are attempting to do here is discover what *you* meant by those words.

Statement

The flight of the middle class to bedroom communities, leaving the poor and disadvantaged in the inner cities, is segregating metropolitan areas, economically and racially.

What do I mean by "flight"? By flight, I mean . . .
What do I mean by "middle class"? By middle class, I mean . . .
What do I mean by "poor"? By poor, I mean . . .
What do I mean by "disadvantaged"? By disadvantaged, I mean . . .
What do I mean by "inner cities"? By inner cities, I mean . . .
What do I mean by "segregating"? By segregating, I mean . . .
What do I mean by "metropolitan areas"? (In the world? In the U.S.? In the northeastern part of the U.S.? New York City?) By metropolitan areas, I mean . . .
What do I mean by "economic segregation"? By economic segregation, I mean . . .
What do I mean by "racial segregation"? By racial segregation, I mean . . .

Statement

Socialism is the best form of government for Kenya.

What do I mean by "socialism"? By socialism, I mean . . .
What do I mean by "best"? By best, I mean . . .
What do I mean by "Kenya"? (Kenya in the nineteenth century? Kenya before independence? Kenya today?) By Kenya, I mean . . .

After you define all key terms in your own words, you may want to check your definitions against the definitions in a dictionary. Does the word "socialism" mean what you thought it meant? Is "socialism" the word you want? Your working hypothesis/thesis must say what you want it to say. The words on the page must reflect what you have in your head. Don't change your ideas; just find the right word for what you want to say.

These three strategies are designed to help you come up with a statement that is precise, that says directly and clearly what you want it to say. When you finish these exercises, you ought to have a statement that tells you what kind of evidence you need to look for, and that also tells you how you are going to go about assessing the information you find.

Working Theses

I assume that the flight of the white middle class to bedroom communities, leaving the poor and disadvantaged in the inner cities, is segregating metropolitan areas like New York City and Detroit, economically and racially.

I assume that, in the history of popular music in the 1960s, the Beatles transformed rock 'n' roll into acid rock.

I assume that scientific studies show that doses of vitamin C, larger than the recommended daily allowances, allow the body to resist colds and the flu.

I assume that the government takeover of industries in Kenya will make Kenya an economically independent country because it will reduce her dependence on imported capital and machinery, and it will improve the living standards of her people because they will be hired as managers and supervisors as well as laborers.

Looking over these examples, you may be thinking that they are too narrow and specific. You may be struck by the "But-I-can't-write-a-ten-page-paper-on-*that*" panic. Let me help you drive away this specter by saying that, in my experience as a teacher, students' working theses are generally too broad rather than too narrow. If you knew the material as well as an expert does, you would realize how broad a so-called narrow thesis really is. Let me remind you that your obligation, in doing your research, is to find as much available information as possible on your working hypothesis/thesis. The odds are that there is much, much more information available on your subject than you suspect right now.

Besides, your final paper is not going to be a laundry list of facts. You are going to be making meaning of these facts, and you will have to make your meaning clear to the people who will be reading your paper. Explaining ideas to others in such a way that they understand takes space. How many times have you seen "please explain" or "develop this idea" written in the margins of your essays?

Of course, if you are still nervous that your working hypothesis/thesis is too narrow, by all means show it to your instructor. As a matter of fact, in subsection G.3 I recommend that you prepare a proposal of your research project for your instructor so that you can be reassured that you are heading in a profitable direction.

F. Step 5: Choosing Your Research Strategy—Research Questions

You now have your initial research question and a refined statement of an answer you assume you will find. You are ready to decide on your research strategy, to determine what you need to know and where you are going to look for this evidence. As I promised, your working hypothesis/thesis provides you guidance. It raises all sorts of questions that point you toward information you need and decisions you will have to make.

In the Research Strategy section of your Researcher's Notebook, write out your thesis/hypothesis and make as complete and detailed a list as you are able of these questions.

Working Thesis

I assume that the government takeover of industries in Kenya will make Kenya an economically independent country because it will reduce her dependence on imported capital and machinery, and it will improve the living standards of her people because they will be hired as managers and supervisors as well as laborers.

Questions

1. Who now owns Kenya's industries?
2. What are Kenya's main industries?
3. Where does the capital for these industries come from?
4. What are Kenya's balance of trade figures (1980 to now)?
5. Who now work as managers in Kenya's industries?
6. Who work as supervisors in the industries?
7. Can the government afford to buy the industries?

8. Will the government takeover make Kenya more economically independent? How?

9. Where does the machinery in the plants come from now?

And on and on.

Working Thesis

I assume that the flight of the white middle class to bedroom communities, leaving the poor and disadvantaged in the inner cities, is segregating metropolitan areas like New York City and Detroit, economically and racially.

Questions

1. What period of time am I talking about? the present? the last ten years? I must decide.

2. Am I correct in assuming that the white middle class has moved out of the inner cities?

3. What metropolitan areas am I actually talking about? Just New York City and Detroit? I'd better decide.

4. How am I defining "metropolitan area"? If I stick to Detroit and New York City, what are the metropolitan areas?

5. How am I defining "inner city"? What are the "inner cities" of Detroit and New York City?

6. What is the racial minority population of these inner cities?

7. I imply that the racial minorities are the major portion of the inner-city population. Is this accurate?

8. What do I mean by "bedroom communities"? What are the "bedroom communities" of Detroit? Of New York?

9. How am I defining "poor"? "disadvantaged"? How do the experts define these groups?

10. What is the average income of people who live in the inner city of Detroit? Of New York?

11. What is the average income of people in Detroit's bedroom communities? New York's?

12. What is the population of racial minorities in New York City's bedroom communities? Detroit's?

13. I say that metropolitan areas are segregated economically. If they are, do I think this is healthy or unhealthy? Why? What do the experts say about economic segregation?

And on and on.

G. A Few More Words about Research Projects and Testing

Throughout this section I've been referring to working hypotheses/theses; now I'll explain why I have been using these two terms. If you remember, I said in Section 1 that we can talk about two kinds of research projects, primary research projects and secondary research projects. Since there are differences in the research procedures (and the final papers) for these two types of projects, you need to have a clear notion of the category into which your present project falls.

1. Primary Research Projects

Primary research projects are usually called experiments or studies. As the term implies, in primary research projects the researcher is going directly to the original source to gather his or her facts. A second characteristic of primary research projects is that the researcher carefully selects and uses systematic, accepted procedures both for gathering facts (data) and analyzing them.

You are engaged in a primary research project if your project focuses on setting up, and carrying out, an experiment in the lab. You are doing a primary research project if your project focuses on gathering specific information from a select group of people and then analyzing that information using some statistical analysis or other procedure. You are doing a primary research project if your project focuses on systematic observation of a specific group of people, animals, or plants.

If you are engaged in a primary research project, valid testing procedures are critical, both those procedures you use to collect your data and those you use to analyze them. The development of a sound hypothesis is also critical. Most experienced researchers depend on the work of other experts to help them develop their hypotheses and testing procedures. Thus, before you do your actual study or experiment, you will want to do some research in the library to find out what other researchers in the field have already done.

If you are engaged in a primary research project, I recommend that you turn right now to Section 5.B in this book and read about primary research reports. I also urge you to write your hypothesis and methodology (testing procedures) *before* you do your study or experiment and show them to your instructor. A flawed study or experiment will produce meaningless results.

2. Secondary Research Projects

In secondary research projects, the researcher is looking at the work that has already been done by others. Therefore, he or she will be reading and studying the primary research projects of others, reported in periodicals and books, and the theories and opinions of others. Most research projects assigned to students fall into this category.

In general, there are two kinds of secondary research papers: reviews and critical papers.

a. Reviews and Reviews of the Literature

A *review,* or a *review of the literature,* is a report to the reader about the trends in a particular field in a given period of time. The research procedures you would use to do a review are the research procedures covered in the next two sections of this book. You will also be expected to think about the material you are reading and formulate conclusions. Because your basic task in a review will be to summarize the trends and developments in a particular area of a field, your research question should be: "What are the basic trends and developments in X?" Begin writing your answer to this question—your working thesis—as soon as you are able after you start gathering your evidence.

If your instructor has asked you to do a review or a review of the literature, you should now turn to Section 5.C and read about this form of research paper.

If you are not sure that your instructor wants you to do a review or a review of the literature, ask right away if he or she wants a review or a critical paper.

b. Critical Papers

Doing a *critical paper* involves formulating a working thesis and then testing that thesis by gathering and analyzing the available facts and evidence. The paper that you write at the end of this process will focus on a claim or assertion (thesis) that you feel confident in making because you have critically examined your evidence. In some cases your final thesis may be the same as the working thesis you began with. Very often, however, your working thesis will change as you learn more about the subject. Such changes are natural, and you must be flexible enough to let the thesis change.

- If, as you research, you find that the facts suggest that your working thesis was incorrect, rewrite your thesis to fit the facts. You may find that you need to rewrite the thesis several times.

- As you research, you may find that the scope of your original thesis is too large to research thoroughly in the time you have, or you may find that your interests shift to one aspect of the larger thesis. This often happens to researchers, and they respond by writing a new thesis that now covers the specific area in which they have become interested.

Individuals who have done a lot of research are used to these various changes in the direction of their research, and they do not let such changes frighten or panic them. Neither should you. From the beginning you should be aware that your research may take you into areas that your original research question did not include.

If you are doing a research project that does not involve testing your data with statistical analysis, here are some ideas for ways in which you can test your original thesis. Use a theoretical model or a theory that is currently popular or generally accepted in the field. To determine whether a violent change in government in a particular country was a revolution, you could use a Marxist model of a revolution. If you are studying a work of literature, you could use one of the accepted literary theories (such as the sociological approach) or you could compare the approaches of the critics who are considered the experts on that literary work. If you are studying a piece of music or art, you could begin by comparing the work with a description of the style (baroque, romantic, expressionist) in which it is normally classified.

3. A Research Proposal

Don't be surprised if your instructor, in the early stages of your project, asks you to hand in some kind of description of what you propose to research for your paper. Even if such a proposal isn't required, it would be a good idea to do one anyway. If you are doing a primary research project, I strongly urge you to do such a proposal, including in it a complete description of your research design.

In the real world, writing research proposals is fairly standard practice. Research usually costs money, and researchers have to convince the people with the money—government agencies, private foundations, corporations—that their particular projects are worth the investment. Your professor will probably have different reasons for wanting to know what you are planning to do. Asking for such a proposal is a convenient method of encouraging you to get an early start on a research paper. But handing in such a proposal can profit you in another way. Before you do too much work, your instructor can give you an expert's opinion, warning you about trouble you may encounter, giving you useful information about sources of evidence that you may not be aware of, or helping you to refine your sense of direction even further. There is no standard format for a proposal you would write for a classroom instructor. In deciding what you want to say, remember that your general purpose is to let your instructor know the problem on which you are working and the type of investigation you intend to pursue. You will want to inform your instructor about

- your general area of investigation (liberation theology, the function of enzymes) with a *short* narrative of how you became interested in this topic and/or how your investigation fits in with the material you are studying in this class;

- your initial research question and your working hypothesis/thesis, explicitly labeled as such;

- your general research strategy—what kinds of evidence you will be looking for and where you will be looking for it. Often instructors will ask you to include a bibliography. To respond to this request, you will need to have started the next stage of the process, which is covered in Section 3, "Finding the Evidence."

There are no rules about the length of proposals. Just remember that the better your instructor understands what you have in mind, the more help he or she can give you.

4. Summary

I hope that you have noticed, as you've followed my suggestions in this section, that they revolve around a pattern of questioning and answering. This pattern of asking questions, developing your own answers for them, but questioning the answers you develop is what critical thinking is all about. This pattern will characterize the thinking and writing you'll be doing in your Researcher's Notebook. Regardless of the subject you are examining and the method of testing you decide to use, you are beginning with a hypothesis/thesis that you are opening up to question. As objectively as possible, you are going to examine your assumption critically to determine how valid it is. *Testing* is a very different process from *rationalizing, justifying,* or *proving* (as this word is often used in debate). A person may be able to give several good reasons why marijuana should be decriminalized; but simply being able to give a few good reasons for (or against) a particular position does not necessarily mean that a person has carefully studied all of the available facts, critically reviewed the various opinions of the experts, and developed a final conclusion from his or her critical thinking, based on those facts and the opinions of the experts.

Because your goal is to develop your own conclusion, based on your critical assessment of the facts and the opinions of experts, you are obliged

- to find as much information as you can about your subject;
- to consider *all* of the evidence you find, even if it seems to be saying that your original hypothesis/thesis is incorrect.

H. A Final Note

The solution or conclusion you are seeking is not tucked away in some book or article in the library. Researching is not a game of treasure hunt.

Your conclusion is just that—the conclusion or idea that *you* develop as you examine, analyze, and consider the evidence you discover. You are, as I will remind you constantly, a detective. Like a detective, you cannot know where your search will finally end. But you can, and must, constantly give *direction* to your search. For this reason your Researcher's Notebook is your most important tool.

As your experience as a researcher increases, you will learn that research projects, especially complex research projects, often take unexpected twists as they develop. The puzzle you intended to solve at the beginning of your search gradually changes shape and turns into a new puzzle as you learn more about the subject you are investigating. As a researcher, then, you must remain flexible and alert; you must be willing to change, but you must always know which path you are taking.

If you are doing a secondary research project, once you have your working thesis and research questions, you are ready to start looking for the evidence. You should now turn to the next section of this book.

The next section of this book is also very important for the researcher involved in a primary research project. Although your final goal is to collect and analyze raw data directly from the source, you must first have a sound hypothesis and valid testing procedures. The work that others have done in your field is critical to you in developing the design of your study or experiment. The following section of this book, which offers strategies for using libraries, can help you discover what others in your field have done.

I. Planning Ahead: Developing a Work Schedule

Begin with the date on which the paper is due, and work backward.

Date	*Stage in the Process*
[ ]	Due date, the date on which you will give your paper to your instructor.
[ ]	Polished final draft ready to type (one to three days before due date: be realistic about the amount of time the typing will take, and allow time for proofreading the typed copy).
[ ]	First rough draft complete (two to two-and-a-half weeks before the due date).
[ ]	If you are working on a critical paper, the date on which your research is essentially complete and you begin to develop the thesis for your paper; if you are working on a primary research project, the date on which you have all the necessary data from your study or experiment in your hands (at least three weeks before due date).
[ ]	Date on which you begin the research process by selecting an area of investigation, developing your research question, and starting your Researcher's Notebook (within a week of the time you receive the assignment).

Once you have set the deadlines above and you have developed your research strategies, you will be able to—and should—set deadlines for yourself for intermediate steps in the process. If you are doing a secondary research project, you should set deadlines for such things as gathering your first list of sources from indexes and bibliographies, having certain books and articles read, doing interviews, and the like. If you are doing a primary research project, it is crucial for you to set a number of deadlines: when your research design will be complete; when you will put together your apparatus or find your subjects or pass out your questionnaires; when you will run the experiment or study itself; and so on.

SECTION 3

Finding the Evidence

It is still not quite time to head for the card catalogue in the library.

Although the card catalogue will be a helpful tool in your quest for the information you need, it is in no way the only tool the library has, nor is it always the best place to start. Before you head for the library, I want you to read the major parts of this section. In these parts I will point out and explain some important resources the library has, resources that will allow you to jump from your research questions to the books and articles that are likely to hold answers to your questions. As you read this section, make notes in the Research Strategy section of your Researcher's Notebook about those reference materials in the library that will be most helpful to you. You will notice that this section is set up so that you can come back to individual parts and read them when you are actually in the library, looking for or using these reference materials.

But, to return to my main image of directions and paths, I must warn you that often a research process can look like a swamp to a researcher. No matter how carefully you plot your way through the territory, you can feel bogged down; your course will not always be smooth. Unfortunately, some of the time and effort you expend on this project will feel like mindless busywork. Compiling lists of books and articles and other sources will itself take time; so will finding these books and articles. You will be running from one area of the library to another. You may be running from one library to another. You may be spending time running around town, interviewing people. Unless you were born under a very lucky star, you will discover that your library doesn't have a periodical that you need or that a book you want has been checked out or that a person you want to interview cannot see you until a week from next Thursday. There isn't much you can do to prevent these sorts of snafus. But you can cut down on the frustration that often results when obstacles are placed in your path, and you can turn mountains into molehills if

- you recognize that you will be doing some mindless busywork and that snafus will occur; in other words, assume that some time will be "wasted";
- you give yourself plenty of time to do your research;
- and, above all, you use the information in this section to plan, wisely, the way you use the library.

A. *Potential Sources of Information*

Libraries are a logical place to look for your evidence because libraries, by definition, are repositories of published information. But not all information is in libraries. In your quest for an answer to your research questions, be flexible and imaginative in considering potential sources of information, and think of a library as a valuable tool in your quest rather than just the place where you will pursue your quest.

Depending upon the working hypothesis/thesis you have developed for your current project, it is possible that you will find valuable evidence outside the library as well as in books and articles you will find in the library. Evidence you need might lie in printed material not normally housed in a college library—the annual report of a corporation, for example, or a pamphlet published by a local social service agency, or a magazine or newsletter published by a trade association for its members.

Moreover, I don't need to remind you that much information today is disseminated in nonprint form. Perhaps radio or television programs contain evidence you could use, or maybe some of your evidence is to be found in a recording or on a videotape; it's also possible that one of your sources might be a live performance: a concert or the production of a play or a public lecture. And people you can speak with face to face may provide you with information you need; thus interviews might be a potential source of evidence.

In other words, as you review your working thesis/hypothesis and research questions and develop your research strategy, don't trap yourself by assuming that sources can be only books and articles in a library; and don't be trapped by a narrow view of libraries—either limiting yourself only to books and articles you assume your library has or thinking of libraries as having only books and articles on specific subjects. Focus directly on what your research questions indicate that you need to know. Even if you are doing a project in which you will be mainly using books and articles, don't overlook the possibility of doing some primary research.

- If your working thesis involves a subject with which you have or can have personal contact, would it make sense for you to gather information about your personal experiences with this subject? If you are investigating the work of a composer, should you attend a concert in which her music is played or listen to tapes of her work? If you are doing research on advertising on television or in magazines, would it make sense for you to look at certain ads yourself, recording what you see and how the ads affect you? If your working thesis has to do with mass transit, would it be valuable for you to plan a few trips on various parts of your local mass transit system?

- If your working thesis involves institutions that still exist or work that is still being done, think about gathering information from people who are employed by such institutions or whose jobs involve the kind of work you are researching. If you are investigating a subject related to a government or private agency, perhaps you should contact that agency for relevant printed material. Maybe some well-chosen interviews with key people in an organization would tell you what you need to know. If you are researching a foreign country, have you thought about contacting one of its embassies or consulates for information?

- The term "expert" is a word we use to describe a person whom we consider to have valuable knowledge about a subject, but not all experts' opinions or views are published in books and academic journals. If your working thesis is about an academic subject, you might want to talk to the "experts" who teach this subject at your school or on a nearby campus. Officers in an organization can tell you a great deal about that organization. But also think about others who might be able to give you an "expert's view" of the subject you're investigating. Who knows the pros and cons of a computer software program better than a person who uses it every day? While an official who works for a mass transit system certainly has one view of that system, the people who ride the buses and subways every day also have knowledge and opinions about it that could be exactly the type of evidence you need.

Even if you decide to seek out sources beyond the materials normally housed in a library, I think you will still find the library an important tool in your search. In the "Using a Library" subsections of this section, I focus on tools that a library provides to enable you to move from your research questions to sources where you are likely to find your evidence. These tools are reference materials—and here let us not forget librarians, too.

If you decide that your research strategy involves contacting businesses, corporations, or government or private agencies, you should be aware that most libraries have directories that list the names and addresses of businesses, organizations, or people involved in a particular endeavor; most libraries also have telephone books for cities across the country. If you want to find a videotape or a recording, ask a librarian about catalogues of such nonprint materials. Whether you are looking for sources that you will find in the library itself or you need information that will take you to sources outside your library, reference materials and librarians can give you a great amount of help.

B. *Interviews*

Depending upon the type of research project you are involved in and the specific working hypothesis/thesis you have developed, you may decide that potential sources of evidence are people with whom you would talk directly. But interviews involve a great deal more than dropping in on a person for a casual chat about your subject. Effective interviews take prior thinking and planning, just as the whole research process does. If you are considering doing interviews, I'd suggest that you read this whole section first; come back to especially relevant parts as you get ready to do your interviews.

The suggestions I give you here are a combination of common sense, my own experience, and the wise words of Leslie Baxter, who has used interviewing extensively in her own research and who has taught interviewing techniques to students for a number of years. These suggestions are divided into four stages: determining what you need, preparing for the interview, the interview itself, and writing up the interview.

1. Determining What You Need

Before I go on, I need to distinguish two different purposes for interviewing. Some research projects rely completely on evidence gathered through interviews; these types of projects fall into the category of primary research projects, in which the researcher develops a working hypothesis (for example, "I predict that women use different language than men do in talking about romantic relationships"), then tests this hypothesis by interviewing a random sampling of subjects. In these primary research projects, the answer to the research question is developed from a systematic analysis of the responses of the interviewees. While the advice I give here applies to such studies, it doesn't go far enough. If I have just described the type of research you are doing, you must work very closely with your instructor in determining whom you will interview and preparing your interview script. In writing this section on interviews, I have had in mind those of you who are thinking of interviews as one of many kinds of sources you will be using in gathering your evidence.

Determining specifically whom you should interview, what kinds of questions to ask—even whether an interview is necessary—will depend on your answer to the question: What do I need to know? So you will start by going back to the Research Strategy section of your Researcher's Notebook. If you are considering interviews, follow these two rules of thumb:

- You do not want to carry out an interview if the information you need can be obtained in other ways.

- Assume that you interview a person because that person is the best and most direct source of a *specific kind of evidence.*

Let us say, for example, that you are contemplating interviews to gather some data about an organization: How many buses does Rose City Transit operate? What are the goals and objectives of the Helping Hand Child Care Center? Before you set up any interviews, especially face-to-face interviews with senior people in the organization, you should do enough homework to know whether this information is available in printed form, or whether it could be obtained through a short telephone interview with a person in the public information office of the organization. Obtaining some facts about an organization may be part of the reason to set up an interview, but I would assume that you want to talk to a person to obtain information about how that person carries out his or her job, or the opinions, perspectives, point of view this person has about your subject. When you set up an interview, you are to some extent imposing on an individual; you certainly use his or her time. For these reasons, set up interviews only when you really need them, and set up the type of interview that meets your need.

If you decide that an interview would be valuable, study your research questions to decide whom you want to interview. If your working thesis has to do with female executives, for example, you will have to decide how you are defining "executive," and you will then need to answer some other questions. How much of a sample do you want? Do you want to talk only with the female executives in one company or female executives in one industry or type of business? Or do you want a cross section of female executives involved in a wide variety of organizations? Do you want to interview only the executives themselves, or do you want to talk to people who work for these women? If your working thesis, on the other hand, is focused on one organization or one type of organization, then you'll need to decide how many people to interview and which employees have the information you need (accountants? supervisors? marketing specialists? sales people?). You can make these decisions only by first knowing precisely what information you want, then doing some research on the organization itself. If this research isn't enough, try calling the personnel office or the public information office and asking who could best answer your questions.

Before you can walk into an interview or even conduct a short interview on the phone, however, you still have preparation to do. Television talk shows make interviewing look easy and spontaneous; as in any endeavor, these interviewers are so skilled in their craft that the work that lies behind it doesn't show. For your part, you cannot assume that all you need to do is ask a question or two, and then wait for your source to reel off a gold mine of evidence into your tape recorder. If you want the interview to be productive, if you want to receive the information that led you to consider interviews in the first place, then you need to have a plan for the interview.

2. Preparing for the Interview

Your preparation for the interview involves four steps:

- Educating yourself about the subject matter of the interview;
- Preparing an interview script;
- Pilot testing the interview;
- Contacting potential interviewees.

a. Educating Yourself about the Subject Matter of the Interview

By the "subject matter of the interview," I mean first of all the topic that you and the interviewee will be discussing, which is probably embodied in your working thesis and research questions. Second, I mean having a clear idea of the context in which this person operates as an "expert." If you are interviewing someone who works for an organization, for example, you need to know what the organization does, and you should also have a general idea of what your interviewee does in his or her job. Let me repeat: An interview should never be a substitute for other kinds of research. You should not be interviewing the president of Electronics, Inc., to find out what kind of products Electronics makes. Like a good investigative reporter, you will have learned what you could learn from other sources; now you have come to this person because she and only she can answer the questions you have. For these reasons, it is wise to conduct your interviews after you have had an opportunity to do some preliminary investigations.

b. Preparing an Interview Script

You will be walking into the interview with a script, a carefully prepared list of questions that you have developed. The fact that you are going in with a script doesn't mean that the interview is going to resemble an oral exam, with your marching in lockstep from one question to another regardless of the answers you are receiving. But it does mean that you want to be absolutely sure that you get the information you need, and thus that you intend to guide the conversation in a certain direction. Interestingly enough, you will find that this script (and the work that goes into it) is the best way to prepare yourself to engage meaningfully in the conversation you will have; it will allow you to pick up on and pursue relevant points your interviewee raises and to ask questions that may not have been in your original script. And you needn't worry about the interviewee thinking you are too forward or aggressive. This isn't an ordinary conversation. You set up the interview; the interviewee wants and expects you to take charge.

Writing your script involves deciding not only the content of your questions but also the way you will phrase the questions and the order in which you will ask them. In preparing your script, here are some things you will want to keep in mind.

Questions can be thought of as falling along a spectrum from closed questions to open-ended ones. Closed questions are the kind that invite a short, simple answer: How long have you been an accountant? Did Electronics show a profit this year? Open-ended questions invite longer, less restricted and less directed responses: What are some of your thoughts on X? In preparing your questions, you should be aware that closed questions tend to be questions that are easy to answer, but they restrict the kind of information you receive—and to an extent they may bias it in the sense that they force the interviewee to put himself or herself in a camp or category. Compare the closed question "Do you favor quotas for minorities?" with the open-ended "I'd like to hear what you think about quotas for minorities."

But open-ended questions also have their pitfalls. They can encourage directionless, rambling answers. So when you use open-ended questions, you must also write out a series of follow-up questions, designed to move the interviewee to talk about the specific points you are most interested in. If, for example, your open-ended question was "What do you think about the proposal to put in a light-rail system on the west side of the city?" some possible follow-up questions might be: What route do you think would be the best? Do you think the plan to build a tunnel under the West Hills is feasible? desirable? How would you respond to the neighborhood associations that are opposed to the Sunset Corridor plan? If the topic of your interview is complex (What makes a business person successful?), it is wise to start with closed questions and move to more open-ended ones.

In this area of open-ended questions, Leslie Baxter called my attention to the problem of the "unanswerable" question. Often, she told me, novices at interviewing will go into an interview and ask their major research question, which, as you have already discovered, tends to be general and abstract. In an interview, such a question could stop your interviewee cold as he or she tries to figure out how to approach it or tries to figure out what you want. You can solve the problem by asking for more concrete, specific answers that will reveal the interviewee's thinking on the larger question. Let's say, for example, that you want to know what makes a businessperson successful. Instead of asking that question point blank, you say, "Think of the last time you had a feeling of real success on the job. Could you describe that experience for me?" You could elicit similar information by saying, "I'd like you to think of an incident at work in which you felt you failed to achieve what you thought you should have achieved. Could you describe that incident for me?" By listening to these answers and using the paraphrasing technique ("So you believe that making decisions quickly is important to success?"), you will gradually accumulate a rich, clear picture of this person's answer to your big question.

In writing the script for your interview, you must keep coming back to this major point: what do I want to know? Here are some further guidelines for phrasing and ordering your questions:

- You will probably want to start the interview with a few closed and/ or easy questions; questions about the person's exact title and how long he or she has worked for this company or done this sort of work are naturals. You could also ask some questions that confirm information you have already uncovered ("I understand that Helping Hand takes care of 300 children a day; is that correct?"). These questions should be designed to elicit or confirm specific background information that you need about the person or organization; they should set the topic and direction of the interview; and you make them easy in order to build rapport with your interviewee. Since most interviewees are distracted by a tape recorder for the first two or three minutes it is on, you do not want to start the interview with any major questions.

- In general, order your questions from "easy" and/or closed ones to more open-ended and/or probing ones. This ordering is especially important if your topic is complex or sensitive or both.

- Use every strategy you know to be sure the questions in your script are eliciting the kind of information you want, and be sensitive to a series of questions that may either unnecessarily restrict the answers you receive or inadvertently bias them.

- If you use open-ended questions, be sure you put a series of follow-up questions in your script.

- Your last question should always be one that invites the interviewee to express his or her point of view on your topic clearly (and catches anything important you may have missed): Is there anything else you'd like to say that would provide me with a better understanding of X?

c. Pilot Testing the Interview

Even the most carefully prepared script won't give you a completely clear picture of how the interview will go, so you should always test your script in a trial interview. Find someone whose area of expertise is like that of your real interviewee. If you are going to interview business executives, for example, do your trial interview with one of the instructors in the business department; or find a friend of your parents who is in business, or a parent of one of your friends. Go through the whole interview as if it were the real thing. This trial interview has several purposes:

- to develop an accurate estimate of how long the interview will take;

- to be sure your questions are really eliciting the information you want;

- to give you a chance to make any adjustments you need to in your script (changing the wording of questions or the order of questions, adding or deleting follow-up questions, and the like); and

- to test your general performance as an interviewer.

When you make arrangements for the trial interview, be sure to ask the "interviewee" to be prepared to critique the whole interview and your behavior as an interviewer.

When your script is in its final form, memorize it.

d. Contacting Potential Interviewees

Plan to make your initial contact with interviewees over the phone or in person. *Never* conduct the interview itself in this initial contact. Leslie Baxter advises her students to write what they are going to say in this initial contact so that they are sure they've covered everything and so that they pay close attention to the words they use. In your initial contact, here's what you need to cover:

- Identify yourself (in addition to your name, tell the person that you are a student at X).

- Tell the person how and why you selected him or her for an interview.

- Tell the person the purpose of the interview and how your record of the interview will be used (e.g., "I am doing a research project on what makes business people successful. The information I gather from you will be used in a paper on this topic that I am writing for X class").

- Settle the issue of confidentiality. Before you make this contact, you will need to decide whether you want to acknowledge your sources by name in your paper, or if you intend to keep the identity of your interviewees confidential, referring to them in your paper only in general terms like "an executive in a large company in Portland." In your initial contact, tell the person you intend to keep his or her identity confidential, or ask permission to acknowledge the person by name in your paper. Unless you have decided to keep all of your sources confidential, keep a written record of those people who have given you permission to use their names and those who wish their identities to be kept confidential.

- Tell the person how long the interview will last; it is crucial that your estimate be accurate.

- Set up a time and place for the interview (and be sure you write it down in your engagement calendar!).

It is a good idea to call the day before the interview to reconfirm.

3. The Interview Itself

When you leave for the interview, be sure you have

- a tape recorder and a blank tape. Before you leave, start the tape, and identify the interview ("This is a record of my interview with John Doe, May 3, 1991"). As you are setting up the tape recorder at the beginning of the interview, you can say, "I prefer to tape this interview so that I can give my full attention to you and what you are saying." Leslie Baxter tells me this statement normally overcomes any qualms an interviewee has about being recorded.

- a clip board, your script, a pen, and blank paper. During the interview you are going to check off your questions as you ask them—just another guarantee that you haven't missed anything important. You want to have paper so that you can jot down any follow-up questions that occur to you during the interview, to make a quick note of any part of the interview you particularly want to use, and to take full notes in case your interviewee really doesn't want to be tape-recorded.

Your script and the trial test you've done should give you a fairly clear sense of how the interview *should* go. But here are some further observations and advice:

- Remain flexible, open, and, above all, attentive. Just because you have a script and a tape recorder doesn't mean you can become a passive sponge. You are going to be an active participant in a conversation, and to do that you have to listen closely to what your interviewee is saying. As long as you are getting the type of information you need, you can change the order in which you ask your questions. You can also abandon parts or all of your script if the situation calls for it.

- Throughout the interview, give clear signals, verbal and nonverbal, that you are paying close attention (nod your head, say "That's interesting," or "I see," or give other such "encouraging" cues). Always give positive feedback; never give the impression that what the interviewee said was wrong or beside the point (don't frown, don't say "That's not what I asked" or "Let's move on to the next question"). As often as you can, try to integrate the questions on your script with what the interviewee has said ("A minute ago you mentioned X; I'd like to ask you something more about that").

- Throughout the interview, plan to use paraphrase as feedback. Restate to the interviewee what you heard him or her say: "If I understand correctly, you are saying that . . ." or "So you mean X?" or "You are saying, then, that . . ." It is particularly useful to paraphrase those points that get at the heart of the information you need.

- If you have an interviewee who isn't talking enough, it probably means either that you have not established enough rapport, that the person doesn't understand what the interview is about, or that the questions you are asking are unanswerable. You will have to try to read the situation on the spot and make amends. Try increasing the positive feedback you are giving, and see what happens with a "Could you describe a personal experience you've had with X?" approach.

- If you have a person who is talking too much, you need to regain control of the conversation—in a tactful manner (you don't want your interviewee to shut up completely!). Interrupt the interviewee at a natural speech pause, but don't switch the topic or go on to a new question. Rather, pick up something he or she has said that is relevant or potentially relevant to your interests, and gradually get the conversation back on track ("What you have been saying is very interesting. It brings X to mind. Could you talk a bit more about X?")

- If, during the interview, the person says something that strikes you as very important, feel free to say, "That's very nice. May I quote you on that?" Otherwise, on the issue of permission to quote, at the end of the interview, while the tape is still running, ask, "Is there anything you have said during our conversation that you would not want me to quote or to attribute to you?" Ask this question in such a way that the interviewee will feel free to be honest. On your part, you will have to abide by his or her response.

- You really need to repay the interviewee in some way for his or her time. As you are leaving, offer to send him or her a copy of your final paper. (I hope the person says yes; it is a good incentive for you to do your best on this paper!)

4. Writing Up the Interview

As soon as possible after the interview is over, sit down and freewrite about it in your Researcher's Notebook. If you are doing a series of interviews, you might want to create a special section for them in your Notebook; otherwise, do your freewrite in the Reading section. Don't listen to the tape; write your freewrite from your memory of the interview:

- Try to capture the flavor of the interview; record your general impressions.
- Write about what stands out in your memory about what the interviewee said.
- If the interview had any glitches, write about what went wrong, and give yourself some advice about how to avoid such problems in the future.

At this point your tape becomes a document, just like a book or a journal article. The rest of my advice follows my general advice for taking notes; you will find more detailed information in Section 4.D.

- Write a reference card (see Section 4.B.3), recording the following information:
  - the full name of the interviewee
  - his/her official title
  - the full official name of the company or organization for which this person works
  - the date of the interview

Be sure to write the name of the interviewee and the date on the cassette, too.

- After listening to the tape and rereading your interview notes, write a summary card (sec. 4.D.2) and make notes on specific information. If you are quoting the interviewee on a notecard, play back the tape after you've written down the words to be sure they are accurate.
- Plan to keep the tape until your paper is turned in, just in case you need to refer to it while you are writing your drafts.

If you took written notes rather than tape-recording the interview, plan to rewrite all your notes in "clean" form as soon as you can after the interview is over. If you have not done so already, put quotation marks around the words you know are the exact words your interviewee used. Your clean notes now become the basic document of the interview, just as a tape recording would be. From these notes you should write a reference card and a summary card and take specific notes, following the process I outlined above.

When it is time to write your final paper, you can use the appendixes in this book to see some methods of documenting interviews, both in your text and in your reference list or bibliography (see the "Forms for Other Types of Sources" sections of Appendixes A, B, C, and D). But you can document the interviews in this formal way only if the person you interviewed gave you permission to use his or her name.

If you have agreed to keep the identity of one or more of the interviewees confidential, I recommend the following:

- The first time you refer to one of these confidential interviews, include an explanatory note (I explain explanatory notes in Appendixes A, B, C, and D). In this note tell your readers that you did X number of interviews in which you agreed to keep the identity of the interviewees confidential; describe these sources as concretely as you can within the limits of your agreement with the sources (officials at Peabody Company, or executives in major lumber firms in Portland, or whatever); and give the date or the period over which the interviews were conducted (December 9–11, 1991).

- In the body of your paper, give as much information as you can about each of your confidential sources within the limits of your confidentiality agreement: "In an interview with me last month an official of a major lumber firm, who wishes to remain anonymous, said. . . ."

Even if you do use the interviewee's name, it is a good idea to give some information about this person in the body of your paper: "John Doe, head of marketing for the large retail chain Clothes Unlimited, thinks. . . ."

C. Using a Library: Introductory Remarks

Every type of research project involves some use of the library. If you are doing a secondary research project, much of your research will depend on material you find in libraries.

One of the first things you should realize is that libraries are not all alike. The material—books, periodicals, documents—housed in a particular library is acquired according to the purpose and clientele that library is designed to serve. If your school library does not have some material you need, this does not mean that your library is a bad library. You should acquaint yourself with other libraries in your town or the surrounding region; you may find that you will have to use libraries other than your school library. Even if you are not allowed to check out materials from these other libraries, most libraries allow the public to use materials on their premises. And don't overlook the possibility of getting material through interlibrary loan (see subsection J in this section).

The collections of libraries are limited. On the other hand, too often I hear the complaint from students that "our library doesn't have what I need." Occasionally the complaint is legitimate. Too frequently, however, the problem is not the library but the student researcher who is using (or not properly using) the library. Many students I know, and you may fit this category, don't know how to use a library.

The key to unlocking the wealth of information available to you in a library is to recognize that all materials and information in it are stored or filed according to particular systems. You are already acquainted with one of these systems if you have used the card catalogue to find the call number of a book; the call number tells everyone where a particular book is stored. In many libraries today the card catalogue has been computerized; in fact, many researchers search for promising sources by sitting in front of a computer terminal. If you enjoy working on computers, you may find this part of the process more enjoyable than you anticipated. But let's not get too starry-eyed about computers doing your work for you. Whether you use a computer or consult traditional printed materials in your search for sources, information in both is filed and stored according to specific systems; you won't find what you need unless you understand the system that was used to compile this information, and do your search accordingly. In subsection H I will say more about computer searches. But first I want to introduce you to some basic—and very valuable—resources in the library that you may not be aware of and explain how to use them.

As I said earlier, you should read the rest of this section now, before you go to the library. Make a note of the types of reference materials that seem directly related to your research project. Then, take this book with you to the library. If you get confused, you can use this guide as a handy reference.

Let me begin with a few words of advice:

- Take your Researcher's Notebook with you to the library, along with your notecards.

  - In the Sources section, write all your citations to books, articles, and other materials you want to read. It is very tempting, I know, to scribble this information on the backs of envelopes and in various class notebooks, but it is very easy to lose these citations. Remember what I have said about saving yourself *needless* frustration and wasted time?
  - In the Research Strategy section of your Researcher's Notebook, jot down ideas about people you want to interview, reference materials you should use, and other parts of your research plan.

- Be very conscious of the dates of publication of the materials you look at. This is discussed at more length in the next section of the book (see Section 4.B.2). Here let me say that unless you specifically want material that is older, you should look for books and articles published in the last ten or five years. When using bibliographies and indexes (see Section 3.F.2), start with the most recent issues and work backward.

- Do you want to hear me say again how important it is to begin your research early?

D. Using a Library: The Subject Catalogue of the Card Catalogue

Most academic libraries now use the Library of Congress (LC) cataloguing system. Library of Congress call numbers look like this:

PN
511
.W 7
1948

Throughout this section I will be talking about the LC system. If your library does not use the LC system, you will have to acquaint yourself with the cataloguing system it does use.

The subject catalogue of the card catalogue is one reference tool that most students think they know. I'll admit that I learned a great deal about the way the subject catalogue works when I wrote this book so I think you may learn something, too, when you read this section.

Let me warn you that the subject catalogue lists *only* books that your library has. Therefore, it is a rather limited source for finding the information you need. Use the subject catalogue, but plan to use other reference materials.

First of all, you must be aware that the Library of Congress system has its own set of subject headings that may not correspond to the subject headings you are using. If you find nothing in the subject catalogue under your key word or term, look in the *Library of Congress Subject Headings*, two large volumes located near the card catalogue.

If you looked under "Culture conflict" in these volumes, for example, this is what you'd find:

Culture conflict *(Indirect) (Psychology, BF740)*
  sa   Interracial marriage
       Marginality, Social
       Marriage, Mixed
       Miscegenation
       North and south
   x   Conflict of cultures
  xx   Ethnopsychology
       Genetic psychology
       Psychology, Pathological
       Race relations

Here's how to read this list:

- The letters and numbers (BF 740) indicate the basic Library of Congress call numbers under which you'd find books on cultural conflict.
- *sa* means "see also," which indicates that you could find sources under the other headings listed here. You may decide that "Interracial marriage" or "Marriage, Mixed" are more precisely the subjects you are interested in; check these topic headings in the subject catalogue.
- The single *x* indicates that this is *not* a heading used by the Library of Congress system. You will not find "Conflict of cultures" in the subject catalogue.
- The double *x* (*xx*) indicates a related heading, usually broader in scope. If the topics listed here under "Culture conflict" do not hit upon the subject you are investigating, you should check "Ethnopsychology" in the Library of Congress volumes.

The *Library of Congress Subject Headings* volumes will also give you the particular heading the LC system uses. For example, if you looked under

Culturally deprived

you would find

See Socially handicapped

Or, if you looked under

Culturally handicapped

you would find

See Socially handicapped

These entries indicate that you should look in the subject catalogue under "Socially handicapped" for your sources.

When using the subject catalogue, pay close attention to the headings typed at the top of each card. These headings indicate subdivisions within a particular topic. The cards are filed in alphabetical order, according to these subheadings. For example, if you checked under "Boston" in the subject section, you would find cards marked with these subheadings:

Boston—Commerce
Boston—Committee of Correspondence
Boston—History
Boston—History—Colonial Period
Boston—Population—History

These subheadings are designed to help you locate information directly related to your special interest.

When using the subject catalogue:

- Look under various subject headings.
- Use the *Library of Congress Subject Headings* volumes to find appropriate subject headings.
- Pay attention to the various subheadings; check the subheadings appropriate to your specific topic.

If you do not find what you need in the subject catalogue, don't give up. There are other reference materials in the library that may be more helpful than the subject catalogue.

E. Using a Library: Periodicals

The word "periodical," if you consider its root, refers to a publication that is issued "periodically" or at regular, recurring intervals—once a year, once a month, once a week. Magazines, journals, newspapers are all periodicals. If you want the most recent, up-to-date information on your subject, your most promising source is periodicals.

One thing you should know is that, in academic circles, a distinction is made between "popular" periodicals and "scholarly" ones. The distinction is based on the audience for whom the periodicals are written.

Popular periodicals are written for the general public. These are the newspapers and magazines you find at your local supermarket or newsstand. *Time, Newsweek, Atlantic Monthly,* the *New York Times* fall into this category. These publications are certainly reputable periodicals, but you should be aware that when you do research for a college class, your instructor will expect you to depend more heavily on scholarly periodicals than on popular ones.

Scholarly periodicals (often called journals) are periodicals that contain reviews, essays, and research reports written by experts and scholars in a field for other experts and scholars in a field. Although they contain the type of authoritative information you want, the fact that experts are speaking to experts in these journals may cause you some trouble, especially at the beginning of your research project. Depending upon how specialized and technical your research subject is, the articles in these journals may be very difficult for you to read. Here are two suggestions for you:

- If you run across journal articles that you find very difficult to read, look at my advice in Section 4.C.2.
- Below I have listed some periodicals that I call "authoritative but accessible." That is, the information in these periodicals is considered sound by scholars in the field, but the articles are not so technical as those in other scholarly journals. Articles in these journals and periodicals may be a good place to start your reading.

As a rule, *popular periodicals* are indexed in the *Readers' Guide*. *Scholarly periodicals* are indexed in the indexes for particular disciplines (see this section, F.2).

Below I have listed some periodicals in various fields that are considered authoritative but which are not so technical as some journals in the field. Thus, they are good periodicals to start with. This list is certainly not exhaustive. Ask your instructor if he or she can give you the titles of other authoritative but accessible scholarly periodicals in your area of investigation.

Authoritative but Accessible Journals

Business

Business and Society Review
Business Horizons
California Management Review
Forbes
Harvard Business Review
Journal of Accountancy

Journal of Business
Journal of Finance
Journal of Marketing
Management Accounting
Sloan Management Review

Communications

Central States Speech Journal
Communication Quarterly
Communications Monographs (for-
    merly *Speech Monographs*)
Journal of Broadcasting
Journal of Communication

Journalism Quarterly
Quarterly Journal of Speech
Quill
Western Journal of Speech Commu-
    nication

Economics

American Economic Review
American Journal of Economics
    and Sociology
Business Economics
Challenge
Economic History Review

The Economist
Inter-American Economic Affairs
Journal of Economic History
Journal of Political Economy
Quarterly Journal of Economics

Political Science

American Political Science
    Review
Congressional Digest
Current Affairs Bulletin
Current History
Foreign Affairs

International Affairs
National Journal
Public Opinion Quarterly
The Washington Quarterly
World Affairs

Psychology

American Psychologist
Community Mental Health
    Journal
Contemporary Psychology: A
    Journal of Reviews

Journal of Social Issues
Journal of Social Psychology
Psychology Today (issues in 1983
    and after)

Science

American Scientist
BioScience
Nature
New Scientist

Science
The Sciences
Scientific American

Sociology

American Journal of Sociology
American Sociological Review
British Journal of Sociology
Current Sociology
International Journal of Compar-
    ative Sociology

Journal of Ethnic Studies
Journal of Social Issues
Social Forces
Social Problems

F. Using a Library: Reference Materials

When people start listing reference books, I find that my eyes glaze over and I simply cannot concentrate because I know, beforehand, that I'll never remember all the information that is being thrown at me. I have this reaction when I am given information in a vacuum. I certainly don't want to cause your eyes to glaze over or you to tune out, so instead of just listing various kinds of reference materials, I've set up this section according to the kinds of information you might need.

Use this section this way: with your Researcher's Notebook and your research questions in front of you, look at the questions that head each part of this section. Make a note of each of those question headings and reference materials that applies to your research questions. Then take this book with you to the library to use as a reference book.

Please note that I have not listed *all* the reference books available in each category, and your library may not have the reference books I've listed. Almost every field of study has sets of bibliographies, indexes, dictionaries, encyclopedias. Be prepared to use the card catalogue to find reference books comparable to those I've listed, or ask your reference librarian or instructor to help you.

1. Do You Need Some General Information about a Subject?

Check an **encyclopedia.**

Encyclopedias contain general summary articles about subjects; some articles also include a short bibliography of books and/or articles you may want to look at.

a. General Encyclopedias

These include such references as:

> *The Encyclopaedia Britannica*
> *The Encyclopedia Americana*

b. Specialized Encyclopedias

Specialized encyclopedias, such as the ones listed here, focus on particular fields of study:

> *The Encyclopedia of Philosophy*
> *The Encyclopedia of Religion and Ethics*
> *The Encyclopedia of World Art*
> *The International Encyclopedia of the Social Sciences*
> *McGraw-Hill Encyclopedia of Science and Technology*
> *Parry and Grant Encyclopaedic Dictionary of International Law*
> *Physics in Medicine and Biology Encyclopedia: Medical Physics, Bio-Engineering, and Biophysics*
> *The Princeton Encyclopedia of Poetry and Poetics*
> *The Social Science Encyclopedia*

There are other specialized encyclopedias in the library. Check the subject catalogue under your general topic; look under the subheading "Dictionaries." Or ask the reference librarian.

2. Do You Need Lists of Books and Articles about Your Subject?

Check **bibliographies.**

Bibliographies are reference books that list books and articles written on specific subjects. They are set up very much like the subject catalogue.

To find a bibliography on your topic, check the subject catalogue. Look under your topic, then check the subheading "Bibliographies." Or use the *Bibliographic Index* (see Section 3.G).

Check **indexes.**

An *index* is also a bibliography, although indexes tend to concentrate more on articles published in magazines and journals.

a. General Indexes

These include various kinds of citations. *The Readers' Guide* is an index containing references to popular periodicals — *Time, Sports Illustrated, Field and Stream*. It will not be very helpful if you want to read scholarly, authoritative articles on your subject.

To find more scholarly articles and books, use

The *Humanities Index*. Subject fields covered include archeology, classical studies, folklore, history, languages, literature, and other areas in the humanities.

The *Social Sciences Index*. Subject fields covered include anthropology, economics, geography, political science, psychology, public administration, and other subjects in the social sciences.

Note: The *Humanities Index* and the *Social Sciences Index* were divided into two separate volumes in 1974. Before 1974 they were combined in the *Social Sciences and Humanities Index*. Before 1965, this index was known as *The International Index*.

b. Specialized Indexes

In addition to general indexes, the library has specialized indexes. The following list is representative but not complete:

American Statistics Index
Applied Science and Technology Index
Architectural Index
Art Index
Book Review Index

Business Periodicals Index
CIS [Congressional Information Service] *Index*
Computer Literature Index
Current Index to Journals in Education
Current Law Index
Current Physics Index
Education Index
Engineering Index
General Science Index
Index Medicus [medicine]
Index to Jewish Periodicals
Index to Periodicals by and about Blacks
Index to U.S. Government Documents
International Index to Film Periodicals
International Nursing Index
Music Index
The Philosopher's Index
Physical Education Index
Science Citation Index
Social Sciences Citation Index

Specialized indexes are one of the most valuable reference tools researchers have. Check your library's collection of specialized indexes carefully to locate those that promise to contain citations for articles and books on your specific topic. Or check the subject catalogue under your topic heading; look under the subheading "Indexes." Finally, see Section 3.G for guidelines on using indexes.

3. Would You Like to Find Summaries of Articles about Your Subject?

Check an **abstract.**

An *abstract* is a summary of the content (the author's thesis/hypothesis, methodology) of an article or book. Abstracts, such as those listed below, contain summaries of thousands of articles (some abstracts also cover books) written during a given year on various topics in the field. Some abstracts available are

Abstracts of English Studies
Abstracts of Popular Culture
Biological Abstracts
Chemical Abstracts
Energy Research Abstracts

Historical Abstracts
International Political Science Abstracts
Language and Language Behavior Abstracts
Metals Abstracts
Mineralogical Abstracts
New Testament Abstracts
Personnel Management Abstracts
Photographic Abstracts
Physics Abstracts
Psychological Abstracts
Science Abstracts
Sociological Abstracts
Urban Affairs Abstracts
Women Studies Abstracts
Work Related Abstracts

When using an abstract, always check the front pages of the volume to see how that particular abstract is set up. Pay close attention to the categories used in the subject section to classify the abstracts. Since the categories used are usually traditional divisions in a field, you will need to know into which field division your particular subject falls.

4. Do You Need to Know What a Particular Term Means, or Who a Particular Fictional Character Was?

Check a **dictionary.**

a. General Dictionaries

These references include

Webster's New International Dictionary, 2nd ed., Unabridged. Definitions in this edition are considered to be *correct* usage.

Webster's Third International Dictionary, Unabridged. Definitions in this edition follow the language as it is currently used. Purists may consider some of these usages incorrect, colloquial, or vulgar. The *Second International,* an older edition, prescribed correct usage.

The *Oxford English Dictionary* (OED); also called the NED, *New English Dictionary.* A British dictionary that gives a history of the meanings of English words. An excellent source if you need to know what a particular word meant in the sixteenth century, or the eighteenth.

b. Specialized Dictionaries

Among these references are

Cinema: A Critical Dictionary
Concise Chemical and Technical Dictionary
Dictionary of American History
Dictionary of Computing
Dictionary of Key Words in Psychology
Dictionary of Life Sciences
A Dictionary of Mining, Mineral, and Related Terms
A Dictionary of Modern Politics
A Dictionary of the Social Sciences
A Dictionary of Twentieth-Century Composers (1911–71)
Encyclopedic Dictionary of Mathematics
Funk & Wagnalls Standard Dictionary of Folklore, Mythology, and Legend
Holman and Harmon's *Handbook to Literature*
McGraw-Hill Dictionary of Scientific and Technical Terms
The New Harvard Dictionary of Music
Oxford Classical Dictionary
Theological Dictionary of the New Testament

There are other specialized dictionaries. Check the subject catalogue under your general topic; look under the subheading "Dictionaries." Or ask the reference librarian.

5. Do You Need Information about a Particular Person, Living or Dead?

Check a **biographical dictionary** or **index.** Here are a few:

Biographical Sources: A Guide to Dictionaries and Reference Works
Biography and Genealogy Master Index
Biography Index
Chambers Biographical Dictionary
Current Biography: Cumulated Index 1940–1985
Current Biography Yearbook
Dictionary of American Biography
Dictionary of National Biography
The McGraw-Hill Encyclopedia of World Biography

Or look in one of the *Who's Whos.* There may also be book-length biographies written about your particular subject. Check the subject catalogue; look under the subheading "Biographies."

6. Do You Need a Specific Fact, like the Population of Sweden in 1960, or . . . ?

Check an **almanac** or **fact book.**

Information Please Almanac
Statistics Sources: A Subject Guide to Data on Industrial, Business, Social,
    Educational, Financial, and Other Topics for the United States and Internationally
Whitaker's Almanac
The World Almanac and Book of Facts
World Statistics in Brief: United Nations Statistical Pocketbook

7. Do You Need to Find Out Where a City Is Located, or the Boundaries of a Country at a Certain Point in History?

Check an **atlas.**

Atlas of World History
The National Atlas of the United States
Rand McNally Bible Atlas
Rand McNally Goode's World Atlas

8. Do You Want to Find Newspaper Articles on Your Subject?

Check a **newspaper index.**

Nationally distributed newspapers like the *New York Times,* the *Wall Street Journal,* and the *Christian Science Monitor* publish their own indexes. Check to see if your library has these indexes.

If local newspapers are indexed, this job is usually done by the local public library. If you are interested in articles that were published in your local paper, find out if your local public library has an index.

The list of **reference materials** given on the last few pages is certainly not complete. However, by now it should be clear that there are many places you can look for the information you need or for sources that will contain the information you need.

G. Using a Library: How to Use an Index

Many students fail to do an in-depth study of their subjects either because they do not know how to use indexes or because they are intimidated by them. Using indexes is really a very simple operation once you understand how they work. In the next few pages I am going to explain how indexes work by using facsimiles of actual pages from the *Bibliographic Index* and the *Social Sciences Index*.

First of all, I will explain how an index is set up. Then I will show you how to read a bibliographic citation (the publication information about a book or article).

Please read the next few pages and compare my explanations with the actual material from these two indexes. I have set up this section so that you can also use it as an aid when you are in the library, working with actual indexes. I should also tell you that every index includes information (usually in the front part of each volume) about how to use that particular index, just in case my explanations do not apply to the specific index you are using.

1. Using an Index: The Format

a. The *Bibliographic Index*

The *Bibliographic Index* refers you to books and articles where you will find bibliographies (lists of books and articles) on your subject.

The first thing you should be aware of is that most indexes are set up like the subject catalogue of the card catalogue. Thus, citations of specific books and articles are listed under general **headings,** alphabetically arranged throughout the volume.

Page 379 of the *Bibliographic Index*, on page 69, begins with the heading

MARITAL status

and goes to

MARKETING research

When a topic is broad, that topic may be subdivided into **subheadings.** The subheadings in this index are in boldface type, centered in each column.

MARITAL status
See also
Married people

Gove, W. R. and Hughes, M. Reexamining the ecological fallacy; a study in which aggregate data are critical in investigating the pathological effects of living alone. Social Forces 58:1174-7 Je '80

MARITIME law
See also
Commercial law

Gounaris, Emmanuel. Die völkerrechtliche und aussenpolitische Bedeutung der Kontinental-shelf-Doktrin in der Staatenpraxis Griechen-lands, der Bundesrepublik Deutschland und der Deutschen Demokratischen Republik; Ägäis, Nordsee, Ostsee; ein Vergleich. (Völkerrecht und int. Politik, v 1) Lang, P. '79 p249-61

Managing ocean resources; a primer; ed. by Robert L. Friedheim. Westview press '79 p203-8

Papadakis, N. International law of the sea; a bibliography. Sijthoff & Noordhoff '80 457p

Latin America

Szekely, Alberto. Bibliography on Latin America and the law of the sea. (Special pub. no5) Law of the sea inst. '76 20p

MARITIME Provinces, Canada

Economic conditions

Barrett, L. G. Perspectives on dependency and underdevelopment in the Atlantic region [bibliog. article] Can R Social & Anthropol 17:273-86 Ag '80 annot

Sacouman, R. J. Semi-proletarianization and rural underdevelopment in the Maritimes. Can R Social & Anthropol 17:242-5 Ag '80

Politics and government

Forbes, Ernest R. Maritime rights movement, 1919-1927; a study in Canadian regionalism. Mc-Gill-Queen's univ. '79 p229-37

MARIVAUX, Pierre Carlet de Chamblain de, 1688-1763
by and about

Spacagna, Antoine. Entre le oui et le non; essai sur la structure profonde du théâtre de Mari-vaux, ltd ed (Europäische Hochschulschriften. Reihe 13. Französische Sprache und Lit. v55) Lang, P. '78 p465-8

MARK, Gospel of. See Bible. New Testament—Mark

MARKET, Capital. See Capital market

MARKET research. See Marketing research

MARKET segmentation

Zinser, Wolfgang. Der Absatz von Investitions-gütern; ein Beitrag zur Bestimmung von Marktsegmenten mit Hilfe von Einstellungs-daten. (Schriften zum Marketing (Berlin) v6) Duncker & Humblot '78 p314-32

MARKET surveys
See also
Consumers' preferences
Store location

Washington researchers. Government market studies; a listing of market studies and repts. produced by the Federal government. The or-ganization '79 426p

United States

Nelson, Theodore A. Measuring markets; a guide to the use of federal and state statistical data. updated version U.S. Ind. & trade adm. '79 p88-97

Washington researchers. Government market studies; a listing of market studies and repts. produced by the Federal government. The or-ganization '79 426p

MARKETING
See also
Bank marketing
Commodity exchanges
Consumers
Export marketing
Market segmentation
Physical distribution of goods
Price discrimination
Price policy
Product life cycle
Sales management
Sales promotion
Selling
also subhead Marketing under the following subjects
Arts
Beef—Kenya
Farm produce
Information services

Anbar yearbook, 8 (to Aug. '79). Anbar pubs. '79 266p

Baker, Michael John. Marketing; an introd. text. 3rd ed Macmillan (London) '79 p475-80

Berekoven, Ludwig. Internationales Marketing. Gabler '78 p249-62

Bloch, Carolyn. Exporting, basics for the small firm. Contax '78 p82-8

Gardner, David Morgan, and Belk, Russell W. Basic bibliography on experimental design in marketing. (AMA bibliog. ser, no37) Am. mar-keting assn. '80 59p

Hahne, Dietrich. Marketing in Entwicklungs-ländern. (Schriftenreihe Wirtschaftswissen-schaftliche Forschung und Entwicklung, v29) Florentz '79 p312-60

Hauser, J. R. and Simmie, P. Profit maximising perceptual positions; an integrated theory for the sel. of product features and price. Mgt Sci 27:54-6 Ja '81

Marketing abstracts. See issues of Journal of marketing

Marketing distribution; a sel. and annot. bibliog [comp. by] Daulatram Lund [et al] (AMA bibliog. ser, no35) Am. marketing assn. '79 118p

Marketing information guide. Trade marketing information guide, inc. See issues

Petermann, Günter. Absatzwirtschaft; unter Mitarbeit von Bernhard Conrads und Reinhard Hünerberg. Kohlhammer '79 p293-308

Regulation of marketing and the public interest; ed. by Frederick E. Balderston [et al] essays in honor of Ewald T. Grether. Pergamon press '81 p261-92

Schiller, Rüdiger, and Kästing, Friederike. Bi-bliographie der Marketingliteratur; Verzeichnis deutschsprachiger Lit. ab 1945. (Kölner ab-satzwirtschaftliche Dok. v2) Poeschel '79 603p

Shama, Avraham. Marketing in a slow-growth economy; the impact of stagflation on con-sumer psychology. Holt, Rinehart & Winston '80 incl bibliog

Zinser, Wolfgang. Der Absatz von Investitions-gütern; ein Beitrag zur Bestimmung von Marktsegmenten mit Hilfe von Einstellungs-daten. (Schriften zum Marketing (Berlin) v6) Duncker & Humblot '78 p314-32

Management

Hénault, Georges Maurice. Le consommateur. (Coll. Eurêka, 2) Presses de l'Univ. du Québec '79 p207-12

Mathematical models

Bagozzi, Richard P. Causal models in marketing. Wiley '80 p276-93

Urban, Glen L. and Hauser, John R. Design and marketing of new products. Prentice-Hall '80 p583-608

Psychological aspects

Britt, Steuart Henderson. Psychological princi-ples of marketing and consumer behavior. Heath '78 p487-523

Underdeveloped areas

See Underdeveloped areas—Marketing

MARKETING channels

Dwyer, F. R. and Walker, O. C. Bargaining in an asymmetrical power structure. J Marketing 45:114-15 Wint '81

Management

Michigan. State university, East Lansing. Dept. of marketing and transportation administration. Management in marketing channels [by] Don-ald J. Bowersox [et al] McGraw-Hill '80 p369-83

MARKETING management
See also
Product management

Enis, Ben M. Marketing principles. 3rd ed Goodyear '80 incl bibliog

Keegan, Warren J. Multinational marketing management. 2nd ed Prentice-Hall '80 incl bibliog

Luck, David Johnson, and Ferrell, O. C. Market-ing strategy and plans; systematic marketing management. Prentice-Hall '79 p455-61

Michigan. State university, East Lansing. Dept. of marketing and transportation administration. Management in marketing channels [by] Don-ald J. Bowersox [et al] McGraw-Hill '80 p369-83

Wilson, Richard M. S. Management controls and marketing planning. Wiley '79 p201-7

Zantow, Roger. Systemorientierte Marketing-analyse der Banken; die Systemforschung als Grundlage generell anwendbarer Analysemo-delle, dargestellt am Beispiel der Bankmarket-ing-analyse. (Schriftenreihe Wirtschaftswi-senschaftliche Forschung und Entwicklung, 10) Florentz '78 p437-72

MARKETING research
See also
Market surveys
Motivation research (marketing)
Sales forecasting

Bagozzi, Richard P. Causal models in marketing. Wiley '80 p276-93

Under the heading MARKETING, there are four subheadings:

Management
Mathematical models
Psychological aspects
Underdeveloped areas

When you are using an index, be sure to look over the entire entry so that you will find the subheading that contains the information you are looking for.

Finally, please notice that an index will always use **cross-references** to help you find the materials you need. The index will tell you which headings it uses and/or it will refer you to related headings where other citations on the same or related subjects are listed. Cross-references are usually indicated by "See" or "See also." Note this cross-reference:

MARKET research. See Marketing research

This line indicates that the *Bibliographic Index* lists works on market research under the heading MARKETING research. You will find this heading at the bottom of the page, alphabetically listed after MARKETING management. Another cross-reference on this page is:

MARKET surveys
  See also
Consumers' preferences
Store location

This notation means that you may also find information on market surveys under the general headings CONSUMERS' preferences and STORE location.

It may take a little more time to check these cross-references, but it is certainly time well spent. It isn't legitimate to say that "nothing's been written on my subject" when the truth of the matter is that the index you are using doesn't use the particular subject headings that you think it should!

b. The *Social Sciences Index*

Page 297 of the April 1980 to March 1981 *Social Sciences Index,* on page 71, shows that this index is set up in a format very similar to that of the *Bibliographic Index.*

Page 297 begins with the general heading

Elasticity (economics) — *cont.*

Elasticity (economics) —cont.
  See also
Substitution (economics)
Elation
  See also
Mania
Elche, Spain
        Description
Date on the Costa Blanca. C. Lim. il map Geog Mag 52:841-2 S '80
Elder, Bruce
Snow seen. il Can Forum 60:46-7 Je '80
Elder, Charles
Does individual behavior cause systems, or do systems cause individual behavior?[review article]. Urb Aff Q 15:232-5 D '79
Elder, Lonne, 3d
Lorraine Hansberry: social consciousness and the will. Freedomways 19 no4:213-18 '79
Elderly. See Aged
Election districts
        Great Britain
Race for seats; boundary commission. Economist 276:58-9 Jl 5 '80
Election expenses. See Campaign funds
Election forecasting
Certain problems in election survey methodology. P. Perry. bibl Pub Opinion Q 43:312-25 Fall '79
        Mathematical models
Electoral forecasting from poll data: the British case. P. Whiteley. Brit J Pol Sci 9:219-36 Ap '79; Reply with rejoinder. N. L. Webb. 10:271-2 Ap '80
Election law
  See also
Voters, Registration of
Voting, Absent
        Ireland
Politicians and electoral laws: an anthropology of party competition in Ireland. R. K. Carty. Pol Stud 28:551-66 D '80
        Singapore
Imposing a new electoral rule. S. Awanohara. Far E Econ R 109:12 Ag 8 '80
        Turkey
        History
Role of the electoral system in Turkish politics [1950-1977]. W. Hale. Int J Mid E Stud 11:401-17 My '80
        United States
Impact of state legislation on political campaigns. A. D. McNitt. State Govt 53:135-9 Summ '80
Political action committees are throwing ringers. J. Rees. il Am Opinion 23:27-9+ Je '80
Primary rules, political power, and social change. J. I. Lengle and B. Shafer. Am Pol Sci R 70:25-40 Mr '76; Reply. T. H. Hammond. W Pol Q 33:50-72 Mr '80
Electioneering. See Advertising, Political
Elections
  See also
Campaign funds
Election districts
Election forecasting
Election law
Local elections
Majorities
Political candidates
Proportional representation
Referendum
Representative government and representation
Voters, Registration of
Voting
        International aspects
Importance of being in government. Economist 275:57 My 10 '80
        Australia
All about petrol? Economist 277:44-5 O 11 '80
Australia's premature Labor pains. Economist 277:107 O 18 '80
Election order out of chaos. A. Summers. Far E Econ R 109:19 Ag 8 '80
Small chance of much change. Economist 276:35 S 20 '80
Three men seeking a swing. H. Ester. Far E Econ R 109:18 S 19 '80
        Bolivia
Where democrats are brave. Economist 276:38 Jl 5 '80
        Botswana
Elections and parliamentary democracy in Botswana. J. A. Wiseman. World Today 36:72-8 F '80
        Canada
Energy and elections. R. C. Paehlke. Environment 22:4-5 My '80
New chapter for Trudeau. Economist 275:39-40 Ap 5 '80

        Denmark
Look at the elections; interview with Ib Nørlund. World Marx R 23:54-5 Ap '80
        Europe, Western
American federalism and European integration. K. Pöhle. State Govt 53:50-3 Wint '80
European elections of 1979: a problem of turnout. J. Lodge. Parl Aff 32:448-58 Aut '79
European policy of Franz Josef Strauss and its implications for the Community. G. Pridham. J Common Mkt Stud 18:313-32 Je '80
        France
Environmental concerns and local political initiatives in France. J. R. McDonald. map Geog R 70:343-9 Jl '80
French elections and the ecology movement. M. J. Kurlansky. Environment 22:4-5 S '80
  See also
Presidents—France—Election
        Germany (Federal Republic)
Brezhnev's present. Economist 276:46 Jl 5 '80
Can Schmidt lose? Economist 276:39-40 Ag 9 '80
Off with the kid gloves. Economist 275:60 My 24 '80
Old firm. Economist 276:14-15 S 13 '80
  See also
Prime ministers—Germany (Federal Republic)—Election
        History
Mass media use and electoral choice in West Germany. H. Norpoth and K. L. Baker. Comp Pol 13:1-14 O '80
        Gibraltar
Rock steady. Economist 274:54 F 16 '80
        Great Britain
How elections elect. Economist 274:49-50 Mr 1 '80
        Greece
  See also
Presidents—Greece—Election
        India
Cynical election. C. Hitchens. New Statesm 99:4 Ja 4 '80
Freestyle power game. M. Ram. Far E Econ R 107:20-1 Ja 11 '80
Stability yes, emergency no. M. Ram; J. Sarkar. Far E Econ R 107:8-9 Ja 18 '80
        Iran
  See also
Presidents—Iran—Election
        Jamaica
Bullets in the ballot. Economist 277:68+ O 25 '80
Off with a bang. Economist 277:45-6 O 11 '80
        History
Racial ideology in Jamaican politics: the People's political party in the parliamentary elections of 1962. J. C. Gannon. Caribbean Stud 16:85-108 O '76/Ja '77
        Japan
Constitution's success. N. Macrae. Economist 274:survey 19-20 F 23 '80
Going into uncharted waters. J. Lewis. Far E Econ R 108:30 Je 13 '80
Japanese splits. Economist 275:14+ My 24 '80
Japan's election: return to the 1960s. G. H. Healey. World Today 36:285-7 Ag '80
Rug pulled out. Economist 275:48-9 My 24 '80
        Kenya
1979 Kenya election: a preliminary assessment. V. B. Khapoya. Africa Today 26 no3:55-6 '79
  See also
Presidents—Kenya—Election
        Lebanon
  See also
Presidents—Lebanon—Election
        Panama
From his hammock. Economist 277:44 O 4 '80
        Portugal
Another battle to win. R. Harvey. Economist 275:survey 11-12+ Je 14 '80
One election at a time. Economist 276:42 Ag 30 '80
Party goes to the polls. World Marx R 23:41-7 F '80
Stained before battle. Economist 276:45-6 Jl 19 '80
        Rhodesia
Africa as usual. Economist 274:16 F 9 '80
At least the words are gentler. Economist 274:53-4 F 2 '80
British observer's view of the election. A. Campbell. Round Tab no279:283-9 Jl '80
Explosions before Zimbabwe votes—and afterwards, too? Economist 274:37-8 F 23 '80
Lick at democracy. Economist 274:11 F 16 '80
1980 Rhodesian elections—a first hand account and analysis. M. Gregory. World Today 36:180-8 My '80
Now, how will the soldiers vote? Economist 274:18 Mr 1 '80
Other battle. Economist 274:50 Ja 19 '80
There will still be too many guns about after the voting. Economist 274:35-6 Mr 1 '80

and goes to

> Elections
>> Rhodesia

You will notice that Elections is a broad topic, because it is subdivided on this page into twenty-one subheadings:

International aspects	[a general subdivision]
Australia	
Bolivia	[divisions according
Botswana	to region/country]
Canada	

Here we see that the *Social Sciences Index* further subdivides its subheadings, so that we have this category:

> Germany (Federal Republic)
>> *History*

This page has a number of cross-references. If, for example, you wanted information on elections in Iran, the cross-reference "See also" tells you to look at

Presidents	[general heading]
Iran	[subdivision]
Election	[further subdivision]

You will also notice that the index tells you that articles on Electioneering are listed under the general heading Advertising, Political:

> Electioneering. See Advertising, Political

I'd like to call your attention to another feature of this index, namely **names.** Names are used in the *Social Sciences Index,* as they are in many other indexes and bibliographic indexes, as general headings.

- The names of people important in history or important in a field of study are used as general headings. For an example, turn back to the sample page from the *Bibliographic Index* and check "MARIVAUX, Pierre Carlet de Chamblain de, 1688–1763."

- The names of authors of articles are also used as general headings. What this means for you as a researcher is that you can use the *Social Sciences Index* (and other indexes) to locate the bibliographic information about an article if you know who wrote the article. On the *Social Sciences Index* page, see "Elder, Bruce" and "Elder, Charles." To find the bibliographic information, of course, you have to know in what year the article was published and to check the volume of the index that lists articles published in that year, or you will have to be prepared to look through several volumes of the index until you locate the citation.

Another advantage of knowing that authors' names are used as headings is that you can check to see if a particular expert in a field has published anything recently. You could find out, for example, whether Lester Thurow has had anything to say in print lately, or whether Richard Leakey has published any articles.

c. General Summary

By this point it should be obvious that a very common method of classifying information about books and articles—used in the subject catalogue of the card catalogue, in abstracts, and in computer data banks, as well as in indexes like the *Social Sciences Index*—is a system of classifying information according to sets of general categories and subdivision of those categories. Once you understand that this is the general pattern, the job of tracking down the information you need becomes much easier. But there is a catch—you must use the **key terms** used by a specific index or system to identify the general categories and subdivisions. Your ability to be flexible and alert becomes all-important at this point. Individual indexes help by providing cross-references, which lead you to the key terms (headings) that those indexes use. If you do not find the information you need under the first key term you have checked and there are no cross-references, don't give up. Using your research questions and your knowledge of the subject, have a list of other possible key terms. When I was looking for reviews of a particular movie several years ago, I had to try several headings (movies, film, cinema, the director's name, the title of the film) before I found the reviews I wanted. If you get stuck, always feel free to ask a reference librarian for help; I do.

2. Using an Index: Reading Citations

After you have found the proper heading (and, if necessary, subheading) in an index, you have before you a list of books and/or articles on your subject. You will have trouble finding these books and articles, however, if you don't know how to read the citations.

In the next couple of pages I will show you how to read citations, using examples from the sample pages of the *Bibliographic Index* and the *Social Sciences Index*. Right now you should carefully look over these pages to familiarize yourself with the general form of a citation. And a word of warning: always copy down *everything* in a citation, *exactly* as it is in an index, in the Sources section of your Researcher's Notebook. Be sure to copy it neatly and clearly, because you will need to be able to read it later. Leave room next to each citation so that you can fill in the library call number.

a. Reading Citations in the *Bibliographic Index*

Sample Citation 1

> Urban, Glen L. and Hauser, John R. Design and marketing of new products. Prentice-Hall '80 p583–608.

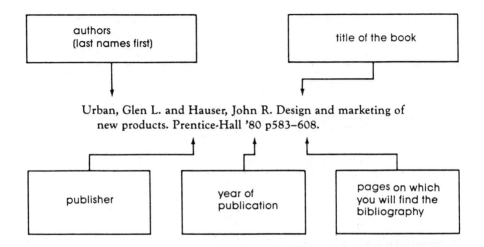

Sample Citation 2

> Barrett, L.G. Perspectives on dependency and
>   underdevelopment in the Atlantic region [bibliog. article]
>   Can R Social & Anthropol 17:273-86 Ag '80 annot

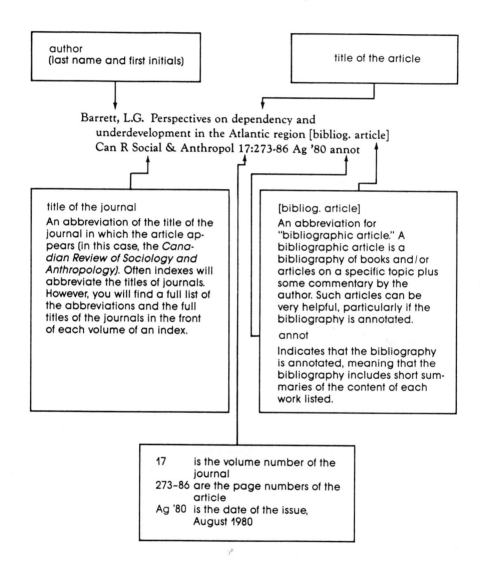

author
(last name and first initials)

title of the article

Barrett, L.G. Perspectives on dependency and
    underdevelopment in the Atlantic region [bibliog. article]
    Can R Social & Anthropol 17:273-86 Ag '80 annot

title of the journal
An abbreviation of the title of the journal in which the article appears (in this case, the *Canadian Review of Sociology and Anthropology*). Often indexes will abbreviate the titles of journals. However, you will find a full list of the abbreviations and the full titles of the journals in the front of each volume of an index.

[bibliog. article]
An abbreviation for "bibliographic article." A bibliographic article is a bibliography of books and/or articles on a specific topic plus some commentary by the author. Such articles can be very helpful, particularly if the bibliography is annotated.

annot
Indicates that the bibliography is annotated, meaning that the bibliography includes short summaries of the content of each work listed.

17   is the volume number of the journal
273-86 are the page numbers of the article
Ag '80   is the date of the issue, August 1980

b. Reading Citations in the *Social Sciences Index*

Sample Citation 1

Bullets in the ballot. Economist 277:68+ 0 25 '80

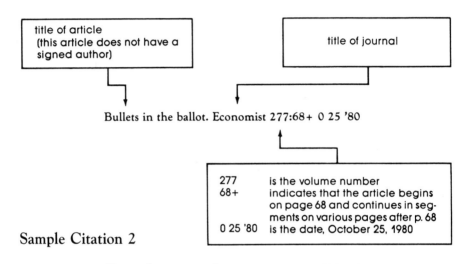

Bullets in the ballot. Economist 277:68+ 0 25 '80

277   is the volume number
68+   indicates that the article begins
           on page 68 and continues in seg-
           ments on various pages after p. 68
0 25 '80   is the date, October 25, 1980

Sample Citation 2

1979 Kenya election: a preliminary assessment. V.B. Khapoya.
   Africa Today 26 no3: 55–6 '79

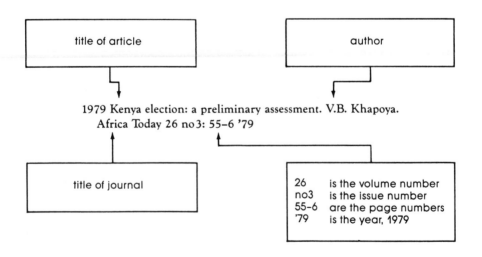

1979 Kenya election: a preliminary assessment. V.B. Khapoya.
   Africa Today 26 no3: 55–6 '79

title of journal

26   is the volume number
no3   is the issue number
55–6   are the page numbers
'79   is the year, 1979

Sample Citation 3

Date on the Costa Blanca. C. Lim.
il map Geog Mag 52:841–2 S '80

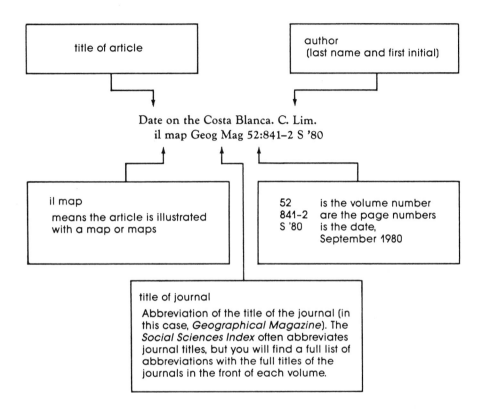

Volume numbers are usually assigned to a journal or magazine for a full year; thus fifty-two issues of *Newsweek* will carry the same volume number. But each of the fifty-two issues of *Newsweek* published in that year begins with page 1. If you found a citation for an article in *Newsweek* that read 26:15, how would you know which of the fifty-two issues to look in? Each would have a page 15. The key is the issue number ("no3" in the Sample Citation 2). When a magazine or journal begins each issue with page 1, you will normally be given either the specific date of the issue (O 25 '80) or the issue number. Thus, when you find an issue number in a citation such as the one in Sample Citation 2, be sure to copy it down; you will need it.

Many journals use a different system to make it easier to locate specific articles: they number the pages of an entire volume consecutively, rather than starting every issue with page 1. In a volume that is paginated consecutively, the first issue (January, perhaps) would contain pages 1 through 80; the second issue (February) would contain pages 81 through 123; the third issue (March) would contain pages 124 through 174; and so on until December. Thus, when you are looking for an article in which the volumes are paginated consecutively, you actually need only the volume number and the page numbers.

Before leaving this discussion of reading citations in indexes, let me call your attention to the *Social Sciences Index* citation under the heading "Elder, Charles." After the title, in brackets, the citation says "review article." A **review article** is an essay in which the author summarizes major theories and/or research on a specific topic in a field. Such articles can be very helpful to a researcher, and you should make a special effort to find any articles on your subject that have the words "a review" in the title or which are classified as review articles (as Elder's article is classified here by the *Social Sciences Index*).

H. *Using a Library: Computer Searches*

The information sources I outline here are telecommunication services— that is, those which hook you up through telephones to databases throughout the country. Your use of such databases will depend on the type of information you need and the computer services available to you, either through your library or through your own home computer. I'll remind you that if you want to retrieve the information you need from these databases, you need to know what kind of information they contain and the system that was used to file this information.

Two basic kinds of computer services that can be helpful to researchers are:

- **On-line bibliographic searching.** Many libraries subscribe to information services that give them access to bibliographic databases. These bibliographic databases are, in essence, electronic indexes housed in computer memory banks rather than in bound volumes. Like indexes, these bibliographic databases contain lists of books and articles; as in printed indexes, the citations are classified under specific headings and subheadings.

  Ask the reference librarian whether your library subscribes to a service that provides on-line bibliographic searching, and ask if this service is available to you. Or, if you own a computer or have access to one, ask at your local computer store to see what equipment you would need to hook into a service that provides on-line bibliographic searching.

If you intend to do a bibliographic on-line search, here are some things you should know:

○ Many of these bibliographic databases contain only recent citations. Few will list books and articles published before the late 1960s, and the dates of most citations will probably be more recent than that.

○ To locate a list of books and articles directly relevant to your subject, you must use headings and subheadings used to file these citations in the database. You must study the list of headings and subheadings for each database and determine which headings and subheadings are most appropriate to your specific area of investigation. If the headings you use are too broad, you could end up with a printout of thousands of titles. Even if you use the proper key terms, you may not find the citations you expected. Some databases classify citations by using only the key terms that appear in the titles of books and articles; thus the list of citations this database provides may not contain all the books and articles in which your subject was discussed or referred to. Don't expect miracles!

● **Information databases** that include the data themselves. Computer owners can subscribe to telecommunication services that give them access to such information as trading statistics on stock and bond exchanges, financial reports of companies listed with the Securities Exchange Commission, documents generated by the United States Congress, and so on. These databases are particularly appealing because the information they provide is obviously up-to-the-minute.

Let me end by saying that computers can help researchers, but they are not a substitute for an intelligent researcher who knows what she needs to know and knows how and where to look for this information. If you don't know which buttons to push on the computer it is no more helpful than a library whose resources you do not know how to tap.

I. Using a Library: Finding the Books, Articles, and Newspapers on Your List

When you have citations for books, articles, and newspapers, the next step is to see if your library has these books, articles, and newspapers.

The **books** that your library owns are catalogued in the author and title catalogues of the card catalogue. I prefer to check the author catalogue first. When you use the author catalogue, be sure that you know the correct spelling of the author's name and that you carefully check first name and middle name or initial. Many authors have common surnames (Williams, Smith, etc.). If you use the title catalogue, remember that *the* and *a* at the beginning of a title are disregarded in alphabetizing. *A History of the Civil War* will be alphabetically listed under H.

Copy the call number of the book next to your citation in the Sources section of your Researcher's Notebook. If this book is not on the shelf the first time you check, you will need this call number when you check the shelf a second time. If the book is still missing after you've checked the shelf several times, ask about it at the circulation desk.

In looking for **articles,** your first task is to see whether the library subscribes to the periodical in which the article appears and then to see if the library has the volume of the periodical in which it is printed.

In some libraries, periodicals are catalogued along with books in the Library of Congress system. In other libraries, separate indexes list the library's periodical holdings. You will have to find out which system your library uses.

If your library catalogues periodicals in the LC system, check the title catalogue of the card catalogue; remember that *the* and *a* are disregarded in alphabetizing titles. *The Southern Speech Communication Journal* will be catalogued under S.

If you find the title of the periodical you need, your next step is to find out whether the library has the volume you need. A series of numbers is on the card that catalogues the periodical. Here's what these numbers mean:

Entry

    Communications Monographs
      formerly Speech Monographs
    v. 27 (1960) —
    Microfilm B 737 v.1–32
    (1934–65) 3 reels

Explanation

First of all, notice that this journal has changed its name. *v. 27 (1960) —* means that the library has volumes 27 through the current volume on the shelves. Whenever you see a dash after a volume number and no number follows the dash, you know that the library has all volumes printed after the volume number given. *Microfilm B 737 v. 1–32 (1934–65)* means that the library has the first through the thirty-second volumes on microfilm. *B 737* is this particular library's code for its microfilm collection. You will need this number if you want to use this microfilm.

Entry

Comparative Literature Studies

   v. 1 (1964); 6 (1969)—

Explanation

The library has volume 1 and volumes 6 through the present volume on the shelves. Volumes 2 through 5 are *not* in the library.

- If the library has the volume you need in a printed copy, copy the call number next to your citation in the Sources section of your Researcher's Notebook. You will then have to find out where this periodical is shelved in your library.
- If the library has the volume you need on microfilm, copy the appropriate information next to your citation in the Sources section of your Researcher's Notebook. You will then have to find out where this microfilm is housed in your library. You may also need a librarian's help in using the microfilm reader.

Different libraries subscribe to different **newspapers.** Very often newspapers will be put on microfilm. Find out which newspapers your library has, where they are stored, and in what form they are stored. If newspapers are on microfilm, you may need the help of the librarian in locating the issue you want and in using the microfilm reader.

J. What If Our Library Doesn't Have the Books and Periodicals I Need?

When you have checked the card catalogue and/or the periodical index and you have noted the call numbers of the books and periodicals your library has, then make a list of the books, the periodical volumes, and newspaper issues that your library does *not* have. You will now have to look for these materials in other places.

   Check **other libraries** in your town or city. If you need only one book or one periodical, it is acceptable to call a library to find out if it has this book or periodical. Ask for the main reference desk. If, however, you are looking for a number of books and/or periodicals, you will have to check the card catalogue of these libraries yourself.

Most libraries, particularly college and university libraries, participate in the **interlibrary loan** network. This system allows you to obtain books and articles from other libraries across the country. If your library participates in this network, ask the reference librarian how to go about ordering the books or articles you need. You will need complete bibliographic information on the book or article, so check your citations carefully and be sure to give the librarian accurate information. Put in interlibrary loan requests *as soon as possible.* Processing requests and obtaining materials takes time, sometimes weeks. A book or article will not do you much good if it arrives two days after you have handed in your paper.

K. Summary

Because there is quite a bit of specific information in this section, let me summarize for you the main points you will want to remember.

- Not all information is stored in libraries, and not all libraries house the same material. When you begin looking for your evidence, check your research questions and ask yourself whether some of your information might be obtained from sources other than those in libraries. If you decide to look for sources in places other than the library, plot your strategies for finding these sources.

- A great deal of information is stored in libraries. Because there is so much information stored in them, libraries must have systems for storing and retrieving this information. If you are going to find the information you need, you must know some of the library's systems and you must use them. You must also realize that a library contains information about sources (books, articles, and documents) that the library itself may not have.

   ○ One stepping-stone to sources is the subject catalogue of the card catalogue. It lists materials your library has. Among the materials it lists are reference materials.

   ○ Other stepping-stones to sources are indexes and bibliographies. These reference materials are an excellent place to start your search. Indexes and bibliographies are put together according to general disciplines (humanities, social sciences), according to fields (art, business, etc.), or according to specific areas within a field. To find an appropriate index or bibliography, you must know in which discipline or field your subject falls.

○ Another stepping-stone to sources is abstracts. Abstracts will give you not only the titles of books and articles but also some information about the content of those books and articles. They allow you to decide which books and articles are most likely to contain the information you need.

○ Certain reference books, like encyclopedias and specialized dictionaries, can provide you with important "background" information in the subject you are pursuing.

○ Certain reference books may themselves contain the information you need (biographical dictionaries, fact books, atlases, specialized dictionaries, etc.).

● If your library does not have a book or article you need, your search is not over. Check other libraries in your town or city. Use the interlibrary loan service.

● If you have questions or run into trouble using your library, ask a librarian for help. But don't turn into a passive sponge here. Use the information I have given you. Use the maps and brochures and tours provided by your library to help you find materials. If you ask a librarian for help, approach him or her with a *specific* question.

● Your search for sources will not be limited to your first search of the subject catalogue and indexes. Throughout your research you will come across references to other sources, particularly in the books and articles you read. Check the notes, bibliographies, and reference lists of each book and article you read. Copy citations of promising sources in the Sources section of your Researcher's Notebook.

● As you read and think about the sources you collect, your research questions—and even your working thesis—will change. With each change of direction your research takes, you will need new information. You will therefore be consulting indexes, bibliographies, the card catalogue, and other reference material throughout the research process.

SECTION 4

Reading Critically and Taking Notes

A. Some Opening Remarks . . .

If you have done a research project before, you are used to the idea that part of your time will be spent making lists of books, articles, and other published materials, and running about gathering this material. But what then? What do you do after your desk is piled high with books and articles? This is the point in the process when many students are tempted to turn into passive sponges. From their sources, they copy sentence after sentence onto notecards or into notebooks. They have a wonderful time highlighting passages in yellow, pink, and green. For what purpose?

Notetaking is not the mindless activity of a passive sponge. It is not the process of pointlessly transcribing sentences from one piece of paper to another.

Notetaking, if it is to be a meaningful activity, must be the product of reading and studying.

A researcher gathers books and articles so that he or she can learn about a subject by reading what others have said and done and then by thinking about—analyzing, synthesizing—what he or she has read. In this section I will discuss notecards and notetaking, but always in the context of reading, thinking, learning. The research process has no point if it is not a process of thinking and learning.

In the research process, you will be taking two kinds of notes:

- On notecards, or in some similarly systematic fashion, you will be recording the evidence you find.
- In your Researcher's Notebook, you will be recording *your own thoughts* about the evidence you have gathered and the material you are reading.

You will be making both kinds of notes throughout the research process.

In order for you to know what belongs on notecards and what belongs in your Researcher's Notebook, you will have to be able to distinguish between the ideas of others and your own ideas.

I realize that when I say that you have to be able to make such distinctions, you may be responding: "But you have just hit the problem right on the head. I can't always distinguish between my own thoughts and those of my sources. I don't know very much about the subject I'm researching; that's why I'm doing the research. The experts—they're the ones who know. I have to depend on them."

All researchers, as I noted in Section 1, rely on the work done by others in the field. You will want to use these sources; what you want to avoid is having them use you. "Reading critically" has a prominent place in the title of this section to reflect my belief that the secret of distinguishing your own thinking from that of your sources lies in the act of reading them critically. A major purpose of this section is to help you reach this goal. You will find in this section several keys to developing a healthy relationship with your sources.

The first is to recognize that, except for the special cases of almanacs and compilations of statistics, the books and articles you will be studying are not conglomerations of facts or truths. They are, instead, *interpretations* of evidence, interpretations that have been formulated by human beings. An easy way to remind yourself that what you are reading are the thoughts of other human beings is to use the author's name whenever you refer to one of these sources: Valdez says . . . , Jones looks at . . . , The way Greenberg and Yamada see it . . . .

Another way to avoid the trap of looking at your sources as collections of facts and truths is to recognize that if you want to understand what an author is *saying,* you also need to see what he or she is *doing* in this piece of prose. Later in this section I will elaborate on this idea and give you specific strategies for focusing on what an author is doing. For right now, let me say that since an author obviously believes in the validity of her perception of a subject, one thing she is doing is trying to persuade you to see the subject as she does. You can avoid *mindlessly* falling into her pattern of thinking by distancing yourself from it. Talk to yourself about what she is doing at various points in her presentation: here she is telling me about the problem she wants to unravel; here she is giving me her hypothesis/thesis; here she is explaining to me the mode of analysis she is using; here she is summarizing the conclusions she has drawn. Look at your sources as other human beings' constructions of meaning. After you have read a number of books and articles in this manner, you will see for yourself that there is no central "truth" for you to find. Not all experts interpret the evidence in the same way; not all experts use the same evidence. If you think in these terms, you should see for yourself that the authors of your sources are carrying on a conversation about the best way to understand this subject.

You are perfectly capable of joining this conversation. You are perfectly capable of thinking. You are perfectly capable of formulating a point of view. You have already taken a major step in this direction by beginning this research project with your own working hypothesis/thesis. Now you need to have confidence in yourself. You want to listen to what the experts have to say; you want to understand their points of view. But take the attitude of the little boy in "The Emperor's New Clothes": never mind what others see; what do *you see?* What matters most is *what makes sense to you.*

"What makes sense to you" brings us to the heart of the distinction between your own ideas and those of others. The authors you are reading give you what they see as good reasons for thinking the way they do. You may accept, reject, or qualify all or part of what they say, but you need *good reasons* for doing so. You will know that you are thinking for yourself when you can explain to yourself *how* and *why* one way of looking at your subject makes more sense than another. It doesn't matter if your thinking is similar to that of the experts (in all likelihood it will be); what matters is that you yourself have found a way to make the evidence mean something.

As you dive into that pile of books and articles on your desk, you must resist the temptation to become a passive sponge. You must assert yourself as an intelligent person capable of thinking for yourself. Maintaining your own point of view in the research process is going to be much easier if you use your Researcher's Notebook.

In Your Researcher's Notebook . . .

In the Reading section of a Researcher's Notebook, I expect to find passages like these:

> Latour's ideas on power are really hard to understand. I've got to see if I really am grasping what he's talking about. It sounds like he's arguing that if you have power you really don't HAVE power. You have power when other

people do what you want them to do. Let's see . . . if my boss tells me to move these crates over to the loading dock, he has power because *I* moved the crates. I could refuse to move the crates, or I could ignore what he tells me to do—then we could say he has no power. That I can see. But I still think of somebody like my boss as HAVING power. Let's go back to what "power" means. Latour is saying that power = exertion, something/someone DOING something. Me, moving or not moving the crates. So Latour is saying that if the whole crew moves crates like the boss wants, the power = the crates being moved. The boss doesn't have power because he didn't move one crate himself, although he was the source of the crates being moved. OK. Let's say that is what Latour means. So what? Why is Latour defining power this way?

Or

Chin and Murphy make a pretty convincing argument that individuals 16 and older should be tried in adult court for major felonies like murder and rape. They base their argument on case studies of 5 teenage murderers and rapists who were released from the juvenile court system when they were 18 and went on to commit the same crimes again. C&M's views aren't really very typical. Most of the other experts I've read feel that the best way to deal with juvenile offenders is intense therapy designed to change both their behavior and their thinking. I should see if I can get any statistics on the criminal histories of juveniles—do most become adult criminals, or are they rehabilitated? Are C&M's cases representative? Does intense therapy work? And what about this age business? Why 18, or 16, or 14? Where do we draw the line between children and adults?

Freewrites in your Reading section may well prompt you to turn to other divisions of your Notebook. In the second example, the question about the histories of juvenile offenders may be one to transfer over to the Research Strategy section. The second example also illustrates how freewrites in the Reading section can move into freewrites on the more general research question. When you reach a point like this, you may want to flip over to the Working Hypothesis/Thesis division of your Notebook and continue your inquiry there.

These examples illustrate the type of record you should be keeping of what is happening in your head *as* you go through your sources. You should notice that it will be easy to distinguish between what you are reading and what you are thinking because you will be referring to what you've been reading, as you do the reading, and you will be commenting on it.

Write frequently in your Researcher's Notebook. Talk to yourself about the books and articles you read. Keep going back to your working hypothesis/thesis and measure what you've learned against it. Keep asking questions, and looking for answers.

On Notecards . . .

At the same time that you are writing to yourself in your Researcher's Notebook about your thoughts on your readings, you must also be keeping a clear, clean record of the evidence you are finding in your sources. The evidence will usually fall into one of two categories:

- facts, or data;
- the theories, hypotheses, conclusions of the experts.

This evidence is vital to your research project. It is the solid material you are using to test your working thesis. The conclusions and ideas that you are formulating as you write in your Researcher's Notebook should be based directly on this evidence. Such evidence, therefore, must be recorded in a clear, systematic, easy-to-use way.

I am going to urge you to keep your records of your evidence on notecards and reference cards. Many students seem to find notecards a waste of time, so let me explain why I use this system.

If you are like many students I know, you may be accustomed to taking notes by putting slips of paper in books, writing your notes in spiral notebooks, or highlighting books and articles you read. These systems do work, up to a point. But you should realize their limitations.

One limitation is people like me who get very angry with individuals who deface library books and periodicals by underlining, highlighting, or writing in the margins. At the very best, such defacing is distracting; at the worst, it destroys the text itself because it renders the words and sentences unreadable.

I become even more angry when I discover that someone has cut out a page or a whole article from a periodical or a book. I am not the only user of libraries who feels this way about the defacing of public property. When you find that you are unable to use a book or an article because the material has been damaged, you will know how I feel. The availability of photocopying machines in libraries today makes defacing books and periodicals all the more unforgivable.

Now let's turn to the limitations of underlining books and articles, along with other notetaking systems, for you as a researcher.

Putting slips of paper in books, highlighting photocopies of book pages or articles, and taking notes in spiral notebooks work well as long as (1) you remember all the material that you have marked in this way and (2) you remember where each piece of information is to be found. These two qualifications are precisely the limitations of these systems. It is all too easy to forget much of the information you have marked in these ways; or, even when you remember that you did mark a piece of information in one of your sources, you must waste time looking through all the books and articles until you find it. These systems are too dependent on your memory, which in essence becomes the heart of these record-keeping systems.

If you are in the habit of making notes haphazardly in notebooks, on slips of paper, or on the backs of envelopes, you have already discovered that these random pieces of paper can get lost in the shuffle. When you make notes randomly, it is also very easy to forget to record critically important information, like the author of the source or the page number(s).

As you will see in a moment, in addition to urging you to put your notes on notecards, I also strongly advise making reference cards for each source you read. If you don't have a systematic record of the bibliographic information (author, title, publisher, date, etc.) of your sources, you may have to waste valuable time tracking this information down when you are writing your paper.

As I have said so many times that I know you are sick of hearing me say it, research is by its nature a time-consuming process. One of the reasons I have written this book for you is to help you avoid *wasting* time, and you can avoid wasting time if you use a record-keeping system for your evidence that has these features:

- There is a complete record of all the bibliographic information for all your sources, and this information is easy to retrieve, to sort, and to manipulate.

- Each piece of evidence is easy to retrieve when you need it.

- Pieces of evidence are easy to sort and classify, making it easy to review the evidence.

Using notecards for notes and bibliographic information is a common method of notetaking that meets these criteria. I have used it for years and find it especially helpful for longer research projects.

At first, you may find the system of taking notes that I outline in the next few pages cumbersome and hard to get used to. But if you force yourself to follow the steps outlined in the next few pages, you will soon develop habits that become as simple and automatic as brushing your teeth or tying your shoes. You will find that your notecards and reference cards will save you an amazing amount of time and frustration when you are writing up your paper. You will be able to double-check specific pieces of evidence easily. Because you can sort and put your notecards into individual piles, you won't leave out critical evidence. The reference cards will give you the precise information you need for citing your sources in your text, and you can put these reference cards into alphabetical order and type your bibliography or reference list straight from the cards.

I hope I have persuaded you to try my system. The headings in the rest of this section will give you a clear sense of the process you will be following in reading and taking notes. Read subsections B and C first to get a general sense of what to do before you actually start taking notes. When you are ready to take notes, keep this book close by to use as a guide.

B. Before Reading Your Sources

1. Deciding Which Sources You Should Read First

Making this decision is not always easy, but here are a few guidelines:

- Choose the material that is written as introductory material or material for nonexperts (look at the prefaces to books; here the author usually states his purpose and the audience for whom he is writing).

- Choose the material that seems directly aimed at your working thesis/hypothesis and research questions.

- If you are already aware that certain people are considered *the* experts in the field, or if you know that Dr. X's theory is the most influential one in the field, read the work of these people first.

- Put aside more technical, difficult reading until later (see Section 4.C.2).

- If the focus of your working thesis is a primary source—a painting or paintings, a poem, a piece of music, a "classic" work like Machiavelli's *The Prince* or Darwin's *Origin*—study this primary source yourself and record your own reactions before you begin your research. Obviously you will have to come back to this source and study it several times in light of the evidence you collect.

2. Determining the Quality of Your Sources

Before you expend time and energy reading a source and taking notes on it, it would be wise to evaluate the quality of the sources you have collected, especially material that was published more than fifteen or twenty years ago.

In the world of scholarship, the work of some people is considered more valuable than the work of others. The more knowledgeable you become in a subject, the more you will become aware of this fact and the more aware you will become that the world of scholarship sometimes resembles the fashion world—there are trends, and trends change. Theories and studies that were popular in the 1950s may be considered out of date in the 1990s.

The less you know about a field, the harder it will be for you to determine the quality of the sources you look at. However, here are a few basic guidelines:

- If you are doing a research project that is essentially historical,

    ○ how did Darwin's contemporaries in nineteenth-century England react to his theories?
    ○ what did dramatists in seventeenth-century France think of Shakespeare's plays?
    ○ how did the Church in the Middle Ages portray Eve and the Virgin Mary?

    you will clearly need primary material from the historical period your question covers. But if your study is not essentially historical, you will want to focus on the most recent research and theories on your subject; concentrate on studies and data gathered in the last ten, or even five, years. Regardless of whether your research project is historical or not, you will want to know how the experts now interpret the evidence. Therefore, you should focus on secondary sources that have been published in the last ten, or five, years.

- If you do your research properly, gathering as much evidence as possible about your working thesis/hypothesis, you will notice that particular authors and/or works are referred to often. These references are clues that these authors and/or works are considered important in the field, regardless of when they were originally published. You will be expected to read and study this material yourself.

- The fact that a book or article has been published, or the fact that it is on the shelf of a library, does not automatically make that book or article a sound piece of scholarship or what experts today would call a sound piece of scholarship. In the social and natural sciences, particularly, you should be skeptical of work published more than fifteen years ago unless you have good reason to believe that the work is still considered authoritative.

3. Writing Reference Cards

Usually, when I am doing research, the *first* thing I do when I pick up one of my sources—a book, an article in a journal, an article in a collection—is to write a reference card for that source. I am going to encourage you to develop the same habit.

A reference card (or bibliography card) is a card on which you record all necessary publication information (also called bibliographic information), the kind of information you find in the card catalogue, in citations in indexes, and in authors' bibliographies and reference lists. In writing a reference card you could, of course, copy everything you imagine you might need, but it is safer to record this information in some standard form, and it is smartest to use the documentation form you will be using in the final draft of your paper. Writing up your reference cards in a documentation form appropriate for the final draft of your paper will not only mean that you will know you have taken down all the information you need, but it will also save you time and trouble when you are facing your final deadline. If your reference cards are already in proper form, you can type your final bibliography or list of works cited straight from your cards.

In Section 7, documentation systems are presented in more detail. Briefly, a documentation system is a formal or standard way of letting your readers know the sources you have used in a paper. You will notice as you do your research that documentation forms vary from field to field and sometimes from journal to journal. But we can divide documentation systems into those appropriate to the humanities and those proper for the sciences.

A humanities documentation system is used in papers and publications that take a humanities approach to a topic; these are the forms that you will find in papers written in such fields as art history, music, literature, philosophy, history, and religious studies. Papers and books that approach a topic scientifically, using empirical or quantitative approaches, will follow one of the standard scientific systems. These are the forms usually found in studies in economics, sociology, anthropology, psychology, biology, and the applied and theoretical sciences.

Appendixes A and B at the end of this book tell you more about two standard documentation forms for the humanities—the MLA style and the notes and bibliography form as given in *The Chicago Manual of Style*. In Appendixes C and D you find two variant forms of scientific systems, one commonly used in the social sciences (the APA style) and a popular form used in the natural sciences (the author-date form as given in *The Chicago Manual of Style*).

To decide which documentation system is most appropriate for your current research project, you can read Section 7.C, "Selecting an Appropriate Documentation Style." I would suggest, however, that you also check with your instructor. You may find that you will have to use a form that isn't in this book. But if your instructor asks you to follow the MLA, the APA, or the Chicago style (either the humanities or the scientific form), you will find specific information about these styles in Appendixes A through D in the back of the book. I have separated this material from the rest of the book so that you can use the appendixes as a handbook, referring to them when you need to look up something related to documentation. You can use Appendixes A, B, C, or D now, as you write your reference cards. So keep this book handy when you are doing your reading and notetaking.

I will now show you some sample reference cards so that you can see, generally, what they look like. Remember that these samples follow a particular form; your cards may look different if you are using a style other than the MLA or the APA.

You will notice that I have also included the Library of Congress call number for each of these sources on the reference card in the lower right-hand corner. I discovered this trick in my student days after I wasted valuable time having to look up the call number of a book two or even three times when I wanted to check that source again. Another time-saving trick.

To summarize: your first step is to make out a reference card for each of your sources, in the proper documentation form, before you even read the source. I take this step so that I have my own clear record of every source I consulted and so that I do not forget to record information that I will need later. Another advantage of these cards, as you will see in subsection D.2, is that they give you the information you need to look these works up again—either to take down information you missed in your first round of notetaking or to study more carefully because they have become central to your more clearly defined working hypothesis/thesis.

Reference Card for a Book: MLA Style

```
Lukacs, Georg.   The Destruction of Reason.
     Trans. Peter Palmer. Atlantic Highlands,
     NJ: Humanities Press, 1981.




                                 B
                                 2743
                                 .L7813
                                 1981
```

Reference Card for a Journal Article: MLA Style

```
Schacht, Paul.  "The Lonesomeness of Huckle-
    berry Finn." American Literature  53
    (May 1981): 189-201.




                                    P
                                    1
                                    .A6
```

Reference Card for a Book: APA Style

```
Kegan, R. (1982).  The evolving self: Problem
    and process in human development.
    Cambridge: Harvard University Press.




                                 BF
                                 713
                                 .K44
                                 1982
```

Reference Card for a Journal Article: APA Style

```
Hansen, G. L. (1982). Measuring prejudice
    against homosexuality (homosexism)
    among college students: A new scale.
    Journal of Social Psychology 117, 233-36.




                                 HM
                                 251
                                 .A1J6
```

C. *Reading Your Sources*

1. In General . . .

After you have made a reference card for a source, the next step is to read this material. This advice sounds so simple that you may reply, "But that's obvious!" However, reading is far more than passing your eye across pages of print. I must now talk to you about what reading is because one problem that many untrained researchers run into is that they don't read their sources properly.

For example, many students I have worked with are in the habit of opening one of their sources, then immediately copying sentences, sometimes whole paragraphs, onto their notecards. These students are saying to themselves, "There is lots of important information here. I must write it down." In one sense they are very right. Clearly the author felt that every sentence he/she wrote was important or he/she wouldn't have written it. But let's consider what the student researcher is actually doing when she copies a sentence. She is not reading; she is transcribing. It is difficult to read and transcribe at the same time. They are two different kinds of activities. A typist is a transcriber, and many professional, expert typists will tell you that they are able to type a paper or report without being able to tell you what the report or paper says. In fact, some typists say that if they try to read while they are typing, their typing suffers.

But, as a researcher, your task is not to transcribe. Your task is to learn, to educate yourself about your subject, to understand what others think. Your job, in other words, is to read. And since transcribing interferes with the comprehension process, you must first read to comprehend. Actually, it is only by reading that you can decide what to put in your notes. We know that every fact and statement in a work was important to the author; the question is, what do *you* consider important in this work?

So let's talk about reading. *Reading* has been defined in a number of ways. The definition that I prefer is Frank Smith's. Smith contends that reading is a very selective activity; we are "deliberately seeking just the information that we need. Need for what purpose? *To answer specific questions that we are asking.*"[1]

Do you notice that Smith's definition of reading is almost exactly the same definition I have been using for the research process? As researchers we are looking for information that we need. We are looking for answers to questions we have asked. We have gathered books and articles and other

---

[1] Frank Smith, *Reading without Nonsense* (New York and London: Teachers College Press, 1979), 105.

sources because we believe that they contain information that will help us answer our research questions, that will give us help in testing our working theses and give us the solid basis we need on which to draw conclusions.

Sometimes the question a reader asks is very specific and narrow:

- When was Julius Caesar assassinated?
- Where did the popes live during the Babylonian Captivity?
- Who developed penicillin as a drug?
- What was the average price of a loaf of bread in 1915?

When your question is this narrow and specific, you read by skimming a page, looking for a visual clue (like numbers or names) to the answer you need. You are not concerned about everything the author is saying about Julius Caesar, or the Babylonian Captivity, or penicillin.

Skimming pages to find answers to very specific questions is a perfectly natural and legitimate form of reading *when your purpose is to answer very specific questions.* You will be doing this type of reading in the course of your research project. But it is not the only kind of reading you will be doing, and it is certainly not appropriate when your purpose is to educate yourself about the perceptions the experts have of your subject. Earlier in this section I reminded you that your working hypothesis/thesis reflects your perception or point of view of a subject. I said that the process of testing your working thesis is to discover the perceptions or points of view of others, particularly those considered experts. You will not really understand these perceptions or points of view simply by skimming. Instead, you will have to read complete books, or sections of books, or complete articles, and you will be asking a series of more complex questions:

- What is the author's hypothesis or thesis?
- What evidence does this author use to test his hypothesis or to support his thesis?
- What meaning does the author give to the facts/data she uses? How does she put the facts/data together?
- What conclusions/results does the author come up with?
- How do the parts of the study or argument fit together? To me, do the parts fit together logically?
- Am I aware of facts or evidence the author did not use? Do I think he or she should have used them? Do the facts and evidence I know support this author's argument, or do they weaken it?
- How does this author's approach compare with that of other authors I have read? How do this author's conclusions and results match the

conclusions and results of other authors I have read? Do I consider this point of view more persuasive than another point of view?

To answer these questions, you must read the entire text as a whole. You must follow the author's line of thought from beginning to end. At the same time, you must keep in mind what you have learned about the subject from other sources. You won't get satisfactory answers to these questions by reading just one sentence or one paragraph. Trying to copy down specific sentences as you read will interfere with your ability to find your answers to these questions.

When you pick up a particular source, ask yourself why you are reading this particular source. The broader the questions you are asking ("How does this author see my subject?"), the more obvious it is that you must read for comprehension. As you pick up each book and article, ask yourself,

- What do I expect to learn from this source?
- What do I need from this source?
- What are the questions for which I expect to find answers?

There are some tricks you can use to help answer these questions, particularly when your source is a book or a collection of essays. Review your working hypothesis/thesis and your research questions. Then

- Check the book's table of contents. Are certain essays or chapters more directly relevant than others? Why are they more directly relevant? What information do you expect them to give you?
- Check the book's index. Look for key words in your working hypothesis/thesis and in your research questions. Look for these key words, or related words, in the index. Do you need to read only those pages, or should you read whole sections or chapters?
- If a book seems to be written directly on your subject, read the preface, the introductory and concluding chapters. In these parts of the book, the author will spell out his or her approach and conclusions. Use them as a framework for reading the entire book.

2. How to Read Material You Find Difficult to Read

As fields of study become more and more specialized and as more and more complex and sophisticated methods of testing become popular, research in many fields becomes more and more difficult for novices to read and interpret. If you come across articles and books written for experts in the field, you may find them very hard going; the vocabulary may sound like gibberish to you, and you will probably sense that the author is assuming that you have knowledge that you, in fact, do not have.

Whenever possible, you should try to use this material, but you will have to use your common sense. You are having trouble reading the material because it was written for experts.

- Do not attempt to read the material until you have spent some time educating yourself about the subject. Go back to textbooks, introductory works, specialized encyclopedias, and accessible but authoritative periodicals before you try to tackle this material.

- Isolate key terms (words or phrases) that are clearly important terms in these more difficult works. Look these terms up in a textbook or specialized dictionary. Write out the definitions on cards. Try to understand the concepts for which they stand. Use these definition cards when you come back to this difficult reading material.

- When you do read this material, be prepared to read slowly and carefully. You may not understand the work completely, but you want to try to understand the author's basic approach. Concentrate, therefore, on introductions and conclusions; look for the author's thesis or hypothesis, results and/or conclusions.

- Whatever you do, do *not* mindlessly copy notes from these works. Do not take down anything in the author's words that you feel you don't understand. If you do take down some of the author's statements, it may be wise for you to include on the notecard your own paraphrase of what you think the author is saying.

D. Taking Notes

1. In General . . .

After you have read one of your sources to comprehend the author's point of view, you are ready to take some notes on it. Before you do, however, let's consider what kinds of notes will be most helpful to you. Keep in mind that it is pointless to recopy massive amounts of a source onto notecards. If you decide that a portion of a source has a great deal of information you need, it would make more sense to photocopy that portion of the source than to transcribe it onto notecards. But these photocopies are not a substitute for notecards. You need to have your information both in a form that is readily accessible to you and in a form that is meaningful to you and your current project. There are two basic kinds of notes that fit these criteria:

- summaries of a source;
- notes on specific information:
  - facts or data, concrete and specific pieces of information (results of studies, statistics, names and identities of particular people, definitions of terms, and so on);
  - the hypotheses, theses, conclusions, opinions of the experts.

In a moment I'll describe these two types of notes, but I probably should alert you here to the need to be careful about plagiarism. Plagiarism is a scary word; the last thing I want to do is to make you uptight about it. Let me reassure you that this whole book is designed to keep you from falling into the really serious traps of *plagiarism*, which essentially means passing off someone else's ideas or words as your own. I discuss plagiarism in some detail in Section 6, and if you are concerned about the problem, you may want to read subsection A of Section 6 now. Here let me say that you need to be careful when you are making your notecards, so that you know which language belongs to the author of a source and which language is your paraphrase of an author's ideas. You need to be careful in writing your notes because these notes are going to be your "sources" when you are writing the final drafts of your paper. If you copy an author's sentence word for word but forget to put quotation marks around that sentence, then you will assume that these are your words. Similarly, if you follow an author's train of thought, simply changing a word or a phrase here or there, your note will be a piece of illegitimate paraphrase like the example of the Gettysburg Address I give in Section 6.B.3. If you use this note in your paper, someone might accuse you of illegitimate paraphrasing.

Don't go into a panic about plagiarism; just be careful. In the next two sections on taking notes, I will give you some advice that will show you how to "be careful."

2. Writing Summaries

After you read each of your sources, your first step will be to write a short summary of the whole work, whether it is a journal article, the chapter in a book, or a whole book. You should also write summary cards on nonprint sources; using the general strategies I give in this section, you can capture the gist of an interview, a concert you have attended, or a film you have seen.

Your summary is a natural consequence of the process you have been through of reading for comprehension. In it you will capture the gist of the author's argument or study. Writing such summaries is a common practice in the world of research. If you have consulted any of the abstracts listed in Section 3, what you read in them were summaries or abstracts of sources; if, in the course of your own research, you look at any primary research reports in the social sciences or the natural sciences, you will notice that most of them are prefaced with an abstract. These summaries are called abstracts because they "abstract" the major points of the author's argument or study or experiment, boiling it down to its central points. That's just what you will be doing in your own summaries.

These summaries are really the most valuable notes you can make. They will help you in several ways.

- They are some of your most valuable evidence. They pull together the general conclusions and approaches of experts who have done research in your subject. In most cases in your own research paper you will be referring only to this summary information.

- As your research progresses and the direction of your search becomes more focused, you will realize that certain works are more important to you than others. Your summaries will tell you which works you should go back to and study more carefully.

- If, as your research progresses, you find that you need more specific information about a particular topic, your summaries will tell you where you can find this specific information.

- Writing these summaries will prevent you from wasting your time recopying massive amounts of a book or an article onto notecards. They will keep you from becoming a passive sponge. The act of writing these summaries is an act of digesting your reading, of pulling out the most important parts of the work and getting them into your head, which is where the information needs to be if you are going to think about it.

Summaries should be written essentially in your own words, although you could include *short* quoted excerpts if you decide the author's words summarize a point most precisely. Probably the best way to write a summary is to put your source away, out of sight. Then ask yourself the following questions:

- What problem or issue was the author trying to understand or resolve in this work?
- What was his or her thesis or hypothesis?
- What were the author's results or conclusions?
- What was the author's method or approach in developing his or her argument or testing his or her thesis?
- Are there particular features of this work that could be especially helpful later in your research? If so, make a note about them in your summary. For example, if the author gives extensive statistics that you know you will want to refer to, jot this information down.

Write enough so that what you write makes sense to you (remember that it will be a few weeks before you use these notecards); but you don't need to use full sentences. Capture the gist of what the author was doing. Another technique you could use is one that Linda Flower calls "nutshell and teach."[2] Pretend that you are on a television talk show. The moderator turns to you and says, "We're running out of time. In a minute or two could you give us the essence of this author's work?" If you are having trouble with your summary, try doing a freewrite first in the Reading section of your Researcher's Notebook.

After you have written your summary, quickly double-check to be sure that all facts you include are correct (the number of subjects in a study, the dates of an historical event, and the like). You will probably be aware of parts of your summary where you are close to the language of your source; you can then go back to your source and decide whether it would be easier to quote those words directly.

I usually write these summaries on the back of my reference cards. If you don't choose this system, *be sure* that on the notecard with your summary you write at least the full name of the author or authors and the title of the work. If you quote any of the author's words, be sure to jot down the page number or numbers.

Writing summaries or abstracts is really an art in itself. Doing them well depends upon many things: your ability to see the main ideas in a longer piece of prose and your confidence in your ability to see the main points; your awareness of different points of view on a topic; your knowledge of a subject area—to name a few. It is an art that is closely associated with growing intellectually, so it is worth working on. But don't get discouraged if you sometimes find it difficult.

[2] *Problem-solving Strategies for Writing*, 2nd ed. (San Diego: Harcourt Brace Jovanovich, 1985), 94–95.

Examples of Summaries

To Smith, the major conflict between the North and the South was the very different perceptions of slavery each region had. To the North, a moral issue; to the South, an economic necessity. Good detailed discussion of the kinds of work slaves did (insights into Southern agricultural practices). Lots of statistics on numbers of slaves in each Southern state, 1850–60 (pp. 186–97).

Wilson & Jones were testing the hypothesis that violence on TV encourages people to resolve problems physically. Longitudinal study—60 subjects—all male. Results inconclusive. Note date: a recent study.

Murphy & Nolan studied the effects of temperature on the germination of sugar pine seeds. Looked at oxygen uptake, ATP levels, moisture content of seeds imbibed at 5°C and 25°C. Results: seeds wouldn't germinate at temperatures above 17°C. Murphy & Nolan suggest reason is the effects of high temperatures on membrane properties.

Pretty technical study of how bees learn. Specifically, how they use landmarks to find their way home. Common assumption—insects have to store in memory exact "photographs" of the area. But Gould's hypothesis is that they can form more flexible mental maps, as vertebrates do. Experiments involved turning bees loose in various landscapes some distance from the hive and timing how long it took them to get home. Results section full of math I don't understand, but Gould claims these results support his hypothesis that bees can form " 'cognitive maps' " (863).

Review of 1st exhibit of impressionists by French critic, published in Paris newspaper in 1874. Written as a little story in which the reviewer and an Academy painter walk around the exhibit and comment on the paintings. VERY sarcastic. Could use to illustrate how "avant-garde" impressionism was—& differences in Academy, impressionist styles.

In this book Edwards looks at all of Waller's plays in relation to her life and to what was going on in theater in 1920–30. Chpt. each on *Lovers, Molly, Window.* Good background info on American regional theater. I like his reading of *Molly* as picture of Waller's struggle to free herself from family/escape oppression of Smalltown.

3. Taking Notes on Specific Information

Now, and only now, should you consider taking specific notes on a work. As I said in the previous subsection, the most important notes you will take will probably be the summaries you write of your readings. Other notes you take will fall into one of two categories of evidence:

- Facts or data, concrete and specific pieces of information, such as the results of studies, statistics, names and identities of particular people, definitions of terms, etc.

- The hypotheses, theses, conclusions, opinions of the experts (in certain cases, you may want to take down the author's specific words).

While you are in the process of educating yourself in general about your subject, you should probably keep these types of notes to a minimum. As you develop specific research questions and as the whole research process becomes more focused, you will probably find yourself taking more of these specific notes.

a. Facts or Data

When you are taking down basic facts and figures, you can usually just abstract the pertinent facts you want and jot them down for yourself in shorthand fashion (see Sample Notecards 1 and 2). But you should make a couple of distinctions here.

The first is between facts and figures that come directly from the work the author has done and facts and figures he or she has taken from somewhere else. Your reading of the text—the context of the fact—will normally tell you which is which. Obviously numbers given in the methods section of a study or experiment, for example, or the numbers in the results section of such a work, are the author's own. When I talk about facts and figures that the author has taken from somewhere else, I mean facts and figures like those italicized in the statements below:

When the battle of Sanchez was over, *1,500 men lay dead* on the field.

Because *anything above 5 parts xenocane per million will kill plant and animal life,* xenocane should not be dumped in landfills; it can too easily seep into water sources.

Here you want to pay close attention to context. If the author you are reading gives no source for this fact, *and* if it is clear that this is not the author's own "fact," then you can consider this information a commonly accepted fact in the field and make a notecard like Sample Notecards 3 and 4. But if the author gives a source for this information (in a note or citation), you should deal with it the same way you deal with material the author has taken from other sources (see subsection D.4).

In some cases, what looks like a simple fact is really the author's interpretation of data. Let us say, for example, that the context makes clear

Sample Notecard 1

```
world military expenditures

     1971                  1980
USA 32%              USA 24%
USSR 25%             USSR 24%
Third World 9%       Third World 16%

                      p.xix, Stockholm
                      International
                      Peace Research Inst.,
                      SIPRI Yearbook,
                      Armaments 1981
```

Sample Notecard 2

```
subjects of study = 75 high school students

1/2 = SAT verbal scores over 600

1/2 =    "     "       "    under 400

instrument used = Howard-Smith Reading
Comprehension Test

                      Sorensen
                      "Comprehension &
                      Thinking"
                      pp. 40-41
```

Sample Notecard 3

```
1500 died in the Battle of Sanchez

                      Vandervoort
                      Glorious Victory
                      p. 176
```

Sample Notecard 4

```
xenocane—lethal above 5 parts per million

                        Samuelson
                        "Xenocane" in
                        Greene & Walters
                        Protecting Our Water
                        p. 87
```

Sample Notecard 5

```
Samuelson considers anything above 5 parts per
million of xenocane lethal

                        Samuelson
                        "Xenocane" in
                        Greene & Walters
                        Protecting Our Water
                        p. 87
```

that when the author says that anything above 5 parts xenocane per million can kill plants and animals, this figure is the *author's* estimate of the danger level of this chemical; in such cases, your note should read accordingly (see Sample Notecard 5).

b. To Paraphrase or to Quote Directly

It is in the area of an author's general interpretation of factual material and those parts of texts in which an author is clearly stating his or her opinions that you normally face decisions about paraphrasing or quoting. Here are a few pointers to keep in mind.

Except in those cases in which you are abstracting a simple fact or number, it is very difficult to paraphrase a short excerpt of a text (two or three sentences) because the text is so closely tied to the author's point of view. Trying to paraphrase such short excerpts can often lead you into illegitimate paraphrasing, where, although you change a word or phrase here or there, you are really recapturing the author's line of thought. To avoid any hint of plagiarism in your notes, remember what I've been encouraging you to do throughout this book:

Step back from the author's words and write about what the author *is doing* rather than recording what the author is *saying* right here.

If you follow this general guideline, you will see that paraphrase usually works best for more extended parts of a text; it's really the same thing as summarizing (see Sample Notecard 6). Stepping back and writing about what the author is doing can also work in paraphrasing shorter excerpts when you realize that what you are doing in the paraphrase is putting a specific idea in a context; take a look at the first sentence of Sample Notecard 9, and compare it with the first sentence of the original passage from Lasch.

In my own notetaking, my habit is to isolate ideas that I consider central to the author's point of view and to quote these ideas directly. Sometimes I quote full sentences, but often I abstract key ideas in sentences and quote only the central parts. Unless a quotation I take down is self-evident, I usually put this idea into context by telling myself how this quoted excerpt fits the author's general argument (see Sample Notecards 7 and 8). Taking down critical ideas in the author's own words has several advantages. Not only do I not have to worry about illegitimate paraphrase, but when I read over my cards later, I know precisely what the author said. I usually do most of my paraphrasing later, when I am writing my paper. At that point I know what my own point is, and I can then express how this author's ideas "fit" with mine.

Sample Notecard 6

```
DiMarco shows how traditional readings of
Williams' poem "Victory" are generally
religious interpretations and emphasize the
Christian symbolism

                         DiMarco
                         "Poetry of
                         Williams"
                         pp. 776-82
```

Sample Notecard 7

```
As Jamison sees it, there are two main schools
of historians: The "'I was there' school," with
the historian attempting to "record a past
event as if the historian were an eye-witness"
(p. 240) and the "analytical school," where
"all historical data become grist for the
statistician's mill" (p. 241).

                            Jamison
                            "History Today"
```

Sample Notecard 8

```
Valdez sees the anthropologist as "walking the
fine line between objectivism and subjectiv-
ism" (p. 876). Her solution: "observational
subjectivism ... the ability to watch both
what is happening outside oneself and to
observe one's own reaction at the same time"
(p. 890).

                            Valdez
                            "Dilemma"
                            in White and
                            Campbell
                            Anthro. Today
```

When you quote authors, you must do so carefully. See my advice below in "Some General Advice about Making Notecards."

c. Some General Advice about Making Notecards

- Put only one piece of information on each card. It may seem as if you are wasting paper, but you are really saving time. When you are writing your paper, you will want to be able to stack these cards in piles that correspond to each section of your paper.

- Get in the habit of putting at least the following information on each card (if you put this information in the same place on each card, you will be developing a habit that makes it less likely that you will forget to record this information):

- ○ the author's last name
- ○ a short title of the work
- ○ the page number

Please note that if you do not make reference cards, you will be forced to put all bibliographic information on *each* notecard.

- On Sample Notecards 4, 5, and 8 I give an author and a title and then, after "in," another set of authors and a title. These are references to collections of articles. Valdez' article, with the shortened title of "Dilemma," was published in a book edited by White and Campbell titled *Anthropology Today*. Whenever you come across edited collections in your research, be sure to take down the author and title of the article and the inclusive pages on which the article appears, as well as full bibliographic information on the book itself on your reference card; you will need it for documentation purposes (see the "Work in a Collection" sections of Appendixes A, B, C, and D). On my notecards, as you can see, I usually record both the author and title of the article and the editor(s) and title of the collection.
- If you have made any photocopies of sources or portions of sources, be sure you take notes on this material (and be sure you have reference cards for each source). If there is an extensive amount of material that you want to remember you have, you could make notes that read like these:

  For Allen Jones's view of the sources of racism, see my copy of *The Plague of Racism*, p. 42, paragraph 3.

  or

  I have complete statistics for mortgage rates for the last 15 years. See copy of pp. 165–66 of John Brown, *Financial Vagaries*.

- If you are quoting the author's words, be very careful that you quote accurately and completely.

  - ○ Be sure to put the quoted material in quotation marks (if you don't, you won't know that these words are quoted).
  - ○ Copy the phrase, sentence, or sentences *exactly* as they are in the text—capital letters, punctuation, spelling, and all.
  - ○ If you want to leave out a word or words, indicate their omission with ellipses (. . .). Be sure that the material you omit does not leave a statement that misrepresents the author's message.
  - ○ If you need to add any information or words, put this added material in brackets [ ]. Note that brackets have square corners. They are not parentheses (). If you were to put this material into parentheses, you

wouldn't know, later, if this material was material you added or material that the author herself had put in parentheses. (See Section 6.B.4 for a more detailed discussion of conventions for omitting and adding words in quotations.)

Check Sample Notecards 9, 10, and 11 and compare the quoted material on the notecard with the original passage to see how these guidelines work in practice.

The Original Passage

Psychoanalysis, a therapy that grew out of experience with severely repressed and morally rigid individuals who needed to come to terms with a rigorous inner "censor," today finds itself confronted more and more often with a "chaotic and

Sample Notecard 9

```
Lasch is comparing the nature of the problems
that psychoanalysis dealt with in its earlier
years and the problems of patients it sees today.
Today psychoanalysis "must deal with patients who
'act out' their conflicts instead of repressing
or sublimating them. These patients ... tend to
cultivate a protective shallowness in emotional
relations."

                              Christopher Lasch
                              Narcissism
                              p. 37
```

Sample Notecard 10

```
"A military scholar who had written and
translated several works on strategy ...,
[General Henry W.] Halleck was a cautious
general who waged war by the book."

                              James McPherson
                              Ordeal by Fire
                              p. 158
```

Sample Notecard 11

```
Commenting on the traditional drug treatment
of depression, Leavitt writes: "For the
approximately 30% of depressed patients
refractory to TCAs [tricyclic antidepres-
sants], MAOIs [monoamine oxidase inhibitors]
provide a useful alternative. The MAOIs
irreversibly inactivate MAO, an enzyme of
major importance in the metabolism of epine-
phrine, norepinephrine, dopamine, and 5-HT
[serotonin]."
                              Fred Leavitt
                              Drugs and
                              Behavior
                              p. 248
```

impulse-ridden character." It must deal with patients who "act out" their conflicts instead of repressing or sublimating them. These patients, though often
ingratiating, tend to cultivate a protective shallowness in emotional relations.

> Christopher Lasch, *The Culture of Narcissism: American Life in an Age of Diminishing Expectations* (New York: W. W. Norton and Co., 1978), 37.

The Original Passage

A military scholar who had written and translated several works on strategy
(which earned him the sobriquet "Old Brains"), Halleck was a cautious general
who waged war by the book.

> James M. McPherson, *Ordeal by Fire: The Civil War and Reconstruction* (New York: Alfred A. Knopf, 1982), 158.

The Original Passage

For the approximately 30% of depressed patients refractory to TCAs, MAOIs
provide a useful alternative. The MAOIs irreversibly inactivate MAO, an enzyme
of major importance in the metabolism of epinephrine, norepinephrine,
dopamine, and 5-HT.

> Fred Leavitt, *Drugs and Behavior*, 2nd ed. (New York: John Wiley and Sons, 1982), 248.

4. Dealing with Material an Author Has Taken from Other Sources

When I discussed, in Section 1, what research is about, I said that
researchers build on the work of others. So in the reading that you do,
you will find that the authors of your sources are themselves referring

to the work of others. These references may be summaries, or they may be direct quotations.

Example 1

In general, the research literature suggests that good readers tend to have more positive self concepts than poor readers (Athey & Holmes, 1969; Hallock, 1958; Lockhart, 1965; Lumpkin, 1959; Malmquist, 1958; Padelford, 1969; Seay, 1960; Stevens, 1971; Zimmerman & Allebrand, 1965).

> Irene Athey, "Reading Research in the Affective Domain," in *Theoretical Models and Processes of Reading,* ed. Harry Singer and Robert B. Ruddell, 2nd ed. (Newark, DE: International Reading Association, 1976), 357.

Example 2

Recent evidence suggests that the toxin provokes the ADP-ribosylation of the same GTP-binding component discussed above (Moss and Vaughan, 1977; Gill and Meren, 1978; Cassel and Pfeuffer, 1978; G. L. Johnson *et al.,* 1978; Gilman *et al.,* 1979).

> Peter J. Roach, "Principles of the Regulation of Enzyme Activity," in *Gene Expression: Translation and Behavior of Proteins,* ed. David M. Prescott and Lester Goldstein, vol. 4 of *Cell Biology: A Comprehensive Treatise* (New York: Academic Press, 1980), 238–39.

Example 3

Andrew D. White asserted in 1890 that "with very few exceptions, the city governments of the United States are the worst in Christendom—the most expensive, the most inefficient, and the most corrupt."[6]

> Richard Hofstadter, *The Age of Reform From Bryan to F.D.R.* (New York: Random House, Vintage Books, 1955), 176.

When you run across such references (summaries or direct quotations) that are relevant to your subject, you will probably be tempted to take this information from the source that you are reading and be done with it.

I must warn you that experienced researchers don't stop here. Instead of copying the information on their notecards, they make a note to themselves to find the author's sources and to look at these works firsthand. You should do the same.

Thus, when you see a reference to a list of studies (as in the first and second examples), you should copy the bibliographic information for each source from the reference list or bibliography. This information goes into the Sources section of your Researcher's Notebook, with a note from you about what to look for in these sources.

When you come across a quotation that you want (as in the third example), again copy down the bibliographic information for its original source and be sure to note the page number(s). If you decide to use such a quotation in your paper, you should be quoting it from its original source.

If you have honestly made every possible effort to locate the original source but find that you cannot do so, you may quote from the secondary source. On your notecard:

- Be sure to put *your* source's words in double quotation marks and the material your author quotes in single quotation marks.

- Put all bibliographic information about the original source (see the author's notes) as well as the necessary information about your source.

Your notecard for Example 3 would look like this:

```
"Andrew D. White asserted in 1890 that 'with
very few exceptions, the city governments of
the United States are the worst in Christendom
-- the most expensive, the most inefficient,
and the most corrupt.'"
                          White, Forum,
                          Vol. X (Dec.
                          1890), p. 25,
                          quoted by
                          Richard
                          Hofstadter,
                          Age of Reform,
                          p. 176
```

As the authors you read give credit where credit is due, so must you when you write your paper. Under no circumstances may you imply in your final paper that you have read and studied works which, in reality, you have only seen referred to in works of others. Your notes must clearly indicate the source of all ideas and the authors of specific words.

E. Summary

Because reading critically and thinking about the evidence you gather is the heart of the research process, I'd like to make a few final summary remarks about this stage of the research process.

Notecards and reference cards are important tools for the researcher. You need an easy-to-manipulate, systematic way of recording your evidence. This evidence, after all, is the essential material you will use to test your original assumption; it constitutes the building material of the conclusion you are drawing about your subject. However, if the evidence on your notecards is only on your notecards and not in your head, you have missed the whole point of the research process. The notecards should be reminders of what you have already learned.

At this stage in the research process, the most important work you are doing is in your Researcher's Notebook.

In the Reading section of your Notebook, you are critically examining the work of others. You are asking questions of the texts you are looking at; you are digesting the work of others, comprehending it, comparing it with what you've learned about your subject. In the Working Thesis section of your Notebook, you are writing to yourself about the picture that is forming in your mind as you put the pieces of the puzzle together, take these same pieces apart and put them together in different ways, decide which pieces in the puzzle are missing, and ask the questions that will allow you to find those pieces.

If you use your Researcher's Notebook wisely, you will realize that you have started writing your research paper *as* you read and study your evidence.

The writing you do in your Researcher's Notebook is a very important part of the writing process. You are figuring out what you want to say. The final paper you are going to produce, I will remind you, is *not* going to be a "memory dump" paper (to use a computer term). You are *not* going to *list* what others have said (John Doe says this about X, and Mary Brown says that about X, and Sally Smith says something else again). Rather, your paper is going to focus on the conclusions *you* have reached about X from your critical reading of John Doe and Mary Brown and Sally Smith and everyone else who can help you draw this conclusion. If you gather all of your evidence first and then attempt to make some sense of it, you will be overwhelmed. I've seen it happen too often to students I've worked with. Besides, as I've now said over and over again, how do you know what evidence you need if you have not, throughout the entire research process, been asking questions, if you have not been the one to give your research direction?

This sense of direction, I repeat, is critical to you as a researcher. As you have already now discovered for yourself, the process of gathering evidence is not as straightforward and neat as all of us would like it to be. Experienced researchers know that their first visit to the library will not be the only visit they will make in the course of a research project. They will return as they come across the titles of promising sources in the bibliographies and reference lists of the books and articles they are reading. As their research changes direction, or as they realize that they are finally zeroing in on the real question they want to ask, they return to indexes, reference materials, the subject catalogue. I have found myself in the library, tracking down the answers to one or two final questions, when I have been in the second or even third draft of my papers. If your experience is like that of other researchers, you will also find yourself rereading important sources several times at different stages of your research, gleaning more information from that source as your knowledge of the subject grows and deepens.

Finally, I should alert you that the research process rarely ends naturally. You will feel that you have more to learn, more sources to read, more to think about, more directions to explore. Experts have spent years, even decades, investigating a subject. As time passes and you get more deeply into your research, you will want to make a conscious effort to isolate and narrow down the area of investigation you want to focus on. Be prepared for the fact that, approximately three weeks before the final paper is due, you will have to say, "The major portion of my research is finished. I must now decide what I am going to say in my paper." Obviously, by this point the major portion of your research must be finished; you must have found, read, and studied the important evidence about your subject. If you are doing a primary research project, you must set a deadline for the time when all your raw data will be in your hands, a deadline that leaves you plenty of time to analyze those data, draw your conclusions, and write your report.

Use your time during this collecting/reading/studying stage of your project wisely. Plan to spend an hour here, a couple of hours there, *every day*, reading, searching, thinking, writing in your Researcher's Notebook. Give your brain as much time as possible to mull over what you are putting into it.

Then about three weeks before the final paper must be handed in to your instructor, when it is time to start work on this paper, turn to the next section of this book.

SECTION 5

Writing Your Paper

If you are on schedule, you should have about three weeks before your final paper is due. I cannot say that it is time for you to start writing, because you have already been doing a great deal of writing over the past weeks in your Researcher's Notebook. But in your Researcher's Notebook you have been writing to yourself, for yourself. As you have tested your working hypothesis/thesis, you have been making sense of your subject. If the Researcher's Notebook has worked for you the way it should, by this stage your own view of your subject ought to be fairly clear to you. This doesn't necessarily mean that the learning process is finished. The final test of how clear your ideas are to you comes in this last stage of the research process, presenting your view of your subject to other people. In showing others how you make sense of the subject, in showing others one way to put the parts of the puzzle together, you will be determining the exact shape of each piece of the puzzle and carefully and precisely fitting the pieces together. As you work on presenting your ideas to others, you will be honing and refining your own thinking.

In some very important ways, writing a research paper is no different from writing other kinds of prose. With and in this paper you are talking to other human beings and your main concern is going to be that they understand what you are saying. You have had enough experience with writing to know that one of the significant differences in addressing others on paper and talking with them face to face is that your readers can't interrupt you when they become lost or confused. Thus, one of the major challenges now before you is finding a mode of presentation that your readers will find clear, coherent, and convincing.

The shape a paper takes is determined by a writer's answers to four basic, interrelated questions:

- What do I want to say about my subject? What is the message I want to convey to my readers?

- Who are my readers? What do they know about my subject? What do they expect me to say? What do they know about the specific idea I am trying to express?

- What persona or speaker do I want to present in this paper? What kind of person do I want my readers to hear speaking to them from this paper?

- What is my purpose in writing this paper? What impact do I want to have on my reader? What do I want my readers to think or feel when they have finished reading my paper?

Often the answers a writer develops for these questions lead him or her to use a particular genre. Genre, which means "type" or "kind" in French, is a term usually used to categorize literary works, but it can also apply to nonfiction writing. Book reviews, biographies, ethnographies, poetry analyses, grant proposals, even various forms of business documents could be called genres. A research paper is not a genre, but certain types of papers based on research are: primary research reports and reviews of the literature are definite categories of academic writing, conventional modes of conveying ideas and information. I am raising the issue of genres here for two related reasons. The first is to alert you that I am breaking down my discussion of the writing process into separate sections on primary research reports, reviews of the literature, and critical papers. The second reason accounts for these divisions. A genre is not a mold or an equation into which the writer mindlessly inserts ideas or information. A more reasonable way to conceptualize a genre is to see it as a conventional form of language use, like the greeting "how are you?" It is a form of verbal shorthand adopted by a particular group of people to facilitate the exchange of common types of messages. Just as "how are you?" is recognized by us all as a gesture to acknowledge another person and make contact with him or her, so a genre automatically signals to readers the general intentions or purposes a writer has for a particular piece of writing. When a reader recognizes that a text is a primary research report, he knows not only that the writer wants to describe a study or experiment she did but that she will follow a pattern that makes it easy for the reader to locate certain kinds of information, to evaluate the writer's work, and/or to set up a similar study.

I've divided some of my discussion of the writing process according to genres because advice I may give you if you are doing a critical paper will differ from the advice I'd give you if you are writing a primary research report. But one point about writing is general enough that it applies to all three kinds of papers: Composing a paper is the process of making decisions. And the only way for you to make the numerous "micro" decisions you will need to make—about which word to use, about how to structure a sentence, about how to organize a paragraph, about which evidence belongs where—is for you to have a clear sense of the overall purpose you have for the paper as a whole. In subsections B, C, and D you will find a great deal of discussion about purpose. At times I will be informing you about purposes that are built into a genre—what readers will expect you to be doing. At other times I will be offering strategies that will enable you, by adopting these generally accepted purposes, to decide the most effective way to present your ideas and points.

There are a few more general words of advice I can offer you about the writing process that you are now beginning, so before you turn to the subsection relevant to the paper you are writing, read over "The Writing Process: An Overview."

A. The Writing Process: An Overview

1. Writing for Readers

It's hard to tell why so many students seem to think that research papers have to be dull and dry. Perhaps it has something to do with the pointlessness of those "reports" on dinosaurs you copied out of encyclopedias in the seventh grade. Or maybe it is because, for you, "formal" means "dull and dry." For me, dullness and dryness have nothing to do with subject matter or style per se, and everything to do with my sense of the writer's involvement with his or her material, and the writer's interest in me, the reader. The whole process you've been following up to this point has been intended to involve you with your subject matter. Now you must attend to the challenge of getting your readers equally involved.

When experienced researchers write a paper, they are usually addressing an audience (readers) of other experts who are interested in the general subject the writer is writing about. The purpose of these writers is to inform this audience about the work they've done and the conclusions they've reached. By presenting their work as thorough and their conclusions as logical, sound conclusions, they therefore wish to persuade their readers that the readers should see their subject as they see it. These writers usually, then, present themselves as serious, thoughtful, reasonable people, confident that the work and thinking they have done is worthy of consideration.

You are not an experienced researcher speaking to other experts. But you will write a much more successful paper if you can imagine yourself in a situation like the one I just outlined. You will write a much more successful paper if you can avoid the traps of "writing for the teacher." If you think of your reader only as your instructor, two bad things may happen to you as a writer:

- You may fall into the trap of feeling that your purpose in writing the paper is to prove to the instructor that you have done your research properly. You will be tempted to drag in every source you have examined, whether it applies to your main point or not, just to show your instructor that you read this material. In other words, thinking that your purpose is to prove to your instructor that you did your research properly may cause you to write a "memory-dump" paper.

- You may fall into the trap of feeling that you have no right to say anything about this subject because your reader (the instructor) knows far more about your subject than you do. This perception will hurt the paper you produce because you will be tempted to leave out some essential information since, you will say to yourself, "My instructor already knows what X is." This perception will hurt the paper you produce because you will fail to explain ideas that need to be explained, simply because you assume your instructor already knows what you are talking about.

The best way to avoid the traps inherent in writing only for your instructor is not to think of your instructor as your audience (reader).

Plan to address your paper to other students.

The students you address may be either the other students who are enrolled in your class or the students who are majoring in the field or department in which your course is offered. Assume that these students are interested in your general subject; surely they have demonstrated their interest by taking the course or majoring in this field. Because you have been going to class regularly and reading the required material, you know what your fellow students in the class already know. But remember that they have not done the research you have done and that they certainly do not know what your conclusions are. Therefore, you legitimately have to assume that you will have to show these readers what the parts of your idea look like, and you will have to explain clearly how the parts fit together. Addressing an audience of your peers will put you in the position of experienced researchers, whose purpose is to inform their peers about the work they've done and the conclusions they've reached. Because you want to persuade other students to accept your view of your subject as a valid and legitimate view, you will present yourself as a serious, thoughtful, reasonable researcher. You will have a sense of confidence because you know that you have done a thorough job of researching and you have given your subject much thought, and you will not be intimidated because you know that you know more about your subject than your readers do.

2. Working from Whole to Part

Your readers are going to expect your paper, in the words of my students, "to flow"; they will expect your paper to be clear and coherent from beginning to end. In my experience as a writer, clarity and coherence do not just happen; they are the result of conscious effort. Too many students I talk to think that the mark of a good writer is "getting it right" in the first draft; they seem to feel that the need to do a series of drafts—the need to revise—is a clear sign that they are unskilled writers. If that's true, then you'll have to classify me as an unskilled writer, because what I want to say rarely comes out "right" in my first attempt to put it on paper. My major concern, like that of all experienced writers, is to be sure that my readers understand exactly what I mean. I am willing to experiment with different organizational patterns, to try out various ways of expressing an idea, to look for just the right word or phrase—to go through as much revising and rewriting as necessary to reach this goal. Considering all the time and effort you have expended on this research project up to this point, I hope that your goal, too, is to do as much revising and rewriting as is necessary to develop a paper that precisely and clearly reproduces the ideas you have in your mind.

Ironically, the goal of getting it right in the first draft runs counter to everything we know about effective problem solving. Trying to make all kinds of decisions at once ties your brain into knots, potentially leading to a major case of writer's block. The reasonable way to write is to focus your attention on one thing at a time, writing first to discover your answers to "macro" questions, and in subsequent drafts working your way down to the "micro" ones.

- Your first concern should be the *general shape* of your presentation, which means translating your purpose into a skeleton of the paper as a whole. At this stage you want to work on deciding what your main points will be, where they should be placed, and, generally, what type of support you will need for each.

- After you are satisfied that you have a meaningful, coherent overall shape, then you can focus on sharpening and outlining individual sections. Your attention in these first two steps is on your ideas—getting them into words that come closer and closer to expressing what you have in your mind.

- When you have a good sense of what a particular section is supposed to do, you can give your attention to each paragraph, considering its organization, working with specific sentences, concentrating on word choice, making sure you provide transitions that link this paragraph to what you said earlier, and preparing us for what is coming next.

- Finally, when the paper has reached the point at which all these earlier problems have been satisfactorily resolved, you can worry about editing and proofreading. Don't waste time early in the process correcting spelling, punctuation, subject-verb agreement, and the like. There can be real dangers in polishing your prose too soon. The more you polish, the less willing you will be to throw out a paragraph or do a major revision, even though you know what you have isn't right.

I want to introduce two basic strategies that will give you a way to focus on the shape of the entire paper. One strategy is making a map of the territory; the other is writing an abstract of your paper. They are slightly different means of achieving the same end: enabling you to make the macro decisions upon which your micro decisions will be based.

a. Maps of the Territory

You are no doubt familiar with outlines—in theory, if not in practice. Traditional outlines are one kind of map. I prefer the broader term "map of the territory" because it so precisely expresses the functions of this strategy. Like a road map, a map of your paper gives you a detailed picture of your entire paper at one glance. With a map you represent to yourself

- the *direction* of your ideas (what idea comes first, second, third, etc.);
- the *level* of each idea (what is a main point and what is a subordinate point, what is illustration, evidence, explanation);
- the *relationships* of ideas (Y causes Z, or Y is part of Z, or if Y, then Z).

Outlines are essentially a verbal map. The common division markers

> I.
>> A.
>>> 1.
>>>> a.

indicate the relationships of ideas, both temporal and logical. Concepts marked by the same number or letter are of equal importance (I = II = III), while the letter or number that follows in the pattern indicates a subordinate idea (A is a part of I, 1 is a part of A, and so on). You can express items in an outline as topics (II. Latin American debt) or by making full grammatical statements (II. In the past ten years Latin American debt has risen at an alarming rate).

Writers who are more visual than verbal may prefer maps that represent temporal and logical relationships in forms that look like diagrams. To see what visual maps might look like, turn to subsection D.3; there you will also find two samples of sentence outlines. What is important for you to recognize are the main purposes and advantages of making a map:

- At a glance, a map enables you to plot out your paper as an organic whole. A map is an easy way to work out what will be your major points, what are subordinate concepts, and, most importantly, how they are connected to each other. With a map, you are deciding what needs to be said, what should go where, and why. It doesn't really matter if your map doesn't make much sense to another person, but it must make perfect sense to you.

- It is much easier to try out different organizational patterns by shifting around the small units of a map than by trying to push around chunks of written prose.

- Perhaps the greatest advantage of a map comes when you are writing. You probably know how easy it is to lose track of what you are doing when you are writing a particular section or paragraph of a paper, how easy it is to go off on tangents. If you have a map to guide you, you can always check on

where you've been,
where you are going,
and where you should be now.

b. Writing an Abstract: Your First Rough Draft

As a strategy for the first stages of the writing process, composing an abstract has the same goals as a map: An abstract is a map in prose form. In earlier sections of this book I talked about abstracts as brief summaries of the major points made by an author in a book or article. And if you are doing a paper in the social or natural sciences, you may be expected to write an abstract of your own paper after it is finished. I risk confusing you a bit here by calling this first draft of your paper an abstract; it *is* different in some ways from abstracts of finished work, but the term captures perfectly what this type of first draft is supposed to do—to abstract or focus on the central shape of your thinking. This first, preliminary sketch of your paper should have three characteristics: In it you will be telling yourself

- where you are going to discuss specific main ideas;
- generally speaking, what types of supporting evidence and explanations you will later include;
- and, most importantly, you will be explicitly telling yourself *why* you are discussing a particular idea in a certain place and how it is related to other points.

An abstract should go something like this:

Now that I have explained X, I can go on to show how Y fits into the category of X. In doing this, I want to be sure to emphasize the idea that _____ . Once I have established this point, I'll illustrate and support it with evidence I have that _____ .

Don't worry about polished prose; the abstract is just a sketch. It would be best to write it all at one sitting. Because the abstract is your paper in capsule form, it will probably be short. My abstracts are usually about a quarter of the length of my final paper.

As you stand poised to begin writing this research paper, you could start with a quick map, and then do an abstract; or you could write an abstract first, and then do a map; or you write only an abstract or only a map. Do what feels best for you. The longer the paper is going to be and/or the more complex its structure, the greater are the advantages of having a map to use at all stages of drafting and revising. Work back and forth between your map and your first draft, making changes in either as your ideas become clearer to you. Maps and abstracts are simply strategies for making decisions at the macro level, for getting at the skeleton of your thinking. As a first step in getting started on a paper, writing maps and abstracts makes a lot more sense than spending three days struggling to write a beautifully polished introduction for a paper that does not yet exist.

3. Reviewing Your Evidence: Your Notecards

The point in the writing process when you should review your notecards will depend on the type of paper you are writing and other factors. In general, however, you are better off putting your notecards aside and developing your first maps and abstracts from the Working Hypothesis/ Thesis section of your Researcher's Notebook.

Looking at those notecards before you've established the shape for your paper can seduce you into becoming a passive sponge, focused on getting all of this evidence into your paper or choosing an outline that is nothing more than a mindless catalogue of what other people have said. As hard as you have worked to focus on your view of your subject, I'd really hate to see you turn into a passive sponge at this point in the process.

On the other hand, the evidence you have collected on your notecards is important to this paper. In Section 6 you will find a detailed discussion about how to decide which evidence to use and how to incorporate it into your drafts. At this early stage of the drafting process I just want to say a few words about a mechanical issue, keeping the record straight.

As you write your paper, your mental energy must be focused on presenting your ideas to your readers. But because your explanation must include the evidence you've gathered from a variety of sources, you must keep a record *in your text* of the sources of the various pieces of evidence you use. In the final draft of your paper, you must be able to document, accurately, all of the material you have taken from others.

Here are some techniques that should help to keep track of the sources of each piece of information as you write. You may use these systems or develop your own. Whatever system you use, it must meet these criteria:

- You must use a system that tells you, in the text of your paper, that the information you have just used is taken from one or more of your sources.

- You must use a system that tells you, in the text of the paper, what that specific source is.

- You must use a system that allows you to go directly from the text to the appropriate notecard, so that you can double-check the information to make sure that what you have in your text is accurate.

- You should use a system that will allow you to document your sources in the final draft with a minimum of wasted time and energy.

One system you could use is a system very close to the final citation form of the MLA style and the author-date style:

- Whenever you use information from one of your notecards, in the text of your paper, immediately after the sentence that contains the information, write the following information in parentheses:

- ○ the author's full name
- ○ a short version of the title
- ○ the page number

Include all this information for each source you refer to.

Example

Several experts in the field of diplomatic history have pointed out that the United States tends to take a confrontive rather than a conciliatory stance in its dealings with other countries (John Williams, *Dip. History of US,* p. 497; *Looking at Diplomacy,* pp. 297–300; Elwin Carter, "US and Other Nations," p. 406). Confrontation certainly characterizes the way the United States handled the Cuban missile crisis. The US acted immediately, creating a blockade around Cuba to prevent the delivery of more missiles from the USSR and declaring that the firing of these missiles would be met with full military retaliation (Robert Corwin, *Cuban Crisis,* pp. 905–30). . . .

If you use this system of keeping track of your sources, you will also have to have a method of double-checking the accuracy of your information, either facts or direct quotations. Perhaps the easiest thing to do is simply to make a separate stack of the notecards you use, keeping them in the order in which you used them.

If you find that you will be using a great number of reference cards and notecards, a more elaborate system might be more efficient. A system I developed for myself involves coding reference and notecards, then using these codes in the text of the paper. Here's how I code my cards:

- Pull all of the *reference cards.* Put them in alphabetical order, according to the author's last name.

- Code these cards by using the alphabet. In the upper right-hand corner, put an A on the first card, a B on the second, a C on the third, and so on. If you have more than twenty-six cards, go on with double letters (AA on the twenty-seventh, BB on the twenty-eighth, CC on the twenty-ninth, and so on).

- Now separate the *notecards,* making a separate stack for the notes taken from the sources indicated by each reference card. For example, make a stack of all the notes you took from the source indicated on reference card A, another stack for the notes taken from the source indicated on reference card B, and so on.

- When all the notecards have been separated and stacked, code them with the reference card letter, and simply number them. Thus, the first card in stack A will be A1, the second will be A2, the third A3, and so on.

When you are writing, you will code your information with the letter and number of the card from which the information is taken. No matter how much rewriting you do, you will always be able to identify the source of the information because you will be able to get straight back to the original notecard. When your final draft is complete, you can document the source *and* double-check the notecard to be sure that the information or quotation you have used in your paper is absolutely correct. The system can save you time and frustration.

You are now ready to turn to subsection B, C, or D, depending on which type of research project you have been engaged in:

- If you have designed and carried out an experiment or study, turn to subsection B, A Primary Research Report.
- If you have concentrated on discovering exactly what's been done recently in a specific area of a field so that you can write a review or a review of the literature paper, turn to subsection C, A Review or a Review of the Literature Paper.
- If the paper you are writing will focus on your answer to the research question you have posed for yourself, turn to subsection D, A Critical Paper.

When you have accomplished the part of the writing process covered in subsection B, C, or D, then turn to subsection E, Drafting and Revising.

B. A *Primary Research Report*

A primary research report applies only to those research projects that have focused on studies or experiments in which you have gathered raw data directly from sources through a carefully designed series of tests or procedures, and in which you have analyzed your raw data by using objective, accepted procedures in the field. Primary research projects of the type I will discuss here are the studies or experiments normally done in the social and natural sciences.

1. General Format

In a primary research report, the researcher is laying out his or her study or experiment for the reader in the order in which the study was conceived and carried out. The diagram provides a picture of the overall shape of the report.

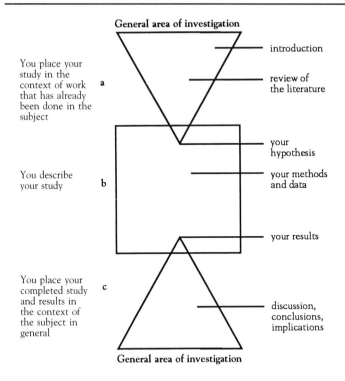

General area of investigation

introduction

You place your study in the context of work that has already been done in the subject **a**

review of the literature

your hypothesis

You describe your study **b**

your methods and data

your results

You place your completed study and results in the context of the subject in general **c**

discussion, conclusions, implications

General area of investigation

The report breaks down into three major parts (a, b, c, on the left of the diagram).

a. The First Section: Introduction, Review of the Literature, Statement of the Hypothesis

In the diagram the first section of the report is an inverted pyramid because, in this part of the report, you begin by introducing your reader to the general area of investigation (the general subject) and then gradually lead your reader to the specific hypothesis you tested. The purpose of this opening segment of the report is to put your study or experiment into the context of other work that has already been done in the field.

If you have worked as other experienced researchers have worked, before you designed your specific study or experiment you investigated the theories that are current in the field and you looked carefully at the studies and experiments that have been carried out by others. Thus, your specific study evolved out of your reactions to these previous studies and experiments, reactions such as "Smith and Jones's hypothesis needs to be tested further with more subjects" or "Dr. X's theory needs to be tested by doing a study that would . . ." or "I wonder if procedure Y would give me more information about the way that DNA . . . ." In other words, you did your study to fill a hole or gap in the knowledge that has already been accumulated about your subject.

In the first part of your report, then, you are doing two things:

- You are *informing* your reader about the theories that your study is based on and about published research projects that you have drawn on to develop your hypothesis and methodology.

- You are *explaining* to your reader where your study fits in the general picture of the current theories and the work that has been done.

An abstract of this section of your paper would go something like this:

I need to tell my reader that my general area of investigation is learning styles. Then I need to say that there are 3 basic views of learning styles: view Y, view X, and view Z. I'll briefly describe X and Y and tell the reader that I'm not following these views. I'll then explain Z's theory in more detail, because, as I'll tell the reader, this is the theory I'm using. Briefly I'll show the reader what kinds of testing procedures have been used to test Z's theory, stressing Smith and Wesson's work. I'll point out that these studies haven't considered age as a variable. I will say that I think age is an important variable, and I will prove it by pointing to the work on age and learning in general done by Wilson, Johnson, and Smedley. Then I will say that age should also be considered when talking about learning styles, which will lead me right into my hypothesis that . . . .

If you look at the research reports you have read as you were doing your library work, you will see that primary research reports are divided by headings in the text. Sometimes this first section is headed Introduction. Sometimes, particularly if this part of the report is long, the writer will use several headings (Introduction, Review of the Literature, Statement of Hypothesis) or will subdivide the introduction, using subheadings or headings that specifically describe the content of that section (Z's Theory of Learning Styles, Age and Learning).

b. The Second Section: A Description of Your Study, including Data and Methodology

The second general segment of the report is a description of the study you did. It includes a description of the material or subjects you used as your source for raw data, the procedures you used to acquire your data, the data themselves. The common headings for this section are Methods, Methods and Procedures, Materials and Methods, and Experimental Section. Use the heading or headings that best describe the work you did. Check the published reports you read as you were doing your library research.

In the sciences and social sciences one purpose of writing up a study is to allow other researchers to replicate or redo a study or experiment exactly as it was first done. This principle, then, can provide you with a good rule of thumb in writing the methods section of your report. Ask yourself what another researcher would need to know about your materials (and/or subjects) and your research procedure in order to reproduce your study or experiment exactly as you did it.

After you have jotted down this information, try to organize it so that this part of your report is easy to follow. You could, for example, first talk about your materials—the chemicals, instruments, and apparatus you used—then describe your research design.

You will notice that experienced researchers sometimes divide this section with several headings or subheadings if it is complicated or long.

c. The Third Section: Results, Discussion, Conclusions

The final section of the body of the report is devoted to a presentation of the results you came up with when you analyzed your data and a discussion of the results and the study as a whole. It begins with a straight forward report of your results or findings and an explanation of the procedures you used to obtain those results. Once this is accomplished, the researcher is free to step back from the study or experiment he or she did and comment on the study as a whole, or parts of it. This section allows you to critique your work and the results of your work (thus Discussion) and to draw conclusions or to discuss the implications of your study for the field as a whole.

In preparing to write this section, then, what do you want to say about your results? What do you want to say about the whole study? If you feel that your procedures were flawed in any way, discuss that here. If you wished you had used other instruments or tests to generate more data, say so here. If you feel that you should have analyzed your data in other ways, say so here. You will want to compare your results with your original hypothesis. Do your results support the hypothesis? Were they inconclusive? Have your results suggested certain implications for the direction further research should take?

In other words, after you have described your results, you will be doing what you did in the beginning of your paper—you will be putting your specific study and the information you obtained from it back into the context of the general search for knowledge in this area of investigation. Thus, on the diagram, this segment appears as a regular pyramid. You are moving from your specific study back to the general area of investigation. In the Discussion and the Conclusions sections of this segment of your report, you will be telling your reader what you learned, in more general terms, by doing this study. If you look at the published studies you read as you were doing your library research, you will notice that some researchers label this part "Results and Discussion" and that others divide their reports into separate Results and Discussion sections.

d. Appendixes and the Reference List

If you need to include appendixes in your report (see the following guidelines in B.2), you will place them after the text of your report. The report will end with your list of references (see Section 7 and Appendix C, D, or E).

e. The Abstract

After your report is finished, you should write an abstract of the entire report, which you will type on a separate sheet of paper and insert between your title page and the first page of the body of your report. Clearly the abstract I am talking about here is not the preliminary draft that I've recommended as a strategy in the writing process, but a formal summary of your finished paper. Authors of published papers often preface their articles with these succinct overviews of the main points in their papers to allow readers to determine quickly whether an article contains material of interest to them. To get started, you can try writing one sentence each on the basic area of the study, your hypothesis, your methods, and your results. Work with it until you have one, tight paragraph.

Two of the sample student papers at the end of this book, "The Study of Fossil Flowers" and "The Effectiveness of Lithium Carbonate and Imipramine in the Treatment of Bipolar Affective Disorders," are prefaced by abstracts; you might want to take a look at them.

As you can see from this general description of the order in which you present your information, you are approximating the order in which you conceived and carried out your study. In this report, you are telling your reader what you did and explaining why you did it. Your information is complete enough that your reader, if he or she wished to, could duplicate your study and compare his or her results with yours. The text is divided by headings so that the reader can quickly distinguish the parts, and the headings allow a reader who is most interested in your methodology, or results, to go straight to that specific part of the study.

2. General Guidelines for Writing the Report

Here are some pointers that will help you produce a coherent, readable report.

- The three divisions I've just described give you the basic outline of your paper, but it would be wise to "fill in the blanks" by doing a map of each section. In my experience, many students have trouble with the review of the literature section of primary research reports. Starting with an abstract of this section, and of your discussion section, would be particularly helpful. Plan on writing several drafts, working from whole to part in each section. Once you have your first rough draft of one or more of the divisions, read over subsections E, F, and G of this section and continue to write with the issues and suggestions you find there in mind.

- Because your report is divided into separate segments, you can begin to write the introduction and methodology sections even while you are analyzing your data and considering your conclusions/discussion.

- Because this paper is a formal, scientific report, you will want to use a style appropriate to such a report. Do *not* write in an informal, chatty way. You may want to avoid using the first person (*I* did this; this is *my* study); ask your instructor. Use technical language where it is appropriate, but keep your audience in mind. Will your readers know what these terms refer to?

- Throughout your report, your goal is to be as clear and precise as possible. Even if your instructor helped you design your study and analyze your data, you may not assume that your readers know what you did in this study. Think of your readers as people who had no idea that you were working on any research project until they picked up this report.

- You must be precise and specific, but you do not want to overwhelm your reader with details to the point that your reader can't see the forest for the trees. Try these techniques:

  ○ In each division of the text, begin with a summary statement of the material in that section, then go into more detail. Use this same summarize-then-explain pattern in each subdivision, and even each paragraph. For example, your results section might begin, "Results indicate that males prefer tasks that require physical activity and interaction with other people, while females prefer to work alone in sedentary jobs. On the Hansen Job Inventory Scale, 92% of the male subjects ranked 'Be physically active' as their first priority;

the other 8% ranked this criterion either second or third (see Table 3)."

- ○ Whenever possible, use graphs and charts to report results or to summarize data. In your text, do not simply write your data in prose. The prose parts of your text should be statements you make to draw your reader's attention to numbers you consider important or significant and to tell your reader why you consider these numbers important.

- ○ Do not attempt to put all your raw data in the body of your paper. If you feel obliged to give data that cannot be represented in summary charts and graphs, put these data in appendixes at the end of your report. If and when you want to refer to these data, you can refer your reader to the proper appendix.

- ○ If you were gathering data from people by using tests or instruments that your reader could not easily obtain (such as a questionnaire that you made up), you should include a copy of this test or instrument. However, put this material in an appendix at the end of the paper and refer your reader to the appropriate appendix when you talk about this material in your text.

- Whenever you refer to the work of other researchers and experts, you must document your sources. See Section 7, and Appendix C, D, or E.

- As suggested in subsection B.1. of this section, your text should be divided by headings. If you are not sure how to divide your text, either look at the studies you have read as you were doing your library research, or ask your instructor. Mainly, in cases like this, you should use your common sense. Your object is to isolate the important parts of your report so that readers can go directly to those specific portions of your study that particularly interest them.

C. A Review or a Review of the Literature Paper

In addition to describing one section of a primary research report, the term "review of the literature" also applies to an entire research paper, one that is based on material you have gathered from books and articles. In the natural sciences, this type of paper is often called simply a review. Don't confuse this type of review with an evaluation of a specific book, play, or film. The review that I am describing here is a review of the research that has been done in a specific field.

A review of the literature, or review, is a summary of the "state of the art" of a particular area of investigation. A researcher selects a particular subject (clinical therapies for depression, field dependent–independent learning theory, Legionnaire's disease, etc.); the objective is to point out to readers the patterns and trends that have been developing in research done on this subject. Unless the writer has a particular reason for doing a historical study, she is usually interested in the most recent trends and patterns of research (what has happened in the last ten, or even five, years).

Reviews of the literature are a common form of paper in academic disciplines. As the knowledge explosion increases and experts become more specialized, these experts find it difficult to keep abreast of developments in areas outside their own fields of interest. Reviews help them stay informed about subjects in their general field about which they have not had time to read in depth. An instructor may ask students to write reviews on topics outside his or her area of specialization as one means of keeping informed about developments in the field in general.

If your research project assignment was to write a review of the literature, then your obligation has been to find and read *everything available* on the topic. Since this has been your obligation, I would expect that you have narrowed the topic if you have found that a great deal has been written on the general subject with which you started. The two most common ways to narrow down the topic are to narrow the area of investigation (the function of vitamin E in the body rather than the function of all vitamins) or to restrict your research to a given period of time (what clinical therapies for depression have been used in the past five years?)

When you write a review or review of the literature paper, the most valuable evidence you have are the summaries of books and articles that you have written (see Section 4.D.2).

The trickiest part of writing a review of the literature is deciding how to organize your paper. The one thing you *do not* want to do is simply to *list* the studies you have read. Let me remind you that your purpose in writing a review is to tell your reader about the main *trends* and *patterns* you see in the work that has been done on this subject. Thus, as you have researched, you should have been looking constantly for trends and patterns (and considering these in the Working Thesis section of your Researcher's Notebook). In determining the overall structure of your paper, you should use the basic trends and patterns you see as the focal point of the paper.

Here are some strategies you can use in determining what the basic trends and patterns are:

- What theory or theories seem to be the most popular? (Which theories are referred to most often? Which theories are the basis for most of the studies or experiments you looked at?) Has there been a shift in the popularity of theories?

- What basic assumptions do most of the researchers seem to be making about the subject?

- Can you categorize the research reports you've read according to the test procedures used in the studies and experiments?

- Can you categorize the research reports you've read according to the kinds of subjects or material tested or observed?

- Can you see any patterns in the results reported?

- Are there any patterns in the conclusions drawn by the researchers?

- What experts' names pop up most frequently? Are certain experts associated with certain types of research, certain theories, certain areas of investigation?

If it helps you, make actual charts by putting these questions in categories at the top of the page and the works you've read along the left-hand side; then fill in the blanks. Or create a chart by putting the following categories at the top: theories used, hypothesis, methods, results, major points made in the discussion section. Then list each article along the left-hand side, and fill in the blanks.

Here are some other strategies to use in writing your paper:

- When you have determined what you consider to be the two or three most important trends or patterns in the subject you've researched, you need to summarize these trends or patterns in one sentence (your thesis statement) and use that sentence as the key to the organizational pattern of your whole paper. Some of the strategies I give in subsection D for critical papers could be helpful to you. But if you read subsection D, remember that in a review of the literature your purpose is *not* to focus on your personal ideas about the topic. Your thesis statement must be a statement of the conclusions you have reached about *the major trends and developments you see in the research that has been done on your subject.* I would urge you to do a map and abstract of the whole paper; use as your major points those aspects of the studies that reveal the trends or developments you've nutshelled in your thesis statement.

- Another word of caution: in a review of the literature, your obligation is only to indicate the *type* of work that is being done or has been done and the most *influential* theories. Of course you will illustrate and support your argument by referring to specific works, but this can be done with summary statements and *some* descriptions of actual studies. Do *not* turn your paper into a list in paragraph form, giving a summary of one work in one paragraph, then a summary of the next work in another paragraph, and so on. It is not necessary for you to give a complete description of every study or book you looked at. Use detail where it is important to make your point. A review is not a memory-dump paper.

- At the end of your review, you should devote a few paragraphs to your conclusions about the work that still needs to be done in the field. You won't be able to do this unless you have thought about the general picture you have seen emerging in the research to date.

- Obviously, your reader will expect you to refer to specific books and articles as you support and illustrate the points you are making (it would be very difficult indeed to write a review of the literature without a large number of these references, since your job was to survey the field). All works you refer to must be documented in your paper. So see Section 7 and the appropriate appendix.

- Plan to write several drafts, working from the overall shape of your paper to specific parts. Once you have a rough draft of your paper, read subsections E, F, and G, and keep in mind the suggestions and strategies there as you continue to pull your paper into its final form.

One of the sample student papers at the end of this book, Sarah Jo Chaplen's "The Effectiveness of Lithium Carbonate and Imipramine in the Treatment of Bipolar Affective Disorders," is a review of the literature. You might find it helpful to see how she followed the basic guidelines just given. Remember, though, that there is no set format for a review of the literature paper; the organizational pattern you use will be determined by the trends and patterns you find in the sources you read.

D. A Critical Paper

The most common type of research paper assigned to students in college courses falls into the broad category of critical papers. The focal point of a critical paper is an assertion or claim the writer makes about a particular subject:

The Beatles composed very sophisticated music.

The uncontrolled building of homes and industrial parks on the edges of cities is ecologically unsound.

Clearly you don't need eight or ten pages to write out a statement like these. What constitutes the body of a critical paper—and holds the key to its purpose—is nicely explained by Stephen Toulmin:

> Whatever the nature of the particular assertion may be . . . we can challenge the assertion, and demand to have our attention drawn to the grounds (backing, data, facts, evidence, considerations, features) on which the merits of the assertion are to depend. We can, that is, demand an argument; and a claim need be conceded only if the argument which can be produced in its support proves to be up to standard.[1]

In the paper you are now starting, your readers will expect you to make one central claim or assertion about your subject. Because they value critical thinking, their willingness to accept your claim will be based on your providing grounds for this assertion; in other words, your readers expect you to provide an argument.

Writing your paper, then, involves two central tasks: first, determining the specific claim you'll be making in this paper, then working out an argument. Actually, you've already spent a great deal of time doing the necessary groundwork. Your whole investigation has been directed by a tentative assertion, which we've been calling your working thesis. Determining your claim simply involves moving from a "working" thesis to a final thesis statement. The terms "thesis" or "thesis statement" are probably more familiar to you than "claim" or "assertion"; as I continue my discussion, think of the four terms as synonymous. In your Researcher's Notebook you've been continually testing—and perhaps changing—your working thesis by putting together the evidence you've found into patterns that make sense to you. Now you'll be taking the lines of reasoning you've been working out in your Researcher's Notebook and transforming them into the argument you'll present to your readers. The specific shape your argument takes will be the overall shape—the organization—of your whole paper. And since the argument you work out is, in turn, determined by the assertion you decide to focus on, let's go now to strategies for developing your thesis statement.

1. Developing Your Thesis Statement

In this process of developing your thesis, it could be helpful to think about the claim or assertion you will make as the statement of a conclusion you've arrived at about your subject after all these weeks of studying and thinking

---

[1] Stephen Toulmin, *The Uses of Argument* (Cambridge: Cambridge University Press, 1958), 11–12.

about it. It's time now to determine exactly what conclusion you feel strongly enough about that you want to base your paper on it. So take out your Researcher's Notebook, and in the Working Thesis section answer these questions:

- Was my original assumption/working thesis valid?
- Based on the evidence I have found, what conclusions have I drawn about my subject?
- What statements do I feel comfortable making about my subject? (You want inferences and judgments here, not factual statements.)

Freewrite on these questions.

Don't worry if you decide that your original assumption or working thesis was not correct; don't worry if you find that the conclusions you are drawing cover only a part of the general area you began investigating. You should know by now that the more you research, the more you realize how broad and complex a subject is.

As you are developing your thesis, let me address two common fears that seem to drive students to write poor critical papers. Do *not* try to find a conclusion that will cover everything you read just so you can refer to all your research in your paper. If you have done a thorough job of investigating your research assumption or working thesis, you will find yourself referring to a variety of sources as you develop the argument of your paper, even though your thesis seems narrow. But the main thing to remember is that the *quality* of the assertion you make and the argument you present is the real test of a critical paper. The more evidence you studied, the more time you spent thinking about your subject, the higher will be the quality of the thesis you develop.

Your objective, at this stage, is to express your thesis in one sentence.

When I insist that the thesis be expressed in one sentence, my students often groan and complain and beg for a couple of sentences or a paragraph—but I stand firm, and here's why. You could draw many conclusions about your subject, as you've already discovered in the freewrites you've been doing. If you want to end up with a successful paper—one that presents one, sharp, clear-cut argument—you must begin with one, sharp, definite point. The strategy of expressing your point in one sentence forces you (1) to decide exactly *which* claim you want to make, and (2) to bring that claim into sharp focus. The task won't be very difficult at all if you remember a couple of things. First of all, a thesis statement by definition is a summary statement. It is not self-explanatory; in fact, you are going to write eight or ten or fifteen pages to explain what it means. Second, the structure of sentences in English allows you to qualify assertions made in the main clause with all sorts of dependent clauses, phrases, adjectives, and adverbs. Your thesis statement probably won't be a flat assertion such as "The moon is blue." I assume you'll qualify it by saying something like this: "Under certain atmospheric conditions the moon can appear to be blue"; or, "The moon can appear to be blue because of X, Y, and Z." To see how much you can say in one sentence, take a look at the sample thesis statements I offer below.

It may take a while to come up with the sentence that feels exactly right. Don't put it off. Here are a few strategies to follow:

- What claim do you feel confident in making about your subject?
- You may come up with several statements. In these cases you will have to choose one. Which statement comes closest to expressing what you want to say about your subject?
- Don't just stare at a blank page, forming and dismissing statements in your head. Write down something, anything. If the first statement you write is "wrong," don't erase it or scratch it out. Move down on the sheet of paper and write another statement.
- If you write a statement that is not quite right, underline the parts of the statement that are wrong and rewrite those parts until they say what you want them to say.
- As you write and rewrite these statements, keep saying to yourself, "*Exactly* what do I want to say about X in this paper?"
- Be sure the statement you end up with covers only what you want to say in your paper and that it does cover what you want to say, precisely and completely.

Your thesis should look like this:

When men and women in our society talk to each other, they can fail to communicate because research indicates that men and women have different concepts of what "communication" means.

In their efforts to learn more about human evolution, physical anthropologists and paleontologists focus their investigations on the development of three human characteristics—bipedalism, brain size, and tool use; their purpose is to attempt to determine when these characteristics developed, and under what conditions.

Once you have a statement that you are sure states clearly and precisely the assertion you want to make, you are ready to begin sketching out your paper.

Don't let the specter of "how can I write ten pages on this?" get to you now. You now *know* that you have a great deal of knowledge of your subject. Never forget that it takes a great deal of space to make your ideas clear to other people. And the abstract you will write in the next step will immediately calm your fears, because you will immediately begin to fill in pages with your prose.

2. Writing an Abstract of Your Paper: Your First Rough Draft

I believe that writing an abstract is a very important strategy to use in doing a critical paper. Having a clear sense of your line of reasoning is crucial for two reasons. First, the success or failure of your paper depends upon your argument; if your readers find your thinking logical, they will be willing to accept your claim or assertion. Moreover, the line of reasoning you choose automatically becomes the organizational pattern or outline of your paper. So the more you concentrate on the skeleton of your argument—which is what you are doing in the abstract—the higher your chances of writing an A paper.

This is probably a good place to say a few more words about arguments. Let me begin by talking about what an argument is not. An argument is not a story. It is neither the story of what you've been reading over the past few weeks (John Doe says this and Mary Brown says that . . .), nor is it the history of your subject (first this happened, and then that happened). In certain sections of your paper you may use a few short stories to explain or illustrate a point, but the overall organization of the paper has got to mirror some pattern of logical, analytical thinking.

The claim you are making, expressed in the thesis statement you developed in the last step, is your whole paper in a nutshell. You know what the statement means to you, but nobody else but you knows all those "meanings." Therefore you must write a paper which will be a full explanation of how and why you arrived at this conclusion. That is, you will now be reconstructing, in all its detail, the way you've put this puzzle together. Do *not* use your notecards at this stage of the process; do not even look at them. Write your thesis statement on a card or a slip of paper so that you can have it in front of you at all times. Then, as you've been doing in the Working Thesis section of your Researcher's Notebook, write your abstract by using only the ideas and information you have in your head. A few more words of wisdom:

- Very often an organizational pattern is built into your thesis statement; see if yours has one, and if so, start with it.

- After you sketch out a possible introduction (which probably should include your thesis statement), go to your first central point. Avoid giving us "background" material; it is a trap that can lead you into telling us the story of your subject. The odds are that relevant background material is really an explanation of or evidence for one of your main points, and should be presented as such.

- Remember: If you find, as you sketch out your thinking, that your thesis statement is not quite right, stop and revise the thesis statement.

- And don't try to write polished prose. You are still writing for yourself, attempting to discover what you mean by the claim you've summarized in your thesis statement.

In writing your abstract, you have two objectives:

- to express the *major* ideas or parts of your argument;
- to express clearly the ways these ideas are related to each other.

Here are examples of abstracts for the two thesis statements I gave in the last section:

Abstract for the Paper on Gender and Communication

A good way to start this paper would be to find an actual short dialogue between a male & female that my readers would recognize as familiar and that would illustrate my central point about problems in communicating. Then there are two things I need to do in this opening section—(1) establish that enough research has been done to show that men and women do communicate differently—(2) give my thesis statement. *Also,* somewhere in this paper I need to *define* communication. Tricky, since my whole paper is about definitions of communication, but I need some measure of effective communication. Should I put this here, or wait until section 3, where I go into talk between males and females? Anyway, I'll say that just because a person hears the words another person is uttering, it doesn't mean that the listener interprets the speaker's messages the way the speaker intends them to be interpreted. Effective communication = hearer tries to interpret the message the way the speaker intends, then tries to respond along the same lines. I'll use this basic idea as a touchstone for effective and ineffective communication.

I'll start right in, then, with the different ways that boys and girls learn to use language when they are young because my point is that these different styles are established early in life and are practically unconscious. I'll break this section into 2 parts, one about research in boys' language use in all-male groups and one about girls' talk in all-female groups. For boys, my main point is they use language in larger groups to establish their place in the hierarchy, to dominate and control the group. In these groups boys attempt to "hold the floor" with stories meant to impress their peers. Goal: to complete the story in spite of challenges and heckling from others. Boys' style: competitive and aggressive. Be sure to illustrate, provide evidence. Then on to girls, where my main point is that, in contrast to boys, girls use talk to form and maintain personal relationships. Girls' talk is in smaller groups (2 or 3), topics are their feelings and everyday lives. Girls' style: cooperative, inclusive. Give illustrations, evidence.

If I devote quite a bit of space to the section above, this next section, on adult communication styles, can focus mainly on evidence. My main point: by the time we are adults, males and females have established definite and different concepts of communication. I'll again break down into males in all-male groups, then females in all-female groups. Main point about males: communication = establish status and authority. Main point about females: communication = establish and maintain personal relationships. Use this section to give lots of evidence that these are the definitions that males and females operate on.

This third major section is probably the most important—may be the longest. Using what I've said in the first 2 sections, I can now say that it isn't surprising that a man and a woman may run into trouble when they want to communicate with each other. I want to break this section down into (1) relationships at work; (2) relationships "at home" (romantic, marriage). I want to make the point that male-female relationships in the workplace are more and more relevant as women move into positions of authority in businesses and corporations. Here I want to tie the research I've done on women's managerial style in with this research on male/female communication styles; my point—you "manage" people through communication, verbal and nonverbal! So, if your messages are misinterpreted, that will lead to poor working relationships. Then I'll go into intimate relationships. Here I think I'll break it down into "male's view," then "female's view," focusing on females' frustrations. Male view: if talk establishes status and control, no need to talk much at home unless he feels need to re-establish dominance or control. Not interested in mate's desire to talk about feelings, mundane experiences—sees it as idle chitchat. Female view—talk about feelings, mundane experiences creates and maintains relationship. VERY frustrated if mate not interested in what she says, if he shows no interest in talking about his feelings, how his day went. TROUBLE is brewing.

Right now, I come to a paradoxical conclusion. Conflict resolution tends to stress the need for "more communication," "talking it out"—but this isn't going to work very well in male-female relationships—intimate or working relationships—if males and females see different purposes in talk! Is "talking it out" a "female" form of conflict resolution? Does "talking it out" just mean different things for all-male, all-female groups? HMMMM. Something else to think about: Do I want to reword my thesis statement slightly so that the "frame" is conflict resolution between males and females? The paper then would be about the limitations of the approach of "talking it out" when it comes to problems in male-female relationships because of gender differences in definitions of communication.

Abstract for the Paper on Human Evolution

I will begin my paper by making the point that the history of evolution is recorded in fossils. I will have to show the reader that paleontologists and physical anthropologists look for certain characteristics of skeletons to decide if the fossil is of the ape family or is a hominid (the primate family of which *homo sapiens* is the only remaining species). Apes are distinguished from hominids by such physical features as the shape of the jaw, the kind and shape of teeth, the way the backbone connects with the skull, and the size and shape of the skull. In trying to determine if a fossil is an ape or a hominid, paleontologists and physical anthropologists also make note of the type of rock in which the fossil is embedded and how old the fossil is believed to be. I also need to note that the scientists' task is made harder by the fact that, usually, only fragments of skeletons are found.

Based upon this information, I will say then that most paleontologists and physical anthropologists agree that bipedalism was the first human characteristic to evolve. It is also generally agreed that bipedalism evolved about 4 million years ago in the grasslands and savannas of Africa. Using specific examples, I will show that it is known that fossils found in the African savannas are bipedal hominids because of specific skeletal features. Then I will say that the scientists infer that the environment encouraged the development of bipedalism. In wide open spaces, standing on one's rear legs allows a creature to spot predators from a distance (a survival technique). An added advantage of standing on one's rear legs is that it frees the hands—for such human activities as carrying and manipulating objects, a prerequisite for using tools. Then I will point out that these bipedal organisms in Africa 4 million years ago (*Australopithecus*) had small brains, and that no tools have been found with these fossils.

My next major point will be that fossils indicate that the next evolutionary step was increasing brain size (skulls found in Africa that date between 4 million and a half-million years ago). Then I will go into detail about the fossil record of hominid skulls and growing size (*homo habilis, homo erectus,* modern man). My big point here is that the advantages of larger brains and the conditions under which they evolved are controversial subjects among paleontologists and physical anthropologists. I need to be sure the reader sees that the various statements made by these scientists on these issues are strictly inferences; there is no solid evidence for these speculations and conclusions.

My last point has to do with the third human characteristic, tool use. I will say that, right now, most speculation among paleontologists and physical anthropologists is that the evolution of larger brains is tied to tool use. Most people, I will point out, assume that using tools gives an organism a measure of control over the environment and thus the development of tool use is an important step in human evolution. I will say that some scientists infer that the larger the brain, the greater the potential for tool development. Then I want to get into a really interesting issue; to me it seems that some paleontologists and physical anthropologists want to draw a causal relationship between increasing brain size and tool use (as brains got bigger, hominids had more potential to develop tools). But the point I want to make is: isn't there another, complicating factor? In this same period of increasing brain size, there is evidence of the development of culture (living in groups, cooperative food gathering, specialization of tasks— some members of a group hunt, others fix the food, etc.). Larger brains, in general, allow for more flexible behavior and adaptation. If culture is developing, behavior (like using tools) could be as easily influenced by the culture as by physical environmental factors (like standing on one's rear legs to spot predators). Is increasing tool use simply a factor of increasing brain size, or was the increasing development and use of tools an indirect result of increasing brain size—that is, was increasing tool use encouraged by a variety of cultural factors?

When you are satisfied that the have all the main points of your argument in their proper places, and when you have explained to yourself how the parts fit together (the argument "flows" smoothly from one point to the next), you have your first rough draft. Before you do any more drafting, I encourage you to make a map of the territory.

3. Creating a Map of the Territory

You are now going to take what you've learned from your abstract and put it into the form of a map so that, from now on, you have a convenient way of keeping the overall shape of your argument before you as you continue the writing process. On the following pages are samples of two more visually oriented maps (Samples 1 and 2), as well as a couple of sample sentence outlines (Sample 3). Try each to see what works best for you, although it is very likely that you will develop your own particular form.

When I help students write outlines for arguments, I insist that they write sentence outlines, outlines in which each item is a full grammatical statement. My reason is simple. Topic outlines, the kind of outline that uses only key words, for example,

I. Fossils

II. Bipedalism

III. Brain Size

are often a hindrance rather than a help because *the writer fails to tell herself what she wants to say about the key word(s)*. With this type of topic outline you could easily be inclined to natter on about everything you have learned about fossils, bipedalism, and brain size, thus creating a sprawling mess rather than a tight, focused argument. Topic outlines work for writers if and when the writers remember what they intend to say about each of those key words. Writers who are still getting used to generating cogent, tight arguments usually function better with sentence outlines since a sentence, by definition, forces them to say something about that key word:

Fossils record the history of evolution from ape to hominid.

Bipedalism evolved before large brain and tool use.

The sentence outline, as a good map should, reproduces your central argument and thus keeps the argument on track. Another aid in keeping your argument on track is to repeat key words in the statements you write:

I. *Latin American debt* is *increasing* at an alarming rate.

A. One reason for this *increase* . . .

II. As a consequence of their *debt* burden, the economies of *Latin American countries* . . .

When you have a map and an abstract you are satisfied with, read subsections E, F, and G, and continue to write with the issues and suggestions there in mind.

A Map of the Territory: Sample 1

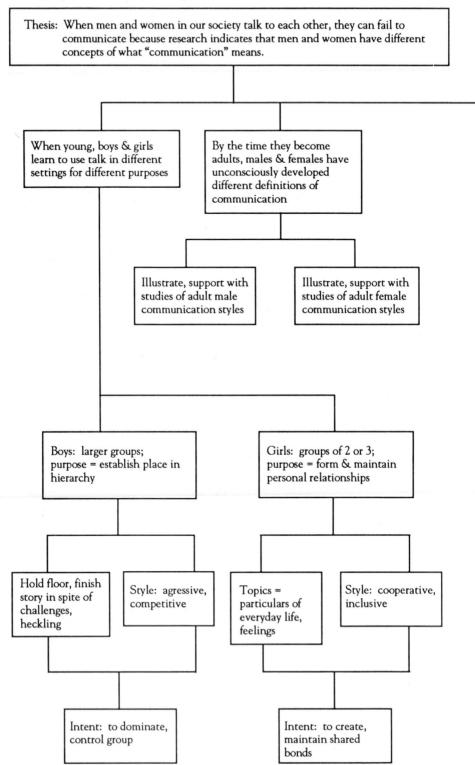

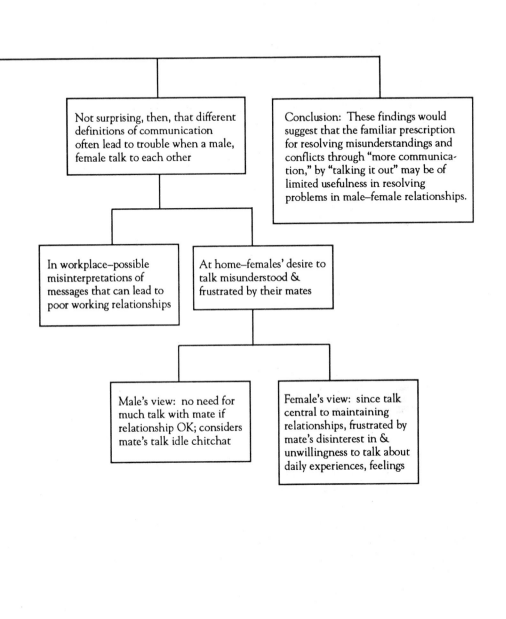

A Map of the Territory: Sample 2

Thesis: In their efforts to learn more about human evolution, physical anthropologists and paleontologists focus their investigations on the development of three human characteristics—bipedalism, brain size, and tool use; their purpose is to attempt to determine when these characteristics developed, and under what conditions.

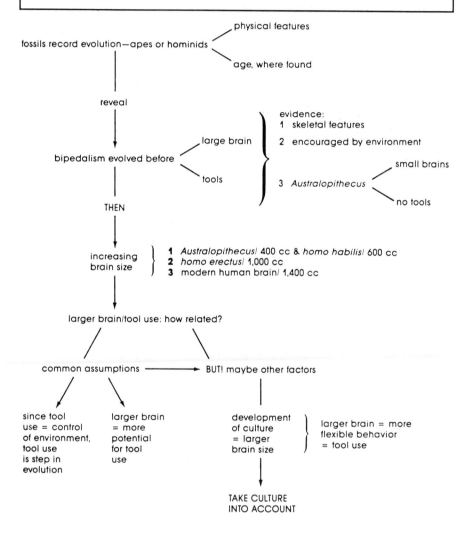

A Map of the Territory: Sample 3

Thesis: When men and women in our society talk to each other, they can fail to communicate because research indicates that men and women have different concepts of what "communication" means.

I. When they are young, boys and girls learn to use language in different settings for different purposes.
   A. Boys use talk in groups of three or more other boys for the purpose of establishing their place in the group's hierarchy.
      1. In these settings, boys attempt to "hold the floor" with stories meant to impress their peers; their goal is to complete the story in spite of challenges and heckling from other members of the group.
      2. Boys' communication style in these settings is competitive, and verbally and nonverbally aggressive.
      3. Thus, boys learn to use language to dominate and control groups.
   B. In contrast, girls use talk in smaller groups of two or three other girls for the purpose of forming and maintaining personal relationships.
      1. In these settings, "girl talk" revolves around details of everyday life and what the girls are feeling as well as thinking.
      2. Their communication style is cooperative and inclusive.
      3. Thus, girls learn to use language to create and maintain shared bonds with one another.
II. As a consequence of this early socialization, adult males and females have unconsciously developed different definitions of what "communication" means.
   A. Studies of men's communication style in all-male groups reveal that the objective of talk is to establish status and authority in the group, which men do in talk about activities and things (cars, football, fishing trips, sexual conquests, etc.).
   B. Studies of women's communication style in all-female groups reveal that the objective of talk is to establish personal relationships which they do by sharing personal experiences and feelings.
III. It is not surprising, then, that these different definitions of communication can lead men and women into trouble when they attempt to communicate with each other in both working relationships and intimate relationships.
   A. In the workplace, differences in male and female communication styles can lead to misinterpretation of messages and thus to poor working relationships.
   B. In intimate relationships, females' desire for "more communication" with their mates can be misunderstood and frustrated by their mates.
      1. Since males view language essentially as a means to establish their status and authority, they will tend to talk less when they judge their relationship with their mate to be satisfactory; they will dismiss the talk of their mates about daily experiences and feelings as idle chitchat.

2. Since females view language as an essential means of establishing and maintaining personal relationships, they will be frustrated by their mate's disinterest in and unwillingness to engage in talk about daily experiences and feelings.

IV. These findings would suggest that the familiar prescription for resolving misunderstandings and conflicts through "more communication," by "talking it out" may be of limited usefulness in resolving problems in male-female relationships.

Thesis: In their efforts to learn more about human evolution, physical anthropologists and paleontologists focus their investigations on the development of three human characteristics—bipedalism, brain size, and tool use; their purpose is to attempt to determine when these characteristics developed, and under what conditions.

I. The history of evolution is recorded in fossils; therefore, paleontologists and physical anthropologists will distinguish the ape from the hominid (family of humans) by certain skeletal features.
   A. Apes and hominids are distinguished by certain physical features.
      1. One difference is the shape of the jaw.
      2. Another difference is the kind and shape of teeth.
      3. Another difference is the way the backbone connects with the skull.
      4. Another is the size and shape of the skull.
   B. Other observations paleontologists and physical anthropologists make in distinguishing the ape from the hominid are the type of rock in which a fossil is embedded and how old the fossil is believed to be.
II. Using observations of physical characteristics, the type of rock in which a fossil is found and the age of the fossil, paleontologists and physical anthropologists generally agree that bipedalism evolved before large brain and tool use; it is generally agreed that bipedalism evolved in the expanding grasslands and savannas of Africa about 4 million years ago.
   A. It is known that the fossils found in the African savannas and grasslands represent bipedal hominids because of specific skeletal features.
   B. Paleontologists and physical anthropologists infer that the environment encouraged the development of bipedalism.
      1. In grasslands, standing on the rear legs allows a creature to spot predators coming across these wide-open spaces.
      2. A consequence of standing on the rear legs is that it frees the hands for carrying and manipulating objects (a prerequisite for tool use).
   C. Evidence shows that these bipedal organisms found in Africa 4 million years ago (*Australopithecus*) had small brains, and no tools were found with the fossils.
III. After the development of bipedalism, there is rapid evolution toward increasing brain size, as clearly evidenced in fossil skulls found in Africa that date between 4 million and a half-million years ago, the period in which the first recognizable humans appeared.

A. The evidence for the evolution of brain size is clear.
   1. *Australopithecus* fossils had a brain capacity of 400 cc.; by 3 million years ago, hominids (named *homo habilis* by Louis Leakey) had brain capacities of around 600 cc.
   2. By 2 million years ago an organism called *homo erectus* had a brain capacity of about 1,000 cc.
   3. Modern-day humans have a brain capacity of 1,400 cc.
B. The advantages of larger brains, however, and the conditions under which they evolved are controversial subjects among physical anthropologists and paleontologists; speculations and conclusions about these issues are strictly inferences at this time.

IV. Most current speculation among paleontologists and physical anthropologists about why larger brains developed is tied to tool use.
   A. It is axiomatic among these scientists (as it is in the culture as a whole) that tool use gives humans a measure of control over the environment and thus tool use is an important step in human evolution.
   B. It is inferred by some scientists that the larger the brain, the greater the potential for tool development.
   C. Some paleontologists and physical anthropologists want to draw a causal relationship between increasing brain size and tool use. However, it may not be that tool use alone encouraged the development of larger brains.
      1. During this period in human evolution, there is evidence of the development of culture — living in groups, cooperative food gathering, specialization of tasks among members of the group, etc. The development of culture is clearly related to brain size.
      2. Larger brain size allows for more flexible behavior and adaptation; within a culture, behavior (such as tool use) can easily be influenced by the culture itself as by physical environmental factors.
      3. Is increasing tool use a simple factor of increasing brain size alone, or was the increasing use and development of tools an indirect result of increasing brain size — that is, was increasing use and development of tools encouraged by a variety of cultural factors? Any answers to this question would now have to be inferences and speculations, but I believe that the variable of culture should be taken into account by paleontologists and physical anthropologists as they continue their search for more knowledge about human evolution.

E. Drafting and Revising

No matter which type of research paper you are writing — a primary research report, a review of the literature, or a critical paper — you should plan on working through several drafts. Writing your paper will be far easier if you focus on one mental activity at a time rather than trying to accomplish several tasks at once. In the overview of the writing process, I advised you to work on your paper from whole to part, and what I say now is premised on the assumption that you have already done a map and/or an abstract and that you have a first draft. But just as the research process is not a neat, clean progression from one step to the next, so the writing process tends to be recursive. Some sections of your paper may work according to your plan. But it is also possible that as you develop specific sections and paragraphs, you will discover that your original scenario isn't going to work—or, more interestingly, that you are writing new insights, making connections you hadn't anticipated. As you write, your ideas can change. This happens to writers all the time. The trick is to avoid being overwhelmed by these new possibilities, to avoid feeling as if you are losing control. You can avoid this trap by going back to the whole, going back to the macro level, and making some conscious choices. If a new idea feels "right," revise a main point to accommodate it; change things on your map; try out new connections by sketching a quick abstract. If you remember that the most important thing is to have a coherent picture of the whole paper based on some central purpose, you will always have a sense of direction, even if the particular direction changes. In fact, my major piece of advice as you move into this drafting and revising stage is this: Be prepared to keep moving back and forth from whole to part and part to whole.

- After you have a map and/or an abstract that pleases you, you are ready to decide what evidence you are going to use. Review your notecards and the summaries of sources that you have written. Read each section of your abstract or outline to remind yourself of the major points you want to make in each section. Select the specific evidence you want to use in each section by using these criteria:

  ○ What information or evidence helps you *explain* this point?
  ○ What information or evidence helps you *substantiate* this point?
  ○ What information or evidence helps you *illustrate* this point?

  Your goal is to end up with separate stacks of cards that correspond to each section of your paper; these stacks should include *only* that information or evidence directly relevant to each section. It is very possible that when you have finished sorting you will have a stack of cards left over that you will not use in the paper. That's fine. Your goal is to write a cogent argument, not to squeeze in everything, whether it fits or not.

  If you've looked at the table of contents of this book, you will have noticed that I've devoted a separate section to the topic of how to, and how not to, incorporate evidence into your paper. The topic deserves extended discussion because there are ways of incorporating your evidence into your text that can make you seem like a passive sponge. Since you have taken such pains to avoid this trap in the research process up to this point, you don't want to fall into it now. You want to handle your evidence in your paper the way the experts do. When your draft has reached the stage at which you are ready to start using your notecards and after you've decided how you are going to keep track of your sources as you write, you've reached a good point to stop and read Section 6.

- You can save yourself a great deal of time and energy once you start your second draft if you

  - write on only one side of the piece of paper;
  - write only on every other line of each sheet;
  - leave wide margins on each sheet.

  These simple devices will allow you to change parts of your draft without having to recopy parts of the text that don't need to be changed. By writing on every other line and leaving wide margins, you can add sentences or change sentences without having to recopy. If you write on only one side of each sheet of paper, you can cut your draft apart and paste paragraphs and sections together in different ways if you decide to introduce an idea in a different part of the paper. All of this advice will be easy to follow if you are composing on a word processor. But whether you have the advantage of using a computer or you are composing with pen and paper, the point is still the same: You want to have a flexible, open attitude toward your draft, being ready, willing, and able to make changes that will make your paper stronger—and you want to have a draft that is clean enough for you to read. If certain pages become so messy that you can't read them, recopy them right away. If you can't easily read what you've written, you're losing control. Finally, number the pages of your draft; how can you read your draft if you don't know which page goes where?

- Plan to write a more elaborated, although still rough, draft of the whole paper, working from section to section. If you realize that you don't have a clear picture of some section, take time to map it out, or do a brief abstract of it. At this stage you should be writing in complete sentences, and you should be looking for the words and sentence structures that best express your ideas—but your focus should still be on capturing those ideas and the flow of your thinking. Don't distract yourself by worrying about spelling or punctuation; if a sentence is clumsy, mark it in some way, so that you can revise it later, and keep moving ahead.

Remember that you are explaining to other people what your ideas are and how they are related. If you expect your readers to understand the point you are making, then you must explain clearly what you are talking about, and you must *show* your readers *exactly* how each idea is related to the others. Never assume that your readers know what you mean. Even if these readers are acquainted with your subject matter, they cannot know how you see this subject until you *tell* them how you see it. Such explanations apply to all parts of the paper.

Never introduce facts or information unless you have shown your readers what to do with these facts or this information. Each section, each paragraph of your paper should include a statement (the sooner, the better) that clearly states the point you are making here. As you complete one point and move on to the next, show your readers how the two points are related. Don't assume they know; spell it out. If you feel at any point that you are going off on a tangent or that you are getting lost, refer back to your map. Say to yourself, "What is the point I want to make here?" Or go back and reread the two or three pages that precede the paragraph. Remind yourself where you are going.

- Plan to reread the entire draft frequently, matching it against your outline or abstract. As you reread, you are checking to make sure that each section is fitting properly into the overall shape of the paper. When you see a problem, write a note to yourself in the margin, telling yourself what the problem is. You should finish your reading before you stop to revise. Keep working in this fashion, from whole to part to whole, until you feel you have a draft that is ready for a final polish.

- Since you are going to be addressing your paper to your fellow students, you may want to involve one or two of them actively and directly in your writing process. Think about asking one or two members of your class, or someone you know who is a major in the field, to read and respond to your paper as you are writing it. While you can ask for help in spotting mechanical problems (spelling, punctuation, grammatical errors), help of this sort should be requested late in the process, when you consider your paper almost finished. Earlier in the process, while your paper is still in draft form, ask a classmate to *read*—not to edit or to proofread—it to see whether your ideas are coming across clearly and to see how convincing your presentation is. If you ask for help of this sort, tell your reader to concentrate on what you are saying; tell him or her that you are most interested in whether or not your draft is making sense. Some of the points you could ask this reader to respond to are listed below. You will probably want to add to the list, especially requesting information on sections of your draft that don't seem to be working or that you are worried about. Your readers could give their responses to you orally, but if you asked your readers to write their responses, you would have them in front of you when you sit down to revise. And a word of caution: Since your purpose here is to "test" your draft to see whether it is saying what you want it to say, don't prejudice your readers by explaining ahead of time what your main point is or what you are trying to accomplish in this paper. Let the draft speak for itself.

Responses to ask of your reader:

○ Tell me the main point of my paper.
○ After you have read my paper, sketch out the general direction of and the main points of my argument.
○ Did you understand all of my technical terms and language? Were there any that I could have made clearer?
○ If there are any places in my paper where you were confused, even for a short period of time, point them out to me and explain to me what confused you.
○ Are there any places where you are not convinced by what I say? Where? Why weren't you convinced?
○ Do you have any advice or suggestions that you think would make my paper stronger?

Don't feel as if you are obliged to follow every suggestion but do pay close attention to the responses you receive from these readers because they will give you a good notion of the way other readers will process or comprehend your words. Compare your readers' reactions with your intentions for your paper, and make any changes that will clarify your points and make your ideas easier to follow.

F. May I Use the First Person in My Paper? And Other Issues Related to Style

One question that students often ask me when they are writing their research papers is, "May I use *I* in this paper?" I cannot always answer the question for them. Because conventions of style differ from discipline to discipline and from type of paper to type of paper, your instructor is the person who can tell you whether the first person is appropriate in the specific paper you are preparing for him or her. So your safest course is to address specific questions about style to your instructor. However, there are general guidelines that experienced writers use for determining the style and tone of papers (not only research papers but all types of expository writing). In the rest of this subsection I'll briefly discuss some of these guidelines; they could help you determine the most appropriate style for your paper.

At the beginning of this section I talked about the audience for whom you are writing your paper and the image of yourself that you want to project to this audience. If you think of yourself as a speaker and think about the audience you are addressing, you put your paper in a communication context. If, when you write, you consider yourself communicating with a group of readers, an issue that then arises is, "What is my relationship with the members of my audience?" Determining the relationship between themselves as speakers or writers and their audience or readers helps experienced writers decide the style and tone of the prose they are composing. Let us say, for example, that you are a senior psychology major who has done a research project on teenage drug abuse. You would discuss your work differently if you were writing a letter to a close friend, if you were talking to a class of junior high students, and if you were presenting your work at a conference of social workers, psychologists, and school officials. The differences in the way you present your work are determined by the differences in your relationship with each of these groups.

In writing a letter to a close friend, you would probably be casual. You might use slang and colloquial expressions. You probably wouldn't worry about your sentence structure and punctuation. Instead of presenting your ideas in a tight, logical fashion, you'd probably dash off ideas as they came into your mind. It would be natural to make connections between what you've learned in your study and instances of drug abuse that you've noticed among the people you know. You'd probably refer to events that you and your friend have shared. In other words, a casual or informal style is most appropriate for this communication context because you are "talking" to someone you know very well, someone with whom you share a certain intimacy.

However, in making a presentation on this same study on teenage drug abuse at a conference, your style and tone would change because you have a different relationship with this audience. In a group of psychologists, social workers, and school officials, there would be many people you do not know. Even if some of the members of the audience are friends of yours, this is a "professional" communication situation and you are playing the role of "budding professional." You want the members of the audience to see you as a knowledgeable, reasonable, thoughtful researcher. Because the situation is more formal, you would use a more formal style.

The communication context of the research paper you are now writing is much closer to the presentation of the study on teenage drug abuse at a conference than to writing about the subject to a close friend. Thus your paper will be in a more formal style.

In writing your paper in a more formal style, here are some of the features of your prose that you will want to pay attention to.

- You will want to avoid slang, colloquialisms, and such informal speech mannerisms as "well," "you know," "as I was saying," etc.

  This diction is usually inappropriate in a more formal communication situation because it implies a casual, more intimate relationship with your audience than actually exists. Even if you address your paper to your classmates, you are speaking to them in the more formal context of the classroom. You want them to take you and your work seriously. In formal situations, slang will work against your efforts to communicate, not only because some of your readers may not know what the slang words mean but also because slang tends to be very vague and thus imprecise. Some instructors may consider contractions (*don't, wasn't*) too informal; it would be wise to ask your instructor about this and other stylistic matters before you polish your final draft.

- You will use the technical terminology associated with your subject because it is the most precise language to use; at the same time, in using this language of the discipline, you will always consider the amount of knowledge your audience has about this subject.

  If you are positive that your readers know what a term means (and thus know the concept that it represents), you will use the term without explaining it. If you know your readers do not know the term (and thus the concept it represents), you must be prepared to educate your readers about this concept as you make your own point. And remember: explanations need not be exhaustive. You can tell your readers only what they need to know in order to understand the point you are making.

- In deciding whether to use the first person in your paper, Mary-Claire van Leunen offers a nice rule of thumb: "When you're a part of your story, bring yourself in directly, not in a submerged or twisted way. . . . When you have nothing to do with your story, leave yourself out."[2]

[2] Mary-Claire van Leunen, *Handbook for Scholars* (New York: Alfred A. Knopf, 1978), 39–40.

This simple guideline can also help you decide whether your own personal experiences belong in your paper. From the beginning, were you and your experiences meant to be a part of the subject you were researching? If they were, then references to yourself are an appropriate part of your paper and should be presented in the first person. If you and your personal experiences were not intended to be a part of the subject you were researching, then they probably do not belong in your paper.

Many of you may have been taught not to use the first person in any expository prose. This ban on the first person is all tied up with the development of the modern scientific method and an approach to knowledge that could be summed up this way: "The role of the scientist or researcher is to observe and record phenomena that have no connection with the scientist or researcher herself. Thus, in reporting what she has observed, the researcher or scientist will obviously not appear in the paper." If you are writing a critical paper, however, you are certainly a part of that paper since the inferences and judgments you have made—your ideas—are the major informing element of the paper. This fact does not automatically mean that each of your inferences or judgments should be prefaced with "I think," "I feel," or "It is my opinion." Your readers will assume that inferential and judgmental statements are your inferences and judgments unless you indicate otherwise. It is for this reason that I urge you in Section 6 (see 6.B.2) to name in your sentences the authors of the ideas that you have taken from your sources.

If you feel comfortable that you know which ideas are yours and which belong to your sources, and if you realize that your readers will assume that an inference or judgment is yours unless you tell them otherwise, you should find that you really won't have to use the first person very often. You will probably notice that frequently, when you are not reiterating the opinions of other authors, you are saying that the facts speak for themselves; the most accurate way of expressing this idea is, "However, it is clear from the evidence that . . ." or "There is no substantial evidence for these positions." On those few occasions when you feel that you need to tell the reader directly that a certain idea is yours, you should feel free to do so in the first person. If your instructor has told you not to use the first person, you will have to refer to yourself in the third person: "This author has concluded . . ."; "It is the opinion of this author that . . ."

- Be very careful about the use of the first person plural (*we, us, our*). Such pronouns are appropriate only when they are used to represent a specific group of which you are actually a member and only when you have made it clear to your reader which group you are referring to. If a music teacher is addressing other music teachers about common teaching experiences, he or she could appropriately write, "We music teachers often find that our students . . . " But don't use the editorial *we* as a roundabout way of saying *I*. And, if the group you are referring to is the human race, it is clearer to say *people* or *human beings* than *we*, at least in initial references to this group.

- Whether or not you use the second person (*you, your*) will again depend on your relationship with your readers and the purpose you have in writing your paper.

  A *you* in a paper automatically means *me* to the reader; if the remark seems to me, the reader, to apply to me, all is well; but I resent it when you make a remark in your paper about *you* (me) that I don't think applies to me. Perhaps you've noticed that the second person is usually found in prose intended to instruct readers how to do something or to exhort them to think, feel, or behave in a particular way. If the purpose of your paper is to instruct (as it is the purpose of this book) or if it is to exhort your readers to change their ways, then the second person is appropriate. If your paper is not a "how-to" paper or a piece of exhortation, the second person isn't appropriate. Also, watch out for *you* as it is used in informal prose to represent *anybody* or *everybody* as in "When a dog growls, you assume it will bite." In more formal writing, it is better to use either *a person, people,* or *one:* "When embarrassed, a person (one) is likely to become hostile or defensive."

- Finally, formal style is usually characterized by paragraphs and sentences that are self-explanatory.

  Because your readers cannot know how you have put your ideas and evidence together, all of these relationships must be made absolutely explicit. This is the reason that writers, in formal communication contexts, usually use a topic sentence that gives their readers an overview of the point that is being introduced; this is the reason that sentences in formal writing tend to be longer and to fall into the category of complex sentences (sentences with one or more dependent clauses).

  In talking to a friend, you might appropriately say, "I left the party early. I was sick" and to leave it to the listener to infer a cause-effect relationship. In formal writing, you don't want to take the chance that the reader might not see the cause-effect relationship, so you make it explicit: "I left the party because I was not feeling well."

The need for precision is the other reason that sentences tend to be longer in formal writing. You want to qualify your point so that the statement is exact: "In this case, Outer Slobovia felt that if it did not send troops to the Isle of Herron, it risked losing the support of its allies, Inner Slobovia and Alcimene."

As a writer addressing a group of people whom you do not know very well, your major objective is your readers' complete understanding of your exact point. Thus, above all, you want your prose to be clear and precise. You can judge the clarity of your prose by asking, "Will my readers comprehend my point after one reading of this sentence or paragraph?" You can judge the precision of your prose by asking, "Will my readers see exactly what I mean here?" Because it is not always easy to answer these questions on your own, you can see the advantage of asking one or two other students to read and respond to your drafts.

Before I leave this issue of formal style, I must warn you that formality of style is not measured by the "look" or the "sound" of the words on the page. To put it another way, you are not making your paper more formal if you simply search around for the longest, classiest words you can find and then string them together in phrases that have a certain "ring" to them—"the proposition of annihilation tactics"; "integrated monitored hardware."

I realize that you may be tempted to throw big words around in long, convoluted sentences because such sentences seem to look and sound like the sentences of the authors you've been reading. It is natural for you to assume that you need to impress your readers and that the best way to impress them is to sound impressive. I see papers every day that are collections of such impressive-sounding sentences; unfortunately, very often they don't communicate any ideas. A few years ago when I was discussing a collection of such sentences with Tony Abena, the student who had written them, he had a flash of insight: "I'm writing to impress, not to express," he said. I am borrowing Tony Abena's phrase because it says so well what many students do when they are trying to write in a formal style.

My usual response to the student who is working harder to impress me than to communicate with me is this. Words carry meanings for me. If a particular group of words doesn't make sense to me, I'm not impressed; I'm confused, frustrated, and angry. What impresses me is the idea that is expressed, the idea that is carried by the words. So if you want to impress your readers, choose those words and phrases that best represent the idea you have in your mind. Those people who are worth impressing are too smart to be snowed by an avalanche of meaningless verbiage.

G. *Summary*

Some students tend to lose momentum when it comes time to write the paper that ends the research process. When they feel they have figured out their answer to their research question, it seems bothersome, boring, or redundant to have to put it all down on paper. The pressure of the deadline doesn't help, especially since other papers, tests, or assignments are usually due about the same time. If you find yourself being tempted to slack off at this stage, here are some things you should tell yourself.

First, writing the paper is still a very critical part of the thinking process. You may "feel" you know what you think, but you won't really *know* until you say it to yourself or another person. Writing the paper gives you the opportunity to go through this process. It is the final and crucial "sharpening" phase of the whole thinking/research process. I know this from my own experiences with writing and from the hours I have spent with students. Students tell me they know what they think, but as they try to express their ideas, they often just give me disconnected bits and pieces. Our talking together about a paper has the effect of bringing these pieces into a unified whole and often brings to light connections they didn't realize they saw. What students and I are doing together in these conversations is going through the same mental processes that a writer goes through in composing a paper. So think of the whole formal writing process, from determining the paper's overall shape and purpose through the various drafts, as an important intellectual challenge—the challenge of refining your ideas into a form that is clear and meaningful and the challenge of giving other people good reasons for accepting your view of your subject.

Second, it is also very important for you to attend to details that may be more mechanical than creative. When you have read over the entire draft from beginning to end and you are satisfied that your ideas are spelled out so clearly that your readers will have no trouble following you, you have a final rough draft. Only three more steps are left.

- When you have a final rough draft, you must double-check the accuracy of the information you have taken from your sources, and you must document these sources. Using the coding system in the text, begin with your first reference to a source. Check what you have in the text against the information or quotation on the notecard. Then document the source (using notecard and reference card), using the proper documentation form. For more information on documentation and documentation systems, see Section 7.

- The next step is to proofread your final rough draft. Examine each sentence and paragraph carefully. Make sure all words are spelled correctly, make sure all sentences are punctuated properly (including quotation marks), make sure that you have used one basic tense for the paper, check pronoun references, and so on.

- Making the final clean draft of the paper should be a simple act of transcription. You should never make a substantive change in sentences or paragraphs at this stage. A substantive change in a sentence changes its meaning; this in turn calls for changes in other sentences in the paragraph, and you are, suddenly, back to revising. You should not be revising when you make your final clean draft.

In this final polishing stage, you should consult Appendix F, which gives you pointers about careful editing, proofreading, and proper manuscript form. These final steps will be easier if you have had the advantage of doing your paper on a word processor, but whether you are using a computer or an ordinary typewriter, all these steps are important and worth the time and effort they take. If you need some encouragement here, call upon your pride of ownership, or the value you place on putting your best foot forward, or the perfectionist in you—the one who says, "If it's worth doing, it's worth doing well." Attention to detail is important in writing. Misspelled words, errors in grammar, and sloppiness in documentation form can dominate readers' perceptions—and judgment—of your work. At best, these technical problems will irritate readers and distract their attention from what is being said in the paper. At worst, readers can interpret a writer's lack of attention to such details as a sign that the writer doesn't put much value on his or her work. Thus, readers may conclude that they shouldn't take the work very seriously either. You have put a great deal of time and energy into developing your views of your subject. I would assume that now you want your readers to focus on what you have to say, that you want to hear what your readers think about your ideas. Is it worth taking the risk that your readers' first comments will be about technical mistakes?

SECTION 6

How to and How Not to Incorporate Your Evidence into Your Paper

A. If You Don't Use and Acknowledge Your Sources Properly, You May End Up Plagiarizing

I don't like beginning this section with an unpleasant subject, but plagiarism is a serious offense and, after all the time and energy you have put into your research project up to this point, you certainly do not want your instructor to accuse you of having plagiarized parts of the paper you hand in. In my experience in working with students who are writing research papers, I have found that much plagiarism is unintentional. Papers, or parts of papers, are plagiarized not because the student intended to plagiarize but because the student either did not know how to use sources properly or because the student did not know how to acknowledge sources properly. To express it negatively, the purpose of this section is to save you from falling into unintentional plagiarism; to express it more positively, the purpose of this section is to show you how experienced writers follow the basic rule of using the ideas and works of others: giving credit where credit is due.

1. What Plagiarism Is

Quite simply, plagiarism is theft. Common thieves take cars, stereos, silverware, and other material goods that legally belong to others, then use this property as if it were rightfully theirs. Plagiarists steal the words, the ideas, and/or the work that rightfully belong to others. Plagiarists then present these words, ideas, and/or work as if this material were their own words, ideas, or work.

Just as there are laws against taking the material goods that belong to another, so there are laws against plagiarism. If you were to copy an article or the section of a book and publish this work under your own name, clearly implying that this work was yours, you could be taken to a court of law. But you do not have to publish plagiarized material to be in serious trouble. College instructors put plagiarism in the same category as cheating on exams and offenders can be punished with stiff penalties.

Obviously, you'd be in serious trouble if you intentionally passed off the work, the ideas, or the words of another person as your own. You'd be in serious trouble if you put your name on a paper that was, in fact, copied from a published book or article. You'd be in serious trouble if part of your paper were words copied from a book or article but not enclosed in quotation marks. You'd be in trouble if all or part of your paper was illegitimate paraphrase (see subsection B.3).

Occasionally, students are guilty of premeditated or intentional plagiarism. They consciously attempt to pass off the work of others as their own, or they buy a term paper written by someone else. But as I've said, many cases of plagiarism are cases of unintentional plagiarism. I am sure that you don't want to be one of those students who plagiarize without realizing that they are plagiarizing.

2. Common Sources of Unintentional Plagiarism

If plagiarism is the act of presenting the words, ideas, or work of others as if they were your own, then the proper use of the work of others requires that you

always give credit where credit is due.

Or, to put it another way, in our papers we frankly tell our readers that we are making use of the material of another, and we give our readers all the information they need to find and read the original source. In academic circles the two basic ways we give credit where credit is due are these:

- We frankly acknowledge to our readers that certain ideas or work has been taken from other sources by saying so in the text of the paper and/or by documenting the sources of these ideas in our papers. In Section 7 of this book and the appendixes that follow, I show you five of the basic modes of documentation. Although these forms differ, each is an accepted system for giving credit where credit is due.

- We frankly acknowledge to our readers that the words we are using are the words of another person by putting these words in quotation marks *and* documenting that source by using one of the accepted modes of documentation. I talk more about the proper ways of quoting material in subsection B.4 of this section.

Often students neglect to follow these simple procedures for giving credit where credit is due. Here are some of the reasons I've discovered for unintentional plagiarism.

- One major source of unintentional plagiarism is carelessness in the research process.

    In Section 4 I stressed the importance of using notecards or a comparable system for keeping track of your sources; one reason for this emphasis on careful notetaking is to help you avoid the risk of unintentional plagiarism.

    You can, if you are sloppy, fail to make a record of the source of a piece of evidence (forgetting to record the author or the title of the work or the page number on which this information was given). Or you can fail to keep a complete record of the necessary bibliographic information for the source. If, when you write your paper, you want to use this information, you are going to have trouble giving the credit you are expected to give.

    In Section 4, I also stressed how important it is to put quotation marks around the exact words of an author on your notecards. If your notecard doesn't indicate that the words are the words of the author, you will assume that these words are yours and thus fail to give credit where credit is due. If you are not careful to paraphrase properly, you may have notecards that are illegitimate paraphrases (see subsection B.3).

    Thus, carelessness in the research process can lead to inadvertent plagiarism.

- Another source of unintentional plagiarism is sloppiness while writing your paper.

    You may fall into plagiarism if you fail to keep track of the sources of your evidence in your drafts as you write and revise your paper. You can easily avoid this source of unintentional plagiarism by developing a system of noting your sources as you write (see Section 5.A.3).

- A more general source of unintentional plagiarism is ignorance of the "giving-credit-where-credit-is-due" rule.

  Many students fall into plagiarism because they do not know that they are obliged to give credit where credit is due or because they do not know the proper ways to give such credit.

- Perhaps the most common source of unintentional plagiarism is the "passive-sponge" approach to research.

  If a student mindlessly gathers great quantities of information without digesting, thinking about, and assessing this information as she researches, it is very easy for her to plagiarize because she can easily assume that everything she reads is, somehow, *the truth*. She will not see a need to document sources or to give credit to specific experts because she will assume that all of the evidence she has gathered falls into the category of received truth or common knowledge.

  A passive sponge may panic when he sits down to write his paper. Suddenly he may realize that all he has is material that belongs to others. Because he has not been developing his own ideas, he is trapped into following the ideas in his sources. He may conclude—probably accurately—that everything in his paper will have to be acknowledged as belonging to others. He may find himself using long passages from his sources, either quoting directly or falling into illegitimate paraphrase. Overwhelmed and oppressed by the idea of having to document everything in the paper because the paper actually belongs to his sources, he may rebel and document haphazardly.

Throughout this book I have attempted to save you from falling into the traps that lie in wait for passive sponges. Saving you from unintentional plagiarism is only one reason I have stressed taking control of your research project from the beginning of the process. But obviously one of the advantages of taking control of the research process from the beginning is that when you reach the point of writing your papers, you have a clear sense of your own ideas and the debts you owe to others. Thus, if you have taken your notes carefully and systematically, if you have been careful to make reference cards, and especially if you have used your Researcher's Notebook as I have advised you to do, you have the necessary basic foundation for avoiding plagiarism.

However, you may still have questions about the best way of incorporating your evidence into your text and the best way of giving credit where credit is due. These are the issues I will discuss in the rest of this section. So when you have a good, solid first rough draft of your paper, when you have developed a system for keeping track of your sources as you write and revise, and when you have reviewed your evidence and decided what you want to use, you should stop and read all of the subsections of this section.

B. *Using and Acknowledging Your Sources . . . Properly*

Obvious signs of plagiarism are not the only problems instructors find in the way that students use, or abuse, sources. Whenever I read a student paper that includes a large number of direct quotations, particularly a large number of *long* direct quotations, I worry that I am reading the paper of a student who has allowed herself to be used by her sources. Instead of writing a paper in which she expresses her own point of view, supported by evidence from various sources, she is letting others write her paper for her. Whenever I read a paper in which the same source is footnoted in paragraph after paragraph, or page after page, I worry that I am reading another paper in which a student has allowed himself to be used by his sources. Instead of developing and formulating his own point of view, this student is content to repeat the argument of one of his sources.

Throughout the research process your goal has been to use your sources, rather than having your sources use you.

Now, at this last stage of the research process, you do not want to fall victim to your sources. So I will repeat, one last time, that in your paper you are articulating and presenting *your* perception of the subject you have been investigating. The phrase "your perception of the subject" should not be read as "a completely new, original, unique perception of the subject." Your conclusions will probably not be startlingly new; but coming to radically new perceptions of a subject isn't the ordinary experience of experts, either. Teachers do not expect your paper to be original in this sense. Rather, what they will expect to see in your papers are obvious and clear signs that *you* have made *your own decisions* about the way the intellectual puzzle you have been working on should be put together. A passive-sponge paper sounds like a person who would say to you, "Mom has told me not to major in chemistry because . . . ." A researcher-as-detective paper sounds like the person who says "I have decided to major in geology because, as my dad says, geology is . . . . Also, as Aunt Jane points out, a geology major would . . . . Besides, several people who have majored in geology have found that . . . ."

Confidence is the key, the confidence that you have drawn your own conclusion and that there is a solid basis for it. Just as it is natural for my hypothetical student to explain her decision to major in geology by calling on the arguments and facts offered by her father and her Aunt Jane and other majors, so in your paper you should find that you automatically refer to the sources upon which you have drawn to form your conclusion. You should find it natural to say, "After considering the theories of X, Y, and Z, I find that Z's argument is most convincing because . . ." or "I agree with Doe's assessment of the problem." Because you have worked out your own picture of the puzzle, you won't be tempted to present Sarah Doe's or Z's argument in great detail because you know that their arguments are *their* perceptions of the puzzle, and, while you agree with their general perceptions, you have your own reasons for doing so. You will use Doe's work, or Z's, and that of your other sources as it suits your needs.

I urged you to do your first full draft without your notecards so that you would have the confidence that I've been talking about. Now that you have this confidence, let's talk about using those sources you've decided to use.

1. Use What You Need, Where You Need It—and Document What You've Used

In most cases, as you write your paper, you should find that the evidence you are using is either

discrete pieces of information from your sources

or

summaries of the conclusions, work, or opinions of one or more of the experts you've read.

Using sources does not imply quoting the sources directly, and, in fact, you should be very judicious in using direct quotations. Look upon direct quotations only as supporting evidence, never as a substitute for your own expression of the point you want to make. You should use the exact words of others *only* when the expert's words are the best or most direct illustration of the expert's point of view. In subsection B.4, I talk at length about how to quote your sources effectively and properly. But here let me illustrate what I mean when I say that in most cases you will be using discrete pieces of information or summarizing the work or conclusions of others.

a. Using Discrete Pieces of Information

Example 1

Your Paper
(Documented in the Chicago Humanities Style)

Breakdowns of expenditures on arms throughout the world between 1971 and 1980 show that the Third World countries increased their military expenditures while, in comparison, the amount spent by the U.S. and the U.S.S.R. decreased. In 1971, Third World countries accounted for only 9 percent of worldwide military expenditures; by 1980, the proportion had increased to 16 percent of the total.[9]

Your Notecard

```
world military expenditures

        1971                1980
USA 32%              USA 24%
USSR 25%             USSR 24%
Third World 9%       Third World 16%

                      p.xix, Stockholm
                      International
                      Peace Research Inst.,
                      SIPRI Yearbook,
                      Armaments 1981
```

Your Documentation
(Endnote or Footnote)

9. Stockholm International Peace Research Institute, *SIPRI Yearbook of World Armaments and Disarmament, 1981* (London: Taylor and Frances Ltd., 1981), xix.

Example 2

Your Paper
(Documented in the MLA Style)

When considering the reign of the Ayatollah Khomeini in Iran, one must always keep in mind two central points about the Islamic religion. The first is that the essence of Islam is submission (Goldziher 3–4). The other is that the Islamic religion pervades all aspects of the state. Whereas in Western countries one can distinguish between the laws of a particular religion and the secular laws of the state (i.e., civil and criminal codes), in an Islamic state all the laws of the country are dictated by the religious laws (Goldziher 54).

Your Notecards

```
"Islam means submission, the believer's
submission to Allah. The word expresses, first
and foremost, a feeling of dependency on an
unbounded omnipotence to which man must submit
and resign his will .... Submission is the
dominant principle inherent in all
manifestations of Islam: in its ideas, forms,
ethics, and worship."

                              Goldziher
                              Islamic Theology & Law
                              pp. 3-4
```

```
"But the conduct of life in conformity to the
law includes more than ritual. For in Islam,
religious law encompasses all legal branches:
civil, criminal, and constitutional."




                         Goldziher
                         Islamic Theology & Law
                         p. 54
```

Your Documentation

Readers will find full documentation for the Goldziher book in the list of works cited at the end of your paper:

Goldziher, Ignaz. *Introduction to Islamic Theology and Law.* Trans. Andras and Ruth Hamori. Modern Classics in Near Eastern Studies. Princeton, NJ: Princeton UP, 1981.

b. Summarizing the Work of Others

Example 1

Your Paper
(Documented in the Chicago Author-Date Style)

Recent studies indicate that the medical benefits of DMSO outweigh potential side effects (Jones 1981; Smith 1989; Wilson and Johnson 1985).

Your Documentation

The reference to the articles by Jones, Smith, and Wilson and Johnson in the body of your paper is comparable to a footnote citing these three articles. The reference tells us that the studies of these experts all point to the conclusion you've stated. In the reference list at the end of your paper, you will give complete bibliographic information about these three sources.

Example 2

Your Paper
(Documented in the Chicago Humanities Style)

In his recent study of Supreme Court Justice Felix Frankfurter, H. N. Hirsch joins other historians and political scientists who are exploring the possibilities of psychobiography.[21]

Your Documentation
(Endnote or Footnote)

21. H. N. Hirsch, *The Enigma of Felix Frankfurter* (New York: Basic Books, 1981). See pp. 3–10.

Since your reference is to the entire book, your note need not give any specific page numbers. Here, however, you suggest that your reader look at the first chapter (pp. 3–10) because on these pages Hirsch discusses the how's and why's of his use of psychological theories in this biography.

Example 3

Your Paper
(Documented in the MLA Style)

Irene Athey points out that research indicates a strong correlation between a child's self-concept and his or her reading achievement (357). These findings, combined with other research on the self-images of dyslexics, would suggest that college-level students who suffer from dyslexia would have more negative self-concepts than would college students who have always had average or better-than-average reading skills.

Notice that in your paper you must give credit to Athey for summarizing the results of the research.

Your Notecard

```
"In general, the research literature suggests that good
readers tend to have more positive self concepts than
poor readers (Athey & Holmes, 1969; Hallock, 1958;
Lockhart, 1965; Lumpkin, 1959; Malmquist, 1958;
Padelford, 1969; Seay, 1960; Stevens, 1971; Zimmerman &
Allebrand, 1965). More specifically, feelings of
adequacy and personal worth, self-confidence and self-
reliance seem to emerge as important factors in the
relationship with reading achievement. Conversely,
underachieving readers tend to be characterized by
immaturity, impulsivity, and negative feelings
concerning themselves and their world (Blackham, 1955;
Bodwin, 1957; Schwyhart, 1967; Toller, 1967)."

                          Athey in Singer & Ruddell
                          Theo. Models
                          p. 357
```

Your Documentation

Readers will find full bibliographic information about this source under "Athey" in the list of works cited at the end of the paper:

Athey, Irene. "Reading Research in the Affective Domain." *Theoretical Models and Processes of Reading.* Ed. Harry Singer and Robert B. Ruddell. 2nd ed. Newark, DE: International Reading Association, 1976.   352–380.

To give you a clearer sense of the way that information from other sources is digested and used by a researcher for her own purposes, I am now going to show you a short excerpt from a research paper I wrote several years ago, and excerpts from the sources I used in this paragraph of my paper.

First of all, you should read the two paragraphs carefully, noting specifically how I develop the main point of the second paragraph, that "once come to Court . . . the nobleman found the road to power and riches anything but a primrose path." Then, on the next four pages, compare the sources I used with my use of this information. Pay close attention to the focal points, or points of view, of my paragraph and the paragraphs from which I took my ideas and information. My main point was developed from my reading of Zagorin, Cheyney, Stone, and others. I built my idea from their ideas and the information they used. But notice—it's fairly obvious from the first sentence of each paragraph—that each of us has a different point to make, a different point of view, a different argument.

The Final Draft of My Paper

Thus, as the Queen called on her nobility to live up to their responsibilities and return to the land, economic realities and the centralization of power created a counterforce, pulling them toward London and the Court.

Once come to Court, however, the nobleman found the road to power and riches anything but a primrose path. The golden apples of "titles and places of honour, . . . rewards of land or money, grants of valuable fiscal privileges under the royal prerogative, such as monopolies and customs farms, miscellaneous rights in the crown's gift . . . and appointment to office" were tightly held by Elizabeth and her intimates.[14] To earn such an apple the courtier had to attract the Queen's eye and ear, and this meant working one's way up the ladder of preferment by winning patrons whose "letters of introduction" were paid for with promises and gold. The process was costly, in moral as well as monetary terms. The constant need to jockey for favorable positions, and the whimsies of the Queen herself, bred envy and hatred among her courtiers. Often the Court was split into dangerous and vicious factions; the infighting of the friends of the Earl of Essex and the Cecils darkened the last years of Elizabeth's reign.[15] Moreover, the Virgin Queen, who was always frugal with her favors, became excessively parsimonious in her later years.[16] In the 1590s a courtier often found the efforts of many years rewarded with only bitterness and a long list of debts.

14. Perez Zagorin, *The Court and the Country: The Beginning of the English Revolution* (New York: Atheneum, 1970), 47–48.

15. Zagorin, 47; Edward Cheyney, *A History of England from the Defeat of the Armada to the Death of Elizabeth* (London and New York: Longmans, Green, 1914), 1:49–50.

16. Lawrence Stone, *The Crisis of the Aristocracy 1558–1641*, abridged ed. (New York: Oxford University Press, 1967), 94; Cheyney 1:9. Stone ties James I's notorious granting of knighthoods in part to a "fierce pressure from below from a squirearchy too long starved of titles" (*Crisis of the Aristocracy*, 42).

My Paper

Thus, as the Queen called on her nobility to live up to their responsibilities and return to the land, economic realities and the centralization of power created a counterforce, pulling them toward London and the Court.

Once come to Court, however, the nobleman found the road to power and riches anything but a primrose path. The golden apples of "titles and places of honour, . . . rewards of land or money, grants of valuable fiscal privileges under the royal prerogative, such as monopolies and customs farms, miscellaneous rights in the crown's gift . . . and appointment to office" were tightly held by Elizabeth and her intimates.[14] To earn such an apple the courtier had to attract the Queen's eye and ear, and this meant working one's way up the ladder of preferment by winning patrons whose "letters of introduction" were paid for with promises and gold.

14. Perez Zagorin, *The Court and the Country: The Beginning of the English Revolution* (New York: Atheneum, 1970), 47–48.

My Source

Original passage from Perez Zagorin, *The Court and the Country: The Beginning of the English Revolution* (New York: Atheneum, 1970), 47–48:

The Court's resources for gratifying the hope of preferment were of diverse kinds. They ranged from the bestowal of titles and places of honour, through rewards of land or money, grants of valuable fiscal privileges under the royal prerogative, such as monopolies and customs farms, miscellaneous rights in the crown's gift that could be a source of profit to their recipients, and appointment to office. The commonest aim, however, of the seeker after advancement was office, which might also afford access to other benefits obtainable in the Court. We shall therefore confine our attention to the nature and significance of office.[1] In particular, we shall wish to consider how far officials constituted a *bloc* committed to the support of the King's power and whether they were a body socially distinct from men without Court affiliation.

My Paper

The process was costly, in moral as well as monetary terms. The constant need to jockey for favorable positions, and the whimsies of the Queen herself, bred envy and hatred among her courtiers. Often the Court was split into dangerous and vicious factions; the infighting of the friends of the Earl of Essex and the Cecils darkened the last years of Elizabeth's reign.[15]

15. Zagorin, 47; Edward Cheyney, *A History of England from the Defeat of the Armada to the Death of Elizabeth* (London and New York: Longmans, Green, 1914), 1:49–50.

My Sources

Original passage from Zagorin, 47:

> Beyond all these considerations, great rising and an eminent career in the Court were attended by envy, hatred, and faction. 'Happy the favourite,' wrote Fuller, 'that is raised without the ruin of another.'[2] The actors on the Stuart political scene long retained the memory of the rivalry between the Essex and Cecil factions and of Essex's fall and execution at the setting of Queen Elizabeth's reign. The reigns of James and Charles likewise witnessed the disgrace of such Court personages as the earls of Somerset and Suffolk, Bacon, and Bishop Williams, whose calamity pointed up the perils incident to high office. . . .

Original passage from Edward Cheyney, *A History of England from the Defeat of the Armada to the Death of Elizabeth* (London and New York: Longmans, Green, 1914), 1:49–50:

> These relationships and instances of favoritism combined with influences of temperament and interest to group the men surrounding the queen into factions. These showed themselves sometimes in the council, but more frequently outside. The Cecils and Howards against the friends of Essex, the Norrises against the Knollys, Sir Walter Raleigh against his rivals, and many other factions and temporary intrigues divided the courtiers, fretted the queen, and weakened the government. The greater ministers for the most part rose above these quarrels, but they played a conspicuous part in the routine of court life and increased in bitterness in the later years of the queen's reign. Elizabeth's court was not characterized by high-mindedness or appreciation of the more delicate sentiments of life, and if actual violence and disorder were repressed, and if there was less open immorality than in some of the other courts of Europe, it was nevertheless filled with petty jealousies, conflicts and intrigues.

My Paper

Moreover, the Virgin Queen, who was always frugal with her favors, became excessively parsimonious in her later years.[16] In the 1590s a courtier often found the efforts of many years rewarded with only bitterness and a long list of debts.

16. Lawrence Stone, *The Crisis of the Aristocracy 1558–1641*, abridged ed. (New York: Oxford University Press, 1967), 94; Cheyney 1:9. Stone ties James I's notorious granting of knighthoods in part to a "fierce pressure from below from a squirearchy too long starved of titles" (*Crisis of the Aristocracy*, 42).

My Sources

Original passage from Lawrence Stone, *The Crisis of the Aristocracy 1558–1641*, abridged ed. (New York: Oxford University Press, 1967), 94:

The instability of landed fortunes at this period was not the product of some strange freak of genetics which caused an abnormal proportion of stupid and dissolute children, or no children at all. To the inevitable changes wrought by the eccentricities of human reproductive capacity were added in the late sixteenth century exceptional temptations and compulsions to overspend on conspicuous consumption, royal service, or marriage portions, exceptional need for adaptability in estate management, novel opportunities and exceptional dangers in large-scale borrowing. Compensations were lacking during the reign of Elizabeth, owing to exceptional stinginess in the distribution of royal favours and snobbish objections to marriage with heiresses of lower social status. To make matters worse, legal obstacles to breaking entails and selling land were exceptionally weak, and moral objections to the dismemberment of the family patrimony exceptionally feeble. A landed aristocracy has rarely had it so bad.

Original passage from Cheyney 1:9:

Elizabeth had few generous impulses. No one of the great men of her time, in literature, learning, civil, military or naval life was fully recognized or adequately rewarded by her. She was occasionally liberal to her favorites, but never lavish, except for her own personal adornment or gratification. While her mariners and soldiers starved, her unpaid servants suffered and patriots found themselves neglected or disowned, her signature was being affixed to warrants for £1,700 for a pearl chain for herself, or 1,200 "for a great diamond with a pendant," or "761, 4s, 4d for fine linen for her Majesty's own person."[2]

Original passage from Stone, *Crisis of the Aristocracy*, 42:

Knighthood was the first dignity which the Crown openly allowed to be sold, not by the King himself but by deserving courtiers and servants. The causes of this development are clear enough. Fierce pressure from below from a squirearchy too long starved of titles, a financial stringency that precluded the distribution of direct cash gifts to servants and followers, a laudable desire to please both courtiers and clients, the fact that offices, monopolies, and favours were already being granted to courtiers for resale, all led the easy-going James to succumb to temptation and make knighthood a saleable commodity. Fluctuating according to the conflicting needs to reward followers, to keep up the price, and to preserve the dignity from falling into complete contempt, sales continued until Charles's decision after the death of Buckingham to put a stop to all such practices.

2. Experts Openly Acknowledge Their Sources in the Body of Their Papers; So Should You

If you look carefully at articles in popular magazines and newspapers, you will notice that the authors of these articles constantly give the sources of their information in the body of their stories.

The office [Congressional Budget Office] . . . said in its annual economic report the economy will grow 4 percent in 1983 and 4.7 percent in 1984, and the budget deficit will be $194 billion this year. . . .

The report estimates unemployment, which reached 10.8 percent in December, will be 10.6 percent this year and then slowly decline to 7.5 percent by 1988. The [1984] Reagan budget predicts unemployment of 10.9 percent this year, 10 percent in 1984 and 6.6 percent by 1988.

> Robert MacKay, "Congressional Budget Office Says Recession Ending," *The (Portland) Oregonian*, 4 Feb. 1983, Business Section, C1.

Thanks to new engines and wings, and the use of lighter composite materials, United [Airlines] says that the 767 is 30% to 54% more fuel efficient than the older planes it replaces. Boeing claims that airlines can save up to $2.5 million annually for every 767 they fly.

> Janice Castro, "Boeing Buckles Up for Takeoff," *Time*, 24 Jan. 1983, 60.

Journalists must indicate the sources of their information in the body of their stories because this is their only opportunity to document their sources. But if you look at the scholarly books and articles you've been reading, you will see that the experts also take every opportunity to name the source of their information in the body of their texts, as well as giving complete bibliographic information in notes or reference lists. They recognize a principle that journalists have long been aware of—naming the source of certain information not only acknowledges the source of the information but also lends more credibility to the information.

Thus, as you work on the drafts of your paper, whenever possible you should name the source of the information you are using in the sentence you write. Particularly, you should give the names of the experts whose opinions you are summarizing or quoting.

Here are a few examples from published works that show how the experts acknowledge the sources of their evidence in the body of their texts.

Professor E. H. Carr has recently reminded us that the historian does not exist who is unaffected by his upbringing and background.

> Lawrence Stone, *The Crisis of the Aristocracy 1558–1641*, abridged ed. (New York: Oxford University Press, 1967), 4.

However, as recently discussed by Ulrich (1975), paleoclimate evidence concerning the long-term temperature variations on the earth suggests that the sun's luminosity has not changed from its present value by more than about 3% over the past million years, although the Dilke and Gough mechanism would induce at least a 10% change in the solar luminosity over that time scale.

> Robert W. Noyes, "New Developments in Solar Research," in *Frontiers of Astrophysics*, ed. Eugene H. Avrett (Cambridge, Mass.: Harvard University Press, 1976), 45.

Within the United States, Clifford Shaw and Henry McKay are considered to have pioneered this approach (see Shaw 1929; Shaw and McKay 1931, 1942, 1969), providing the empirical and theoretical standards that have guided many subsequent large-scale studies.

> Robert J. Bursik, Jr., and Jim Webb, "Community Change and Patterns of Delinquency," *American Journal of Sociology* 88 (July 1982): 24.

Fukui, who has studied this phenomenon back as far as 1890, has shown how there has been a steady decrease in the proportion of members of the House of Representatives with a background in local politics.

> Nobutaka Ike, *Japanese Politics: Patron-Client Democracy*, 2d ed. (New York: Alfred A. Knopf, Borzoi Books, 1972), 86.

Wagner[31] has recently published the far-infrared spectrum of liquid bromine, and Chantry *et al.*[32] have studied the long-wavelength absorption of various nonpolar liquids using interferometric techniques. This group of authors attribute the long-wavelength absorption to a vibrational motion of the disordered lattice in the liquid, the so-called 'liquid lattice absorption.'

> Karl D. Möller and Walter G. Rothschild, *Far-Infrared Spectroscopy*, Wiley Series in Pure and Applied Optics (New York: John Wiley and Sons, Wiley-Interscience, 1971), 409.

The urban gangster was also a striking departure from the nineteenth-century criminal figures of the outlaw and the domestic murderer. His legend was, as Daniel Bell and Robert Warshow have noted, a complex mirror image of the American myth of success and social mobility.

> John G. Cawelti, *Adventure, Mystery, and Romance: Formula Stories as Art and Popular Culture* (Chicago and London: University of Chicago Press, 1976), 59.

For the field of reading, Robinson *(73)* has suggested that confusion might be reduced if models would be subgrouped into three categories: models representing 1) theories or procedures of teaching, 2) processes utilized or mobilized in reading, and 3) skills and abilities required for reading attainment.

> Harry Singer, "Theoretical Models of Reading: Implications for Teaching and Research," in *Theoretical Models and Processes of Reading*, ed. Harry Singer and Robert B. Ruddell (Newark, Del.: International Reading Association, 1970), 147.

In Iran, Bharier's data for the 1960s show output growing faster in the larger establishments but employment growing faster in the small-scale sector. For Pakistan, Falcon and Stern[12] show the output of large industrial plants growing faster than total manufacturing output: 10.7 percent per year compared with 7.4 percent per year over the period 1954/55–1968/69.

> Lloyd G. Reynolds, *Image and Reality in Economic Development* (New Haven and London: Yale University Press, 1977), 316.

To live for the moment is the prevailing passion—to live for yourself, not for your predecessors or posterity. We are fast losing the sense of historical continuity, the sense of belonging to a succession of generations originating in the past and stretching into the future. It is the waning of the sense of historical time—in particular, the erosion of any strong concern for posterity—that distinguishes the spiritual crisis of the seventies from earlier outbreaks of millenarian religion, to which it bears a superficial resemblance. Many commentators have seized on this resemblance as a means of understanding the contemporary "cultural revolution," ignoring the features that distinguish it from the religions of the past. A few years ago, Leslie Fiedler proclaimed a "New Age of Faith." More recently, Tom Wolfe has interpreted the new narcissism as a "third great awakening," an outbreak of orgiastic, ecstatic religiosity. Jim Hougan, in a book that seems to present itself simultaneously as a critique and a celebration of contemporary decadence, compares the current mood to the millennialism of the waning Middle Ages. "The anxieties of the Middle Ages are not much different from those of the present," he writes. Then, as now, social upheaval gave rise to "millenarian sects."

Christopher Lasch, The Culture of Narcissism: American Life in an Age of Diminishing Expectations (New York: W. W. Norton and Co., 1978), 5.

Look at each of these examples. Notice how, in each, the author includes at least the last name of the expert whose work he refers to and makes it clear in his statement that the ideas outlined belong to the person named. These published writers show you how you can acknowledge your sources directly in the body of your paper.

I have included the longer example from Christopher Lasch to show you how one expert, Lasch, uses other experts to make his own point. Lasch's point is stated in the third sentence: "It is the waning of the sense of historical time—in particular, the erosion of any strong concern for posterity—that distinguishes the spiritual crisis of the seventies from earlier outbreaks of millenarian religion, to which it bears a superficial resemblance." He points out that others (Fiedler, Wolfe, and Hougan) have seen a resemblance between the cultural revolution of the seventies and millenarian movements of the past but continues with his own argument that the resemblance is superficial by arguing that Fiedler, Wolfe, and Hougan fail to see important differences between the previous millenarian movements and the cultural movement of the seventies. In the paragraph following the one I have quoted, Lasch shows what he considers the flaws in their thinking. But first he must establish that these three men do see the current spiritual crisis as a religious awakening. The purpose of this paragraph is to make Lasch's idea clear to his readers; he uses Fiedler, Wolfe, and Hougan to make his own argument.

3. Summarizing the Work and Ideas of Another Expert: How Experienced Writers Do It

Because, in your paper, you are using the work of others, rather than having the work and ideas of others use you, in most cases you will need only a sentence or two to summarize the work and ideas of others. You will have selected what you need from these sources and you will put this material into a paragraph, similar to the one I quoted from Lasch in the last subsection, in which you are developing your own idea. Occasionally, however, you may decide that you need to give more information about the ideas or argument of a particular author.

If you find yourself giving a detailed, extended summary of an author's idea or argument, be very careful. In these situations you run the risk of letting your source take over your paper, which can all too easily lead you into a form of plagiarism that I will call illegitimate paraphrase. Let us say, for example, that you are reading a paper on the American Civil War and you come across this passage:

> Eighty-seven years earlier the Founding Fathers had brought forth a new nation on this continent, born in liberty and dedicated to the idea that all men are created equal. But this nation was now engaged in a great civil conflict, testing whether the United States or any country set up on the principles upon which the United States was founded could continue to endure. People on the Union side met on a famous battlefield of this civil war. They were there to dedicate part of this battlefield as a final resting-place for those who gave their lives that the nation might live. They were there to dedicate themselves to a large task that still remained before them. From those who died they would take increased devotion to the cause for which these men died. They resolved that these dead should not have died in vain; that this nation, under God, should have a new birth of freedom; and that government of the people, by the people, for the people should not perish from the earth.

Your first reaction will probably be, "Why, that's Lincoln's Gettysburg Address!" You recognize Lincoln's famous speech because this passage is the Gettysburg Address with only a few words and phrases changed here and there. If I ran across this passage in a paper, I would consider this passage plagiarized. I would consider it plagiarized first of all because there is no mention of Lincoln or his speech. But even if the author of this passage had prefaced the passage by saying, "As Lincoln said at Gettysburg," I'd still consider the passage an illegitimate paraphrase because what are expressed in this passage are essentially Lincoln's ideas and words, not the writer's. The ideas are introduced in the same order in which Lincoln introduced his ideas, and the relationship among the ideas expressed here is exactly the relationship Lincoln expressed. The writer has done nothing but change a few words and phrases; the difference between Lincoln's address and this paraphrase is that the passage is slightly less precise than the actual Gettysburg Address, and much less eloquent.

In your efforts to understand the ideas of others you may find it helpful to take a passage from a work and do a paraphrase like the preceding one. Your purpose would be to change unusual language into words that are more meaningful to you in order to increase your comprehension of the author's ideas. But such direct paraphrases do not belong in the papers you write. You would go through the exercise of doing a paraphrase so that ultimately you could express your understanding of the author's idea, so that you could reach your own conclusions about what the author means. Having digested the basic ideas of another person, in your paper you will want to express, in your own words, your understanding of what this author is saying. In your paper you will use summaries, not paraphrases; and in these summaries you will clearly indicate to your readers that you are talking about the ideas of another person, and you will put in quotation marks those phrases and sentences that are taken directly from the source.

A legitimate summary of Lincoln's address would look like this:

> In his short but eloquent dedication of the cemetery at Gettysburg in 1863, Lincoln focuses his audience's attention on the Union's cause, the preservation of the United States as it was constituted eighty-seven years earlier. Time and again he returns to ideas formalized in the Declaration of Independence and the Constitution, reminding the audience that the United States was "dedicated to the proposition that all men are created equal" and that it is a "government of the people, by the people, for the people."

If, as you are writing your paper, you find yourself slipping into close paraphrase of one of your sources, it is time to step back from your paper and ask yourself why you are following your source in such detail. Is this author's argument or idea central to *your* argument? How? What is your point? What is the relationship between the author's point and your point? You should not continue with a detailed summary of an expert's argument until you know exactly why you are using this material and until you know what point you want to make about it.

If, after considering the issues I have just raised, you decide that a more extensive description of another person's idea is critical to your argument, follow these guidelines in doing your summary:

- Determine what *your* point is. Write your point in a sentence (that sentence would probably make a good topic sentence for your paragraph). If you have decided that the author's analysis of the problem is the most convincing analysis, then I would expect you to write a statement like "Richard Jones's analysis of the problem of welfare fraud is the most convincing analysis because Jones stresses the role that desperation plays in the lives of people who are likely to commit such fraud."

- Acknowledge the source of the idea in your paragraph by naming the person to whom the idea belongs.

- Do not get caught in the trap of simply reiterating the author's argument. Pull out those points that are critical to the point you want to make. Use only those ideas that you want and need.

- Throughout your summary, explicitly indicate which ideas belong to your source ("according to Smith," "he notes," "Smith goes on to say"), so that your readers know what is yours and what belongs to your source.

- Put quotation marks around words and phrases that are taken directly from the source.

To illustrate ways to follow these guidelines, I am including some examples of ways that published writers give more extended summaries of the work of others. Study these examples carefully. Note how each writer follows the guidelines I have just laid out.

Example 1

Virgil Whitaker, in his biographical-analytical study, *Shakespeare's Use of Learning,* asserts this current religious view of Shakespeare's comic and tragic art with admirable boldness. Shakespeare as a man of the Renaissance, he assures us, had accepted the basic religious training of his youth and had never experienced "a genuine skepticism." It follows from such a premise that Shakespeare "did believe profoundly that God had made man in His own image and that, as all men had fallen once in Adam, so each man might fall again if he disobeyed the fundamental laws of God."[4] Whitaker, when he turns to aesthetics, is therefore led to argue, for example, that "Macbeth's sin is so awful simply because, like Shakespeare, he knows and believes in the foundations of human morality and in their ultimate basis in the mind and will of God."[5] This is no doubt to praise Shakespeare and Macbeth as sternly religious men, rather than as superlative playwright and brilliantly conceived character. Moreover, the implications seem to be that the sternness of the religion begot the strength of the play. And some such assumption of a highly self-conscious, febrile religious orthodoxy, both in Shakespeare and in his audience, seems to underlie the critical comments on Shakespeare by the whole contemporary school of Christian aesthetics.

> David Lloyd Stevenson, *The Achievement of Shakespeare's "Measure for Measure"* (Ithaca, N.Y.: Cornell University Press, 1966), 94–95.

The first and last sentences of Stevenson's paragraph indicate very clearly why he is summarizing Whitaker's work. Stevenson wants us to see the Christian approach to Shakespeare in detail. Stevenson's point is that the critics who take this approach assume that Shakespeare, Shakespeare's characters, and Shakespeare's audience were highly conscious of Christian teaching and that these Christian ideas were the essence of the meanings of the plays. So that we see clearly what he is talking about, and in order to support his argument, Stevenson summarizes the argument of one of these Christian critics, Virgil Whitaker, and quotes passages from Whitaker that illustrate this religious view.

Example 2

Shaw and McKay never claimed that they were the first to investigate the geographical distributions of juvenile delinquency. In their introduction to the 1942 volume, they cite not only the spatial work of European criminologists (especially in France and England; see Morris [1957] or Phillips [1972]) but also the American research of Breckenridge and Abbott (1912), Blackmar and Burgess (1917), and McKenzie (1923) that preceded their first major report in 1929. However, Shaw and McKay were not satisfied with the descriptive emphasis found in these studies and sought to interpret the spatial distributions within a general macroscopic theory of community processes. It was this important empirical/theoretical synthesis that gave the Shaw and McKay research its significance. Broadly stated, they proposed that the spatial distribution of delinquency in a city was a product of "larger economic and social processes characterizing the history and growth of the city and of the local communities which comprise it" (1942, p. 14).[2]

> Robert J. Bursik, Jr., and Jim Webb, "Community Change and Patterns of Delinquency," *American Journal of Sociology* 88 (July 1982):25.

In this paragraph, Bursik and Webb's major point is that although Shaw and McKay were not "the first to investigate the geographical distributions of juvenile delinquency," Shaw and McKay's research is very important because they "sought to interpret the spatial distributions within a general macroscopic theory of community processes." The body of the paragraph provides specific illustration and support for this major idea. Notice how Bursik and Webb constantly refer to their source (Shaw and McKay never claimed . . . they were . . . their introduction . . . they cite . . . their

first major report . . . Shaw and McKay were not satisfied . . . the Shaw
and McKay research . . . they proposed . . .).

Example 3

The idea of writing the earlier essay on the "Utility of Religion," its title and its
specific theme, had first originated with his wife. Her proposal was clear in
intention if incoherent in expression:

> Would not religion, the Utility of Religion, be one of the subjects you would
> have most to say on—there is to account for the existence nearly universal of
> some religion (superstition) by the instincts of fear, hope and mystery etc., and
> throwing over all doctrines and theories, called religion, and devices for power,
> to show how religion and poetry fill the same want . . . —how all this must
> be superseded by morality deriving its power from sympathies and benevolence
> and its reward from the approbation of those we respect.[4]

The essay, as Mill then wrote it, reflected most of these views. Religion, he wrote,
was indefensible both on the grounds of truth and of utility, the appeal to the
latter being a form of "moral bribery or subornation of the understanding."[5] There
was, he concluded, nothing in Christianity that was not better supplied by the
Religion of Humanity. At the same time, using her very words, he subtly altered
their effect: religion, he suggested, had a more honorable origin than fear; the idea
of religion as a device for power was only the "vulgarest part" of his subject; and
religion, while comparable to poetry, was also distinct from it, for it addressed
itself to reality in a way that poetry did not.

> Gertrude Himmelfarb, "The Other John Stuart Mill," in *Victorian Minds: A Study
> of Intellectuals in Crisis and of Ideologies in Transition* (New York: Harper & Row,
> Harper Torchbooks, 1970), 151–52.

Himmelfarb's focus in this paragraph is an early essay written by John Stuart
Mill entitled "Utility of Religion." Using a proposal for the essay by Mill's
wife as a convenient summary of the major ideas in the essay, Himmelfarb
shows us major changes Mill made in the essay he wrote. In the paragraph
that follows this one in "The Other John Stuart Mill," Himmelfarb goes on
to compare "Utility of Religion" with an essay on religion that Mill wrote
later in his life. Himmelfarb's overall concern is the way Mill's thinking
changed and evolved.

Example 4

In June 1905, *Annalen der Physik* published an article by Einstein entitled "On
a Heuristic Viewpoint Concerning the Production and Transformation of Light."
Physicists usually refer to this as "Einstein's paper on the photoelectric effect,"
but that description does not do it justice. Einstein himself characterized it at the

time as "very revolutionary," and he was right. This is the paper in which he proposed that light can, and in some situations must, be treated as a collection of independent particles of energy—light quanta—that behave like the particles of a gas. Einstein was well aware that a great weight of evidence had been amassed in the course of the previous century showing light to be a wave phenomenon. He knew, in particular, that Heinrich Hertz's experiments, carried out less than twenty years earlier, had confirmed Maxwell's theoretical conclusion that light waves were electromagnetic in character. Despite all this evidence Einstein argued that the wave theory of light had its limits, and that many phenomena involving the emission and absorption of light "seemed to be more intelligible" if his idea of quanta were adapted. The photoelectric effect was one of several such phenomena which he analyzed to show the power of his new hypothesis.

> Martin J. Klein, "Einstein and the Development of Quantum Physics," in *Einstein: A Centenary Volume*, ed. A. P. French (Cambridge, Mass.: Harvard University Press, 1979), 134.

Klein is clearly not reproducing Einstein's argument in detail. Rather, in the last five sentences he abstracts the main points in the argument, beginning with Einstein's hypothesis (light is a collection of particles of energy) and then giving, in their logical order, the major points that Einstein makes in his article. Notice that Klein constantly reminds us that this is Einstein's argument by using either "Einstein" or "he" in each of these five summary sentences. Notice also that Klein tells us first of all, in sentences two and three, why this article is important and thus worth summarizing.

4. Using Direct Quotations Properly

If you review the examples I have used in the last two subsections of this section, you will see that published authors occasionally quote directly from their sources. You will notice, however, that they don't use direct quotations as a way of letting other people write their essays for them. Rather, they quote the words of another person when the idea they are developing involves the perspective or point of view of another person, a point of view that is best established or illustrated by this person's exact words. You will also notice that in most cases this point of view can be established or illustrated by quoting just a few words, or perhaps a sentence, and these few words are always integrated into a statement or sentence by the writer, a sentence that usually includes a direct acknowledgment of the source of the words quoted.

> "The anxieties of the Middle Ages are not much different from those of the present," he writes.
>
> Christopher Lasch, *The Culture of Narcissism*, 5.

Religion, he wrote, was indefensible both on the grounds of truth and of utility, the appeal to the latter being a form of "moral bribery or subornation of the understanding."

> Gertrude Himmelfarb, "The Other John Stuart Mill," in *Victorian Minds*, 152.

Broadly stated, they proposed that the spatial distribution of delinquency in a city was a product of "larger economic and social processes characterizing the history and growth of the city and of the local communities which comprise it."

> Bursik and Webb, "Community Change and Patterns of Delinquency," 25.

Einstein himself characterized it at the time as "very revolutionary," and he was right.

> Martin J. Klein, "Einstein and the Development of Quantum Physics," in *Einstein: A Centenary Volume*, ed. A. P. French, 134.

From these examples, we can develop our first four guidelines for using quoted material.

Guideline 1

Quote directly from the source *only* when the point you want to make involves calling the reader's attention to the point of view of the author you are discussing, and his or her point of view is *best* established or illustrated by using this person's exact words.

Guideline 2

Quote only those words, phrases, or sentences necessary to make your point about the author's point of view. Don't use the words of another to express ideas that you should express in your own words.

Guideline 3

Quoted material should never stand alone in your paper. Always incorporate the words of others in your own sentences.

- *Avoid* using quotations this way:

  The value of many diet drugs is highly questionable. "Starch blockers are a fraud."[14] "Many hunger suppressants are dangerous because they raise the blood pressure."[15]

- Use this approach:

  The value of many diet drugs is highly questionable. Based on a series of studies he has conducted, Dr. Benjamin Stokely flatly states that "starch blockers are a fraud."[14] Tests of other diet drugs reveal potentially dangerous side effects. A report by the Science Research Institute concludes that "many hunger suppressants are dangerous because they raise blood pressure."[15]

Guideline 4

Punctuation before and after direct quotations is determined by the grammar of your sentence.

Dr. Carl Smith has stated that "there is no evidence that large doses of vitamin C have any beneficial effect."[17]

Dr. Carl Smith doubts the value of taking large amounts of vitamin C; "there is no evidence," he states, "that large doses of vitamin C have any beneficial effect."[17]

Dr. Carl Smith doubts the value of taking large amounts of vitamin C: "There is no evidence that large doses of vitamin C have any beneficial effect."[17]

The fifth guideline for using direct quotations properly pertains to the use of material that is quoted in the source you read. If you remember, in Section 4.D.4 I alerted you that you should make every effort to find the work in which the quotation originally appeared and, if you decide to use this material, to quote from the original source. If, however, you want to use quoted material whose original source you have not been able to locate, here are guidelines to follow.

Guideline 5

When quoting material that is quoted in your source:

- Be sure to name the source of the words you are quoting in the body of your paper.

- Be sure to put the material in quotation marks. If you quote words of the author of the secondary source you are using as well as the words of the person he or she is quoting, put double quotation marks around the material from your source and single quotation marks around the material quoted *in* your source. If you use only the words quoted in the source, use double quotation marks alone, but be sure that you acknowledge that this work is quoted in your documenting note or parenthetical citation (see examples).

Example 1

The Secondary Source

"If our civilization is destroyed, as Macaulay predicted," wrote Henry Demarest Lloyd in an assessment of the robber barons, "it will not be by his barbarians from below. Our barbarians come from above. Our great money-makers have sprung in one generation into seats of power kings do not know. . . ."

> Richard Hofstadter, *The Age of Reform from Bryan to F.D.R.* (New York: Random House, Vintage Books, 1955), 141.

Your Paper

Writing about the nineteenth-century robber barons in 1894, Henry Demarest Lloyd did not paint a very flattering portrait of men whom he called "barbarians." These men had ascended, Lloyd said, to "power kings do not know."[11]

Example 2

The Secondary Source

Collins (1970, 1975), on the other hand, has argued for an extreme environmental position, suggesting that handedness is transmitted from one generation to the next by means of cultural and environmental biases. In this, he echoes the earlier conclusion of Blau (1946) who, after careful review of the evidence, wrote as follows:

> Preferred laterality is not an inherited trait. There is absolutely no evidence to support the contention that dominance, either in handed-ness or any other form, is a congenital, predetermined human capacity. Despite the popularity it has enjoyed with many investigators and the attempts to prove it by various techniques and in relation to different organs of the body, the theory of heredity must be put down as erroneous [p. 180].

> Michael C. Corballis, "Is Left-Handedness Genetically Determined?" in *Neuropsychology of Left-Handedness*, ed. Jeannine Herron, Perspectives in Neurolinguistics and Psycholinguistics (New York: Academic Press, 1980), 159.

Your Paper

On the side of those who argue that handedness is strictly the product of environment or culture is Blau, who wrote in 1946: "Preferred laterality is not an inherited trait. . . . Despite the popularity it has enjoyed with many investigators and the attempts to prove it by various techniques and in relation to different organs of the body, the theory of heredity must be put down as erroneous."[10]

- When you document this quoted material, you must clearly acknowledge that the words you have quoted are taken from a secondary source. If you are documenting your sources with notes (see Appendix B), give at least the author and title, as well as the date, of the original source (you can find this information in the documenting note of the secondary source); then give full bibliographic information about the secondary source you used. Your notes for the two examples given above would look like this:

Example 1

11. Henry D. Lloyd, *Wealth Against Commonwealth* (1894; ed. 1899), quoted by Richard Hofstadter, *The Age of Reform from Bryan to F.D.R.* (New York: Random House, Vintage Books, 1955), 141.

Example 2

10. A. Blau, *The Master Hand* (New York: American Orthopsychiatric Association, 1946), quoted by Michael C. Corballis, "Is Left-Handedness Genetically Determined?" in *Neuropsychology of Left-Handedness*, ed. Jeannine Herron, Perspectives in Neurolinguistics and Psycholinguistics (New York: Academic Press, 1980), 159.

- If you are using the MLA form (see Appendix A), you would indicate that the material is quoted in your parenthetical citation; your paper for Example 1 would look like this:

Writing about the nineteenth-century robber barons in 1894, Henry Demarest Lloyd did not paint a very flattering portrait of men whom he called "barbarians." These men had ascended, Lloyd said, to "power kings do not know" (qtd. in Hofstadter 141).

- If you are using the APA form (see Appendix C), you would indicate that your quotation comes from a secondary source in your parenthetical citation; your paper for Example 2 would look like this:

On the side of those who argue that handedness is strictly the product of environment or culture is Blau (cited in Corballis, 1980), who wrote in 1946: "Preferred laterality is not an inherited trait. . . . Despite the popularity it has enjoyed with many investigators and the attempts to prove it by various techniques and in relation to different organs of the body, the theory of heredity must be put down as erroneous" (p. 159).

The sixth guideline concerns the methods you can use to indicate to your readers that certain words in your paper are the words of another person. The most common method is to put these words in quotation marks. Longer quotations, however, can be marked as quoted by setting this material off from the text of your paper.

Guideline 6

Indicate that material is quoted by using quotation marks, unless the quotation you are using is a long quotation. The general definition of a "long" quotation is one that consists of 100 words or more, or a quotation that will run for four or five lines in your paper. This is the format for a long quotation, called a block quotation:

- Double-space before and after the quotation.
- Single-space the text of the quotation.
- Indent all lines of the quotation four spaces from your left-hand margin.
- Do *not* use quotation marks around block quotations. Setting the quotation off from your text is equal to putting this material in quotation marks.

Note: A quick survey of style manuals (see Section 7.C.1) shows that formats for block quotations vary. Turabian, for example, recommends indenting four spaces; the APA, five spaces; the MLA *Handbook,* ten spaces. In Elizabeth Cookson's "The Forgotten Women," one of the sample papers at the end of this book, block quotations are indented ten spaces and double-spaced to conform to MLA manuscript style. Since most style manuals are addressed to scholars preparing manuscripts for publication, authors are asked to double-space block quotations to make it easy for editors to proofread and for compositors to set the text into type. Since you are not submitting your paper for publication, my suggested format fulfills the ultimate objective of this convention: to display the quoted material in a form visibly distinct from that of the body of the text. If you aren't sure which format is proper for a particular paper, ask your instructor. As in all matters of style, consistency is of utmost importance. In a specific paper, all block quotations must be formatted the same way.

Example

Much of the material that Smith used in his novel about Napoleon is based on historical fact. In a letter to his friend Sam Spade in 1924, Smith explained that

> I am starting work on a novel on Napoleon that I've spent the last six years researching. Don't misunderstand. I do not intend to write an historical romance, those so-called novels that pretend to be historical by piling up all sorts of accurate detail about furniture and clothes and architecture. Such bits and pieces of history do not add up to any real sort of authenticity. My novel is going to be a novel that recreates Napoleon himself. When I am finished, I will have made Napoleon a living, breathing person that the reader will feel he has met and lived with for years and years. I can do it. I've read everything that has been written about the man, and everything he wrote.[8]

Smith did not have to worry about someone who actually knew the Emperor calling his portrait into question, since all those people have long ago turned into dust; but ignoring the issue of the authenticity of the portrait for a moment, there is no doubt that Smith has created a three-dimensional character.

Guideline 7

Occasionally it will be necessary to alter quotations slightly to meet the needs of your prose. Such modifications are acceptable only if you do not misrepresent the meaning of the original words and only if you use the accepted means of indicating that quoted material is being modified.

- Indicate *omission* of a word or words by inserting ellipsis points (. . .) where a word or words are omitted.

Original

In the corporate structure as in government, the rhetoric of achievement, of single-minded devotion to the task at hand—the rhetoric of performance, efficiency, and productivity—no longer provides an accurate description of the struggle for personal survival.

> Christopher Lasch, *The Culture of Narcissism: American Life in an Age of Diminishing Expectations* (New York: W. W. Norton, 1978), 61.

Omissions Indicated by Ellipses (. . .)

In the corporate structure as in government, the rhetoric of . . . single-minded devotion to the task at hand . . . no longer provides an accurate description of the struggle for personal survival.

- Indicate *additions* or changes of certain words by putting your changes in brackets [ ].

Original

Was the King regulating trade in the national interest, or to oblige his friends?

Lawrence Stone, The Crisis of the Aristocracy 1558–1641, abridged ed. (New York: Oxford University Press, 1967), 202.

Modification Indicated by Brackets [ ]

Stone asks, "Was [King James] regulating trade in the national interest, or to oblige his friends?"

Original

Knipling believed the most significant implication of his theoretical results was that the two complementary techniques allowed a pest controller to overcome the law of diminishing returns.

John H. Perkins, Insects, Experts, and the Insecticide Crisis: The Quest for New Pest Management Strategies (New York and London: Plenum Press, 1982), 118.

Modification Indicated by Brackets [ ]

Perkins writes: "Knipling believed the most significant implication of his theoretical results was that the two complementary techniques [of using insecticides and releasing sterile male insects] allowed a pest controller to overcome the law of diminishing returns."

Please note that brackets have squared-off corners and are clearly different from parentheses. If your typewriter has no bracket key, you can draw the brackets neatly with a pen. Do not use parentheses for additions or changes of words in direct quotations. You always want a clear distinction between material you have modified or added and material that the author of the passage may have put in parentheses.

Modifications or additions to quotations should be limited to changes of pronouns to nouns, changes of verb tense, additions of the first name of a person mentioned or of the full name of an event or company, and other such changes for clarification and readability. If you find yourself adding a great deal of information in brackets in a quotation, you should probably write the statement you want to make and then put in quotation marks those words that are taken from your source. Other examples of modifications of quotations can be found in the beginning of subsection B.2 of this section and on sample notecards 9–11 in Section 4.D.3.c.

Note: Normally, when you are quoting only a phrase or a part of a sentence from a source, it is obvious that you are quoting only a part of the author's original sentence. It is, therefore, not necessary to put ellipsis points at the beginning and the end of these quotations.

Not Necessary

In John Frederick's view, this minor confrontation represented " . . . a critical turning point . . . " in the relationship of these two countries.

Accepted Form

In John Frederick's view, this minor confrontation represented "a critical turning point" in the relationship of these two countries.

You may, however, want to use ellipses in a few cases where it may not be obvious from the context that you are using only a part of what is a larger whole. For example, I used ellipses at the end of the quotation by Henry Lloyd quoted by Hofstadter on page 186 to let you know that Hofstadter quoted more of Lloyd than I did.

Guideline 8

Finally, there are a few things you should know about quoting from novels, short stories, poetry, and plays. In general, when quoting from a work of literature, you should use the same guidelines I have just outlined. Thus, you should quote from the actual text of a piece of literature only when the specific words of the text are essential to the point you are making. Otherwise, as in using other kinds of sources, you will find that the most effective way for you to make your point is to summarize, in your own words, the material in the text to which you refer.

If you decide that you must quote the exact words of the text in order to support your point, be sure to introduce the quotation by giving your readers enough information to put the quotation into its proper context. If you are quoting the words of a character in a novel or a play, for example, be sure to tell us which character is speaking. Similarly, the words you quote often will be more meaningful if you tell your readers, briefly, the circumstances that led that character to speak these words.

Example 1

As he draws toward the end of his story of the "great" Jay Gatsby, Nick Carraway passes judgment on Daisy and Tom Buchanan—"they were careless people," Nick decides; "they smashed up things and creatures and then retreated back into their money or their vast carelessness, or whatever it was that kept them together, and let other people clean up the mess they had made. . . ."[11]

11. F. Scott Fitzgerald, *The Great Gatsby* (New York: Charles Scribner's Sons, 1953), 120.

Example 2

In *To the Lighthouse*, Mrs. Ramsey is constantly giving of herself to her husband, her children, her neighbors. This self-giving is what brings other personalities into harmony and communion. At the dinner with which section I ends, Mrs. Ramsey surveys the group seated around the table: "They all sat separate. And the whole of the effort of merging and flowing and creating rested on her."[7]

7. Virginia Woolf, *To the Lighthouse* (New York: Harcourt, Brace, 1927), 126.

Example 3

Richard's helpless self-pity is eloquently expressed as he prepares to give up his role as king, and his identity:

> What must the King do now? Must he submit?
> The King shall do it. Must he be depos'd?
> The King shall be contented. Must he lose
> The name of king? a' God's name let it go.   (3.3.142–45)

As Example 3 illustrates, several lines of poetry may be quoted by setting them off from the text in a block quotation. Shorter passages of poetry, however, should be put in quotation marks and integrated into the prose of your text. If the passage you quote runs from one verse line to another, you should indicate the end of the verse line with a slash mark and the beginning of the next verse line by capitalizing the first letter of the first word.

Example 4

The tragedy in the story of Michael is that his only son, heir to his land and to his life, is forced to apprentice himself to a kinsman, "a prosperous man,/Thriving in trade" (Wordsworth, "Michael," lines 249–50.)

SECTION 7

Documenting Your Sources

A. General Overview

If you have paid careful attention to the preceding sections of this book, you will realize that you have one important step left before you are ready to type your paper: you must find a method of documenting your sources. Documenting your sources involves letting your reader know, in the body of your paper, that certain information and ideas have been taken from specific sources and giving your readers complete publication information about each of the sources you have used.

If you are like many students with whom I have worked, you face the process of documenting your sources with a mixture of dread and exasperation. Perhaps in the past you have written a research paper, struggling to get the footnotes and bibliography right, only to find that your instructor has scribbled corrections all over the notes and bibliography and he or she has taken off points because of these mistakes. Or perhaps your instructor has asked you to use the APA style or the MLA style in the paper you are now finishing, and you don't have the foggiest idea what the APA style or the MLA style is. Your attitude may be that you ought to be able to document your sources in your own way and that instructors who insist that you follow a specific form exactly are tiresome nitpickers.

In one sense, this kind of attitude toward documentation is reasonable. Not many people find documenting sources correctly very exciting or creative work. It can be especially troublesome for novices who have not had much experience with a particular documentation system. On the other hand, documenting sources correctly is an important part of learning how to become a responsible detective-researcher, and you do not want to endanger your research project at this late stage of the process by becoming sloppy and careless. I cannot promise you that I will make this final step quick and painless for you, but I think that I can make it reasonably easy by helping you to understand what documentation systems are all about.

In this section I will give you a general overview of documentation systems, explaining the purpose that lies behind all documentation systems and helping you to select the style that is most appropriate for the paper you are now writing. In the appendixes that follow this section, I have laid out basic information about four basic documentation modes, two appropriate for papers written in the humanities and two often used in the social and natural sciences. Before you turn to these appendixes, though, you should read over the rest of this section.

From your experience in doing research papers in the past, you may be aware that there are different documentation forms. The form that your psychology instructor wants you to use is not the form your literature teacher wants, and the form recommended by your chemistry professor may be different from these other two. Perhaps you have noticed, as you've checked the notes and references of different books and articles you've been reading for this research project, differences in documentation form from one of your sources to the next. Such variations do exist, and they can seem bewildering. It would be natural for you to assume that there is no such thing as a correct form and that people like me and your instructors pretend there is a correct form simply to increase the burdens and suffering of an overworked student like yourself. Because you have not spent time studying documentation systems, it is difficult for you to see that in this seeming chaos there is an order. It is true that there are variations within actual documentation systems, but behind these variations there lie two basic premises.

B. The Basic Premises of Documentation Systems

Premise 1

A writer must clearly signal his or her readers, in the body of a paper, where he or she is using material that is taken from someone else, and this writer must also give the readers full information about each source so that the readers, if they chose, could locate each source themselves.

Regardless of the specific form it takes, each documentation style is designed to allow you to give credit where credit is due. In addition to paying your debt to your sources by acknowledging them, you are also being a generous researcher. In giving your readers full information about each of your sources, you are sharing these sources of information with your readers. By allowing them to locate and read this material themselves, you are enlarging their knowledge of your subject. If you think about it, you yourself have profited from the generosity of other researchers when you have taken the titles of books and articles from their notes, bibliographies, and reference lists.

Premise 2

The information about the writer's sources should be given in a form that is least obtrusive and that takes the least amount of space without sacrificing completeness or intelligibility.

As the costs of publishing books and journals have risen, space itself has become an increasingly valuable commodity. Publishers would rather devote as much space as possible to an author's ideas, limiting the amount of space necessary for documentation to a minimum. The result of this need to save space in documentation has been the development of systems of shorthand. Thus many citations in footnotes and bibliographies on the surface seem to be mysterious series of words and numbers:

Proc. Nat. Acad. Sc. 7:186.

But this shorthand system allows this author to say "you will find this article in volume 7 of *The Proceedings of the National Academy of Sciences* on page 186" in much less space than it took me to write all that.

Obviously, shorthand systems won't work unless there are rules that govern the "code" and unless both readers and writers know these rules. You could, of course, develop your own system of shorthand, but that would involve working out a complete system and then providing your readers with the key. Why reinvent the wheel? Over the years workable systems have been developed by publishing agencies and professional academic organizations that nicely meet the needs expressed in the two basic premises of documentation. Following one of these established systems saves you the trouble of having to develop your own code, and it has the advantage of being familiar to your readers.

Thus, my advice to you is to resolve that, as a responsible researcher, each time you do a research paper you will have this as your goal:

Select a style of documentation that is appropriate for the subject matter and audience of your paper, and follow this style exactly.

C. Selecting an Appropriate Documentation Style

While there are variations in documentation style, in academic circles it is possible to talk about humanities systems and scientific systems. One way to decide which particular style is appropriate for a paper you are writing is to decide whether your paper is a humanities or a scientific paper, and one way to do this is to consider the approach taken by experts in your area of investigation to their subject matter. The scientific approach is generally characterized by objective measurement; data are collected and assessed by use of machinery or instruments, mathematical formulas, statistical procedures. Thus in the natural and applied sciences experts use a scientific system of documentation. Experts who gather information and test hypotheses by means other than those using machinery or instruments, mathematical formulas, or statistical procedures usually use a humanities form of documentation. A humanities form is one you will usually find in works on history, literature, art, music, religious studies, philosophy. So, to determine which style is appropriate for your paper, you can ask yourself: How has the information I have used in my paper been gathered and analyzed? Have most of the experts I have read used the scientific approach or not?

The audience for which your paper is intended is also a factor you should consider in making your decision. Documentation systems are more effective if they are familiar to the readers you are addressing. A very pragmatic way to determine which style is appropriate for your paper is to ask your instructor which form he or she prefers. Probably the best way to ask the question is this: "Which style or style manual do you want me to follow?"

1. Style Manuals

A style manual is a book or pamphlet that outlines the general style appropriate for manuscripts that will be published by a particular publishing firm or journal. Style manuals cover much more than documentation form. In them you can find answers for such questions as: How wide should my margins be? Should I use headings in the body of my paper? What do I do if I want to use charts and graphs? Should I include a table of contents? Style manuals also cover matters of mechanics: punctuation, capitalization, setting up quotations, abbreviations, and so on. These style manuals can be seen as the professional counterparts of the handbooks often used in English composition courses. Obviously, such manuals can be very helpful to you in answering all sorts of questions you might have about the final form your research paper should take. Style manuals fall roughly into three categories:

- Style manuals developed by publishers for authors who are writing books or articles for that publishing firm;
- "General" style manuals;
- Style manuals developed by professional organizations.

The most "public" of the manuals in the first category are the style manuals of the *New York Times* and the *Washington Post.* Perhaps you've seen copies of them in bookstores. Although these manuals are now being sold to the general public, they were put together for journalists who write for these two newspapers.

As a student, you will probably be most interested in the other two types of manuals.

a. "General" Style Manuals

The Chicago Manual of Style. 13th ed., rev. and expanded. Chicago: University of Chicago Press, 1982.

Turabian, Kate. *A Manual for Writers of Term Papers, Theses, and Dissertations.* 5th ed. Chicago: University of Chicago Press, 1987.

Turabian, Kate. *Student's Guide for Writing College Papers.* 3rd ed., rev. and expanded. Chicago: University of Chicago Press, 1976.

Although I have listed three titles here, the two books by Turabian are really scaled-down versions of *The Chicago Manual of Style.* All present what is generally called the Chicago style. Technically speaking, *The Chicago Manual* should be listed with those manuals developed by publishing firms for its authors because *The Chicago Manual* was created by the University of Chicago Press for use by writers preparing manuscripts for this publishing house. However, *The Chicago Manual* has become accepted as the authoritative manual for people who write scholarly books in academic disciplines and beyond. It is a complete style manual, answering almost any question you could think of about proper manuscript form. I call it a complete style manual also because it fully describes documentation forms for both humanities and scientific papers; thus there is a Chicago humanities style and a Chicago scientific style.

Because *The Chicago Manual* is a complete style manual written for professional writers, it can be intimidating and perhaps bewildering for students taking their first look at it. Recognizing this fact, the University of Chicago Press publishes two books for students that present the Chicago style in a form more in keeping with students' needs. I give you the basics of the Chicago humanities and scientific styles, but I cannot cover them in any depth. You may want to invest in a copy of one of the two Turabian books if you know that you will be writing a number of research papers before you receive your degree. Both of these books are published in paperbacks that are usually stocked by college bookstores.

Of the two books by Turabian, the one more suitable for students who have had little experience with research papers is the *Student's Guide*. It gives a few specifics about the scientific system of documentation, but it focuses on the humanities system. I particularly like the *Student's Guide* because it includes over fifty pages of basic reference works in many subjects and disciplines, a very convenient resource for students who don't know where to start looking for information in a particular subject. A *Manual for Writers*, on the other hand, is written for advanced students; in this book you will find more detailed information about using charts, graphs, appendixes, about how to document legal documents, and about other issues that arise when you are doing more sophisticated research papers.

b. Style Manuals of Professional Organizations

In addition to the general style manuals I just discussed, there are style manuals developed and published by professional academic organizations. Here is a list of a few such manuals:

American Chemical Society. *Handbook for Authors.* Washington, D.C.: American Chemical Society, 1978. (available in paperback)

American Institute of Physics Style Manual. 3rd ed. McGraw-Hill, 1978. Reprinted in the *Bulletin of the American Physical Society* 24 (December 1979).

American Psychological Association (APA). *Publication Manual.* 3rd ed. Washington, D.C.: APA, 1983.

Council of Biology Educators Style Manual. 4th ed. 1978.

Gibaldi, Joseph, and Walter S. Achtert. *MLA Handbook for Writers of Research Papers.* 3rd ed. New York: Modern Language Association, 1988.

The two manuals listed here that I will be referring to are those published by the American Psychological Association (APA) and the Modern Language Association (MLA).

2. Summary: Choosing an Appropriate Documentation Style

In the appendixes that follow, I give you two standard styles appropriate for papers in the humanities and two standard systems for those in the social and natural sciences.

If the paper you are working on falls into the category of a humanities paper, you may use the MLA style, described in Appendix A, or the Chicago form of the traditional notes-and-bibliography style, described in Appendix B. The notes-and-bibliography style is probably the one you are most familiar with. In this system, the reader is alerted to the fact that the author is using material from a source by a number in the body of the paper that is raised above the line—like this.[5] The number refers the reader to a note (at the bottom of the page or on a sheet at the end of the paper) where full information about the source is given. This traditional humanities system usually also includes a bibliography, which is a convenient alphabetized list of all the works the author read and consulted in doing his or her research for this paper or book. The bibliography allows the reader to check at a glance the depth and scope of the author's investigations.

Recently, however, many journals and professional organizations in the humanities have been moving to a system that closely resembles the scientific system in the sense that it eliminates the middle step of notes. The MLA style is one of these new humanities systems. In the MLA form, the traditional bibliography becomes a list of works cited. The list of works cited is like a bibliography in that it is an alphabetized list of sources attached to the end of the paper, but it differs from the bibliography in that it includes only works directly referred to by the writer in his or her paper. In the body of the paper the writer alerts readers that material from sources is being used by giving the name of the author of a source and the page number(s) on which the quotation or information can be found. Readers can find full information about the source by using the author's name to locate the appropriate entry on the list of works cited.

The new MLA form has taken its lead from traditional scientific systems of documentation, which are usually composed of two parts: a reference list and parenthetical citations in the body of the paper that tell readers to consult the reference list. "Reference list" is another way of saying "list of works cited"; it includes only works directly referred to by the writer in his or her paper.

One aspect of scientific documentation systems that differentiates them from one another is the way in which the writer says he or she is using a source. In one standard variation, called the numbered reference list, the writer numbers her reference list and then tells readers that she is using a source by putting the number of the source in brackets or parentheses in the body of her paper, like this [4]. In another standard form, known as the author-date form, the writer alerts readers that he or she is using a source by giving the last name(s) of the author(s) of the source and its date of publication, like this: (Greene & Smith, 1987). Since reference lists at the end of these papers are set up by first giving authors' names and publication dates, it is easy to find full information about the source I just cited by looking in the reference list for a work written by Greene and Smith in 1987.

The numbered reference list form, described in Appendix E, is usually found in professional papers in the natural sciences. I would recommend that you check with your instructor before you choose it.

The author-date system is more widely used in scientific papers, and it is usually considered an appropriate form in both the social sciences and the natural sciences. If you look at Appendixes C and D, you will see that I give you two forms of the author-date style. One of these forms is that recommended by the American Psychological Association, usually called the APA style. It is the style you should use in psychology papers, and it is often found in papers in education, communications, and other social sciences. The Chicago form of the author-date style is the preferred form for papers in the natural sciences.

Please be aware that my appendixes are only introductions to these forms. Nothing so brief can answer all the questions you may have about the proper way to document every type of source. Be prepared to locate copies of the various style manuals I have used in these appendixes, and expect to seek your instructor's help as well.

I believe that if you have read this section carefully, and if you read the introductions to each of the appendixes, you will find the actual style manuals much less intimidating. They are not terribly difficult to use if you know what kinds of questions you have; each has a detailed table of contents and an index that will allow you to find the information you need.

D. Following the Form Exactly

After you have selected the documentation form that is most appropriate for your subject matter and audience, you must follow the form exactly. If you choose a scientific system, for example, you must consistently use either the Chicago form or the APA form in a particular paper; never mix the forms. The reason should be obvious. Since each documentation style is a form of shorthand, the placement of information and such details as punctuation, underlining, and so on, all carry meanings. If you do not follow the form exactly, you run the risk of leaving out important information or of confusing your reader by signaling "this number is a volume number" when you meant to say "this number is a page number." The first time you use a system of documentation it will probably feel awkward to you, and you will have to exercise a little patience to get it right. But after you have used the same system several times, you'll find that it becomes easier and easier as the form becomes familiar to you. By the time you are a senior, you should know the standard form in your major so well that you will have to consult a style manual only for special types of citations.

I hope that I have convinced you that there are reasons, beyond avoiding the ire of your instructor, for learning and using exactly the accepted forms of documentation. In the long run it is much easier to learn a standard form than it is to unlearn sloppy and careless habits.

Let me end by saying that documentation systems, like most other things in this world, grow and change to meet new needs and changing circumstances. Documentation forms are always being updated. So when you use a style manual, make a special effort to find out what the most recent edition of that manual is, and try to use this most recent edition. You may find that some of the forms I give in the appendixes have changed since this book was published.

APPENDIX A

Humanities Systems: The MLA Style

A. General Information

The major difference—and it *is* a major difference—between the traditional notes-and-bibliography style and the MLA style is that the MLA style eliminates the intermediate stage of notes. Instead of a bibliography, you create a list of works cited, in which you give readers full information about the sources you have used in the paper. In the body of your paper you tell your readers which of these sources you are referring to simply by using the author's name. Thus, the reader can go straight from the body of the paper to the appropriate entry on the list, which is attached to the end of the paper. Here's an example.

Body of Your Paper

Many short stories published today leave the reader bewildered because they have no clear beginnings and no obvious endings (Jones 139). But Alvin Peabody's story "Searching" is an exception. When Jed confronts his brother, there is a very clear resolution of the plot (69-70).

List of Works Cited

Jones, Arthur W. <u>The Short Story Today</u>. New York: Nameless, 1999.

Peabody, Alvin. "Searching." <u>An Anthology of Recent Fiction</u>. Ed.

   John Q. Smith. New York: Titanic, 1995. 60–71.

Very simple — in principle. But as in any documentation system, there are specific conventions you must follow. If you decide that the MLA style is the right one for your paper, I suggest that you look over subsection B of this appendix to get a sense of the way this documentation system works. Then, in subsection C, you will learn how to set up your list of works cited.

The version of the MLA style I am following is taken from the *MLA Handbook for Writers of Research Papers* by Joseph Gibaldi and Walter S. Achtert (3rd edition, New York: The Modern Language Association of America, 1988). If I fail to answer any of your questions in this appendix, check this handbook.

B. Citing Sources in the Body of Your Paper

As noted, in the MLA style the way you tell your reader that you are using one or more of your sources is to give the last name of the author(s) of the work(s) in the body of your paper. When you refer to specific parts of a work, you will also include the page number(s).

This form of poetry was very popular in the eighteenth century
(Jones 15).

Sneed wrote that "in our day we rarely saw automobiles" (29).

It's very simple. But as simple as the basics are, the MLA style, like all other forms of documentation, has forms and conventions that you are expected to know and follow. The remainder of subsection B explains the basic form of parenthetical citations, outlines where you place these citations, and gives you variations of the basic form. Obviously, in this system you must have a list of works cited since it is the only place your readers will find such necessary information as title, edition, publication facts, and the like. But before you think about setting up your list, I'd suggest you read this whole section on parenthetical citations first.

When you feel that you understand how the system works, go through the draft of your paper; each time you refer to a source, find the appropriate notecard for that piece of information and the reference card for the source. Insert the proper parenthetical citation in the body of your paper, and put the reference card in a stack that will make up your list of works cited. If a particular reference card does not begin with the name of the person you have cited in your paper, paperclip the notecard to the reference card. In subsection C, I explain how to order your list and I give you the proper forms for various kinds of sources.

1. The Basic Form

You cite a source in the body of your paper by giving the author's last name and the page number(s) in parentheses, normally at the end of your sentence.

Paraphrase, not quote

The poet Wilson was a recluse with odd ideas (Stark 24–30).

If you have used the author's name as part of your sentence, as I encouraged you to do in Section 6, you need to add only the page number(s).

Sheila Stark points out that the poet Wilson was a recluse with odd ideas (24–30).

Similarly, if the context makes it clear whose ideas or words you are using, it isn't necessary to repeat the author's name.

These musical instruments came into vogue about the time of King Henry VI (Harvey 134). The viola da gamba, for example, was being played in court in 1453 (140).

If you are referring to the entire work, the author's name is enough; no page number, obviously, is necessary.

Shakespeare's Richard II is full of images of the sun.

If a work was written or edited by more than one author, you must give the last names of all the authors, just as they will appear in the list of works cited. If your source has more than three authors, give the last name of the first followed by "et al." (Smith et al. 94).

```
Felltham was a fanatic about the royalist cause (Witherspoon and
Warnke 317).
```

2. Where to Place Your Citations and How to Keep Your Paper Readable

As you can see, these parenthetical citations have the potential of becoming obtrusive and thus interferring with your readers' ability to pay attention to what you are saying. For this reason, keep these guidelines in mind when you place your citations in your text.

- Within the rules of the MLA form, keep your parenthetical citations as short as possible. One simple solution to this problem is to use the names of authors in your sentence proper, as I advised in Section 6. If you use the author's name directly in your sentence, you need to add only the page number(s) in parentheses.

- The citation must be placed so that it is clear what ideas have been taken from a source; at the same time, you do not want to impede the flow of your sentence. Whenever possible, place your parenthetical citation at the end of the sentence. Note that the period comes after the parentheses. If you are finishing a quotation, place the parentheses after the quotation mark and before the period. If it is not possible to put the citation at the end of the sentence, try to place it next to a natural "rest" point in the sentence.

  ```
  As she wrote in her journal in May, "inspiration ravishes me"
  (56).
  This policy, although strongly opposed by Carlson (Hindman
  14–16), eventually was adopted by the court.
  ```

- If you are using the block style of quoting, place your citations two spaces after the conclusion of the quotation.

  ```
  Describing the battle as he witnessed it from his bedroom window,
  Kendall wrote to a friend:
          It was fierce and bloody. Bullets flew. Blood was
          everywhere. The noise was deafening. Bodies lay on the
          sidewalk. (34)
  ```

3. Variations of the Basic Form

- If your list of works cited contains more than one work by the same author, be sure to give a short title of the work each time you mention this author.

> In his novel Kingdom Come, Withers often uses the phrase "cold death" (68, 97, 110).
>
> This form of poetry was most popular at court (Hall, "Poems" 48).

- If you cite works from several volumes of a multivolume set, you will need to include the number of the volume (in arabic numbers) before the page number. See subsection C.3.h.

> Freud discussed this notion in Interpretation of Dreams (4: 136–38).

- If you are using the words or ideas of a person you read in a source other than the original, you will have to give your readers the names of both the author of these words or ideas *and* the author of the source where you found them. Use the phrase "qtd. in" (quoted in) to cite such references.

> In 1850 a man who signed himself only "Angry" wrote a fierce letter on the subject to the editor of the Times (qtd. in Wallace 67).

- If you are citing a source that has no author, use a short title of the work as your reference. Be sure to use the first two or three main words of the title since your readers will have to be able to find this title in your list of works cited. If you are referring to a source that is only one page long and this page number is given in the entry on your list, you need not repeat the page number in your text.

> Such were the times that men earned less than a dime a day ("Breadlines" 45).

- If you are quoting from or referring to a poem, play, short story, or novel, it is helpful to your readers if you include in your citation division markers used in the work itself (e.g., chapter numbers, book numbers, line numbers, etc.). In your parenthetical citation, give the page number first; then use a semicolon to separate it from the division reference. Abbreviate chapter, book, and section, but spell out the word "line" since lower case l's can be confused with the number 1. If you are citing a classic poem or play, you can omit page numbers completely and just give the conventional division markers used in the work itself. If an act or book number precedes a line number, you don't have to spell out "line"; convention tells us this is a line number.

```
It is not until the middle of the novel that we meet the heroine
(200; ch. 6).
When Keats writes "what soft incense hangs upon the boughs"
(line 52), we can almost smell this dark garden.
Satan's return to hell was greeted by "a dismal universal hiss"
(Bk. X. 508).
The psychological aspects of Richard II become most obvious
in the moving soliloquy of the deposed and imprisoned king
(5.5.1–45).
```

- If you found the same information in more than one work, give all sources, separating the citations with semicolons. If you decide such citations might be obtrusive in the body of your paper, consider putting this information in a note (see the following).

```
(Smith 645; Clark and Hillsdale, "Keats" 47).
```

- **Notes.** At those times when the citation you feel you must give becomes long and/or cumbersome, or when you want to say something further about a topic you raise, place a note number in your paper, raised a half-space above the line (^{1}), and then include the note itself at the bottom of the page or on a separate sheet headed Notes at the end of your paper.

```
² For further detailed information about the Smith raid, see
Johnson (75–83).
³ Throughout the play the word "cold" is used in reference to
chastity, inactivity, and death. So, for example, in speaking
of the postponement of the sentencing of the Duchess's youngest
son, Spurio says . . .
```

Whenever you refer to a source in such notes, follow the form for parenthetical citations I have given in this section, and be sure this source is included in your list of works cited.

It is perfectly acceptable to use explanatory notes, but you must use your common sense. Material that your reader must have to understand a point that you are making should never be hidden in a note; this information belongs in the body of your paper. And don't forget that note numbers are distracting; they encourage your readers to leave your argument and look at your footnote or endnote. Your readers are going to become very irritated if you use the note system to introduce information or ideas that are outside the bounds of the paper you are writing. So use explanatory notes where you feel they are really needed. Don't use explanatory notes to show off all the knowledge you have about a topic.

C. *List of Works Cited*

1. Putting Your List Together

As the heading Works Cited states, this list includes *only* those works that you refer to *directly* in the body of your paper. If you want to let your instructor know that you read other material, you may add these works, but you will have to label this list Works Consulted. Both types of lists follow the form outlined in the rest of this appendix.

In compiling your list of works cited, keep in mind the basic principles of the MLA style:

- The citation in your text should be as short as possible.
- The name of the author you give in your text must be the name of the person whose ideas or words you are using.
- The entry on your list must begin with this person's name. (Otherwise, how are we to know which entry to look at?)
- You must have an entry for each author you cite.

You will have no problem if you are citing a book written by the author or if you are citing an article in a journal, magazine, or newspaper. If you refer to John Doe's book *Poetry* twelve times in your paper, just be sure you have *one* entry that begins "Doe, John. *Poetry*. . . ."

However, if you are using a work that you read in an anthology or a collection of essays, your task is a bit more complicated. If, for example, you are quoting from a poem by William Blake and a poem by John Keats, both of which you found in the same anthology, you will create *two* entries on your list, one that begins "Blake, William" and one that begins "Keats, John." Similarly, let us say that you are writing about Shakespeare's *Richard II* and you refer in your paper both to the play itself and to the introduction to the play written by Kenneth Muir in the Signet Classic edition. Even though the play and the introduction are in the same book, you will have two separate entries on your list, one that begins "Shakespeare, William" and one that begins "Muir, Kenneth." If you have any works in your paper that fit this description, be sure to read subsection C.3.g in this appendix carefully.

You must also be careful if you are using a work that is made up of several volumes. If you are using only one volume of that set in your paper, you may list just that volume (see subsection C.3.h in this appendix). However, if you cite references to several volumes, list the whole set, and be sure to include the volume number *before* the page number in your citations (see subsection B.4).

Take the stack of reference cards you made of the sources you have referred to in your paper. You will now have to put them in alphabetical order, according to the last names of the persons you cited in your paper. Here's some further advice about ordering your list.

- In alphabetizing your sources, use only the letters in an author's last name; ignore his or her first name and/or initials. If your list includes works by Stephen Green and Aaron Greenberg, the work by Green would come first.

- If you have several authors with the same last name, alphabetize according to the author's first names, and then the middle initials.

  Johnson, Carl X.
  Johnson, Frances H.
  Johnson, Frederick J.
  Johnson, Frederick S.

- If your list includes more than one work by the same author or authors (John Jones):

  ○ List all the works that Jones wrote by himself first. Order the entries according to the titles of the works (ignoring *the*, *an*, and *a* as first words).

>
> Jones, John. *The Continental Congress* . . .
> ———— . "The Political Contexts of . . ."

○ Then list any collections that Jones edited:

> Jones, John, ed. *Papers of the Continental Congress* . . .

○ If Jones has written any works with other authors (or edited any works with others), these co-authored works would then be listed. Alphabetize according to the last names of the second co-author, and so on.

> Jones, John, and Herman Gotz. *America during the Revolution* . . .
> Jones, John, Aaron Greenberg, and Alfred Lutz, eds. *The Papers of Thomas Jefferson* . . .
> Jones, John, Aaron Greenberg, and Louisa Smith. *American Lives* . . .
> Jones, John, and James Jackson. *When We Were Young* . . .

Note: You may substitute a line (three hyphens, no space between them) for the author's name *only* when the author or authors are *exactly* the same. Otherwise, spell out every author's name.

• Books with a corporate author (an agency, committee, institute, etc.) are alphabetized according to the first main word (ignoring *the, an,* and *a*) in the name of the group (see subsection C.3.c).

• If a work has no author, you will place it in your list according to the first main word in the title.

Now you are ready to put together your list. In the following sections of this appendix, I give you the proper form for the most common types of sources. Check the headings, find the one that describes your source, and follow the form *exactly.* Watch details like capitalization, punctuation, and underlining very carefully. If you don't find a heading that matches your source, see subsection C.8. I have also included a sample list of works cited in subsection C.9 of this appendix.

2. Form for Books: Placement of Information

A book entry is divided into four parts; each part is separated from the others with a period. The first line of an entry is flush with the left-hand margin; other lines in the entry are indented five spaces.

```
          author                          title
             |                              |
  |Jung, Carl G.|Four Archetypes: Mother, Rebirth, Spirit,
       Trickster.|Trans. R. F. C. Hull. Bollingen Series, 20.   ⌐
       |Princeton: Princeton UP, 1969.                          |
             |                                                   |
          facts of                              particulars of
          publication                           publication
```

Author   The key to your list of works cited is the name of the person or group responsible for the text. Begin with the last name of the first author listed on the title page of the work, and, whenever possible, give each author's full first name and middle initial. If the party responsible is a corporate group, the name of the group will be used as the "author" (see subsection C.3.c). If the book is a collection of essays, poems, or stories, the editor of the collection is considered its author (see subsection C.3.f). Remember, however, that when you are referring to a particular essay or poem or story in a collection or anthology, your entry will begin with the name of the person who wrote that essay, poem, or story. I give full information about how to deal with these types of sources in subsection C.3.g.

Title   Give the full title of the book, including any subtitles. The main words in all titles are always capitalized (see Appendix F.A). Titles of books are underlined. Notice that the title of essays, articles, and other works that were originally published in a larger collection are placed in quotation marks; periods or commas are placed *inside* the quotation marks. If you are referring to a work in a collection or anthology, you must give the full titles of *both* the work itself and the anthology or collection.

Particulars of publication   You must always include other information about the work because such information will help the readers locate the specific book you used. Give such information in this order after the title of the book:

> name of editor and/or translator
> edition used, if not the original
> number of volumes
> title of series, with volume or number

Please note that volume numbers and other numbers used in documentation should always be arabic numerals (33) rather than roman numerals (XXXIII).

Facts of publication   Publication information is given in this form:

New York: Nosuch Press, 1983.

Always give the *city* of publication. The name of the *publisher* follows. The *date* is the date of publication. Check the title page; if no date is given, turn over the page and use the date with the latest copyright (the most recent date next to the ©). You should be aware that the *MLA Handbook* recommends abbreviating the name of the publisher. Obviously I can't list their recommended abbreviations; if you wish to follow the form exactly, you will have to consult that handbook. Otherwise, spell out the name of the publisher. Also note that if you are using a paperback that seems to have two publishers—Vintage Books, A Division of Random House—MLA asks you to give both names. List the paperback imprint name first, then the name of the parent publishing house: Vintage-Random. Finally, if you are listing a selection within an edited work, end your entry with the inclusive page numbers of the selection (see subsection C.3.g).

3. Forms for Specific Types of Books

In the pages that follow I give you examples of the proper form for various kinds of books. Since each example focuses on one aspect of the citation, in some cases you may need to check a couple of headings to see how to write a specific entry in your list.

a. Book—One Author

Zagorin, Perez. The Court and the Country: The Beginning of the
English Revolution. New York: Atheneum, 1970.

b. Book—More Than One Author

Evans, Rowland, and Robert D. Novak. Nixon in the White House: The
Frustration of Power. New York: Random, 1971.
Easton, Susan, Joan M. Mills, and Diane K. Winokur. Equal to the Task:
How Workingwomen Are Managing in Corporate America. New York:
Seaview Books, 1982.

Note that the name of the first author is inverted (Easton, Susan), but the names of other authors appear in their normal form. Be sure to put commas after the last name *and* first name of the first author.

c. Book with Corporate Author

If responsibility for the contents of the book is taken by an agency, corporation, or institute, use the name of this group as the author. Alphabetize according to the first word in the name (disregarding *the, an* and *a*). Spell out the full name of the group. Give the name of the parent body before listing subdivisions of the organization (in the following example, Brooklyn College is responsible for the Institute of Puerto Rican Studies).

> Royal Institute of Philosophy. Understanding Wittgenstein. Royal
>   Institute of Philosophy Lectures 7 (1972–1973). New York: St.
>   Martin's, 1974.
> Museum of Graphic Art. American Printmaking: The First 150 Years. New
>   York: Museum of Graphic Art, 1969.
> Brooklyn College. Institute of Puerto Rican Studies. The Puerto Rican
>   People: A Selected Bibliography for Use in Social Work
>   Education. New York: Council on Social Work Education, 1973.

d. Book — Edition Other Than the Original

> Lawrence, William W. Shakespeare's Problem Comedies. 2nd ed. New
>   York: Ungar, 1960.
> Stone, Lawrence. The Crisis of the Aristocracy 1558–1614. Abridged
>   ed. New York: Oxford UP, 1967.

e. Book with Author and Editor and/or Translator

> Vygotsky, Lev S. Thought and Language. Ed. and trans. Eugenia
>   Hanfmann and Gertrude Vakar. Cambridge: MIT P, 1962.

If editor and translator are different, list in the order in which they appear on the title page of your source.

f. Book with Editor Rather Than Author — A Collection of Works

> Chambers, William N., and Walter D. Burnham, eds. The American Party
>   Systems: Stages of Political Development. 2nd ed. New York:
>   Oxford UP, 1975.

Wilbur, George B., and Warner Muensterberger, eds. <u>Psychoanalysis and</u>
<u>Culture: Essays in Honor of Geza Roheim</u>. New York: International
Universities Press, 1951.

Witherspoon, Alexander M., and Frank J. Warnke, eds. <u>Seventeenth-</u>
<u>Century Prose and Poetry</u>. 2nd ed. New York: Harcourt, 1963.

g. Work in a Collection or Anthology

Since the citations in the body of your paper should be short, and since the author's name you use in the body of your paper must be the name of the person whose words you are referring to or quoting, you will list *separately* those poems, plays, short stories, articles, and essays that you have found in anthologies or edited collections. This guideline also applies to the prefaces, forewords, introductions, and afterwords you find in books or anthologies; an entry for a preface or introduction will begin with the name of the person who wrote it. Following are the appropriate forms for such entries. Before you look for the example that best fits the work you are using, please read over the following general guidelines.

- Your entry must *always* begin with the name of the person whose words or ideas you are using, followed by the full title of the poem, play, short story, selection, or essay.

- Titles of poems, plays, and other works that were originally published as books will be underlined (see the Dekker example that follows); poems, plays, and other works that were originally published in a collection or journal will be put in quotation marks. Note that titles like Introduction, Afterword, and Preface are simple capitalized (see the Marcus example).

- You will give complete bibliographic information for your source, including the title of the anthology or collection, its editor(s), translator, edition, volumes, and so on. If my examples do not completely match the source you are listing, check other categories in subsection C.3.

- The numbers at the end of your entry are the *inclusive* page numbers of the complete work you are listing: that is, the pages on which we will find the *whole* play, poem, essay.

- If you are using an essay or article that was first printed somewhere else, MLA asks you to include full information about the original source first; you can usually find this information at the bottom of the first page of the essay you read (see the Schwartz example).

- The abbreviation "ed." stands for "edited by," so never write "eds." in these situations.
- If you are using several works from the same collection or anthology, you can shorten your entries by using cross-references. I explain this technique after the following examples.

> Crane, Hart.   "To Brooklyn Bridge." A Little Treasury of Modern
>   Poetry, English and American. Ed. Oscar Williams. Rev. ed.
>   New York: Scribner's, 1952. 393–94.
>
> Dekker, Thomas. The Shoemakers' Holiday. English Drama, 1580–
>   1642. Ed. C. F. Tucker Brooke and N. B. Paradise. Boston:
>   Heath, 1933. 263–93.
>
> Halsey, Louis. "The Choral Music." Robert Schumann: The Man and
>   His Music. Ed. Alan Walker. London: Barrie and Jenkins,
>   1972. 350–89.
>
> Marcus, Steven. Afterword. The Pickwick Papers. By Charles
>   Dickens. New York: Signet-NAL, 1964. 864–86.
>
> Schwartz, Delmore.   "Poetry and Belief in Thomas Hardy." Southern
>   Review 6 (1940). Rpt. in Hardy: A Collection of Critical
>   Essays. Ed. Albert J. Guerard. Twentieth Century Views.
>   Englewood Cliffs: Prentice, 1963. 123–34.

Cross-References

If you are using several works from the same collection or anthology, the MLA style allows you to shorten your list in the following manner. Create an entry for each separate work including the author's name, the full title of the work, the name of the editor(s) of the anthology or collection, and the inclusive page numbers of this specific work. Then create a separate entry for the collection or anthology itself, starting with the name of the editor(s) (see subsection C.3.f for this form). Obviously, if you have two works by the person who edited the collection, you will also have to add a short title of the collection in the entries for the specific works.

> Donne, John.   "IV. Meditation." Witherspoon and Warnke 61–62.
>
> Johnson, Ben.   "A Hymn on the Nativity of My Saviour." Witherspoon and
>   Warnke 765.
>
> Witherspoon, Alexander M., and Frank J. Warnke, eds. Seventeenth-
>   Century Prose and Poetry. 2nd ed. New York: Harcourt, 1963.

h. Book in a Multivolume Set

An Entry for the Complete Set

Morison, Samuel E. The History of United States Naval Operations in
    World War II. 15 vols. Boston: Little, 1947–62.

Bronson, Bertrand H., ed. The Traditional Tunes of the Child Ballads
    with Their Texts, according to the Extant Records of Great
    Britain and America. 4 vols. Princeton: Princeton UP, 1959–72.

Note that these volumes were published over a number of years. Be sure to
indicate the dates of publication of the first and last volumes.

An Entry for One Volume

If you are using only one volume of a multivolume set, you may list only that
volume. Note, however, that you will have to include the number of
volumes in each set plus the inclusive publication dates of the whole set. The
first example shows you how to enter one volume of a set with the same title.
The second example shows you what to do if the titles for each volume are
different.

Bronson, Bertrand H., ed. The Traditional Tunes of the Child Ballads
    with Their Texts, according to the Extant Records of Great
    Britain and America. Vol. 3. Princeton: Princeton UP, 1966.
    4 vols. 1959–72.

Morison, Samuel E. The Rising Sun in the Pacific, 1931–April 1942.
    Boston: Little, 1948. Vol. 3 of The History of United States
    Naval Operations in World War II. 15 vols. 1947–52.

If you are using only one selection from one volume of a multivolume set,
the form is essentially that of a work in a collection. The differences are that
you will indicate the number of this volume before the publication information and, after the inclusive page numbers of this selection, indicate the
total number of volumes in the set plus the inclusive publication dates of the
whole set.

"Robin Hood Rescuing Three Squires" (Child No. 140). The Traditional
    Tunes of the Child Ballads with Their Texts, according to the

> Extant Records of Great Britain and America. Ed. Bertrand
>   H.Bronson. Vol. 3. Princeton: Princeton UP, 1966. 53–57.
>   4 vols. 1959–72.

i. Book in a Series

Occasionally when you look at the title page of a book, you will notice that
this book is part of a series; the series title may refer to subject matter
(Documentary Monographs in Modern Art) or to the publisher (Smithsonian Miscellaneous Collection) or to both (Yale Judaica Series). Include
information about the series in your reference. Give the name of the series
(capitalize the main words but do not underline) and the volume or number
of this work if a volume or number is given.

> Bindoff, S. T. Tudor England. Pelican History of England 5.
>   Harmondsworth, Middlesex, England: Penguin Books, 1950.
> McCoy, Garnett, ed. David Smith. Documentary Monographs in Modern
>   Art. New York and Washington: Praeger Publishers, 1973.
> Moses ben Maimon. The Code of Maimonides. Book 3: The Book of
>   Seasons. Trans. Solomon Gandz and Hyman Klein. Yale Judaica
>   Series. New Haven: Yale UP, 1961.

j. Reprint of an Older Work

Once in a while you will use a book that is a reprint of a text that
was originally published many years ago. A reprint of a work is different
from an edition of a work. In an edition, some part or parts of the text
have been changed; a reprint is a reproduction of the actual text the
author originally wrote. If you give only the publication date of the reprint you are using, you give your reader the impression that this text is
more recent than it actually is. This is the proper form for a reprinted
book.

> Hegel, Georg W. F. Lectures on the Philosophy of Religion, Together
>   with a Work on the Proofs of the Existence of God. Trans. from the
>   2nd German ed. by E. B. Speirs and J. Burdon Sanderson. Ed. E. B.
>   Speirs. 1895. New York: Humanities, 1968.
> Woolf, Virginia. The Second Common Reader. 1932. New York: Harvest-
>   Harcourt, 1960.

4. Form for Encyclopedias, Dictionaries, and Similar Reference Works

When you are referring to well-known reference works—the kind that are updated every few years in a new edition—follow the form below. If the entry in the reference work is signed, begin with the author's name; otherwise, begin with the title of the entry.

> Grimsditch, Herbert B. "Rackham, Arthur." <u>Dictionary of National</u>
> <u>Biography</u>. 1931–40 ed.
> "Nikolsburg, Treaty of." <u>Encyclopaedia Britannica</u>. 15th ed.

Citations of other reference works basically follow the form for works in a collection.

> Wheelwright, Philip. "Myth." <u>The Princeton Encyclopedia of Poetry</u>
> <u>and Poetics</u>. Ed. Alex Preminger. Enlarged ed. Princeton:
> Princeton UP, 1974.
> "<u>Film Noir</u>." <u>The Oxford Companion to Film</u>. Ed. Liz-Anne Bawden. New
> York: Oxford UP, 1976.

5. Form for Scholarly Journals

a. General Form

author   article title

Egan, Robert. |"A Thin Beam of Light: The Purpose of

Playing in <u>Rosencrantz and Guildenstern Are</u>

<u>Dead</u>." |<u>Theatre Journal</u> | 31 (March 1979): 59–69.

journal title   publication information

Author   Give the last name of the author first; if there is more than one author, give second and third authors' names in the normal order.

Article title   Put the title of the article in quotation marks; place a period at the end, inside the quotation marks. Underline words in italic type and capitalize all main words in the title (see Appendix F.A).

Journal title   Although the titles of journals are sometimes abbreviated in notes and bibliographies, you should spell out the full title and underline it. Notice that there is no punctuation after the title.

Publication information   The number before the parentheses is the volume number; always use arabic numerals (31) rather than roman numerals (XXXI). The final numbers are the inclusive pages on which the article appears. Since most scholarly journals are paginated consecutively throughout the year, the volume number and the page numbers provide the readers with enough information to locate the article. The date of the volume is given to let the reader know how old, or recent, this article is; the month or season is not technically necessary, but it is useful information for the readers and you should include it. Some magazines and journals do not paginate consecutively throughout the year but instead begin each issue with page 1. If you cite such a journal or magazine, you will have to give the issue number as well as the volume number (see 5.b below). Magazines, those periodicals written for a general audience, are usually cited by giving only the date of publication (see subsection C.6).

Watch the punctuation carefully. A colon separates the date from the page numbers. Otherwise, notice that there is no punctuation. Put a period after the page numbers to indicate the end of the citation.

Barish, Jonas A. "The Double Plot in Volpone." Modern Philology 51
  (1953): 83–92.

Grose, Lois M. "The Able Student in a City School System." English
  Journal 55 (October 1966): 891–94.

Jones, Jacqueline. "'My Mother Was Much of a Woman': Black Women, Work
  and the Family under Slavery." Feminist Studies 8 (Summer 1982):
  235–70.

b. Journal That Paginates Each Issue Separately

Because the *Journal of Popular Culture* begins each issue with page 1, you will have to give the issue number as well as the volume number.

Wilson, Christopher B. "The Era of the Reporter Reconsidered: The
  Case of Lincoln Steffens." Journal of Popular Culture 15. 2 (Fall
  1981): 52–60.

6. Form for Magazines

References to periodicals that are published weekly or monthly and that are intended for a general reading audience are usually cited by omitting the volume number and using the date of publication instead.

> "Alex and the Awards." The New Yorker 21 June 1982: 32–35.
>
> Myers, Mary L. "Reproducing Raphael." Artnews Apr. 1983: 79–83.
>
> Sragow, Michael. "Ghostwriters: Unraveling the Enigma of Movie
>
>   Authorship." Film Commentary Apr. 1983: 9–18.

Note that when a specific date is given, it is given in the European fashion (21 June 1982). If no author is given, use the title to introduce the entry, and alphabetize according to the first main word in the title, disregarding *the*, *an*, and *a*.

7. Form for Newspaper Articles

> Bonner, Raymond. "A Guatemalan General's Rise to Power." New York
>
>   Times 21 July 1982: A3.
>
> "Madman Attacks Alligator." Smithville Observer [Smithfield,
>
>   Florida] 14 August 1991, late ed., sec. 4: 5+.

Watch page numbers in a newspaper. Some newspapers are divided into sections, and each section begins with page 1. Thus, you must give your reader both the section designation and the page numbers. It would be wise to include the edition if the newspaper you are using appears in various editions.

8. Forms for Other Types of Sources

Here are a few, quick samples of citations for other types of sources. If I do not cover a type of source you are using, check the *MLA Handbook*.

In putting together entries in any of these categories, remember the general principle that your entry begins with the person or aspect of the piece to which you are directly referring in the body of your paper. Thus, if you have been talking about *Rear Window* as an example of Alfred Hitchcock's work as a director, your entry should begin with Hitchcock; if, however, you are referring to some aspect of the plot, your entry would begin with the film's title. Give readers enough information so that they can locate the work you are referring to or so that they have a clear sense of the circumstances in which you acquired the information you are giving in your paper.

Radio and Television Programs

Clear-Cut Crisis. Moderator Charles Ogletree. Prod. Bob Allen. OPB.
    KOAP, Portland, OR. 14 August 1990.

"The Moghul Room." The Jewel in the Crown. Based on The Raj Quartet
    by Paul Scott. Dir. Christopher Morahan and Jim O'Brien. Prod.
    Christopher Morahan. Masterpiece Theatre. PBS. KOAP, Portland,
    OR. 9 Aug. 1987.

Recordings

Beethoven, Ludwig van. Sonata for Violin and Piano, no. 9, op. 47,
    "Kreutzer." Zino Francescatti, violin, and Robert Casadesus,
    piano. CBS, MPT 39054, 1984.

Films and Videotapes

Hitchcock, Alfred, dir. Rear Window. With Grace Kelly and Jimmy
    Stewart. Paramount, 1954.

The Manhattan Transfer Live. Videocassette. Prod. Martin Fischer.
    Atlantic Video, 1987. 80 mins.

Live Performances

Bowie, David. Performing with Carlos Alomar and Peter Frampton.
    Concert. The Glass Spider Tour. Civic Stadium, Portland, OR.
    14 Aug. 1987.

Sunday in the Park with George. By Stephen Sondheim. Dir. Bill
    Dobson. Prod. by Portland Center for the Performing Arts and
    Portland Civic Theatre. Portland Center for the Performing Arts,
    Portland, OR. 1 Sept. 1987.

Lectures, Public Addresses

Logan, Donn. Panel member. "Putting It Together: Art and
    Architecture." Portland Center for the Performing Arts,
    Portland, OR. 29 Aug. 1987.

Smith, Stephen. Lecture. Biology 10: Introduction to Biology.
     Anywhere College, Anywhere, NY. 4 Nov. 1991.

Interviews

Hammerstein, Carl. Personal interview. 5 Dec. 1993.

Miller, James. Interview. All Things Considered. Natl. Public
     Radio. KOAP, Portland, OR. 13 August 1987.

Smith, Louisa. Telephone interview. 7 May 1995.

If you have agreed to keep the identity of one or more of your interviewees
confidential, you should turn back to Section 3.B.4 to review my advice on
how to handle these interviews in your paper.

9. The Final List of Works Cited, including a Sample

Your final list of works cited must be typed on a separate sheet (or
sheets) of paper. Use the proper manuscript margins. Number this page
consecutively with the other pages in your paper. If you are including a page
headed Notes, that page should be numbered and placed between the last
page of the body of your paper and this list. Head the list Works Cited; center
the heading one inch from the top of the paper. Double-space; then start
your first entry. The first line of all entries should be flush with the left
margin. Additional lines within an entry should be indented five spaces.
Double-space all entries and double-space between entries.

Works Cited

"Alex and the Awards." The New Yorker 21 June 1982: 32–35.

Barish, Jonas A. "The Double Plot in Volpone." Modern Philology
     51 (1953): 83–92.

"Daguerreotype." The Focal Encyclopedia of Photography. Rev. ed.
     1965.

Donne, John. "IV. Meditation." Witherspoon and Warnke 61–62.

Jonson, Ben. "A Hymn on the Nativity of My Saviour." Witherspoon and
     Warnke 765.

Muir, Kenneth. Introduction. The Tragedy of King Richard the Second.

By William Shakespeare. Ed. Kenneth Muir. New York: Signet-NAL, 1963. xxiii–xxxvii.

Museum of Graphic Art. American Printmaking: The First 150 Years. New York: Museum of Graphic Art, 1969.

"Robin Hood Rescuing Three Squires" (Child No. 140). The Traditional Tunes of the Child Ballads with Their Texts, according to the Extant Records of Great Britain and America. Ed. Bertrand H. Bronson. Vol. 3. Princeton: Princeton UP, 1966. 53–57. 4 vols. 1959–72.

Shakespeare, William. The Tragedy of King Richard the Second. Ed. Kenneth Muir. New York: Signet-NAL, 1963.

Witherspoon, Alexander M., and Frank J. Warnke, eds. Seventeenth-Century Prose and Poetry. 2nd ed. New York: Harcourt, 1963.

Woolf, Virginia. The Second Common Reader. 1932. New York: Harvest-Harcourt, 1960.

APPENDIX B

Humanities Systems: The Chicago Style

A. General Information

The general system I outline in this appendix is probably the one you are most familiar with. In the body of the paper, the author uses a raised number (^{4}) at the end of a sentence to refer the readers to a note that will contain the necessary bibliographic information about the source he or she used. The notes may appear at the bottom of the page (footnotes) or on a separate sheet at the end of the paper (endnotes). In addition to notes, the author usually includes a bibliography. A bibliography is an alphabetized list of the works this author used in the course of researching his or her paper. If your instructor has asked you to use notes or footnotes, this is the style you should follow.

After you have finished the final draft of your paper and before you make your typed or final clean copy, it is time to set up your notes. I encourage you to follow these steps to guarantee that your notes are completely accurate.

1. Put your reference cards in alphabetical order.
2. Starting with the first page of your paper, locate the first reference you make to a source. Follow steps 3 through 7 for each note.

3. Find the notecard from which you took the information or quotation that you have used in your text. Check what you have written against your notecard to be sure the information or quotation in your paper is accurate; obviously, if anything in your paper is inaccurate, you must correct it.

4. Put the appropriate note number at the end of the sentence that contains the information or quotation you have used. I usually put a circle around the note number, or write it in a different color ink, so that I do not miss it when I am typing the final copy of the paper.

5. Locate the bibliographic information about the source on your reference card.

6. On a separate sheet of paper headed Notes, write the appropriate note number. Then write the note in the proper form (see subsections B.4–11 of this appendix). You will need your notecard for the correct page number or numbers, and you will need the reference card for the rest of the information about the source.

7. Put the reference card in a special stack. When it comes time to put your bibliography together, you want to be certain that these sources are included.

In the next section of this appendix, I explain how to write your notes, and give you the proper form for various kinds of sources. In subsection C I show you how to put your bibliography together, with information about the proper forms for entries in the bibliography.

In this appendix I am following the form laid out in the thirteenth edition of *The Chicago Manual of Style* (University of Chicago Press, 1982). If I do not answer all your questions in this appendix, I recommend that you check *The Chicago Manual of Style* or Kate Turabian's *Manual for Writers of Term Papers, Theses, and Dissertations* (5th ed., Chicago: University of Chicago Press, 1987).

B. Notes

1. Basic Information about Notes

Before I give you the proper form for notes for various kinds of sources, here is some general information about notes that you should keep in mind:

- All notes are numbered consecutively throughout the paper, starting with number 1 for your first note and ending with the number that reflects the total number of notes in your paper.

- The note number is raised above the line (no punctuation) and should be placed, whenever possible, at the end of a sentence.

> According to Richard Allen, the poem is based on a traditional
> Navaho myth.[6]

> Although James Johnson has argued that this battle was "the most
> decisive of the war," other historians disagree with Johnson's
> assessment.[10]

- There are different forms for the first reference you make to a source and subsequent references to the same source. Please read subsection B.2.

- It is not always necessary to repeat information in a note *if* the *full* bibliographic information is given in the body of your paper. Thus, if you have given the author's *full* name in your text, it is permissible to begin your note with the title of the work. Similarly, if you have given *both* the author's *full* name and the *complete* title of the work in the body of your paper, you may begin your note with the next piece of information required by the correct note form for that work. However, it is never incorrect to repeat the author's name and title in the note.

- Most notes will be used to acknowledge sources that you have used in your paper. However, you may also use notes to comment on a point you have made or to explain a point. See subsection B.12.

- If material that you use in one or more paragraphs of your paper is taken from the same source, your note should indicate the scope of your use of this material. The note number for this note should be placed early in the section in which you use this material, ideally after a sentence in which you refer directly to the source.

> 10. Information in the following paragraphs on the Battle of the
> Bulge has been taken from John W. Sweet, World War II . . .

If you quote from this source, each quotation will have to have a separate note. If you are using one work extensively in your paper, read subsection B.11.d.

• I discuss format for notes in subsection B.14, where you will also find a sample endnote page.

2. First Notes and Subsequent Notes

The first time you cite a source in your notes, you must give full information about the source; this note would be a first note. However, if you refer to that source again later in your paper, you can use a shortened form to acknowledge the source; notes that refer to a source after the first full citation are called subsequent notes.

First Note on Hays

1. Samuel P. Hays, "Political Parties and the Community-Society Continuum," in The American Party Systems: Stages of Political Development, ed. William N. Chambers and Walter D. Burnham, 2d ed. (New York: Oxford University Press, 1975), 154.

First Note on Jennings

2. William I. Jennings, Appeal to the People, vol. 1 of Party Politics (Cambridge: Cambridge University Press, 1960), 14.

Subsequent Note on Hays

3. Hays, "Political Parties," in Chambers and Burnham, American Party Systems, 156.

Subsequent Note on Jennings

4. Jennings, Appeal to the People, 42.

In subsections B.3–10, I give you more information about the proper form for first notes. You will find more information for the proper form for subsequent notes in subsection B.11.

3. First Notes for Books: Placement of Information

```
          note number  author                      title
               |         |                          |
           |  14.   |Carl G. Jung, |Four Archetypes: Mother, Rebirth,
               Spirit, Trickster, |  ┌─┤trans. R. F. C. Hull, Bollingen Series,
               ┌──no. 20 |(Princeton, N.J.: Princeton
               |  University Press, 1969), |20.
               |                      |                    |
           other           facts of          page number(s)
           publication     publication
           information
```

Notice that author, title, and other publication information are separated by commas.

Author   Begin your note with the name or names of the author(s) of the material you are referring to in your paper. Names are given in normal order.

Title   Be sure to give the full title of the article, poem, play, or selection if you are using a work in a collection; such titles should be put in quotation marks. Give the full title of the book including any subtitle; titles of books are underlined. Be sure to capitalize the main words in all titles (see Appendix F.A).

Other publication information   Information about editors, translators, series, and editions must be given. *The Chicago Manual of Style* recommends placement of other publication information in the following order:

  editor and/or translator (when the original author is given)
  series and the number/volume of this work in the series
  edition (if not the original)
  number of volumes in the set if the work is a multivolume work

Facts of publication   Facts of publication, following the same form as that in the bibliography, are placed in parentheses. Never put a comma before a parenthesis.

Page or pages   The last numbers in the note indicate the page or pages on which the information you have used appears. If the work you are using is part of a multivolume set, the volume number will also be given here (see subsection B.4.f).

4. First Notes for Specific Types of Books

a. Book—One Author

16. Perez Zagorin, <u>The Court and the Country: The Beginning of the English Revolution</u> (New York: Atheneum, 1970), 100.

b. Book—More Than One Author

4. Rowland Evans and Robert D. Novak, <u>Nixon in the White House: The Frustration of Power</u> (New York: Random House, 1971), 54.

5. Susan Easton, Joan M. Mills, and Diane K. Winokur, <u>Equal to the Task: How Workingwomen Are Managing in Corporate America</u> (New York: Seaview Books, 1982), 17.

c. Book with Corporate Author

15. Museum of Graphic Art, <u>American Printmaking: The First 150 Years</u> (New York: Museum of Graphic Art, 1969), 23.

When you are referring to a book with a corporate author, be sure to begin your note with the same words you will use in the "author" position in the entry in your bibliography, so that your readers can easily find the correct entry in the bibliography (see subsection C.3.c).

d. Book—Edition Other Than the Original

8. William W. Lawrence, <u>Shakespeare's Problem Comedies</u>, 2d ed. (New York: Ungar Publishing, 1960), 42.

e. Book with Author and Editor and/or Translator

10. Lev S. Vygotsky, <u>Thought and Language</u>, ed. and trans. Eugenia Hanfmann and Gertrude Vakar (Cambridge, Mass.: MIT Press, 1962), 85.

f. Book in a Multivolume Set

Reference to a Work in Which All Volumes Have the Same Title

13. G. W. F. Hegel, <u>Aesthetics: Lectures on Fine Art</u>, trans. T. M. Knox (Oxford: Clarendon Press, 1975), 2:100.

The first number after the publication facts (2) refers to the volume; the second number (100) refers to the page.

Reference to a Work in Which Each Volume Has a Different Title

17. William I. Jennings, The Growth of Parties, vol. 2 of Party Politics (Cambridge: Cambridge University Press, 1961), 90.

Notice that in this note you give the title of the volume you are using first and then the volume number and the title of the complete series.

g. Book in a Series

18. Moses ben Maimon, The Code of Maimonides. Book 3: The Book of Seasons, trans. Solomon Gandz and Hyman Klein, Yale Judaica Series (New Haven: Yale University Press, 1961), 101–3.

7. S. T. Bindoff, Tudor England, Pelican History of England, vol. 5 (Harmondsworth, Middlesex, England: Penguin Books, 1950), 70.

10. Letter to Edgar Levy, 1 September 1945, in David Smith, ed. Garnett McCoy, Documentary Monographs in Modern Art (New York: Praeger Publishers, 1973), 196.

Information about series should be given in the same order in which it is given in your bibliography entry. See subsection C.3.i.

h. Work in a Collection

When citing a work in a collection, your note must begin with the name of the person who wrote the words to which you are referring and the title of the selection by this person.

14. E. B. White, "The Years of Wonder," in Essays of E. B. White (New York: Harper & Row, 1977), 172.

5. Clyde Kluckhohn and William Morgan, "Some Notes on Navaho Dreams," in Psychoanalysis and Culture: Essays in Honor of Geza Roheim, ed. George B. Wilbur and Warner Muensterberger (New York: International Universities Press, 1951), 120–31.

7. "Robin Hood Rescuing Three Squires" (Child No. 140), in The Traditional Tunes of the Child Ballads with Their Texts, ed. Bertrand H. Bronson (Princeton, N.J.: Princeton University Press, 1966), 3:53–57.

The last reference begins with the title of the selection because the actual author of these ballads is not known.

If you refer to material in a collection that was written by the editor or editors of that collection (such as introductions), you may begin your note with the names of the editors, or you may begin with the title of the selection.

> 9. "John Donne: Introduction," in Seventeenth-Century Prose and Poetry, ed. Alexander M. Witherspoon and Frank J. Warnke, 2d ed. (New York: Harcourt, Brace and World, 1963), 58.

or

> 9. Alexander M. Witherspoon and Frank J. Warnke, eds., "John Donne: Introduction," in Seventeenth-Century Prose and Poetry, 2d ed. (New York: Harcourt, Brace and World, 1963), 58.

Notice that if you begin with the editors' names, it is not necessary to repeat them after the title of the collection.

i. Reprint of an Older Work

For further information on reprints of older works, see subsection C.3.j.

> 10. Georg W. F. Hegel, Lectures on the Philosophy of Religion, Together with a Work on the Proofs of the Existence of God, trans. from the 2d German ed. by E. B. Speirs and J. Burdon Sanderson; ed. E. B. Speirs (London: K. Paul, Trench, Truber, 1895; New York: Humanities Press, 1968), 85.

> 6. Virginia Woolf, "Donne after Three Centuries," in The Second Common Reader (New York: Harcourt, Brace and World, 1932; Harvest Books, 1960), 17–31.

5. First Notes for Encyclopedias, Dictionaries, and Similar Reference Works

Unsigned Articles

> 10. The Focal Encyclopedia of Photography, rev. ed. (1965), s.v. "Daguerreotype."

> 11. Van Nostrand's Scientific Encyclopedia, 6th ed. (1983), s.v. "Cyanogen."

Signed Articles

> 7. The Encyclopedia of Philosophy, 1967 ed., s.v. "Hobbes, Thomas," by R. S. Peters.

18. The Dictionary of National Biography, 1931–40 ed., s.v. "Rackham, Arthur," by Herbert B. Grimsditch.

6. First Notes for Scholarly Journals

a. General Form

```
    note number    author                        title
        |            |                              |
   |   15.   | Jacqueline Jones, | " 'My Mother Was Much of a Woman': |
       Black Women, Work, and the Family under Slavery," |
      | Feminist Studies | 8 (Summer 1982): 236–37. |
              |                       |
         journal title      publication information
```

Note that the author, title, and journal title are separated by commas.

Author   Give the name or names of the author(s) in normal order.

Title   Give the full title of the article, including subtitles. All main words should be capitalized (see Appendix F.A) and the entire title placed in quotation marks (place the comma inside the quotation marks). The single quotation marks here indicate that the first part of the title was placed in quotation marks in the original article.

Journal title   Although you may see the titles of journals abbreviated, you should spell out the full title.

Publication information   The first number given (8) is the volume number. The information in parentheses is the season and year of the issue. The final numbers are the pages to which you are referring.

13.   Lois M. Grose, "The Able Student in a City School System," English Journal 55 (October 1966): 891–94.

5.   Robert Egan, "A Thin Beam of Light: The Purpose of Playing in Rosencrantz and Guildenstern Are Dead," Theatre Journal 31 (March 1979): 63.

L. Journal That Paginates Each Issue Separately

6. Christopher B. Wilson, "The Era of the Reporter Reconsidered: The Case of Lincoln Steffens," Journal of Popular Culture 15, no. 2 (Fall 1981): 59.

7. First Notes for Magazines

8. Michael Sragow, "Ghostwriters: Unraveling the Enigma of Movie Authorship," Film Commentary, April 1983, 10.

11. "Alex and the Awards," The New Yorker, 21 June 1982, 34.

8. First Notes for Newspaper Articles

14. Raymond Bonner, "A Guatemalan General's Rise to Power," New York Times, 21 July 1982, A3.

16. "Madman Attacks Alligator," The Smithville (Florida) Observer, 14 August 1991, sec. 4, p. 5.

9. First Notes for Other Types of Sources

One form I will give you here is the form for interviews:

14. Sally Knowles, interview with author, Portland, Oregon, 14 October, 1995.

If you have agreed to keep the identity of one or more of your interviewees confidential, you should turn back to Section 3, subsection B.4 to review the advice on how to handle these interviews in your paper.

Unfortunately, I do not have the space to give you the forms for other types of sources—documents of federal and local governments, videotapes, films, recordings, television programs. If you have used these types of materials in your paper, check Kate Turabian's *Manual for Writers of Term Papers, Theses, and Dissertations* or *The Chicago Manual of Style* for the form you need.

10. Notes for Quotations from a Secondary Source

In Section 4, subsection D.4, I alerted you to the fact that you should not get into the habit of quoting material that is quoted in one of the sources you have used. I urged you to locate, whenever possible, the original work and to quote from the original work.

In those cases when you have tried to locate the original source of the quotation but have not been able to, your note must clearly reflect that you have used a secondary source. In your note, you should first give your reader as much information as you are able about the original source; if you have full bibliographic information, give it in the normal order for that type of work. Then, in your note you will write "quoted by" and give full bibliographic information about the source you used. The page number you give will be the page number on which the quotation appears in the source you used.

> 15. Henry D. Lloyd, Wealth against Commonwealth (1894; ed. 1899), quoted by Richard Hofstadter, The Age of Reform from Bryan to F.D.R. (New York: Random House, Vintage Books, 1955), 141.

You can find more information about using material from a secondary source in Section 4.D.4 and Section 6.B.4.

11. Form for Subsequent Notes

A subsequent note, I will remind you, is a note that refers to a work that you have already cited in an earlier note (the first note). After you have given full bibliographic information in your first note, you may use a shortened form if you refer to this work again (subsequent notes).

a. The Shortened Form

In a subsequent note, you will give the author's last name, a shortened title of the work, and the page number.

> 16. Jones, " 'My Mother Was Much of a Woman,' " 240.

> 17. Moses ben Maimon, The Code of Maimonides, 116.

> 18. Morison, The Rising Sun in the Pacific, 56.

b. Some Advice on Using the Shortened Form

- In shortening the title of a work, *The Chicago Manual of Style* recommends that:

  ○ you do not change the order of the words from the order in which they appear in the original title (*The History of England* should not be changed to *English History*).

  ○ if the main title of the work contains five words or fewer, you should use the entire main title (*The Court and the Country: The Beginning of the English Revolution* should be shortened to *The Court and the Country*).

  ○ you should use those words from the main title that best identify the subject of the work (*The Traditional Tunes of the Child Ballads with Their Texts according to the Extant Records of Great Britain and America* should be shortened to *Child Ballads*).

- When you refer to a work that is part of a multivolume set with the same title, you must give the appropriate volume number.

  15. Hegel, <u>Aesthetics</u> 2:118.

- In using the shortened form, you must never forget that your first obligation is to allow your readers to locate easily the work to which you are referring. Develop your shortened form entry so that your readers can easily find the correct entry in your bibliography. Thus your note must contain at least the name of the author by which you have listed a work in your bibliography. This caution is particularly important to remember if you are using a number of selections from a collection and your bibliography entry is an entry only for the edited collection. In these situations, your note will have to contain full information about the selection or article you are using and the name(s) of the editor(s) of the collection, plus a short title of the collection.

Bibliography Entry

Wilbur, George B., and Warner Muensterberger, eds. <u>Psychoanalysis and Culture: Essays in Honor of Geza Roheim</u>. New York: International Universities Press, 1951.

Note

18. Clyde Kluckhohn and William Morgan, "Some Notes on Navaho Dreams," in Wilbur and Muensterberger, <u>Psychoanalysis and Culture</u>, 129.

c. Ibid.

Ibid. is the abbreviation for *ibidem*, a Latin word that means "in the same place." Thus ibid. can be used only when a note refers to the source given in the note that immediately precedes it. If, for example, you had three references in a row to Mary L. Myers' article on Raphael, you could use ibid.

    15. Mary L. Myers, "Reproducing Raphael," Artnews, April 1983, 80.

    16. Ibid.

    17. Ibid., 82.

Note 17 is a reference to the same article, but this note refers to a different page. You must also be aware that you cannot use ibid. if the note to which you are referring contains citations for more than one work. If you have two or three works listed, how would the reader know to which of the two or three you are referring?

Ibid. is the last of a number of Latin abbreviations that used to be used in subsequent notes. Op cit. (*opere citato*, "in the work cited") and loc. cit. (*loco citato*, "in the place cited") traditionally were used instead of a short title of the work. When a reader today encounters a note like "70. Williams, op. cit., p. 14," he or she must read through all of the previous footnotes, thumbing back through page after page, until he or she finds that earlier note in which the author gives the full bibliographic informa-tion for Williams's work. And sometimes the reader finds that the author of this book has referred to two different works by Williams. To which work does footnote number 70 refer? Because op. cit. and loc. cit. can be cumbersome, if not downright confusing, for readers, *The Chicago Manual of Style* and other style manuals discourage their use. Because ibid., like op. cit. and loc. cit., refers the reader to previous notes, it too can be cumbersome, especially if your notes are on the bottom of each page of your text. If, for example, note 15 were on page 12, and note 17 were on page 14, you would have to turn back to page 12 to get any information about this source.

Ibid. is becoming as old-fashioned as loc. cit. and op. cit. Therefore I would advise you to use ibid. only if you are putting all your notes on an endnote page. I think the wisest choice of all would probably be to use the shortened form for *all* subsequent notes. However, ibid. is a legitimate term for documentation; check with your instructor if you aren't sure which form to use.

d. Extensive References to One Source

If you have written a paper in which you use one work extensively—if, for example, you have written a paper on Karl Marx in which you refer frequently to his book *Capital*—you will have many notes that cite this work. An alternative is to put these citations in the body of your paper. Here's the procedure for citing a work in the text.

- The first time you refer to this work, you must give a normal first note. After you document the source, it would be wise to inform your reader that further citations in your paper will be given in the body of the paper.

      1. Sigmund Freud, Interpretation of Dreams (1900), in The
      Standard Edition of the Complete Psychological Works of Sigmund
      Freud, trans. from the German under the general editorship of
      James Strachey (London: Hogarth Press and the Institute of
      Psychoanalysis, 1953), 4:136–38. All references to Freud's
      works in this paper are references to this edition of the
      Complete Works; citations will hereafter be given in the
      text.

      2. Karl Marx, Capital: A Critique of Political Economy, trans.
      from the 3d German ed. by Samuel Moore and Edward Aveling, ed.
      Frederick Engels, rev. according to the 4th German ed. by Ernest
      Untermann (New York: Random House, Modern Library, 1906), 106.
      All references to Capital are references to this edition;
      citations will hereafter be given in the text.

- Each time you refer to this work in the body of your paper, you will put your citation in parentheses at the end of the relevant sentence. The reader must be given the same information that would be given in the normal shortened form. If part of this information (like the name of the author and the title of a specific selection) is given in your sentence or is obvious from the context, this information need not be repeated. If the work is part of a multivolume set, don't forget that you must include the volume number.

      According to Marx, capital is "essentially the command over
      unpaid labour" (Capital, 585).

      Freud covers this subject in the first sections of Interpretation
      of Dreams (Complete Works 4:134–62).

Be judicious about putting any citations in the text itself. I would advise you to put subsequent notes in your text only for one or two works to which you refer extensively in your paper. In using this system, never forget that the purpose of documentation is to allow your readers to locate the specific information to which you are referring. If you are sloppy with subsequent notes, you will not be giving your readers the information they need.

12. Explanatory Notes

You may use notes for purposes other than simple documentation of sources. Notes may also be used to refer readers to more detailed discussions of a particular topic, or they may be used to explain or elaborate upon a particular point.

```
11. For more detailed information about the Smith raid, see Johnson,
Indian Wars, 75–83.

19. Throughout the play the word "cold" is used in reference to
chastity, inactivity, and death.  So, for example, in speaking of the
postponement of the sentencing of the Duchess's youngest son, Spurio
says . . .
```

It is perfectly acceptable to use explanatory notes, but you must use your common sense. Material that your reader must have to understand a point that you are making should never be hidden in a note; this information belongs in the body of your paper. And don't forget that note numbers are distracting; they encourage your readers to leave your argument and look at your footnote or endnote. Some readers become very irritated if you use the note system to introduce information or ideas that are outside the bounds of the paper you are writing. So use explanatory notes where you feel they are really needed. Do not use explanatory notes to show off everything you know about your topic.

13. Citing More Than One Source in the Same Note

Occasionally you will want to tell your reader that the same information or ideas can be found in several different sources. In these situations, use one note number and list the various sources in one note. The various citations will be separated with semicolons. Use the first note form if this is your first reference to a specific work; use the shortened form if you have already cited this work in an earlier note.

14. Charles B. Long, <u>The Civil War</u> (New York: Never Press, 1997),
116–17; Curtis, "Lee and Grant," 108; James G. Gilligam, <u>A History of</u>
<u>the War between the States</u> (San Francisco: Nosuch Publishers, 1984),
2:35–70.

14. Format for Notes, with Sample Endnote Page

Your notes may be placed at the bottom of the pages of your text (*footnotes*)
or on a separate sheet at the end of your paper (*endnotes*).

a. Footnotes

Unless your instructor requires that your notes appear at the bottom of the
page, I would advise you to use endnotes. Putting notes at the bottom of the
page can become a typing nightmare unless you are using a word processing
program that formats footnotes automatically. If, however, you have no
choice, I will describe the proper format for footnotes.

The note numbers on a particular page of your text tell you which notes
must appear at the bottom of that page. The difficulty comes in figuring out
which note numbers will appear on a specific page of the final typed copy
and allowing sufficient space for the notes. The text and notes must all
remain within the margins you've chosen for your paper.

After the final line of the body of your paper on a particular page,
single-space and type a line about an inch and a half long. Then double-
space and begin your first note. Single-space individual notes; double-space
between notes.

15. Jones, <u>If I Were a King</u>, 16.

16. Charles W. Long, <u>The French Monarchy</u> (New York: Instant
Publishers, 1987), 5:167–85.

17. Harold Law, "Louis XIV," <u>European History</u> 35 (Spring 1990): 19.

b. Endnotes

Endnotes are all the notes for the paper collected in one place, on a separate sheet or sheets of paper that you will place at the end of the body of
your paper between the last page of your text and the bibliography. Margins are the same as those in the body of your paper. Endnote pages should
be numbered consecutively with the body of your paper. Center the head-

ing, Notes, at the top of the page, leaving at least one line of space between it and the first note. *The Chicago Manual of Style* advises authors to double-space endnote pages. For reasons I give in Appendix F, subsection B, my advice to students preparing papers for classes is to single-space individual notes, double-spacing between them. As in all matters of style, however, your decision to double-space or single-space should be based on the recommendations of the instructor for whom you are writing the paper.

c. Sample Endnote Page

Notes

1. Lev S. Vygotsky, Thought and Language, ed. and trans. Eugenia Hanfmann and Gertrude Vakar (Cambridge, Mass.: MIT Press, 1962), 85.

2. "Robin Hood Rescuing Three Squires" (Child No. 140), in The Traditional Tunes of the Child Ballads with Their Texts, ed. Bertrand H. Bronson (Princeton, N.J.: Princeton University Press, 1966), 3:53–57.

3. William I. Jennings, The Growth of Parties, vol. 2 of Party Politics (Cambridge: Cambridge University Press, 1961), 90.

4. "Robin Hood Rescuing Three Squires" (Child No. 140), in Bronson, Child Ballads 3:56.

5. Jennings, The Growth of Parties, 110.

6. The Dictionary of National Biography, 1931–40 ed., s.v. "Rackham, Arthur," by Herbert B. Grimsditch.

7. John Donne, "IV. Meditation," in Seventeenth-Century Prose and Poetry, ed. Alexander M. Witherspoon and Frank J. Warnke, 2d ed. (New York: Harcourt, Brace and World, 1963), 61.

8. Vygotsky, Thought and Language, 156.

9. Christopher B. Wilson, "The Era of the Reporter Reconsidered: The Case of Lincoln Steffens," Journal of Popular Culture 15, no. 2 (Fall 1981): 59.

10. Donne, "IV. Meditation," in Witherspoon and Warnke, Seventeenth-Century Prose and Poetry, 61.

11. Wilson, "The Era of the Reporter Reconsidered," 52.

12. Jennings, The Growth of Parties, 120–125.

13. Jennings, The Growth of Parties, 167.

C. *Putting a Bibliography Together*

The content of a bibliography varies according to the purpose of the author. As a student preparing a bibliography for a paper for a college course, you should look upon your bibliography as a direct indication of the scope, depth, and thoroughness of the research you have done. Thus your bibliography should include *all* the sources that you cite in your notes plus those sources that you read or consulted in doing your research, even though you may not refer to them in your notes. You should not include works that you did not read or use in some way.

You may have noticed that in some books bibliographies are divided into different sections (like Primary and Secondary Works, or Books and Periodicals). You should not subdivide your bibliography unless it is very long (let us say over six pages) or unless you have a very good reason for separate sections. If you decide it would be wise to subdivide your bibliography, you should consult *The Chicago Manual of Style*.

I will assume that you have decided there is no reason to subdivide your bibliography. You should then begin to compile your bibliography by putting in order the reference cards of all the sources you read or consulted in investigating your subject. Be sure to review your notes to make certain that you haven't left out any work that you cite in your notes.

1. Ordering Sources in Your Bibliography

Bibliographies are set up by starting each entry with the *last* name of the first author mentioned in the work you are listing. Here are some further hints about ordering your list.

- In alphabetizing your sources, use only the letters in an author's last name; ignore his or her first name or initials. If your list includes works by Stephen Green and Aaron Greenberg, the work by Green would come first.

- If you have several authors with the same last name, alphabetize according to the authors' first names, and then the middle initials.

    Johnson, Carl X.
    Johnson, Frances H.
    Johnson, Frederick J.
    Johnson, Frederick S.

- If your list includes more than one work by the same author or authors (John Jones):

  - List all the works that Jones wrote by himself first. Order the entries according to the titles of the works (ignoring *the, an,* and *a* as first words).

    Jones, John. *The Continental Congress* . . .
    ———— . "The Political Contexts of . . ."

  - Then list any collections that Jones edited.

    Jones, John, ed. *Papers of the Continental Congress* . . .

  - If Jones has written any works with other authors (or edited any works with others), these co-authored works would then be listed. Alphabetize according to the last names of the second co-author, and so on.

    Jones, John, and Herman Gotz. *America during the Revolution* . . .
    Jones, John, Aaron Greenberg, and Alfred Lutz, eds. *The Papers of Thomas Jefferson* . . .
    Jones, John, Aaron Greenberg, and Louisa Smith. *American Lives* . . .
    Jones, John, and James Jackson. *When We Were Young* . . .

Note: You may substitute two or three unspaced hyphens for the author's name *only* when the author or authors are *exactly* the same. Otherwise, spell out every author's name.

- Books with a corporate author (an agency, committee, institute, etc.) are alphabetized according to the first main word (ignoring *the, an,* and *a*) in the name of the group (see subsection C.3.c).
- If a work has no author, place it in your bibliography according to the first main word in the title.

In the following I give you the proper form for the most common types of sources. Check the headings in the rest of this appendix, find the one that best matches your source, and follow the form *exactly*. Watch details like capitalization, punctuation, and underlining very carefully. If you cannot find an example of the source you are recording in your bibliography, see subsection C.8. If you would like to see a sample bibliography, turn to subsection C.9.

2. Form for Books: Placement of Information

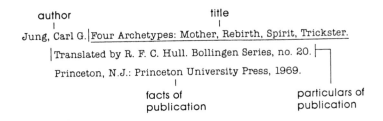

A book entry is divided into four parts; each part is separated from the others with a period. The first line of an entry is flush with the left-hand margin; other lines in the entry are indented five spaces.

Author   The key to your bibliography is the name of the person or group responsible for the text. Begin with the last name of the first author listed on the title page of the work, and whenever possible, give each author's full first name and middle initial. If the party responsible is a corporate group, the name of the group will be used as the "author" (see subsection C.3.c). If the book is a collection of essays, the editor of the collection will be considered its author (see subsection C.3.f).

If you are referring to an article or essay included in a collection of essays, you have two options: (1) you can cite the article or essay, in which case you will enter this work in your bibliography under the name of the author of the article (see subsection C.3.g); or (2) you may cite only the collection itself, in which case you will enter this work under the name of the editor of the collection. If you have used several essays in a collection, it would probably be better to list only the collection itself in your bibliography.

Title   Give the full title of the book, including any subtitles. The main words in all titles are always capitalized (see Appendix F.A). Titles of books are underlined. Notice that the titles of essays, articles, and other works that were originally published in a larger collection are placed in quotation marks; periods or commas are placed *inside* the quotation marks. If you refer to a work in a collection or anthology, you must give the full titles of *both* the work itself and the anthology or collection.

Particulars of publication   You must always include other information about the work because such information will help the readers locate the specific book you used. Give such information in this order after the title of the book:

> name of editor and/or translator
> titles of series, if any, and volume or number
> volume number or total number of volumes if book is a part of a set
> edition (if not the original)

Please note that volume numbers and other numbers used in documentation should always be arabic numerals (33) rather than roman numerals (XXXIII).

Facts of publication   Publication information is given in this form:

> New York: Nosuch Press, 1983.

Always give the *city* of publication. The name of the *publisher* follows. The *date* is the date of publication. Check the title page; if no date is given, turn the page and use the date with the latest copyright (the most recent date next to the ©). You may add the state or country after the city of publication if the city is not well known (Englewood Cliffs, N.J.).

3. Forms for Specific Types of Books

In the pages that follow I give you examples of the proper form for different kinds of books. Since each example focuses on one aspect of the citation, in some cases you may need to check a couple of headings to see how to write a specific entry in your bibliography.

a. Book—One Author

> Zagorin, Perez. The Court and the Country: The Beginning of the English Revolution. New York: Atheneum, 1970.

b. Book—More Than One Author

> Evans, Rowland, and Robert D. Novak. Nixon in the White House: The Frustration of Power. New York: Random House, 1971.

> Easton, Susan, Joan M. Mills, and Diane K. Winokur. Equal to the Task: How Workingwomen Are Managing in Corporate America. New York: Seaview Books, 1982.

Note that the name of the first author is inverted (Easton, Susan), but the names of other authors appear in their normal form. Be sure to put commas after the last name *and* first name of the first author.

c. Book with Corporate Author

If responsibility for the contents of the book is taken by an agency, corporation, or institute, use the name of this group as the author. Alphabetize according to the first word in the name (disregarding *the, an,* and *a*). Spell out the full name of the group. Give the name of the parent body before listing subdivisions of the organization (in the following example, Brooklyn College is responsible for the Institute of Puerto Rican Studies). If your bibliography is going to include a large number of works with group authors, and the names of the organizations are themselves long, consult *The Chicago Manual of Style* for systems you can use to make your citations and the bibliography easier to use.

Royal Institute of Philosophy. Understanding Wittgenstein. Royal
     Institute of Philosophy Lectures, Vol. 7 (1972–1973). New York:
     St. Martin's Press, 1974.

Museum of Graphic Art. American Printmaking: The First 150 Years. New
     York: Museum of Graphic Art, 1969.

Brooklyn College. Institute of Puerto Rican Studies. The Puerto Rican
     People: A Selected Bibliography for Use in Social Work Education.
     New York: Council on Social Work Education, 1973.

d. Book—Edition Other Than the Original

Lawrence, William W. Shakespeare's Problem Comedies. 2d ed. New
     York: Ungar Publishing, 1960.

Stone, Lawrence. The Crisis of the Aristocracy 1558–1614. Abridged
     ed. New York: Oxford University Press, 1967.

e. Book with Author and Editor and/or Translator

Vygotsky, Lev S. Thought and Language. Edited and translated by
     Eugenia Hanfmann and Gertrude Vakar. Cambridge, Mass.: MIT
     Press, 1962.

f. Book with Editor Rather Than Author— A Collection of Works

Chambers, William N., and Walter D. Burnham, eds. <u>The American Party Systems: Stages of Political Development</u>. 2d ed. New York: Oxford University Press, 1975.

Wilbur, George B., and Warner Muensterberger, eds. <u>Psychoanalysis and Culture: Essays in Honor of Geza Roheim</u>. New York: International Universities Press, 1951.

Witherspoon, Alexander M., and Frank J. Warnke, eds. <u>Seventeenth-Century Prose and Poetry</u>. 2d ed. New York: Harcourt, Brace and World, 1963.

g. Work in a Collection or Anthology

If you are using only one work or essay from a collection, you may list only that work; I give you the proper form below. If you are using several works or essays from the same collection, it is probably easier to list only the collection, using the form in C.3.f.

Dekker, Thomas. <u>The Shoemakers' Holiday</u>. In <u>English Drama, 1580–1642</u>, edited by C. F. Tucker Brooke and N. B. Paradise, 263–293. Boston: D. C. Heath, 1933.

Halsey, Louis. "The Choral Music." In <u>Robert Schumann: The Man and His Music</u>, edited by Alan Walker, 350–389. London: Barrie and Jenkins, 1972.

Hays, Samuel P. "Political Parties and the Community-Society Continuum." In <u>The American Party Systems: Stages of Political Development</u>, edited by William N. Chambers and Walter D. Burnham, 152–181. 2d ed. New York: Oxford University Press, 1975.

The numbers that are given immediately after the names of the editors are the pages on which the essay or play appears. *The Shoemakers' Holiday* is underlined because this is a play which, when it first appeared, was published as a separate work.

h. Book in a Multivolume Set

An Entry for the Complete Set

Morison, Samuel E. <u>The History of United States Naval Operations in World War II</u>. 15 vols. Boston: Little, Brown, 1947–62.

Bronson, Bertrand H., ed. <u>The Traditional Tunes of the Child Ballads</u>
<u>with Their Texts, according to the Extant Records of Great</u>
<u>Britain and America</u>. 4 vols. Princeton, N.J.: Princeton
University Press, 1959–72.

Note that these volumes were published over a number of years. Be sure to indicate the dates of publication of the first and last volumes.

An Entry for One Volume

Morison, Samuel E. <u>The Rising Sun in the Pacific, 1931–April 1942</u>.
Vol. 3 of <u>The History of United States Naval Operations in World</u>
<u>War II</u>. Boston: Little, Brown, 1948.

This type of entry is appropriate since the individual volume has its own title but is part of a larger series. Here I indicate only the date of this specific volume.

i. Book in a Series

Occasionally when you look at the title page of a book, you will notice that this book is part of a series; the series title may refer to subject matter (Documentary Monographs in Modern Art) or to the publisher (Smithsonian Miscellaneous Collection) or to both (Yale Judaica Series). Include information about the series in your reference. Give the name of the series (capitalize the main words but do not underline) and the volume or number of this work if a volume or number is given.

Bindoff, S. T. <u>Tudor England</u>. Pelican History of England, vol. 5.
Harmondsworth, Middlesex, England: Penguin Books, 1950.

McCoy, Garnett, ed. <u>David Smith</u>. Documentary Monographs in Modern
Art. New York: Praeger Publishers, 1973.

Moses ben Maimon. <u>The Code of Maimonides. Book 3: The Book of Seasons</u>.
Translated by Solomon Gandz and Hyman Klein. Yale Judaica
Series. New Haven: Yale University Press, 1961.

j. Reprint of an Older Work

Once in a while you will use a book that is a reprint of a text that was originally published many years ago. A reprint of a work is different from an edition of a work. In an edition, some part or parts of the text have been changed; a reprint is a reproduction of the actual text the author originally wrote. If you give only the publication date of the reprint you are using, you give your reader the impression that this text is more recent than it actually is. This is the proper form for a reprinted book.

> Woolf, Virginia. The Second Common Reader. New York: Harcourt, Brace and World, 1932; Harvest Books, 1960.

> Hegel, Georg W. F. Lectures on the Philosophy of Religion, Together with a Work on the Proofs of the Existence of God. Translated from the 2d German ed. by E. B. Speirs and J. Burdon Sanderson; edited by E. B. Speirs. London: K. Paul, Trench, Truber, 1895; New York: Humanities Press, 1968.

When you have full information about the facts of publication of the original text, you give this information first (London . . . 1895); then give publication facts of the reprinted version. If you do not have publication facts about the original, follow this form:

Author, title, date of original publication.

Then write the word "reprint" (capitalize the first letter and put a period after it).

Finish the citation with the facts of publication of the reprint.

4. Form for Encyclopedias, Dictionaries, and Similar Reference Works

Signed Articles

> The Dictionary of National Biography. 1931–40 ed., s.v. "Rackham, Arthur." By Herbert B. Grimsditch.

> The Encyclopedia of Philosophy. 1967 ed., s.v. "Hobbes, Thomas." By R. S. Peters.

Unsigned Articles

> The Focal Encyclopedia of Photography. Rev. ed. (1965), s.v. "Daguerreotype."

> Van Nostrand's Scientific Encyclopedia. 6th ed. (1983), s.v. "Cyanogen."

The abbreviation "s.v." stands for *sub verbo* (under the word). Since most encyclopedias and dictionaries are set up alphabetically according to key terms, the key word that headed the article will allow your readers to find the appropriate entry. In your bibliography, these works will be listed according to the name of the encyclopedia or dictionary (the first information in the entry).

5. Form for Scholarly Journals

a. General Form

```
            author                      article title
              |                             |
     Egan, Robert. |"A Thin Beam of Light: The Purpose of

        Playing in Rosencrantz and Guildenstern Are

        Dead." | Theatre Journal | 31 (March 1979): 59–69.
                        |                      |
                  journal title     publication information
```

Author   Give the last name of the author first; if there is more than one author, give second and third authors' names in the normal order.

Article title   Put the title of the article in quotation marks; place a period at the end, inside the quotation marks. Underline any words that are in italic type. Capitalize all main words in the title (see Appendix F.A).

Journal title   Although the titles of journals are sometimes abbreviated in notes and bibliographies, you should spell out the full title and underline it. Notice that there is no punctuation after the title.

Publication information   The number before the parentheses is the volume number; always use arabic numerals (31) rather than roman numerals (XXXI). The final numbers are the inclusive pages on which the article appears. Since most scholarly journals are paginated consecutively throughout the year, the volume number and the page numbers provide the readers with enough information to locate the article. The date of the volume is given to let the reader know how old, or recent, this article is; the month or season is not technically necessary, but is useful information for the readers and may be included. Some magazines and journals do not paginate consecutively throughout the year, but begin each issue with page 1. If you cite such a journal or magazine, you will have to give the issue number as well as the volume number (see subsection 5.b below). Magazines written for a general audience are usually cited by giving only the date of publication (see subsection C.6).

Watch the punctuation carefully. A colon and a space separate the date from the page numbers. Otherwise, notice that there is no punctuation. Put a period after the page numbers to indicate the end of the citation.

```
Barish, Jonas A.  "The Double Plot in Volpone."  Modern Philology 51
    (1953): 83–92.

Grose, Lois M.  "The Able Student in a City School System."  English
    Journal 55 (October 1966): 891–94.

Jones, Jacqueline.  "'My Mother Was Much of a Woman': Black Women,
    Work, and the Family under Slavery."  Feminist Studies 8 (Summer
    1982): 235–70.
```

b. Journal That Paginates Each Issue Separately

Since the *Journal of Popular Culture* begins each issue with page 1, you will have to give the issue number as well as the volume number.

```
Wilson, Christopher B.  "The Era of the Reporter Reconsidered: The
    Case of Lincoln Steffens."  Journal of Popular Culture, 15, no. 2
    (Fall 1981): 52–60.
```

6. Form for Magazines

References to periodicals that are published weekly or monthly and that are intended for a general reading audience are usually cited by omitting the volume number and using the date of publication instead.

```
"Alex and the Awards."  The New Yorker, 21 June 1982, 32–35.

Sragow, Michael.  "Ghostwriters: Unraveling the Enigma of Movie
    Authorship."  Film Commentary, April 1983, 9–18.

Myers, Mary L.  "Reproducing Raphael."  Artnews, April 1983, 79–83.
```

Note that when a specific date is given, it is given in the European fashion (21 June 1982). If no author is given, use the title to introduce the entry, and alphabetize according to the first main word in the title, disregarding *the*, *an*, and *a*.

7. Form for Newspaper Articles

Bonner, Raymond. "A Guatemalan General's Rise to Power." <u>New York Times</u>, 21 July 1982, A3.

"Madman Attacks Alligator." <u>The Smithville (Florida) Observer</u>, 14 August 1991, sec. 4, p. 5.

Watch page numbers in a newspaper. Some newspapers are divided into sections, and each section begins with page 1. Thus, you must give your reader both the section designation and the page numbers. It would be wise to include the edition if the newspaper you are using appears in various editions.

8. Forms for Other Types of Sources

The proper form for an interview is this:

Knowles, Sally. Interview with author. Portland, Oregon. 14 October 1995.

If you have agreed to keep the identity of one or more of your interviewees confidential, review Section 3.B.4 on how to handle these interviews in your paper.

Unfortunately, there is not enough space to give you the forms for other types of sources such as documents of federal and local governments, videotapes, films, recordings, television programs. If you have used these types of materials in your paper, check Kate Turabian's *Manual for Writers of Term Papers, Theses, and Dissertations* or *The Chicago Manual of Style* for the form you need.

9. The Final Bibliography, including a Sample

Your bibliography will be typed on a separate sheet or sheets of paper, using the same margins as those in the body of your paper. Number the pages consecutively with other pages in the text, remembering that, if you are including endnotes, the endnote page(s) will be placed between the body of the paper and the bibliography. Center the heading, Bibliography, at the top of the page, leaving at least one line of space between it and the first entry. The first line of each entry will be flush with the left-hand margin; other lines in an individual entry are indented five spaces. *The Chicago Manual of Style* advises authors to double-space the bibliography. For reasons I give in

Appendix F, subsection B, my advice to students preparing papers for classes is to single-space individual entries, double-spacing between them. As in all matters of style, however, your decision to double-space or single-space should be based on the recommendations of the instructor for whom you are writing the paper.

Bibliography

"Alex and the Awards." The New Yorker, 21 June 1982, 32–35.

Barish, Jonas A. "The Double Plot in Volpone." Modern Philology 51 (1953): 83–92.

Bronson, Bertrand H., ed. The Traditional Tunes of the Child Ballads with Their Texts, according to the Extant Record of Great Britain and America. 4 vols. Princeton, N.J.: Princeton University Press, 1959–72.

The Focal Encyclopedia of Photography. Rev. ed. (1965), s.v. "Daguerreotype."

Kluckhohn, Clyde, and William Morgan. "Some Notes on Navaho Dreams." In Psychoanalysis and Culture: Essays in Honor of Geza Roheim, edited by George B. Wilbur and Warner Muensterberger, 120–31. New York: International Universities Press, 1951.

Morison, Samuel E. The Rising Sun in the Pacific, 1931–April 1942. Vol. 3 of The History of United States Naval Operations in World War II. Boston: Little, Brown, 1948.

Moses ben Maimon. The Code of Maimonides. Book 3: The Book of Seasons. Translated by Solomon Gandz and Hyman Klein. Yale Judaica Series. New Haven: Yale University Press, 1961.

Museum of Graphic Art. American Printmaking: The First 150 Years. New York: Museum of Graphic Art, 1969.

Sragow, Michael. "Ghostwriters: Unraveling the Enigma of Movie Authorship." Film Commentary, April 1983, 9–18.

Witherspoon, Alexander M., and Frank J. Warnke, eds. Seventeenth-Century Prose and Poetry. 2d ed. New York: Harcourt, Brace and World, 1963.

Woolf, Virginia. The Second Common Reader. New York: Harcourt, Brace and World, 1932; Harvest Books, 1960.

APPENDIX C

Scientific Systems: The APA Style

A. General Information

The APA style derives its name from the documentation form laid out in the *Publication Manual of the American Psychological Association* (the APA). This appendix is a brief introduction to the basics of this style as given in the third edition of the *Manual* (Washington, D.C.: APA, 1983). The APA form is a variant of the author-date system of citing sources, used in the field of psychology and often in other behavioral sciences. Although it is very similar to the author-date form laid out in *The Chicago Manual of Style* (see Appendix D), APA and Chicago should be considered different forms. For example, Chicago, not APA, is the form that should be used for papers in the natural sciences. If you aren't sure if the APA is the appropriate style for your paper, check with your instructor.

The APA style differs in a number of important ways from the documentation style you may be most familiar with, the humanities system that uses footnotes (or endnotes) and a bibliography. The most obvious difference is that in the APA style you use neither footnote numbers nor footnotes. Instead, you let your readers know the source of the information or ideas you are using by giving the last name of the author or authors of a work, and the year in which it was published, right in the body of your paper.

```
Smith and Jones (1976) have found that . . . .

Several studies have been done on sexist language in the workplace

(Aaron, 1986; Clark & Williams, 1978; Taylor, 1984).
```

Full bibliographic information about each of your sources is then given in a reference list which you attach to the end of your paper.

```
Aaron, K. (1986). A study of sexist language in six major
     corporations. Journal of Corporate Behavior, 46, 334–65.

Clark, S., & Williams, E. (1978). Communication styles in the
     executive suite. In J. Doe & G. Smith (Eds.), Corporate
     communication (pp. 297–315). New York: Nosuch Press.

Taylor, M. E. (1984). Sexism and the female worker. San Francisco:
     Gold Coast Press.
```

Like a bibliography, the reference list is a list of works organized alphabetically according to the last name of the first author of a work. But the reference list is a critical element of the APA documentation form since it is the only place where specific information about a source is recorded. In order to use the APA style correctly, you should keep a few basic guidelines in mind.

- The author or authors you cite in the body of your paper must be the names of the individuals or groups whose ideas or words you used.

- The author(s) and date you give in the body of your paper must appear as the first two pieces of information in an entry in your reference list.

These two guidelines are immediately relevant to those cases in which you are using articles published in a collection of works, such as the Clark and Williams example above. Obviously, you couldn't cite the editors of the collection (Doe & Smith, 1978) in your paper because Doe and Smith didn't do the study you are referring to. Neither could you cite Clark and Williams in your paper and list only Doe and Smith's collection in your reference list. How would a reader know that the Clark and Williams article was published in Doe and Smith's collection? You can see in the example above how APA handles such cases; I give another example in subsection B.3.g.

- Similarly, for the APA style to work, each citation in your text must match one, and only one, entry on your reference list. It is not unusual for the same author to write a number of works with various co-authors, and the same author(s) can publish more than one work in the same year. Subsection B.1 shows how to list works that fall into these categories. Here my general advice is to be very careful about recording all authors' names in exactly the same order in which they appear on the title page; and be sure that a citation in your paper matches one and only one entry in your reference list. I'll continue to remind you about this in the next two sections.

Two final guidelines:

- You should be aware that reference lists are different from bibliographies in that reference lists contain *only* the works you refer to directly in your paper. This fact is made clear in such headings as Works Cited or Literature Cited, which you may have seen as alternative headings for reference lists.
- As in all documentation systems, you must follow the APA form exactly. Pay very close attention, in the examples I give, to details, including placement of information, punctuation, capitalization, and underlining.

Probably the best way for you to go about documenting your sources in the APA style is to put a draft of your reference list together first, following the forms in subsection B. Then, using this completed reference list and your notecards, you can go back through the body of your paper, inserting the parenthetical citations where they belong; I give you the proper forms for citations in subsection C.

B. The Reference List

1. Putting Your List Together

Your first step in putting together your reference list is to go through your paper and pull out the reference cards you have made for each of the sources you have referred to in your paper.

The next step is to put these cards in the order in which they will appear in your final list. The basic system used to order works on a reference list is to alphabetize the entries by using the last name of the first author given for every book and article. Put all sources you cite in order according to the last name of the first author given; ordinarily you will not separate books and periodicals or make any other type of subdivision. Remember that the names you cite in the body of your paper must lead your readers to the correct entry in your reference list. Thus, if, in the body of your paper, you cite an article that appears in a collection of articles, the entry that you make in your reference list must begin with the name of the author of the article, not the editor of the collection.

Here are a few more guidelines that will help you order your reference list properly.

- In placing authors' names in alphabetical order, use only the letters in the person's last name. Thus, if your list includes a work by S. H. Roberts and A. R. Robertson, the work by Roberts will come first.

- If your list includes single-author works by people with the same last name, alphabetize using the authors' first initial (and second initial, where necessary).

  Smith, B. C.
  Smith, E. F.
  Smith, H. A.
  Smith, H. B.

- If you have a series of works by the same person (let's say B. C. Smith):

  ○ List all works written by B. C. Smith alone first.
  ○ Then list works that B. C. Smith has co-authored with others, alphabetizing these co-authored works according to the last names of the second author.

    Smith, B. C. . . .
    Smith, B. C., Green, R. J., & Spade, S.
    Smith, B. C., & Weinberg, A. W.

  ○ If you have a series of works by the same author(s), list the works chronologically according to the date of publication, starting with the oldest work and ending with the most recent.

    Smith, B. C., & Weinberg, A. W. (1967).
    Smith, B. C., & Weinberg, A. W. (1972).
    Smith, B. C., & Weinberg, A. W. (1978).

  If Smith and Weinberg have published more than one work in the same year, arrange the works alphabetically according to the first word of the title (disregarding *the, an,* and *a*) and differentiate these works by putting a lowercase *a* after the date of the first work, a lowercase *b* after the date of the second work, and so on.

Smith, B. C., & Weinberg, A. W. (1977a). A case study of sexual
abuse . . .
Smith, B. C., & Weinberg, A. W. (1977b). *Sex abuse and society* . . .

2. Form for Books: Placement of Information

Information is given in the following order:

author
date
title
other publication information:
   editors, translators
   title of series
   volume of series
   volume number, or number of volumes in the set
   edition (if not the original)
facts of publication:
   city
   publisher

Author The author of a book is the person or persons responsible for what appears within the covers of the book. In many cases the person is an actual author, the person or persons who wrote the text. In other cases, the book is a collection of essays and the person responsible is an editor; in a few cases, the responsible party is a group—an agency, an institute, a corporation. In subsection B.3 of this appendix, I will show you how to write entries for books with actual authors, and books where the "author" is an editor or a group. Rather than spelling out authors' first names, use initials only.

Date The date of publication refers to the date on the title page, or the most recent copyright date of the work you use. If there is no date on the title page, check the back of the title page; use the most recent date that has a © before it. Ignore printing dates.

Title Give the full title of the book, including any subtitle. Underline the entire title. Notice that the only words capitalized in the title are (1) the first word of the title, (2) the first word of the subtitle (after the colon), (3) proper names that would always be capitalized. If the entry in your reference list is a reference to an article published in a book, the name of the author of the article and the title of the article will appear first. Titles of articles follow the capitalization rule I just gave; however, titles of articles are *not* underlined nor put in quotation marks.

Other publication information   Since you are responsible for giving your readers as much information as they will need to locate your source easily, you will need to include such information if it applies to the book you are putting in your list. I cover various examples of books with editors, translators, etc., in subsection B.3.

Facts of publication   Give the city in which the book was published. If the city is not a well-known city, also give the state (or country). If you include the state, use the United States Postal Service's abbreviations: MN, CO, TN. Put a colon after the city (and state) and then give the name of the publisher.

New York: Nosuch Press
Albany, NY: Alsono Press

3. Forms for Specific Types of Books

In the pages that follow I give you examples of the proper form for different kinds of books. Since each example focuses on one aspect of the reference form, in some cases you may need to check a couple of headings to see how to write a specific entry in your list.

a. Book—One Author

Lasch, C. (1978). The culture of narcissism: American life in an age of diminishing expectations. New York: Norton.

b. Book—Two or More Authors

Easton, S., Mills, J. M., & Winokur, D. K. (1982). Equal to the task: How working women are managing in corporate America. New York: Seaview Books.

Vacca, R., & Vacca, J. (1986). Content area reading (2nd ed.). Boston: Little, Brown.

The last name of *each* author is given first. You will have to put a comma after each last name and after each set of initials except the final one(s). Use an ampersand (&) rather than the word *and* in these citations.

c. Book with Corporate Author

If responsibility for the contents of the book is taken by an agency, corporation, or institute, use the name of this group as the author. Alphabetize

according to the first word in the name (disregarding *the, an,* and *a*). Spell
out the full name of the group.

    Council on Pediatric Practice. (1967). Standards of child health
        care. Evanston, IL: American Academy of Pediatrics.

    National Council on Crime and Delinquency. (1969). Model rules for
        juvenile courts. New York: Author.

    Office of Technology Assessment (OTA). (1982). World population and
        fertility planning technologies: The next twenty years.
        Washington, DC: Government Printing Office.

There are a couple of things you might want to note here. In the National
Council on Crime and Delinquency example, the publisher is listed as
"Author" since the National Council on Crime and Delinquency (the
author) is also the publisher. In the Office of Technology Assessment
example, you see that I have included a common acronym for this body
(OTA); in citations in the body of your paper, you could use acronyms if they
are commonly used for that organization/agency and if you give the full name
of the organization/agency in your first citation:

First citation

    (Office of Technology Assessment [OTA], 1982)

Subsequent citations

    (OTA, 1982)

If your sources include technical reports, you may want to consult the APA
Manual for detailed information about how to cite these various reports,
although you will find the basic principle for listing such works in my
examples of books in a series (see subsection B.3.i).

d. Book—Edition Other Than the Original

    Lanyon, R., & Goodstein, L. (1982). Personality assessment (2nd ed.).
        New York: Wiley.

e. Book with Author and Editor and/or Translator

    Freud, S. (1961). The future of illusion (J. Strachey, Ed. and Trans.).
        New York: Norton. (Original work published 1928)

In your paper the citation would be (Freud, 1928/1961).

f. Book with Editor Rather Than Author— A Collection of Works

Very often in the social sciences books are collections of articles written by a number of different people and collected by an editor. These books will use the editor (indicated by Ed., or Eds. for more than one) as the author. Subsection B.3.g gives an example of references to specific articles in edited collections.

> Mahowald, M. B. (Ed.). (1978). Philosophy of woman: Classical to current concepts. Indianapolis: Hackett.

> Spiro, R. J., Bruce, B. C., & Brewer, W. F. (Eds.). (1980). Theoretical issues in reading comprehension. Hillsdale, NJ: Erlbaum.

g. Work in a Collection

> Miller, N., & Gentry, K. W. (1980). Sociometric indices of children's peer interaction in the school setting. In H. C. Foot, A. J. Chapman, & J. R. Smith (Eds.), Friendship and social relations in children (pp. 145–77). New York: Wiley.

The numbers following the title are the inclusive page numbers of the article cited.

h. Book in a Multivolume Set

Reference to the Entire Set of Volumes

> Lindzey, G., & Aronson, E. (Eds.). (1969). The handbook of social psychology (5 vols., 2nd ed.). Reading, MA: Addison-Wesley.

Reference to an Article in One Volume

> Moore, W. E. (1969). Social structure and behavior. In G. Lindzey & E. Aronson (Eds.), The handbook of social psychology: Vol. 4. Group psychology and phenomena of interaction (pp. 283–322). (2nd ed.). Reading, MA: Addison-Wesley.

i. Book in a Series

Occasionally when you look at the title page of a book, you will notice that this book is part of a series; the series title may refer to subject matter (Studies in Social Economics) or to the publisher (Smithsonian Miscellaneous Collections) or to both (Wiley Series in Applied Statistics). Include information about the series in your reference. Note that information about the series is included in parentheses.

Schapera, I. (1970). <u>Tribal innovators: Tswana chiefs and social change, 1795–1940</u> (Monographs on Social Anthropology, no. 43). New York: Humanities Press.

Harris, L. S. (Ed.). (1979). <u>Problems of drug dependence, 1979</u>. (National Institute on Drug Abuse [NIDA] Research Monograph 27). Washington, DC: Government Printing Office.

Piaget, J., Grize, J.-B., Szeminska, A., & Bang, V. (1977). <u>Epistemology and psychology of functions</u> (F. X. Castellanos & V. D. Anderson, Trans. Studies in Genetic Epistemology, Vol. 23). Boston: D. Reidel. (Original work published in 1968)

Citation of this reference in the body of your paper would be (Piaget, Grize, Szeminska, & Bang, 1968/1977) or (Piaget et al., 1968/1977). See subsections C.4 and C.8.

4. Form for Scholarly Journals

Fitzgibbons, D., Goldberger, L., & Eagle, M. (1965). Field dependency and memory for incidental material. <u>Perceptual and Motor Skills</u>, <u>21</u>, 743–49.

Pickard, E. (1986). The genesis and development of creative activity. <u>Early Child Development and Care</u>, <u>23</u>, 91–100.

The numbers immediately after the titles are the journals' volume numbers; notice that APA underlines volume numbers. The last sets of numbers in the entries are the pages on which the article appears.

Most scholarly journals are paginated consecutively throughout the year, so a volume number and page numbers are all the reader needs to find an article. However, if you refer to an article in a journal that begins each issue with page 1, you will have to give your reader the issue number as well as the volume number.

<u>The Journal of Social Issues</u>, <u>38</u>(4), 99–110.

Occasionally, you will need to give your readers even more information to help them find exactly the right work.

Lazar, I., & Darlington, R. (1982). Lasting effects of early education. <u>Monographs of the Society for Research in Child Development</u>, <u>47</u>(2–3, Serial No. 195).

No page numbers are given in this entry because the entire issue is devoted to this report. The first numbers in parentheses are the issue numbers.

5. Form for Magazines

General interest periodicals, which are usually published weekly or monthly, are cited by giving the date of publication rather than volume number.

> Anderson, K. (1983, January 24). An eye for an eye: Death row (pop. 1,137) may soon lose a lot more residents to the executioner. Time, pp. 28–39.

> Mazlich, B. (1972, July). Psychohistory and Richard M. Nixon. Psychology Today, pp. 77–80; 90.

If an article does not have an author, begin your entry with the title. Alphabetize by using the first main word, disregarding *the, an,* and *a.*

6. Form for Newspaper Articles

> Kolata, G. (1987, Dec. 17). New research holds promise for dyslexics. The (Portland) Oregonian, Sunrise ed., p. G2.

> School health clinics gain patronage, support. (1987, Dec. 17). The (Portland) Oregonian, Sunrise ed., p. E12.

When listing newspaper articles, give your readers all the information they will need to locate a specific article; here I included the city of publication, since it is not part of the newspaper's title, and the edition. If section numbers are not automatically included with the page number, you should give them, too.

Articles that have no author are entered in the reference list alphabetically under the first main word of the title (disregarding *the, an,* and *a*); the citation in the body of your paper is shortened to the first word or group of words in the title ("School health clinics," 1987).

7. Forms for Other Types of Sources

In the APA style, interviews are not entered in the reference list; they are simply cited in the body of your paper. I show you the proper form in subsection C.10.

Space is too limited for me to give you forms for other types of sources you might be using in your paper. But you can use the APA *Publication Manual* to find the proper form for legal documents, sound and video recordings, reviews of books and films, and the like. If you are in the process of making out your reference cards and you do not have an APA *Manual* handy, then use your common sense. You know, for example, that one of the major purposes of documentation systems is to give readers enough information to enable them to locate your source themselves. What specific information about the source did you need in order to find it yourself? You can also look through subsections B.3 through B.6 to see, generally, the type of information the APA style requires. If you are still in doubt, I'd recommend that you write down as much information about the source as you can find on the title page, as well as page numbers, section numbers, catalogue numbers, the names and titles of various people involved in the production of the work, and the like. It seldom hurts to have too much information, but too little may leave you with a big hole in your final reference list entry.

8. The Final Reference List, including a Sample

Your reference list will be typed on a separate sheet or sheets of paper, using the same margins as those in the body of your paper. Number the pages consecutively with other pages in the text, remembering that any notes and/or appendixes will be placed between the body of the paper and the reference list. Center the heading, References, at the top of the page, leaving a line of space between it and the first entry on the list. The first line of each entry will be flush with the left-hand margin; other lines of individual entries are indented three spaces. In addressing authors preparing manuscripts for publication, the APA *Publication Manual* requires entries in the reference list to be double-spaced. This manual notes, however, that it is acceptable for students preparing papers for classes to single-space individual entries, double-spacing between entries. This is the form I suggest you use (see Appendix F, subsection B). As in all matters of style, however, your decision to double-space or single-space should be based on the recommendations of the instructor for whom you are writing the paper.

References

Freud, S. (1961). The future of illusion (J. Strachey, Ed. and Trans.). New York: Norton. (Original work published 1928)

Harcum, E. R. (1966). Visual hemifield differences as conflicts in direction of reading. Journal of Experimental Psychology, 72, 479–80.

Harcum, E. R., & Filion, R. D. L. (1963). Effects of stimulus reversals on lateral dominance in word recognition. Perceptual and Motor Skills, 17, 779–94.

Harcum, E. R., Hartman, R., & Smith, N. F. (1963). Pre- versus post-knowledge of required reproduction sequence for tachistoscopic patterns. Canadian Journal of Psychology, 17, 264–73.

Lasch, C. (1978). The culture of narcissism: American life in an age of diminishing expectations. New York: Norton.

Miller, N., & Gentry, K. W. (1980). Sociometric indices of children's peer interaction in the school setting. In H. C. Foot, A. J. Chapman, & J. R. Smith (Eds.), Friendship and social relations in children (pp. 145–77). New York: Wiley.

Office of Technology Assessment (OTA). (1982). World population and fertility planning technologies: The next twenty years. Washington, DC: Government Printing Office.

Ortony, A. (1979a). Beyond literal similarity. Psychological Review, 86, 161–80.

Ortony, A. (1979b). The role of similarity in similes and metaphors. In A. Ortony (Ed.), Metaphor and thought (pp. 186–201). Cambridge: Cambridge University Press.

School health clinics gain patronage, support. (1987, Dec. 17). The (Portland) Oregonian, Sunrise ed., p. E12.

C. Citing Sources in the Body of Your Paper

Now I will remind you that this system of documentation will work properly only if the citation you give in the body of your paper matches up with *only one* entry in your reference list. With the reference list you have just completed, go back through your paper, following steps 1 through 3 each time you cite a source in your text.

1. Find the appropriate notecard for each reference. Check what you have said in your paper against your notecard to be sure that what you have in your paper is correct. Check quotations carefully.

2. Find the source of this information or quotation in your reference list

to see that you have the appropriate author(s) and date cited correctly in your reference list. Make any additions or corrections necessary in your list.

3. In the body of your paper, give the last names of *all* authors and the date of each source exactly the way they appear in the reference list, following the forms I give in the rest of this section. Remember that, if you have added an "a" or "b" to a date, the letter must be given each time you cite the work (Smith & Jones, 1987a).

You can cite more than one source in the same citation in your paper; see subsection C.7 for more information.

1. The Basic Form for the Citation

Each citation must give the author or authors of that work and the date of publication of the source. If you are quoting the words of an author, or if you are referring to a specific part of a long work, you will also give page numbers or the number of a section or chapter (see subsection C.6).

The basic forms of the author-date system look like these examples; notice that in the citations in parentheses the authors' names are followed by a comma, and an ampersand (&) is used instead of the word "and."

```
Austin and Smith (1980) argue that behavior modificati n techniques can
be used effectively to enable people to lose weight.
```

```
Behavior modification techniques have been used successfully to enable
people to lose weight (Austin & Smith, 1980).
```

If you mention the name of the author(s) in the sentence you have written, all you need to add is the date. But you must include the names of *all* authors listed in the entry in your reference list.

When you don't mention the name(s) of the author(s) in your sentence, it is preferable to put the citation at the end of the sentence, especially if the citation is long. However, it is acceptable to put a citation after a noun or noun phrase to which the citation refers.

Acceptable

```
Investigations of anorexia nervosa (Jones & Smith, 1973, 1974, 1977a)
indicate that this self-starvation is an attempt to gain control of
one's environment.
```

Better

> Investigations of anorexia nervosa indicate that this self-starvation
> is an attempt to gain control of one's environment (Jones & Smith,
> 1973, 1974, 1977a).

2. Two Sources in Which the Authors Have the Same Last Name

If your reference list contains works by two different authors who have the same last name (Frank Smith and Carl Smith), you will have to use the author's first initial to distinguish the two.

> C. Smith (1980) has argued that the side effects of this drug are
> negligible; other researchers draw different conclusions (Albertson,
> 1976; F. Smith, 1974).

3. Source with Two Authors

> Jones and Welsh (1970) have suggested that . . .

Always spell out the word "and" when you use the names of authors as part of your sentence. When the authors' names are in parentheses, use an ampersand.

> There is evidence that . . . (Jones & Welsh, 1970).

Even if two authors have the same last name, both names must be repeated.

> Robertson and Robertson (1969) tested . . .

> Such investigations (Robertson & Robertson, 1969) . . .

4. Source with More Than Two Authors

When citing works by three to six authors, give the complete set of names the first time you refer to the work. In subsequent references to this work, use the last name of the first author, followed by "et al." (Latin abbreviation for "and others").

First Reference in Your Paper

```
Green, Short, Maximillian, and Witherspoon (1980) have shown . . .
```

Subsequent References

```
This conclusion has been questioned (Green et al., 1980).
```

```
Green et al. (1980) have shown . . .
```

If you have a source with more than six authors, use the "et al." form for all citations.

Be careful with "et al." Once in a while an "et al." could possibly refer your reader to more than one entry in your reference list. If, for example, Green wrote two works in 1980 with two different groups of co-authors, Green et al. (1980) would refer to both. In these cases, you will have to spell out all authors' names in each citation: (Green, Short, Maximillian, & Witherspoon, 1980); (Green, Harnell, Smith, & Jones, 1980).

5. Source with Corporate Author

```
(National Institute of Mental Health, 1972)
```

```
(American Psychiatric Association, 1987)
```

6. Citation That Includes Specific Pages or Sections of a Work

```
The results have been called "poppycock" (Wilson, 1980, p. 70).
```

```
Wilson (1980) has argued that these results are "poppycock" (p. 70).
```

When quoting from a work that is part of a multivolume set, you will have to include the volume number.

```
(Williams, 1986, vol. 3, p. 70)


(Jones, 1979, sec. 18.5)


(Wilson, 1972, chap. 5)


(Clark, 1984, fig. 5)
```

If you are referring to a specific portion of a book or a specific table or figure in a work, your reader would appreciate your including this information in your citation. Use an accepted abbreviation for the material (chapter, section, figure, table) to which you are referring.

7. Citation That Refers to Two or More Sources

If you are citing more than one source by different authors at the same time, arrange the works alphabetically according to the last name of the first author, and separate the references with semicolons.

```
(Hall & Smith, 1982; Kingston, Leonard, & Pepperdine, 1976; Weinstein,
1954)
```

If you are referring to several publications by the same author(s), list the dates chronologically and separate with commas.

```
Winston (1966, 1970, 1972a) has investigated . . .
```


8. Citation of a Reprint of an Older Work

Some works, especially those that are considered classics, are frequently reprinted long after their original publication date. Similarly, a work may be translated into English years after it was published in the author's own language. Because the date of publication indicates when the information in a work was made available to the public, it is important to give your readers an original publication date if the original date is appreciably older than the date of the reprint or translation.

```
(Freud, 1928/1961)
```

For full examples of reprints and translations, see subsections B.3.e and B.3.i.

9. Citation of a Source Referred to in a Second Source

As I pointed out in Section 4, subsection D.4, scholars and researchers always seek out works that are referred to in another source. However, if you wish to use information that has been mentioned in one of your sources and you have not been able to locate the original work, here's the way you should make such a citation.

- In your reference list, enter the work in which you found the material.
- When you cite this material in the body of your paper, give the author of the original work first, then cite the work in your reference list.

Your Reference List

```
Smith, C. E. (1968). The mechanisms of behavior . . .
```

Citation in Your Paper

```
Johnson (cited in Smith, 1968) found . . .
```

10. Citation of Interviews and Other Personal Communications

Sources of information from interviews you have conducted, as well as information you have received from letters, memos, telephone conversations, and other material addressed only to you, are not included in your reference list. However, the source of this information must be cited in the body of your paper, using the following form:

```
Harold Schwartz (personal communication, May 17, 1987) indicated that
the agency . . .
```

```
The agency is not serving its clients (Harold Schwartz, personal
communication, May 17, 1987).
```

If you have agreed to keep the identity of one or more of your interviewees confidential, you should refer to Section 3.B.4 to review the directions on how to handle these interviews in your paper.

D. Explanatory Notes and Appendixes

Once in a while you may feel the need to add information that is not documentation information, nor information that is central to the argument you are developing in your paper. You may include such explanations or commentaries in explanatory notes. However, before you add such explanatory notes to your paper, be sure they are appropriate. An explanatory note should never include information that is necessary to your readers' comprehension of your ideas; such information belongs directly in the body of your paper. Nor should you use notes to add information that you think is interesting but not relevant. Notes are distracting, and they take your readers' attention away from the argument of your paper.

If you decide that you have a legitimate reason to add a note, here's the procedure you should follow.

- In the body of your paper, at the end of the relevant statement, place a number, raised one-half space above the line. Notes should be numbered consecutively throughout the paper, beginning with number 1.

        . . . Freud's concept of the ego.[2]

- The note itself may be written at the bottom of the page on which the note number appears or on a separate sheet of paper headed Notes. If, in your note, you use information from a work listed in your reference list, use the same mode of citing this work that you would use in the body of your paper. If you have questions about the way your notes should be placed and the way they should look, check Appendix B, subsection B.14.

Note pages come after your reference list and any appendixes you may include.

If you feel you should include more extensive information about data you have gathered or procedures you have followed, and this information is inappropriate in your text, consider placing it in an appendix. Each appendix should begin on a new sheet of paper, headed Appendix A, Appendix B, etc., in the order in which you refer to them in the body of your paper. Your references to these appendixes will look like the references I have given to appendixes in this book: "In Appendix A complete data are given . . ." or ". . . with these data (see Appendix B)." Place the appendixes in alphabetical order after your reference list. You will find more information about appendixes in the APA *Manual.*

APPENDIX D

Scientific Systems: The Chicago Author-Date Style

A. General Information

The author-date form of documentation is the form *The Chicago Manual of Style* recommends for all the natural sciences and most of the social sciences. Although it is very similar to the APA style (the style of the American Psychological Association), APA and the Chicago author-date style are different forms. If you are writing your paper in psychology or one of the behavioral sciences, your instructor may expect you to use the APA style, which was covered in Appendix C. Otherwise, if your paper falls into the category of the social or natural sciences, the Chicago author-date style should be perfectly acceptable. If you have any doubts, you should ask your instructor.

The Chicago author-date style differs in a number of important ways from the documentation style you may be most familiar with, the humanities system that uses footnotes (or endnotes) and a bibliography. The most obvious difference is that the Chicago author-date style uses neither footnote numbers nor footnotes. Instead, the writer lets readers know the source of the information and/or ideas he or she is using by giving the last name of the author or authors of a work, and the year in which it was published, in the body of the paper.

```
Smith and Jones (1976) have found that . . .
```

```
Several studies have been done on sexist language in the workplace
(Aaron 1986; Clark and Williams 1978; Taylor 1984).
```

Full bibliographic information about each of the sources is then given in a reference list which is attached to the end of your paper.

```
Aaron, K. 1986. A study of sexist language in six major corporations.
    Journal of Corporate Behavior 46: 334–65.

Clark, S., and E. Williams. 1978. Communication styles in the
    executive suite. In Corporate communication, ed. J. Doe and
    G. Smith, 297–315. New York: Nosuch Press.

Taylor, M. E. 1984. Sexism and the female worker. San Francisco: Gold
    Coast Press.
```

Like a bibliography, the reference list is a list of works organized alphabetically according to the last name of the first author of a work. But the reference list is a critical element of the Chicago author-date documentation form since it is the only place where full information about a source is recorded. In order to use the Chicago style correctly, you should keep a few basic guidelines in mind.

- The author or authors you give in the citation in the body of your paper must be the names of the individuals whose ideas or words you used.

- The author(s) and date you give in the body of your paper must appear as the first two pieces of information in an entry in your reference list.

These two guidelines are immediately relevant to those cases in which you are using articles published in a collection of works, like the Clark and Williams example above. Obviously, you couldn't cite the editors of the collection (Doe and Smith 1978) in your paper because Doe and Smith didn't do the study you are referring to. Neither could you cite Clark and Williams in your paper and list only Doe and Smith's collection in your reference list. How would a reader know that the Clark and Williams article was published in Doe and Smith's collection? You can see in the example above how Chicago handles such cases; I give another example in subsection B.3.g.

- Similarly, for the Chicago author-date style to work, each citation in your text must match one, and only one, entry on your reference list. It is not unusual for the same author to write a number of works with various co-authors, and the same author(s) can publish more than one work in the same year. Subsection B.1. shows you how to list works that fall into these categories. Here my general advice is to be very careful about recording all authors' names in exactly the same order in which they appear on the title page. Also be sure that a citation in your paper matches one, and only one, entry in your reference list. I'll remind you of this in the next two sections.

Two final guidelines:

- You should be aware that reference lists are different from bibliographies in that reference lists contain only the works you refer to directly in your paper. This fact is made clear in such headings as Works Cited or Literature Cited, which you may have seen as alternative headings for reference lists.
- As with all documentation systems, you must follow the Chicago author-date form exactly. Pay very close attention, in the examples I give, to details like placement of information, punctuation, capitalization, and underlining.

Probably the best way for you to go about documenting your sources in the Chicago author-date style is to put a draft of your reference list together first, following the forms in subsection B. Then, using this completed reference list and your notecards, you can go back through the body of your paper, inserting the parenthetical citations where they belong; subsection C covers the proper forms for citations.

B. The Reference List

1. Putting Your List Together

Your first step in putting together your reference list is to go through your paper and pull out the reference cards you have made for each of the sources you have referred to in your paper.

The next step is to put these cards in the order in which they will appear in your final list. The basic system to put works on a reference list in order is to alphabetize the entries by using the last name of the first author given for every book and article. Order all sources you cite according to the last name of the first author given; ordinarily you should not separate books and periodicals or make any types of subdivisions. Remember that the names you cite in the body of your paper must lead your readers to the correct entry in your reference list. Thus, if, in the body of your paper, you cite an article that appears in a collection of articles, the entry that you make in your reference list must begin with the name of the author of the article, not the editor of the collection.

Here are a few more guidelines that will help you order your reference list properly.

- In placing authors' names in alphabetical order, use only the letters in the person's last name. Thus, if your list includes a work by S. H. Roberts and one by A. R. Robertson, the work by Roberts will come first.

- If your list includes single-author works by people with the same last name, alphabetize using the authors' first initial (and second initial, where necessary).

> Smith, B. C.
> Smith, C. F.
> Smith, H. A.
> Smith, H. B.

- If you have a series of works by the same person (let's say B. C. Smith):

  ○ List all works written by B. C. Smith alone first.
  ○ Then list works that B. C. Smith has co-authored with others, alphabetizing these co-authored works according to the last names of the second author.

  > Smith, B. C. . . .
  > Smith, B. C., R. J. Green, and S. Spade . . .
  > Smith, B. C., and A. W. Weinberg . . .

  ○ If you have a series of works by the same author(s), list the works chronologically according to the date of publication, starting with the oldest work and ending with the most recent.

  > Smith, B. C., and A. W. Weinberg.   1967 . . .
  > ————— .   1972 . . .
  > ————— .   1978 . . .

  If Smith and Weinberg have published more than one work in the same year, arrange the works alphabetically according to the first word of the title (disregarding *the, an,* and *a*) and differentiate these works by putting a lowercase "a" after the date of the first work, a lowercase "b" after the date of the second work, and so on.

Smith, B. C., and A. W. Weinberg. 1977a. The effects of pollution on the fish population . . .
——— . 1977b. *Pollutants in the Great Lakes.*

2. Form for Books: Placement of Information

Information is given in the following order:

author
date
title
other publication information:
    editors, translators
    title of series
    volume of series
    volume number, or number of volumes in the set
    edition (if not the original)
facts of publication:
    city
    publisher

Author   The author of a book is the person or persons responsible for what appears within the covers of that book. In many cases the person is an actual author, the person or persons who wrote the text. In other cases, the book is a collection of essays and the person responsible is an editor; in a few cases, the responsible party is a group—an agency, an institute, a corporation. Subsection B.3 of this appendix shows you how to write entries for books with actual authors and books whose "authors" are an editor or a group. In scientific writing, the preferred form is to give only the initial or initials of the author(s) rather than spelling out the first name(s). However, in the Chicago author-date style it is also acceptable to spell out first names.

Date   The date of publication refers to the date on the title page, or the most recent copyright date of the work you use. If there is no date on the title page, check the back of the title page; use the most recent date that has a © before it. Ignore printing dates.

Title   Give the full title of the book, including any subtitle. Underline the entire title. Notice that the only words capitalized in the title are (1) the first word of the title, (2) the first word of the subtitle (after the colon), (3) proper names that would always be capitalized. If the entry in your reference list is a reference to an article published in a book, the name of the author of the article and the title of the article will appear first. Titles of articles follow the capitalization rule I just gave; however, titles of articles are *not* underlined, nor are they put in quotation marks.

Other publication information   Since you are responsible for giving your readers as much information as they will need to locate your source easily, you will need to include such information if it applies to the book you are putting in your list. I cover various examples of books with editors, translators, etc., in subsection B.3.

Facts of publication   Give the city in which the book was published. If the city is not a well-known city, also give the state (or country). Put a colon after the city (and state) and then give the name of the publisher.

New York: Nosuch Press.

3. Forms for Specific Types of Books

In the pages that follow I give you examples of the proper form for different kinds of books. Since each example focuses on one aspect of the reference form, in some cases you may need to check a couple of headings to see how to write up a specific entry in your list.

a. Book—One Author

Lasch, C. 1978. The culture of narcissism: American life in an age of diminishing expectations. New York: W. W. Norton.

b. Book—Two or More Authors

Grawoig, D. E., and C. L. Hubbard. 1982. Strategic financial planning with simulation. New York and Princeton: Petrocelli Books.

Easton, S., J. M. Mills, and D. K. Winokur. 1982. Equal to the task: How workingwomen are managing in corporate America. New York: Seaview Books.

Notice that the name of the first author is inverted; be sure to put a comma after the last name and after the person's initial(s). Names of other authors are given in their normal order.

c. Book with Corporate Author

If responsibility for the contents of the book is taken by an agency, corporation, or institute, use the name of this group as the author. Alphabetize according to the first word in the name (disregarding *the, an,* and *a*). Spell out the full name of the group. Give the name of the parent body before listing subdivisions of the organization. For example, University of Maryland College of Business Administration. Center for Computer Use. Or, Smalltown Public Works Department. Streets and Roads Division. Pothole Section. If your reference list is going to include a large number of works with group authors and the names of the agencies are themselves long, consult *The Chicago Manual* for systems that will make your citations and the reference list easier to use.

> Brookings Institution. 1972. Reshaping the international economic order: A tripartite report by twelve economists from North America, the European community, and Japan. Washington, D.C.: Brookings Institution.

> Environmental Studies Board. Study on Problems of Pest Control. Forest Study Team. 1975. Forest pest control. Washington, D.C.: National Academy of Sciences.

> U.S. Congress. Office of Technology Assessment (OTA). 1982. World population and fertility planning technologies: The next twenty years. Washington, D.C.: U.S. Government Printing Office.

d. Book—Edition Other Than the Original

> Cohen, J. B., E. D. Zinbarg, and A. Zeikel. 1982. Investment analysis and portfolio management. 4th ed. Homewood, Ill.: Richard D. Irwin.

e. Book with Author and Editor and/or Translator

> Freud, S. [1928] 1961. The future of illusion. Trans. and ed. James Strachey. New York: W. W. Norton.

The first date given, in brackets, indicates the year in which the work was originally published; in your paper the citation would be (Freud [1928] 1961).

f. Book with Editor Rather Than Author— A Collection of Works

Very often in the sciences books are collections of articles written by a number of different people and gathered together by an editor. These books will use the editor (indicated by ed., or eds. for more than one) as the author. Subsection B.3.g gives an example of references to specific articles in edited collections.

Mahowald, M. B., ed. 1978. Philosophy of woman: Classical to current concepts. Indianapolis: Hackett Publishing.

Spiro, R. J., B. C. Bruce, and W. F. Brewer, eds. 1980. Theoretical issues in reading comprehension. Hillsdale, N.J.: L. Erlbaum Associates, Publishers.

g. Work in a Collection

Miller, N., and K. W. Gentry. 1980. Sociometric indices of children's peer interaction in the school setting. In Friendship and social relations in children, ed. H. C. Foot, A. J. Chapman, and J. R. Smith, 145–77. New York: John Wiley and Sons.

The numbers following the names of the editors are the inclusive page numbers of the article cited; you do not need to include these page numbers.

h. Book in a Multivolume Set

Reference to the Entire Set of Volumes

Lindzey, G., and E. Aronson, eds. 1969. The handbook of social psychology. 5 vols. 2d ed. Reading, Mass.: Addison-Wesley Publishing.

Reference to an Article in One Volume

Moore, W. E. 1969. Social structure and behavior. In Group psychology and phenomena of interaction, 283–322. Vol. 4 of The handbook of social psychology, ed. G. Lindzey and E. Aronson. 2d ed. Reading, Mass.: Addison-Wesley Publishing.

The numbers following the title indicate the page numbers on which this article appears; you do not have to include these page numbers. If the title of all volumes in a set is the same, give the title of the work and then the editors' names, both followed by commas. Then give volume number and page numbers.

In The history of physics, ed. I. Newton and A. Einstein, 176: 283–322.

or

In The history of physics, ed. I. Newton and A. Einstein, vol. 176.

i. Book in a Series

Occasionally when you look at the title page of a book, you will notice that the book is part of a series; the series title may refer to subject matter (Studies in Social Economics) or to the publisher (Smithsonian Miscellaneous Collections) or to both (Wiley Series in Applied Statistics). Include information about the series in your reference. *The Chicago Manual of Style* recommends that you give information about the series in the following order:

> name of the series, including the agency responsible for its publication if this information is not spelled out in the publication facts (capitalize main words; do not underline)
>
> volume and/or issue number of this book (if such information is given)
>
> publication facts (if the publisher's name is included in the name of the series, it need not be repeated)

Hatt, R. T. 1959. <u>The mammals of Iraq</u>. University of Michigan Museum of Zoology Miscellaneous Publications, no. 106. Ann Arbor.

Schapera, I. 1970. <u>Tribal innovators: Tswana chiefs and social change, 1795–1940</u>. Monographs on Social Anthropology, no. 43. New York: Humanities Press.

Allendoerfer, C. B., ed. 1961. <u>Symposium on differential geometry</u>. Proceedings of Symposia in Pure Mathematics, vol. 3. Providence: American Mathematical Society.

Sherald, J. L. 1982. <u>Dutch elm disease and its management</u>. U.S. Department of Interior, National Parks Services Ecological Services Bulletin, no. 6. Washington, D.C.: U.S. Government Printing Office.

Harris, L. S., ed. 1979. <u>Problems of drug dependence, 1979</u>. National Institute on Drug Abuse (NIDA) Research Monograph 27. Washington, D.C.: U.S. Government Printing Office.

Piaget, J., J. -B. Grize, A. Szeminska, and V. Bang. [1968] 1977. <u>Epistemology and psychology of functions</u>. Trans. F. X. Castellanos and V. D. Anderson. Studies in Genetic Epistemology, vol. 23. Boston: D. Reidel Publishing.

The first date given, in brackets, is the original year in which the work was published. The citation in your paper would be (Piaget, Grize, Szeminska, and Bang [1968] 1977) or (Piaget et al. [1968] 1977). See subsections C.3 and C.7.

4. Form for Scholarly Journals

Fitzgibbons, D., L. Goldberger, and M. Eagle. 1965. Field dependency
    and memory for incidental material. Perceptual and Motor Skills
    21:743–49.

Anthony, R. G., and N. S. Smith. 1977. Ecological relationships
    between mule deer and white-tailed deer in southeastern Arizona.
    Ecological Monographs 47 (Summer): 255–77.

The numbers after the journal title are the volume numbers; if you think it
would be helpful, you may add the month or quarter in which the issue of
the journal appeared in parentheses after the volume number. The last
numbers are the inclusive page numbers of the article.

Most scholarly journals are paginated consecutively throughout the year,
so a volume number and page numbers are all the reader needs to find
an article. However, if you are referring to an article in a journal that
begins each issue with page 1, you will have to give your reader further
information. The usual procedure is to give the volume number and issue
number.

Weymann, R. J. 1978. Stellar winds. Scientific American 239(2):
    44–53.

Dittman, P., D. Glasby, and C. Benenati. 1981. Logic analyzers
    simplify system integration tasks. Computer Design 20(3):
    119–29.

In these entries, the numbers in parentheses are the issue numbers.

Occasionally, you will need to give your readers even more information
to help them find exactly the right work.

Lazar, I., and R. Darlington. 1982. Lasting effects of early
    education. Monographs of the Society for Research in Child
    Development 47(2–3). Serial No. 195.

No page numbers are given in this entry because the entire issue is devoted
to this report.

5. Form for Magazines

Since general-interest periodicals, which are usually published weekly or
monthly, normally begin each issue with page 1, you must always give the
specific date or month of the issue you are referring to.

Hapgood, F. 1987. Viruses emerge as a new key for unlocking life's
    mysteries. Smithsonian, Nov., 116–27.

If the article does not have an author, begin your entry with the title. Alphabetize by using the first main word, disregarding *the, an,* and *a.* For your parenthetical citation, shorten the title by using the first word or two; if, for example, the article above had no author, your citation would be ("Viruses" 1987).

6. Form for Newspaper Articles

The Chicago Manual does not specifically give a form for newspaper articles, as they rarely appear in scientific papers. But we can modify the form for magazines to develop a form that will probably be acceptable for your paper.

```
Shaffer, R. A. 1983. Digital audio already altering recording
    industry's practices. The Wall Street Journal, 29 April, 27.

School health clinics gain patronage, support. 1987. The Oregonian
    (Portland), Sunrise ed., 17 December, E12.
```

If the article does not have an author, begin your entry with the title. Alphabetize by using the first main word, disregarding *the, an,* and *a.* For your parenthetical citation, shorten the title by using the first word or two; thus, the second example here would be cited as ("School health clinics" 1987).

7. Forms for Other Types of Sources

Information from interviews, telephone conversations, and other types of materials addressed specifically to you should be given in the following form:

```
Schwartz, Harold. Interview with author, Smalltown, Nebraska, 17 May
    1987.

Robertson, Joan. Telephone conversation with author, 25 January 1988.
```

In subsection C.9 you will find the proper way to cite such personal communications in the body of your paper. If you have agreed to keep the identity of one or more of your interviewees confidential, review Section 3.B.4 on how to handle these interviews in your paper.

Space is too limited for me to give you forms for other types of sources you might be using in your paper. But you can use *The Chicago Manual of Style* to find the proper form for public documents, sound and video recordings, reviews of books and films, and the like. If you are in the process of making out your reference cards and you do not have a *Chicago Manual* handy, then use your common sense. You know, for example, that one of the major purposes of documentation systems is to give readers enough information to enable them to locate your source themselves. What specific information about the source did you need in order to find it yourself? You can also look through subsections B.3 through B.6 to see, generally, the type of information the Chicago style requires. If you are still in doubt, I'd recommend that you write down as much information about the source as you can find on the title page, as well as page numbers, section numbers, catalogue numbers, the names and titles of various people involved in the production of the work, and the like. It never hurts to have too much information, but too little may leave you with a big hole in your final reference list entry.

8. Shortened Form of the Reference List

Primarily to save space, some scholarly journals, usually in the natural sciences, use a shortened form of the reference list. Sometimes the reference list is omitted and footnotes are used for documentation. These notes are usually given in the shortened form. The main characteristics of the shortened form are that the title of the article in a journal is omitted, and the title of the journal is abbreviated. Since this shortened form is designed for experts in a field speaking to other experts, I advise you not to use the shortened form unless you are writing your paper for an upper-division course in a discipline that normally uses the shortened form *and* your instructor has asked you to use this form. If you are expected to use this shortened form, be sure to use the accepted abbreviations for journal titles. You can learn more about the shortened form by consulting *The Chicago Manual of Style* and by examining carefully the form used in scholarly journals in the field in which you have been doing your investigation.

9. The Final Reference List, including a Sample

Your reference list will be typed on a separate sheet or sheets of paper, using the same margins as those in the body of your paper. Number the pages consecutively with other pages in the text, remembering that any notes and/or appendixes will be placed between the body of the paper and the reference list. You may head your list References or Works Cited or Literature Cited, but notice that the last two headings imply published material and should not be used if your list includes unpublished material. Center the heading at the top of the page, leaving at least one line of space between it and the first entry on the list. The first line of each entry will be flush with the left-hand margin; other lines of individual entries are indented five spaces. *The Chicago Manual of Style* advises authors to double-space reference lists. For reasons I give in Appendix F, subsection B, my advice to students preparing papers for classes is to single-space individual entries, double-spacing between them. As in all matters of style, however, your decision to double-space or single-space should be based on the recommendations of the instructor for whom you are writing the paper.

References

Freud, S. [1928] 1961. The future of illusion. Trans. and ed. James Strachey. New York: W. W. Norton.

Harcum, E. R. 1966. Visual hemifield differences as conflicts in direction of reading. Journal of Experimental Psychology 72:479–80.

Harcum, E. R., and R. D. L. Filion. 1963. Effects of stimulus reversals on lateral dominance in word recognition. Perceptual and Motor Skills 17:779–94.

Harcum, E. R., R. Hartman, and N. F. Smith. 1963. Pre- versus post-knowledge of required reproduction sequence for tachistoscopic patterns. Canadian Journal of Psychology 17:264–73.

Harcum, E. R., and N. F. Smith. 1963. Effect of preknown stimulus-reversals on apparent cerebral dominance in word recognition. Perceptual and Motor Skills 17:799–810.

Lasch, C. 1978. The culture of narcissism: American life in an age of diminishing expectations. New York: W. W. Norton.

Ortony, A. 1979a. Beyond literal similarity. Psychological Review 86:161–80.

———. 1979b. The role of similarity in similes and metaphors. In Metaphor and thought, ed. A. Ortony. Cambridge: Cambridge University Press.

Sherald, J. L. 1982. Dutch elm disease and its management. U.S. Department of Interior, National Parks Services Ecological Services Bulletin, no. 6. Washington, D.C.: U.S. Government Printing Office.

U.S. Congress. Office of Technology Assessment (OTA). 1982. World population and fertility planning technologies: The next twenty years. Washington, D.C.: U.S. Government Printing Office.

Weymann, R. J. 1978. Stellar winds. Scientific American 239(2): 44–53.

C. Citing Sources in the Body of Your Paper

The author-date system of documentation will work properly only if the citation you give in the body of your paper matches up with *only one* entry in your reference list. With the reference list you have just completed, go back through your paper, following steps 1 through 3 each time you cite a source in your text.

1. Find the appropriate notecard for each reference. Check what you have said in your paper against your notecard to be sure that what you have in your paper is correct. Check quotations carefully.

2. Find the source of this information/quotation in your reference list to see that you have the appropriate author(s) and date cited correctly in your reference list. Make any additions or corrections necessary in your list.

3. In the body of your paper, give the last names of *all* authors and the date of each source exactly the way they appear in the reference list, following the forms I give in the rest of this section. Remember that, if you have added an "a" or "b" to a date, the letter must be given each time you cite the work (Smith and Jones 1987a).

You can cite more than one source in the same citation in your paper; see subsection C.6 for more information.

1. The Basic Form for the Author-Date Citation

Each citation of a work in your reference list must give the author or authors of that work and the date of publication of the source. If you are quoting the words of an author, or if you are referring to a specific part of a long work, you will also give page numbers or the number of a section or chapter.

The basic forms of the author-date system look like these examples; in citations in parentheses there is no punctuation between the author's name and the date.

Austin and Smith (1980) argue that behavior modification techniques can be used effectively to enable people to lose weight.

Behavior modification techniques have been used successfully to enable people to lose weight (Austin and Smith 1980).

Notice that if you mention the name of the author(s) in the sentence you have written, all you need to add is the date. But you must include the names of *all* authors listed in the entry in your reference list.

When you don't mention the name(s) of the author(s) in your sentence, it is preferable to put the citation at the end of the sentence, especially if the citation is long. However, it is acceptable to put a citation after a noun or noun phrase to which the citation refers.

Acceptable

Investigations of anorexia nervosa (Jones and Smith 1973, 1974, 1977a) indicate that this self-starvation is an attempt to gain control of one's environment.

Better

Investigations of anorexia nervosa indicate that this self-starvation is an attempt to gain control of one's environment (Jones and Smith 1973, 1974, 1977a).

2. Two Sources in Which the Authors Have the Same Last Name

If your reference list contains works by two different authors who have the same last name (Frank Smith and Carl Smith), you will have to use the author's first initial to distinguish the two.

C. Smith (1980) has argued that the side effects of DMSO are negligible; other researchers draw different conclusions (Albertson 1976; F. Smith 1974).

3. Source with Two or More Authors

Jones and Welsh (1970) have suggested that . . .

There is evidence that . . . (Jones and Welsh 1970).

```
In a recent study Williams, Valdez, and Yamada (1984) found . . .
```

```
There is evidence that . . . (Williams, Valdez, and Yamada 1984).
```

Even if two authors have the same last name, both names must be repeated.

```
Robertson and Robertson (1969) tested . . .
```

```
Such investigations (Robertson and Robertson 1969) . . .
```

In works with four or more authors, use the last name of the first author plus "et al." (Latin abbreviation for "and others"). Thus, Green, Short, Maximillian, and Witherspoon become Green et al.

```
Green et al. (1980) have found . . .
```

```
There is evidence that . . . (Green et al. 1980).
```

But before you shorten a citation in this way, double-check your reference list carefully. If Green is the primary author of two or more co-authored works published in 1980, your (Green et al. 1980) citation could refer to more than one entry on your reference list. In these cases, you will have to spell out all authors' names in each citation: (Green, Short, Maximillian, and Witherspoon 1980).

4. Source with Corporate Author

```
(National Institute of Mental Health 1972)
```

```
(American Psychiatric Association 1987)
```

5. Citation That includes Specific Pages or Sections of a Work

Whenever you quote directly from a source, you must include the page number(s) in the citation.

```
The results have been called "poppycock" (Wilson 1980, 70).
```

```
Wilson (1980) has argued that these results are "poppycock" (p. 70).
```

When quoting from a work that is part of a multivolume set, you will have to include the volume number. Separate volume number and page number with a colon.

```
(Jones 1976, 3:197)
```

If you are referring to a specific portion of a book or a specific table or figure in a work, your reader would appreciate it if you would include this information in your citation. Use an accepted abbreviation for the material (chapter, section, figure, table) to which you are referring.

```
(Jones 1979, sec. 18.5)
```

```
(Wilson 1972, chap. 5)
```

```
(Clark 1984, fig. 5)
```

6. Citation That Refers to Two or More Sources

If you are citing more than one source by different authors at the same time, arrange the works alphabetically according to the last name of the first author, and separate the references with semicolons.

```
(Hall and Smith 1982; Kingston, Leonard, and Pepperdine 1976;
Weinstein 1954).
```

If you are referring to several publications by the same author(s), list the dates chronologically and separate with commas.

```
Winston (1966, 1970, 1972a) has investigated . . .
```

7. Citation of a Reprint of an Older Work

Some works, especially those that are considered classics, are frequently reprinted long after their original publication date. Similarly, a work may be translated into English years after it was published in the author's language. Because the date of publication indicates when the information in a work was made available to the public, it is important to give your readers an original publication date if the original date is appreciably older than the date of the reprint or translation.

(Freud [1928] 1961)

For full examples of reprints and translations, see subsections B.3.e and B.3.i.

8. Citation of a Source Referred to in a Second Source

As I first pointed out in Section 4, subsection D.4, scholars and researchers always seek out the originals of works that are referred to in another source. However, if you wish to use information that has been mentioned in one of your sources and you have not been able to locate the original work, here's the way you should make such a citation.

- In your reference list, enter the work in which you found the material.
- When you cite this material in the body of your paper, give the author of the original work first, then cite the work in your reference list.

Your Reference List

Smith, C. E. 1968. The mechanisms of behavior . . .

Citation in Your Paper

Johnson (cited in Smith 1968) found . . .

9. Citation of Interviews and Other Personal Communications

Harold Schwartz (interview 1987) indicated that . . .

The agency is not financially solvent (Robertson, pers. com. 1988).

In the last example, "pers. com." stands for "personal communication." If you have agreed to keep the identity of one or more of your interviewees confidential, turn back to Section 3.B.4 to review how to handle these interviews in your paper.

D. Explanatory Notes and Appendixes

Once in a while you may feel the need to add information that is neither documentation information nor information that is central to the argument you are developing in your paper. You may include such explanations or commentaries in explanatory notes. However, before you add such explanatory notes to your paper, be sure they are appropriate. An explanatory note should never include information that is central to your readers' comprehension of your ideas; this information belongs directly in the body of your paper. Nor should you use notes to add information that you think is interesting but not relevant. Notes are distracting, and they take your readers' attention away from the argument of your paper.

If you decide that you have a legitimate reason to add a note, here's the procedure you should follow.

- In the body of your paper, at the end of the relevant statement, place a number, raised one-half space above the line. Notes should be numbered consecutively throughout the paper, beginning with number 1.

```
   . . . Freud's concept of the ego.²
```

- The note itself may be written at the bottom of the page on which the note number appears or on a separate sheet of paper headed Notes at the end of the paper, before your reference list. If, in your note, you use information from a work listed in your reference list, use the same mode of citing this work that you would use in the body of your paper. If you have questions about the way your notes should be placed and the way they should look, check Appendix B, subsection B.14.

If you feel you should include more extensive information about data you have gathered or procedures you have followed, and this information is inappropriate in your text, consider placing it in an appendix. Each appendix should begin on a new sheet of paper, headed Appendix A, Appendix B, etc., in the order in which you refer to them in the body of

your paper. Your references to these appendixes will look like the references
I have given to appendixes in this book: "In Appendix A complete data are
given . . ." or ". . . with these data (see Appendix B)." Place the
appendixes in alphabetical order before your reference list. You will find
more information about appendixes in the *The Chicago Manual of Style* or
Kate Turabian's *Manual for Writers of Term Papers, Theses and Dissertations.*

APPENDIX E

Scientific Systems: The Numbered Reference List Form

A. General Information

The numbered reference list form is not as popular as the author-date form, but it is used in some scholarly journals in the natural sciences. Use this system of documentation only if your instructor has asked you to use this form.

The numbered reference list form resembles the traditional humanities system in that numbers are used to refer readers to sources. But there are two major differences between the traditional humanities system and the numbered reference list form. First of all, the numbers in the body of a paper using a numbered reference list are enclosed in parentheses or brackets, like this [12]. Second, whereas the numbers in the traditional humanities system refer to notes at the bottom of the page or at the end of the paper, reference list numbers, as the name implies, direct the readers to a reference list—the scientific equivalent of the bibliography—at the end of the paper. The reference list resembles the reference list in the author-date form, except that each entry in the list has a number in front of it. Thus, when readers see [12] in the paper, they know that they will find full bibliographic information about the source in entry number 12 on the reference list.

There are two variations of this numbered reference list form.

1. In the first variation, the works in the reference list are numbered according to the order in which they are cited in the body of the paper. If, later in her paper, the author refers to a work she has already mentioned, she simply uses the number of that earlier citation.

2. The other variation uses a reference list that is first ordered alphabetically according to the last name of the authors of sources. Then the completed list is numbered.

The numbered reference list system should not be confused with systems, found in many journals in the natural sciences, that use numbers in parentheses or brackets in the body of the paper but which refer to footnotes at the bottom of the page (see Appendix D, subsection B.8).

B. How to Set Up the Numbered Reference List Form

1. Setting Up the Reference List

I have recommended that you not use this system unless your instructor has asked for it, simply because appropriate forms for the reference list can vary; different styles affect the ordering of information in an entry in the list (where you put such things as title of journals, volume number, date of publication, etc.) and the form in which this information is given. Thus, if your instructor wants you to use a numbered reference list, you need to ask him or her for guidance about style. If he or she approves, you may use the reference list form for the Chicago scientific style I give in Appendix D, subsection B. You should not use the APA style in a numbered reference list.

If you decide to list your entries in the order in which your sources appear in your paper, it would be easiest to enter your reference numbers in the body of your paper as you order your list. Thus, you should follow the steps listed in subsection B.2. Since it is critical that the number in the body of your paper correspond with the correct source, plan to write up a rough copy of the reference list as you are entering its numbers in your paper. After you've double-checked the information on your notecard, write the number of the source on the rough draft of your list along with the author and title of that source; also write this number on the reference card itself and put these reference cards in a stack in numerical order as you go along. Then write the proper number of the source in the body of your paper (see subsection B.2.a and b). Remember that you will list a source only once on the list, and all references to that source will have the same number; so if you assign the number 3 to Richard Green's article "Bees," all references in the paper to Green's "Bees," no matter where they come in the paper, will be (3).

If you have decided to list your references alphabetically, make a stack of all of the reference cards of the sources you have referred to in the body of your paper and alphabetize them according to the last name of the first author given. Once the list is complete, you will assign each source a number— 1 for the first entry on the list, 2 for the second, and so on.

Regardless of which of these two variations you use, you will type your reference list on a separate sheet of paper headed References or Works Cited. At the left-hand margin, type the number of the entry and then follow the style your instructor has advised you to use in typing each individual entry. If you would like a *general* idea of what reference lists look like, see Appendix D.B.9.

2. Citing Sources in Your Paper

I would suggest that you follow these steps in citing your sources:

1. Go through the body of your paper, beginning on page 1. Stop at each sentence where you've indicated that you have used one or more of your sources.
2. Double-check the information in the body of your paper against your notecard to be sure the information in your paper is correct.
3. Find the number of the source in your numbered reference list, and insert this number in the body of your paper.

a. Form of Citation

You may put the number in parentheses or in brackets. The number may appear in regular type, or it may be underlined. You may choose which of these forms you like, but once you make your choice, you must use the same form throughout your paper.

b. Placement of Citation

The number should be placed after the name of an author if you mention the author's name in your sentence.

```
According to Jones and Weston (12) . . .
```

If you do not give the name of the author, the number should be placed after the statement that includes the information you have taken from this source.

```
Reduction by ZT3 produces salt and iodine (4).
```

If you wish to cite more than one source, list the entry numbers in numerical order, separated by commas.

```
Investigations have revealed that . . . (1, 12, 17).
```

If you give two pieces of information in one sentence that come from two different sources, place the numbers of the appropriate sources directly after the statement that includes the information.

```
PQR was extracted from the solution (6) and quantified by the
Smith-Jones method (14).
```

C. *Explanatory Notes and Appendixes*

Once in a while you may want to give your readers further explanation of a term or procedure you have used, or you may want to comment on something you have said in the body of your paper. The procedure for such explanatory notes is to put a footnote number in the paper at the end of the relevant sentence. Obviously, this footnote number must look different from your reference list numbers or your readers will think you are referring to a work in your reference list. The normal form for a footnote number is a number raised one-half space above the line.

```
. . . in this procedure, reactive CH4 was used.[2]
```

The note should then be placed at the bottom of the page on which the number appears, separated from the body of your paper with a line. In Appendix B, subsection B.14, you will find more information about the proper placement of footnotes.

Be very careful about explanatory notes. If you decide you want to use an explanatory note, you should ask yourself why you need this note. If the information in the note is critical to the readers' understanding of the point you are making, the information should be in the body of your paper. If the information is interesting but not really relevant to the paper, it probably should be omitted. Footnote numbers are distracting. They encourage the reader to stop reading the text and look down to the bottom of the page. If you interrupt your readers too often, or if you interrupt the readers to give them irrelevant information, they will not follow your paper properly. If you feel you should include more extensive information about data you have used or procedures you have followed, and this information is inappropriate in your text, consider placing it in an appendix or appendixes at the end of the paper. You will find information about appendixes in *The Chicago Manual of Style* or Kate Turabian's *Manual for Writers of Term Papers, Theses, and Dissertations.*

APPENDIX F

The Final Manuscript of Your Paper

After you have documented your sources, you have only three steps left:

- to copyedit the final rough draft;
- to type your paper;
- to proofread the typed copy.

If you have been writing your paper on a word processor, you won't have to worry about the second step because your paper is already "in type." But whether you have been composing on a word processor or your paper still needs to be typed (by you or someone else), you still need to reach a point where you declare your paper finished. Making this decision is important, because with it you will shift from "writing" to "copyediting." The distinction I am making between "writing" and "copyediting" is the distinction between making changes that affect the content of your paper, and making changes that assure that your paper is stylistically and/or mechanically correct. In order to do a good job of editing, you have to resist making any substantive changes and focus all your attention on the type of stylistic and mechanical features that are discussed in subsection A.

If you are working on a word processor, switching from "writing" to "copyediting" could be difficult because it is so easy to begin by changing a word, which may lead to rewriting a sentence, which, since you have changed the meaning and focus of this sentence, may then require revising the whole paragraph. If you find yourself changing from editing to writing, you may want to print out a copy of your paper and do your editing on the printed version. Then you can be strict with yourself, allowing yourself to change only what you have marked on the printed copy. If you have a spell-checker, be sure to use it; and use the guidelines in subsection B to set up the format of the whole paper.

If you don't have a word processor, you should plan to take the time to copyedit the complete rough draft first, to make a clean, easy-to-read final rough copy that you will then simply type. A pair of scissors and glue or transparent tape make it easy enough to create such a clean, easy-to-read manuscript. When you type a paper, you should be simply transcribing; it's the best way to increase your typing speed and cut down on typing errors. When someone else types your paper for you, it is very important to give your typist a clean, easy-to-read manuscript if you expect an accurate typed copy in return.

A. *Copyediting*

Copyediting involves reading your paper from beginning to end, focusing on one paragraph at a time. The following list indicates the types of stylistic and mechanical features you want to pay attention to.

- Be sure each sentence leads the readers clearly from one idea to the next.
- Check your word choice. Be sure the words you've used are words that precisely reflect the ideas you are trying to convey. Eliminate slang and expressions that are too casual for formal papers.
- If you are using numbers in your paper, you should be aware that the commonly accepted style is to spell out numbers if they can be expressed in one or two words and to use numerals if more than two words are necessary.

    two hundred books   1,512 subjects
    a million dollars   412 ships

You should not begin a sentence with a numeral. If you are writing a scientific paper in which there are many numbers, check Turabian, the APA *Publication Manual,* or *The Chicago Manual of Style* for their recommendations about the proper style for numbers.

- If you want to use abbreviations in your paper, be sure you have told your reader what the abbreviation stands for. The first time you refer to the company, chemical compound, or organization, give the full name first and put the abbreviation after it in parentheses.

  ```
  Dimethylsulfoxide (DMSO) is a chemical compound . . .
  ```

  ```
  A leader in this field is International Business Machines (IBM), a
  corporation that . . .
  ```

- To be sure your quotations are in a proper form, check Section 6, subsection B.4.

  A Note on Punctuation and Quotation Marks   Commas and periods are always put *inside* quotation marks.

  ```
  Marble and other cold objects are central images in his poem
  "Death."
  ```

  ```
  Describing the loss as "overwhelming," General Smith promptly
  resigned his post.
  ```

  Semicolons and colons are placed outside the quotation marks. Question marks and exclamation points are placed inside the quotation marks if they are part of the quotation; if they punctuate your sentence, they are placed outside the quotation marks.

  ```
  The speech ends with a question: "What is real?"
  ```

  ```
  Did anyone hear him say "I give up"?
  ```

- Be sure titles in your paper are in their proper form. The rule of thumb is very simple. If a work was published originally as an independent, separate unit, the title should be underlined. Thus the titles of books, journals and magazines, record albums, films, operas are underlined. If a work was originally published within a larger, independent unit, these titles are placed in quotation marks. Thus, if a poem was originally published in a magazine, the title of the poem will be placed in quotation marks. Similarly, the titles of chapters of a book, the titles of essays and articles, the titles of songs or cuts on a record album are put in quotation marks.

A Note on Capitalization in Titles   *The Chicago Manual* gives the following guidelines for capitalizing words in the titles of works:

Capitalized	*Not capitalized*
the first word in title	articles *(a, an, the)*, unless first
the last word in title	word in title or subtitle
all nouns	coordinate conjunctions *(and,*
all pronouns	*but, or, for, nor)*, unless first
all adjectives	word in title or subtitle
all verbs	prepositions *(from, including, to,*
all adverbs	*at, of,* etc.), unless first or last
all subordinate conjunctions	word in title or subtitle
(because, since, unless,	the *to* in an infinitive *(to be, to*
before, after, etc.)	*go, to work,* etc.)

- Be sure the grammar of each sentence is correct.

  - Do pronouns have antecedents? Do the pronouns agree with their antecedents? (. . . the company. It . . .; Scientists. . . . They . . .).
  - Do subjects and verbs agree in number?
  - Is the base tense of your paper consistent? If you are treating an event or events as if they occurred in the past, always refer to these events in the past tense; if you are treating an event or events as if they are occurring now, always use the present tense. What you want to *avoid* is referring to such events in the past tense in one sentence or paragraph, and then switching to the present tense in another sentence or paragraph.

```
        Hamlet was very upset by his father's death, so upset that he
contemplated suicide. . . .
        In this play, Claudius and Gertrude are unwitting villains.
They act as if they are concerned about Hamlet's welfare, at least
at first. . . .
```

- Proofread; correct all errors in spelling and punctuation.
- If you have used the traditional humanities form of documentation, be sure that note numbers in the text correspond with the correct footnote or endnote.

If you have questions about stylistic issues that I have not covered here, check Turabian or an appropriate style manual for the discipline in which you are writing.

B. *Typing: The Format of the Paper*

If you have taken a look at one of the Turabian books or other authoritative style manuals, you know that much of the material in these books is related to the appearance of the final paper. Because most of these manuals are written for authors preparing manuscripts for publication, some of this information may not apply to a paper being prepared for a class. For example, most style manuals advise authors to double-space everything in the manuscript because double-spacing makes it easier for editors to proofread and compositors to set the manuscript into type. Since you are preparing a final manuscript, a text that will be read in the format in which you type it, your concerns should be choosing a format that makes your prose easy to read and that approximates the appearance of printed texts. For these reasons, I have suggested single-spacing block quotations, notes, entries in bibliographies and reference lists. In this section I make other suggestions about the format of your paper. These suggestions are only suggestions. Your guide in matters of manuscript style should always be the recommendations or preferences of the instructor for whom you are preparing your paper. If he or she expects you to follow the manuscript form given in a particular style manual, that is obviously what you should do.

A first step in making your paper easy to read is attending to mechanical matters. Choose a clean and readable typeface—and be sure your printer's ribbon is fresh. If you are using a typewriter, I suggest that you use medium to heavyweight typing paper (sixteen- or twenty-pound). Don't use flimsy paper like onionskin and try to avoid erasable paper that smears when you run your finger over typed lines. If you are using a cloth typewriter ribbon, be sure it is fresh; as a teacher I can tell you that it is very irritating to try to decipher a paper typed with a ribbon that died several papers ago.

Title and title page   In my view, your research paper should have a separate title page. The title of the paper itself should give the reader a clear picture of the content of the paper, even though you may consider such a title boring. Clever titles are fun to create, but they may be very frustrating to the reader, as you yourself may have learned when you were using indexes and the card catalogue.

Frustrating

Fun and Games

Better

`Using Game Theory to Analyze the Ethiopian-Somalian Conflict`

There is no widely accepted form for a title page. If your instructor specifies no preferred format, I recommend this format.

- Center your title about one-third of the way down the sheet of paper. Capitalize only the first letters of central words (see note on capitalization in titles on page 300). In some aesthetically pleasing fashion, give the following information:

  your full name
  the number and title of the course
  the full name of the instructor
  the due date of the paper

Margins   While specific widths for margins vary in the recommendations of different style manuals, any margin less than 1 inch would be unacceptable. I suggest 1-1/4 (or 1-1/2) inches on the left and 1 inch on the other three sides.Remember that footnotes must be placed within these margins. Although I have encouraged you to use these same margins for note pages, bibliographies, and reference lists, you should be aware that some style manuals require deeper top margins for these pages and, sometimes, for the first page of the paper.

Page numbers   I prefer that students put page numbers in the upper right-hand corner of the page, and I like to see the student's last name typed before the page number. Word-processing programs call these "running heads"; setting them up on the computer is very simple.

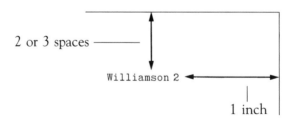

The numbering of nontextual material (endnote pages, bibliography, appendixes, etc.) varies; I would recommend simply numbering all pages in your paper consecutively. Thus, if the last page of your text is page 14, the first page of your endnotes would be page 15, and so on.

Headings and table of contents   If you are doing a primary research report, you will use headings in the body of your paper (see Section 5, subsection B). A table of contents isn't really necessary. If you have written a secondary research paper, whether or not you separate your paper into divisions and subdivisions signaled by headings will depend upon the length and nature of the paper. Headings break the readers' attention, signaling a major transition. Thus, headings would be obtrusive in the middle of a tightly organized argument. On the other hand, if your paper is very long and the argument is rather complex, headings can be helpful to the reader. Again, if you are not sure if it would be appropriate to use headings, consult your instructor.

If you decide that headings are appropriate for your paper, your outline should suggest what headings you should use and where they should be inserted. All headings should follow the parallel-structure rule: express all headings in the same grammatical form (all phrases, or all sentences). For more information on headings, I recommend that you consult *The Chicago Manual of Style*. If your paper is divided into a number of divisions and subdivisions, a table of contents might be useful to the readers. *The Chicago Manual of Style* or Turabian can give you more information about the format.

Tables, charts, and graphs   If you are giving your readers statistical information, charts and graphs can be useful visual aids. To be most effective, such charts and graphs should be placed in the body of the paper at those points where you refer to the information on these charts and graphs. In Turabian you will find helpful guidelines on this subject.

Appendixes   An appendix is what we might call a very long explanatory note. If you wish to include detailed information relevant to some part of your paper, information that does not belong in the text of the paper, you may place it in an appendix, which will be put at the end of your paper. Raw data used in a primary research paper are often compiled in appendixes; in secondary research papers, you will sometimes find documents, like letters or legal documents, reproduced in appendixes for the readers' information. If you decide that you have material that should be put in an appendix, you will find more information about the format of appendixes in Turabian.

C. *Proofreading*

The last step is to proofread the final typed copy. I realize that by the time you have finished typing your paper you never want to see it again. On the other hand, any error that appears on this final copy is, in the eyes of your readers, an error for which you are responsible and errors will detract from the paper. Think about how far you have come since you started this research project months ago. Do you want to risk having all your hard work graded down by your instructor because the paper is full of typos? Ideally (and I realize that I am talking about ideals) you should put the typed copy aside for a day, or at least a few hours, before you attempt to proofread it. Under any circumstances it is hard for people to proofread what they have written; we tend to look at a sentence, say "I know what that says," and not look carefully at the spelling and punctuation (which is what proofreading involves). It is almost impossible to proofread directly after typing a paper. The best solution is to try to type the paper before you go to bed, then to proofread it the next morning, before you turn it in. Correct all errors neatly in pen (black ink looks best). Pages with a large number of errors should be retyped or, if you are using a computer, corrected and printed again.

Four Sample Research Papers

NOTE: In addition to illustrating the documentation form of the MLA style, these two papers also conform to certain recommendations of the MLA regarding manuscript form, such as double-spacing and indentation of block quotations in "The Forgotten Women" paper, and the absence of a title page in the "Willa Cather" paper.

MLA format papers can also be prepared with name, instructor's name, course title, and date appearing in the upper left-hand corner of the first page of the paper

The Forgotten Women:

British Nurses, VADs, and Doctors across the Channel

during World War I

The title page should contain an aesthetically pleasing placement of the paper title, paper author, and course/instructor/date

by

Elizabeth Cookson

History 400

Britain in the Era of World War I

David Savage

June 1, 1981

The thesis is
stated at the
beginning of
the outline

Outline

Thesis: An examination of the writings of British women who
served in the combat areas in World War I as nurses,
doctors, and VADs reveals that, for these women, the
war proved to be a positive and profound experience
that was filled with contradictions.

I. Once the war began, women were eager to serve on the
front.

   A. As the war years went on, the number of women serving
as nurses and members of the VAD (Voluntary Aid
Detachment) grew.

   B. Although the number of nurses, VADs, and women
doctors needed at the front was small, many women
went to great efforts to get to the combat zones.

II. As their writings show, for the British women who worked
as nurses, VADs, and doctors near the lines of fighting,
World War I proved to be a positive and profound
experience which was, nonetheless, filled with
contradictions.

   A. Looking forward to serving at the front, these women
were filled with excitement and considered themselves
setting out on an adventure.

   B. Once in service near the battlefields, these women
reveal in their writings the hardships and stresses
of their jobs; for many, the ability to withstand
these hardships made for a personal triumph of will.

   C. Constant exposure to the grotesque and horrible
sights of severely wounded men had a numbing effect on
these women, most probably a reaction to the
underlying anguish and helplessness they felt in the
face of so much suffering.

D. The shellings, another reminder of their proximity to the fighting, created mixed reactions of distress and a typically British attitude of keeping a stiff upper lip; with the hospitals full of wounded and dying men, the shellings were constant reminders of the carnage and instability of life during war.

E. In spite of the horrors and tragic nature of the work, these women seemed to find it strangely compelling and were reluctant to leave; another instance of their contradictory reactions to their war service is their record of moments of adventure they experienced while in the war zones.

F. Yet, at the same time, they were fully aware of the terrible toll the war was taking on the people and countries of Europe and expressed their hatred of war in their writings.

G. Another indication of the contradictions the war created in them is their record of pleasant times while on service at the front.

III. While it seems strange that many of these nurses, VADs, and doctors greeted the end of their war service with sadness, perhaps their reluctance to return home can be explained by the fact that on the front many of these women had their first taste of freedom, and into what had been retiring and quiet lives, the war brought danger, excitement, fear, and the sense of participating and living life to the utmost.

Cookson 1

Running head with author's name and page number ½ inch from top of page

"The Rose That Grows in No-Man's Land"

It's the one red rose,
The soldier knows;
It's the work of the Master's hand.
In the war's great curse
Stood the Red Cross Nurse,
She's the rose in No-Man's-Land!

Song, 1916

A woman child. She dream'd the dreams of men.
Of fiery purposes, and battle's din.
She left her dolls to play with soldier toys
And glow'd in enterprise of heroes bold.
Such child—
Grown to the kingdom of her woman's heart,
Goes forth with joy beneath her country's flag.
Gives her skill to those who call for aid.
She faces death in many cruel guise,
Holding life cheap, for honour and her King.

A. M. Johns, 1916[1]

Superscript numerals indicate explanatory footnotes at the bottom of the same page

When Great Britain plunged into World War I on August 1, 1914, the British people responded with patriotic enthusiasm. Men volunteered for active duty by the thousands, and women were not far behind in their efforts to help with "The Cause." Responding to the government's pleas for aid, British women took over traditionally male jobs, serving as police officers, tram drivers, munitions workers, and farm laborers.

Text of the paper should be double-spaced

---

[1] "The Rose That Grows in No-Man's Land" quoted in Adam 54; Johns quoted in Matthews ii.

Cookson 2

One more traditional area which attracted thousands of
women was that of nursing and hospital work. By the time World
War I began, nursing was already a well-organized and
respected profession for women. Professional nurses were
supplemented by the Voluntary Aid Detachment, which had been
developed in 1909. VADs received lectures in first aid and
home nursing (Helen Fraser 55-56). The war, however, created
the demand for thousands of extra nurses and VADs. The Times
of May 7, 1915, noted that:

> Every day at Devonshire House a long stream of women,
> varying in age from 23 to 38, are seen by the standing
> committee which has been appointed to deal with the
> application made by the War Office for 3,000 members
> of the Voluntary Aid Detachment to help in military
> hospitals in the coming months. ("Nurses" 1915)

Louise Dalby, in her lecture The Great War and Women's
Liberation, noted that most of the VADs were young women from
middle- and upper-class families to whom farm labor and
munitions work was unappealing (9). Under the orders of the
Joint War Committee, the VADs were to do the cooking, cleaning,
and light nursing tasks in order to relieve the work load of
the professional nurses.

When the war began in August 1914 there were only 463
nurses employed in Queen Alexandra's Imperial Nursing
Service, and on August 12, 1916, The Times reported:

> As a result of the appeal made in The Times on
> behalf of the British Red Cross Society for nurses
> for the military hospitals, more than 3,000 women
> have already volunteered, but many more are urgently
> needed.

Miss Swift, matron-in-chief of the Joint

Author's first name given because list of works cited has two authors named Fraser

Author's name in text; only page number in parentheses

1 inch from bottom of page

Cookson 3

Committee, said yesterday that she has vacancies for
nurses of one or two years' training and also nurses
with fever experience as staff nurses. New hospitals
are being opened, and the work is increasing.

   ("Nurses" 1916; see also Marwick 84)

By November 1918 the number of nurses employed in war work had
risen to 13,000 (Marwick 167-68). The VAD movement grew, too,
from 47,000 women in August 1914 to 83,000 by April 1920
(167-68). During the war, the majority of the nurses and VADs
were employed in civilian and military hospitals in Great
Britain, but a small percentage served near the combat zones in
Belgium, France, Serbia, and elsewhere. In August 1918 there
were 2,396 nurses and 2,547 VADs on the Continent with the
British Expeditionary Force, and 285 nurses and 657 VADs with
the British Red Cross and other independent organizations in
France (167-68). The Times cautioned would-be volunteers
that, "It is impossible to stipulate for foreign service as
the proportion of nurses needed abroad is comparatively small"
("Nurses" 1916). Only about 6 percent of the nursing force was
required for service overseas.

   The British Red Cross Society and the Order of St. John
worked together under the title of the Joint War Committee.
This committee developed extremely stringent terms for
service abroad. VADs, for example, had a one-month
probationary period; thereafter they were required to sign a
declaration to serve six months. They did not receive a
salary, but room, board, and traveling expenses were paid
("Military").

   In spite of these disadvantages, service in France and
elsewhere in Europe was considered to be a thing of great
social status and prestige. Perhaps the thought of nursing

Source of quotation cited first, followed by reference to another source containing similar information; separated by semicolons

Date included with short title to distinguish from another article with same title; no page number necessary when article one page long

Cookson 4

foreign, as well as British, soldiers added to the appeal.
Young women begged to be allowed to cross the Channel. One
woman who worked at the headquarters of the British Red Cross
remembered, "all day long there came an endless procession of
women wanting to help . . . some anxious for adventure and
clamouring 'to go to the front at once' " (Thurstan 3).

*Single quota-
tion marks
indicate words
quoted in
source*

Women doctors were also anxious to help on the Continent.
A few of these women organized and funded groups themselves
when they were denied permission to help. After being told to
"go home and keep quiet," Dr. Elsie Inglis founded the Scottish
Women's Hospitals in Russia and Serbia (Dalby 8). The three
hospitals were staffed entirely by women. Dr. Elizabeth
Garret Anderson and Dr. Flora Murray were similarly dismissed,
so they offered their services to the French, who accepted
their aid with delight (8).

*When source
of informa-
tion obvious,
not necessary
to repeat
author's name*

A number of the British women who finally made it to the
Continent wrote of their experiences in the zones of battle.
While much attention and scholarly effort has been expended in
analyzing the memoirs, letters, and journals of the British
soldiers, little or no attention has been given to the
writings of the women who worked within a few miles of the
actual fighting. As the war had a profound effect on the men
who fought in the trenches, so it affected the women who heard
the noise of battles and attempted to care for the wounded the
war churned out daily. For the British women who worked as
nurses, VADs, and doctors near the lines of fighting, World War
I proved to be a positive and profound experience which was,
nonetheless, filled with contradictions. The women
experienced times of despair and fear, but also enjoyed the
adventures, challenges, excitement, and companionship which
went with service overseas.

Cookson 5

*Text begins 1
inch from
top of page*

For these women, the adventure began upon receiving
notice of being selected for duty abroad. The overwhelming
reaction of the women was one of excitement. In September 1914
one professional nurse noted, "Proudly they [the Territorial
nurses] went away, clad in military uniform, whilst those left
behind envied them with an almost bitter envy" (<u>War</u> 3). When
writing of her own efforts to go abroad, the same nurse said,
"Speaking for myself, to want a thing badly means to get it--if
possible. When the Servians [sic] started I went to the Matron
and asked permission to be released from my services."
Finally, she received a telegram: "ten nurses wanted at once
for Antwerp; must be voluntary" (3,4). She quickly wired her
acceptance, and after weeks of waiting she received a telegram
to "meet the nine-thirty boat train, Victoria, tonight." She
packed "in delighted excitement" and rushed off to catch her
train (51).

*[sic] is placed
after a word to
indicate that
error comes
from original
source*

Nursing Sister Violetta Thurstan could not suppress her
excitement when she was allowed to go to Belgium in the fall of
1914. Thurstan wrote, "On Monday afternoon I was interviewing
my nurses, saying good-bye to friends--shopping in between--
wildly trying to get everything I wanted at the eleventh
hour. . ." (6).

Vera Brittain, a young VAD, volunteered for duty
overseas in 1916 mainly to escape her parents and her thoughts
of her fiance's death. But despite the saddening causes for
her departure, Vera noted "the exhilaration of that day
[of departure] still lives on in the pages of my diary"
(367).

As a volunteer in 1914 for the English Motor Field
Ambulance Corps, Mary Sinclair noted the frustration and
competition involved in getting to Belgium:

Cookson 6

> After the painful births and deaths of I don't know
> how many committees, after six weeks struggling
> with something we imagined to be Red Tape, which
> proved to be the combined egoism of several
> persons all desperately anxious to "get to the
> Front," and all desperately afraid of somebody
> else getting there too, and getting there
> first, we were actually off. (168)

The few positions for service abroad were greeted with eager
competition by the women of Great Britain. The dreams of
adventure and excitement and the mysterious qualities of
foreign peoples and places must have added greatly to the
mystique of serving overseas.

Once overseas, however, the women were inundated by the
frantic and unceasing work demanded by hospitals near the
Front. During a "push" or special attack, the numbers of
wounded men doubled and trebled from the normal load, over 300
arriving in a night in some instances (Marwick 96). In spite of
the long, hard hours and back-breaking work, the nurses and
VADs delighted in the challenge. Vera Brittain, rather
cynically looking back on her early days as a VAD, remarked,
"Every task, from the dressing of a dangerous wound to the
scrubbing of a bed-mackintosh, had for us in those early days a
sacred glamour which redeemed it equally from tedium and

disgust" (210). VAD Sarah Macnaughtan concurred, but noted
that "the girls, of course, and very naturally, were all keen
about ward work. No one had come out to Antwerp to wait on or
cook for an English staff, for instance. They must serve
soldiers!" (27).

As soon as work began, though, it seemed to many to be an
unceasing treadmill. One nurse noted, "How those [first] five

Cookson 7

weeks passed is just a vague impression of constant work,
conflicting rumours, rush and weariness. I can remember
nothing consecutively" (<u>War</u> 10). She went on to describe her
work in further detail:

> My friend and I had a large flat containing fourteen
> wards, with seventy men to attend to. We had no
> orderlies. . . . All the patients were gravely
> wounded; they usually required two dressings a
> day. . . . The meals alone were a perfect nightmare to
> get served, as scarcely any patient could feed
> himself. For the first two weeks there were only two
> of us to do everything. (10-11)

Ellipses within quotations indicate material omitted

A young VAD, in a letter to her uncle, wrote:

> I cannot write properly, as I am dog-tired. We had a
> convoy of wounded, 266 on Friday night and 70 on
> Saturday. They came straight from the trenches into
> the wards after a two days' journey, thick with
> Champagne mud and lice and blood. It is trying to
> cut off clothes and dress wounds by candle-light.
> For two nights and three days we did not take our
> clothes off or our hairpins out. Things are better
> now, but I do forty-one dressings every day and work
> from 7:30 a.m. till 8 p.m., with only one break for
> lunch. (<u>Letters</u> 12-13)

This and other VAD reports conflict noticeably with a general
report issued by the Joint War Committee after the war. The
report stated that "The V.A.D. members were not . . . trained
nurses; nor were they entrusted with trained nurses' work
except on occasions when the emergency was so great that no
other course was open" (qtd. in Brittain 410). The reading of
VAD accounts would indicate that the realities of war nursing

Sources with no author cited by first major word in title; listed alphabetically by this word in list of works cited

made it expedient for VADs routinely to perform professional
nursing duties.

For most of the women who worked in the military hospitals
on the Continent, the hours were long, the breaks few, and the
work many times overwhelming. But though they wrote of the
strains and stresses involved in their jobs, the ability to
withstand the rigor and hardships made for a personal triumph
of will. One woman, a radiographer in France, writing under
the pseudonym of Skia, exulted: "During the battle of the
Somme the strain was terrific--physically, psychologically.
We were stretched taut, and not a strand of the rope was frayed.
We held!" (621).

Though most British women seemed to take the long hours
and pressures of work in their stride, the awful reality of
brutally wounded men proved to be another matter. To the
inexperienced VADs and nurses used to working in civilian
hospitals, the sight of hundreds of grossly wounded men had a
startling and profound impact.

VAD Lesley Smith wrote about the wounded with stark
simplicity. "Day after day," she said,

> we cut down stinking bandages and exposed wounds which
> destroyed the whole original plan of the body . . . [In
> surgery] the leg I was holding came off with a jerk and
> I sat down still clasping the foot. I stuffed the leg
> in the dressing pail beside the other arms and legs.
> The marquee grew hotter and hotter and the sweat ran off
> the surgeons' faces. (qtd. in Mitchell 201)

Vera Brittain recalled

> . . .standing alone in a newly created circle of hell
> during the "emergency" of March 22nd, 1918, and
> gazing, half hypnotised, at the dishevelled boots and

*Quotation
taken from sec-
ondary source;
author of these
words given
in text*

Cookson 9

> piles of muddy khaki, the brown blankets turned back
> from smashed limbs bound to splints by filthy blood—
> stained bandages. Beneath each stinking wad of sodden
> wool and gauze an obscene horror waited me--and all the
> equipment I had . . . was one pair of forceps. (410)

Skia remembered a similar experience as "a nightmare of glaring lights, appalling stenches of ether and chloroform" (622). Violetta Thurstan made use of the same noun:

> It is a dreadful nightmare to look back at. Blood-
> stained uniforms hastily cut off soldiers were lying on
> the floor--half-open packets of dressing were on
> every locker . . . men were moaning with pain, calling
> for water, begging that their dressings might be done
> again. (24)

One nurse wrote simply:

> It becomes monotonous to tell you again that all the
> hundreds and hundreds of men we nursed were far
> spent--suffering from shock collapse, excessive
> hemorrhage, broken to pieces, all in agony. . .
>
>   * *
>
> Some were so terribly burned that it was difficult to
> tell where their faces were; how they lived is a
> marvel to us, for no features seemed left to them. We
> had sometimes to force an opening where the mouth had
> been to insert a tube to feed them. (<u>War</u> 20, 62)

Constant exposure to such grotesque and horrible sights invariably had a numbing effect on the women. Vera Brittain described the effect as a shutter which came down and allowed her to cease thinking (380). Mary Borden, an English nurse who worked in a French hospital, described many of the sensations in a short story she wrote:

*Colon intro-
duces quotation
when quotation
an appositive of
the complete
sentence pre-
ceding it*

*Asterisks indi-
cate a substan-
tial amount of
original source
omitted. In
parenthetical
citation, num-
ber before
comma indi-
cates page from
which words
quoted before
asterisks were
taken; number
after comma is
page number of
quoted words
after asterisks*

She [a nurse] is no longer a woman. She is dead
already, just as I am--really dead, past
resurrection. Her heart is dead. She killed it.
She couldn't bear to feel it jumping in her side when
Life, the sick animal, choked and rattled in her
arms. Her ears are deaf; she deafened them. She
could not bear to hear Life crying and mewing. She
is blind so that she cannot see the torn parts of men
she must handle. Blind, deaf, dead--she is strong,
efficient, fit to consort with gods and demons--a
machine inhabited by a ghost of a woman--soulless,
past redeeming, just as I am--just as I will be.
(59-60)

Mary Borden's words illustrate the underlying anguish and
helplessness the women must have felt when they were
overwhelmed by the severely and mortally wounded men who
seemed to flood the hospitals.

While caring for the wounded served as a constant reminder
of the war, the British women working on the Continent were
reminded in other ways of their proximity to the Front.
Taubes, German airplanes, often flew over the military
hospitals. One VAD working near Verdun said that she was soon
able, from the sound of the shells, to determine the size and
kind of shells being thrown (Bowser 219).

Both author and page number given in parentheses

Reactions to the shellings were mixed. Violetta
Thurstan described the shells as making "a most horrible
scream before bursting, like an animal in pain," but noted
that she found it hard to "realize that all this was happening
to us, one felt rather like a disinterested spectator in a
far-off dream" (136). Lady Helena Gleichen, who worked with a
mobile X-ray unit in Italy, treated the whole experience

Source of quotation introduced in text both by name and by those credentials that give credibility to her words

Cookson 11

as a joke. The shell, she wrote, "finally landed with a tremendous bang in the middle of the road we had at that moment left. . . . And the moral of this little episode is that it is no use fussing where you are, as shells may come anywhere" (158).

One British nurse, however, was understandably upset by the close proximity to her of the falling shells. Her friend thus had to remind her, ''Remember we are British women, not emotional continentals. We've got to keep our heads" (War 22). Sarah Macnaughtan described an incident full of the same stiff-upper-lip attitude. During a prolonged shelling, the nurse and VADs walked through the streets to return to the hospital. It was, she felt, "a matter of honour with us all not to walk too quickly. There is a British obstinacy, of which one saw a great deal during the war, which refuses to hurry for a beastly German shell" (41-42).

Period placed after parentheses

Several women found that the sounds of war were oppressive and served as constant reminders of the carnage and instability of life during a war. Vera Brittain mused that the sounds of war which whispered in the wind created an atmosphere which was always tense and restless, making complete peace impossible (372). Skia concurred that "the bombing, by night, night after night, when from a crowded hospital full of helpless men one hears the sinister sound beating nearer and nearer, with the sure knowledge that death and destruction are in store for some hapless mortal, is horrible" (638). But it was B. G. Mure, a VAD in France, who realistically noted that "at first the sound was nerve-racking, but the human imagination soon tires, and before long a vague sadness, sometimes merely a sense of irritation at the tragic stupidity of the thing to which we listened, replaced our first emotion" (458).

In spite of the horrors and the tragic nature of the work, the women seemed to find it strangely compelling and were reluctant to leave the zones of action. As units and organizations broke up, or left for the safety of England, many of the women stayed behind to offer their services to other organizations. When Violetta Thurstan's unit was forced to leave Belgium under the rapid advance of the German troops, Violetta was seriously ill. She rejoiced at her fever, thinking it would give her a legitimate excuse to stay behind (77). Dr. Caroline Matthews, serving in Serbia, proclaimed, "I was glad I stayed! Looking back I know it was worth it all" (72). One nurse wrote factually:

> We had come to Belgium to nurse the Belgians; what society we served under was a matter of indifference to us. If our party chose to go home to England, we meant to stay. . . . So we quietly went round to the Belgian Croix Rouge and offered our services. They accepted us with open arms. (War 38)

In the strangely contradictory nature of war, the women who worked abroad found moments of excitement and adventure during their service. Mrs. St. Clair Stobart, working in hospitals and ambulance units in Serbia and France, thought that the German airplane which flew over the hospital grounds dropping bombs was "an exciting diversion" (5). Helena Gleichen collected shell-cases as souvenirs (175). B. G. Mure recalled that "there was a certain thrill in the knowledge that we were actually in a country invaded by the enemy" (446).

May Sinclair described the sense of excitement which came from working so closely to danger and death:

> It is only a little thrill, so far (for you don't really believe there is any danger), but you can

Cookson quotes only those specific words that support and illustrate the point she's making

imagine the thing growing, growing steadily until it
becomes ecstasy. Not that you imagine anything at
the moment. At the moment you are no longer a
thinking, reflecting being; you have ceased to be
aware of yourself; you exist only in that quiet
steady thrill which is so unlike any excitement you
have ever known. Presently you get used to it.
"What a fool I would have been if I hadn't come. I
wouldn't have missed this run for the world."
(170-71)

Retreating under a German advance, Violetta Thurston found
that

> Danger always adds a spice to every entertainment,
> and as the wounded were all out and we had nobody but
> ourselves to think about, we could enjoy our
> thrilling departure from Lodz under heavy fire to
> the uttermost. And I must say I have rarely enjoyed
> anything more. It was simply glorious spinning
> along in that car. (141-42)

In another incident, when a Russian regiment began firing on a
Taube, Violetta Thurstan admitted that she ran a much greater
risk "of being killed by a Russian bullet than by the German
Taube." But her overwhelming emotion seems to have been
regret for her failure to bring along a camera to record the
moment (147).

*Period always
inside quotation
marks*

Another nurse, who rode in a car being shelled by a Taube,
noted, "It was great fun! I looked longingly at the fragments
falling all over the road, but could not prevail upon the
parson [the driver] to pull up whilst we gathered a few bits for
presents to our home people" (War 59). It must be mentioned
that this same nurse replied with the true British

understatement of "Rather" when she was asked if she cared to eject a shell at the Boches! (66). Perhaps Violetta Thurstan summed up the seductive nature of the joy rides, daring escapes, and bombing activity when she wrote, "The forbidden has always charms" (103).

In spite of a certain devil-may-care attitude toward the danger to themselves, the British women were made fully aware of the effects of the war on the countries in which they resided and their peoples. The sights and sounds of the war were constant reminders of the bloody turmoil and struggle. One young VAD despaired, "Sometimes I wish I could make governments and politicians spend a month or two working with me. Can anyone justify so much blighting of young lives and crippling of young bodies?" (Letters 24).

After watching refugees stream into Brussels, Violetta Thurstan realized for the first time what war entailed. She discerned, "It was not just rival armies fighting battles, it was civilians--men, women, and children--losing their homes, possessions, their country, even their lives" (11-12). L. E. Fraser, working in the Serbian unit of the Scottish Women's Hospital, complained that

> The men who go home usually do not tell what they have seen,--they think it unfit for women to hear. Being a woman myself I have no such feelings and when I come home I shall tell every one I can what war really means. I believe that if every one quite realised it we should never have another war again. It is a cruel, senseless waste of life, and no one is finally any better for it. (796-97)

L. E. Fraser summed up her feelings succinctly. "War," she wrote, "is still the damn'dest piece of silliness the

Cookson tells us how to interpret words from her source

devil ever invented" (791).

    Though sharing an abject horror of the war, the British women on the Continent also shared some pleasant memories. The nurses, doctors, and VADs did manage to get some time off duty. They went to teas and dinners, visited other villages, and entertained friends. These little everyday activities seemed to bring some semblance of security to the women. In the spring of 1916, one nurse remembered only the pleasant sights, "the quiet country-fields being plowed, birds building nests, larks soaring in the air" (<u>War</u> 94-95). The same woman remembered when she had

> . . .strolled along the banks of the little brooks where forget-me-nots fringed the edges, passed through farmyards where nuns in their quaint costumes sat on three-legged stools milking cows, and soldiers leaned over the gates laughing and chatting. By-the-by the sun sank, a ball of fire, while the mist rose like a veil from the low flat country. (114-15)

A VAD who served in France recalled:

> There were bright moments when friends got down from the line for a 48-hour leave and with another girl as chaperone, as we were never allowed out by ourselves, we could bathe--it was the summer of 1917--and lunch, with someone near the door to see that the Commandant was not about! (qtd. in Marwick 99-100)

Perhaps it was these lighter, more pleasant activities that made it possible for the British women to continue working. Their life was not, after all, sheer unadulterated drudgery and despair. The VADs and nurses were, for the most part, young women. No doubt a touch of romance and beautiful spring weather helped to make their work on the hospital wards more bearable.

In the fall of 1918, however, the war finally ended, and the last of the British nurses, VADs, and doctors could go home to England. But whether the women left while the war still continued or held out until the war ended, they were surprisingly unhappy and sad to leave. Many had found friends and formed close relationships with their fellow workers. While serving near the lines of action, the women had had the satisfaction of knowing that they were directly participating in the war effort.

One nurse remembered:

> In spite of the contact with suffering, misery and death, to us doctors and nurses there was a great share of happiness and the joy of life. It is a great thing to feel that you are fighting death and saving heroes, besides which we were a very happy crowd.
> (War 52-53)

Violetta Thurstan recalled tasting the "joys of companionship to the full, the taking and giving, and helping and being helped in a way that would be impossible to conceive in an ordinary world" (174). One woman remembered the satisfaction of ''real hard work where [I was] . . . really needed" (Stone 183). Vera Brittain was forced by the demands of her parents to leave France to care for her mother. Once back in England she grieved "for the friendly, exhausting, peril-threatened existence [she] . . . had left behind in Etaples" (435).

Thus, the British women who served in Belgium, France, Italy, Serbia, Russia, and elsewhere had mixed feelings about their World War I experiences. For many, perhaps, the war

Brackets indicate words that have been added or changed in original quoted material

Cookson 17

brought the first taste of freedom; the young women were on
their own and out of their parents' houses. The war was,
without a doubt, a shocking and eye-opening experience,
particularly for the relatively sheltered VADs. The sights of
suffering and pain from war injuries had to be seen to be
imagined and understood. Into what had been quiet and
retiring lives, the war brought danger, excitement, fear, and
the sense of participating in and living life to the utmost.
Quiet Dr. Caroline Matthews underlined her passionate words,
"Life was worth living in those days . . . " (72). Other side
products of World War I for these women were the joys of
companionship and the challenges and responsibilities of
caring for severely wounded men. While the women on the whole
felt sickened and saddened by the war debris--the dead, the
dying, and the wounded--they invariably regretted leaving
when their tenure ended.

One nurse wrote sadly upon her return to London, "life
seemed flat after the stirring events through which we had just
passed" (War 47-48). Vera Brittain recalled that for her the
Armistice meant that "already this was a different world from
the one I had known during the four long years. . . . And in that
brightly lit, alien world I should have no part" (463). But
it was Lesley Smith who most acutely discerned that the fun,
adventures, exhilaration, despair, the living and
participating in life to the fullest had ended. On the ship,
returning home to England, Lesley reported with a sad kind of
acceptance the question a kind and interested person asked, "I
suppose you're going to settle down at home now and buy clothes
and do the flowers for mother?" (Mitchell 202). It is
significant that Lesley Smith failed to record her own reply.

Cookson 18

Works Cited

Adam, Ruth. A Woman's Place, 1910-1975. London: Chatto and
     Windus, 1975.

Borden, Mary. The Forbidden Zone. London: Heinemann, 1929.

Bowser, Thekla. Britain's Civilian Volunteers: Authorized
     Story of British Voluntary Aid Detachment Work in the
     Great War. New York: Moffat, Yard, 1917.

Brittain, Vera. Testament of Youth. 1933. London: Wideview
     Books, 1980.

Dalby, Louise Elliott. The Great War and Women's Liberation.
     Skidmore College Faculty Research Lecture. Saratoga
     Springs, NY: Skidmore College, 1970.

Fraser, Helen. Women and War Work. New York: G. Arnold Shaw,
     1918.

Fraser, L. E. "Diary of a Dresser in the Serbian Unit of the
     Scottish Women's Hospital." Blackwood's Magazine June
     1915: 776-797.

Gleichen, Helena. "A Mobile X-Ray Section on the Italian
     Front." Blackwood's Magazine July 1918: 145-177.
     Letters from a French Hospital. Boston: Houghton, 1917.

Macnaughtan, Sarah. A Woman's Diary of the War. London:
     Nelson, n.d.

Marwick, Arthur. Women at War, 1914-1918. London: Fontana
     Paperbacks in association with the Imperial War Museum,
     1977.

Matthews, Dr. Caroline. Experience of a Woman Doctor in
     Serbia. London: Mills and Boon, 1916.

"Military Hospitals an Urgent V.A.D. Appeal." The Times
     (London) 19 April 1917: 9e.

Mitchell, David. Monstrous Regiment: The Story of the Women
     of the First World War. New York: Macmillan, 1965.

"Works Cited" always begins on a new page. Heading centered 1 inch from top of page. All lines double-spaced

Sample book entry

Sample magazine article entry

n.d. [no date] indicates work has no copyright or printing date

Second and subsequent lines in entries indented 5 spaces

Cookson 19

Mure, B. G. "A Side Issue of the War." <u>Blackwood's Magazine</u>
October 1916: 444-469.

"Nurses for Military Hospitals." <u>The Times</u> (London) 7 May
1915: 5c.

"Nurses for Military Hospitals." <u>The Times</u> (London) 12
August 1916: 9c.

Sinclair, May. "The War of Liberation: From a Journal." <u>The
English Review</u> 20-21 (June-July 1915): 168-183, 303-314,
468-476.

Skia. "A Hospital in France." <u>Blackwood's Magazine</u> November
1918: 613-640.

Stobart, Mrs. St. Clair. "A Woman in the Midst of the War: The
Remarkable Recital of a Woman Twice Sentenced to Be Shot,
and Who Went through the History-Making Scenes of Louvain,
Brussels, and Antwerp." <u>The Ladies' Home Journal</u>
January 1915: 4-5, 43-79.

Stone, Gilbert, ed. <u>Women War Workers: Accounts Contributed
by Representative Workers of the Work Done by Women in
the More Important Branches of War Employment</u>. New York:
Crowell, 1917.

Thurstan, Violetta. <u>Field Hospital and Flying Column: Being
the Journal of an English Nursing Sister in Belgium and
Russia</u>. London: Putnam's, 1915.

<u>A War Nurse's Diary: Sketches from a Belgian Field Hospital</u>.
New York: Macmillan, 1918.

*Sample news-
paper articles*

*Sample journal
entry*

*Sample book
by editor entry*

*Work with no
author listed al-
phabetically
according to
first main word
in title*

Jennifer Welsh

Following the English 470
MLA *Hand-*
book, *author's* Professor Berkson
name and in- February 18, 1988
formation
about course
given on first
page of text in
upper left-hand Willa Cather: Challenging the Canon
corner

       The literary canon of American classics of the nineteenth
and early twentieth centuries is composed nearly exclusively
of works by male writers. The fact that this canon was created
by predominantly male writers and critics in a male-dominated
world of academia explains this imbalance to a certain extent.
Yet this canon has had accepted and unchallenged authority for
so long that its sources are rarely questioned. Writers like
Melville, Hawthorne, Emerson, and James are considered the
Text is double- "masters," and other writers are often obscured by the years
spaced
of praise and criticism built up around these "classics."
Only recently, nearly a century later, have the criteria of
establishing a classic been re-evaluated through a contemporary perspective.

       In her article "When We Dead Awaken: Writing as
Re-vision," Adrienne Rich argues the necessity of "looking
back, of seeing with fresh eyes, of entering an old text from a
new critical direction" (18). The "critical direction" she
speaks of is the new basis of feminist theory that has
developed over the past few decades. The "fresh eyes" are
those that have a clearer vision of how gender functions in
today's society and the historical roots of gender-specific
roles. Rich promotes this process of "re-vision" not simply

as a new critical approach but as an "act of survival. Until
we can understand the assumptions in which we are drenched we
cannot know ourselves" (18). The crux of this statement is
"assumptions." This is where literature begins to function
not solely as an art form but as a reflection of the context of
shared values and beliefs that make up the society in which it
is written. These assumptions must be explored and questioned
when re-evaluating the canon of "classics" of the nineteenth
and early twentieth centuries.

Several important theories have been presented
concerning the patterns and common ideals of this body of
literature. R. W. B. Lewis presents the archetypal figure of
the "American Adam," and compares the perceptions of America
found in the literature of the nineteenth century to the
biblical Garden of Eden. In this myth the New World discovered
and claimed by the pilgrims was seen as a fresh start. The land
was wild and untainted by generations of European dominance,
and (so the myth goes) the courageous men who came to conquer
this land left their roots behind and started over, pitting
themselves against the unknown. The "American Adam" was "a
figure of heroic innocence and vast potentialities poised at
the start of a new history" (Lewis 1). Among the many
characteristics of this archetype that Lewis describes,
celibacy is an important factor. Exploring the land and
facing various adventures, the Adam is free from any
restraining ties (i.e., women).

*Author and
page number in
parentheses*

Yet given this myth, which can be identified in the works
of Twain, Melville, Emerson, and many others, where does the
woman find herself in the literature? In her book The Faces of
Eve, Judith Fryer presents four archetypal roles of women
found in this male literature: the Temptress, the American

Welsh 3

Princess, the Great Mother, and the New Woman (24-25). Fryer's
descriptions of these roles are interesting if somewhat
controversial, yet they each offer undeniably distressing
portrayals of women's options. Each archetype defines itself
in relation to men. The American Eve is either tempting Adam
into sin, depending on Adam for protection of her virtue,
striving for power over Adam, or trying to escape Adam by
escaping from life itself. For a woman reading this
literature these are hardly attractive options with which to
identify.

Nina Baym draws on the theory that women are excluded from
the canon and forced to identify with its male figures, and
goes on to explore the reasons for this situation. In her
article "Melodramas of Beset Manhood," she argues that since

American literary criticism is based on content, and since the
quality of this content cannot be compared to the European
traditions from which it is trying to assert its independence,
then the evaluation of its quality must lie in its
"Americanness" itself. Defining this Americanness presents
obvious difficulties. Yet Baym contends that criteria of
"Americanness" did form. She states that two conditions must
be met: "America as a nation must be the ultimate subject of
the work," and the purpose of writing must be to "display, to
meditate" on certain aspects of this nation in order to
"derive from them certain generalizations and conclusions
about the'American experience'" (127). Baym goes on to argue
that women's fiction of the period, although popularly read,
was not considered to reflect American experience: "The
certainty here that stories about women could not contain the
essence of American culture means that the matter of American

experience is inherently male" (130). Baym concludes that

Welsh 4

women are not likely to write successful novels that reflect solely male experience and are therefore excluded from the canon of American authors.

    If these theories are what arise from examination of the traditional canon, then Adrienne Rich's call for "re-vision" does indeed seem crucial. How could today's developing feminist literature ever have taken root with such an imbalanced heritage? Obviously we must look outside the sphere of the male classic to find the missing link. We must make use of our present broader, more egalitarian understanding of gender relations to look again at the literature of the past centuries in order to acknowledge and explore the female literary tradition that has been eclipsed for so many generations. The new, revised canon that appears under this re-examination includes authors such as Dickinson, Stowe, Alcott, Fuller, Chopin, and Cather. In works of these authors one finds a whole new understanding of American experience as defined by the woman's perspective. For each of these authors the experience of developing and fulfilling themselves as women writers living and working in a patriarchal culture had a profound effect on their literature. Some, such as Louisa May Alcott and Kate Chopin, wrote from within the sphere of conventional society, exploring the repression experienced by women. Others, notably Willa Cather, struggled to create characters who formed their identity outside of the conventions. In creating such characters, Cather has developed an alternative conception of women than that offered by the literature of her male counterparts.

    The conventional role of women during the nineteenth century was quite narrow and explicit. Barbara Welter terms

Running head with author's name and page number ½ inch from top of page; text begins 1 inch from top of page

Welsh summarizes author's basic argument; since the source of the information is clear because author and title given in the text, only page numbers need be cited

this phenomenon the "Cult of True Womanhood" in her book

Dimity Convictions: The American Woman in the Nineteenth

Century. These conventions were based on the premise that the

difference between the sexes was total and innate (4). Women

had no place in the men's realm and vice versa. Welter

presents four "cardinal virtues" of femininity: piety,

purity, submissiveness, and domesticity (21). These ideals

were socialized into each generation of women by their mothers

and formed the governing rules of their lives. Piety was

considered the superior domain of women; not only were they

responsible for their own morality but for that of their

husbands as well (21). Religion was the sacred interest

outside of themselves and one of the few worthy causes for

which to use their talent and energies. Purity was the

essential virtue and property of the woman, to be guarded until

the marriage night at which time it, and therefore the woman

herself, would become the property of the man (24).

Submissiveness was the key to obtaining all other rewards.

Only key phrases quoted directly

The subservience of women to men was "the order of the

Universe" itself and not to be tampered with (28). Finally,

domesticity was the happy culminating state of a woman's life.

All of her childhood and adolescence was geared toward

reaching the goal of marriage and only by marrying could she

achieve the status that men achieved through education and

work (8). All of a wife's efforts and good qualities were put

into helping the husband to rise in the world (16). A happy

home and husband made a happy woman (10) and provided security

from the evils of the outside world (31). The state of being

a woman was equated with these virtues to the end that failure

in any one category made them, in Welter's words,

"semi-women . . . mental hermaphrodites" (40). Like Judith

Fryer's archetypal figures the True Woman derived her identity
and satisfaction only from her role in relation to men and
rarely sought fulfillment of her own self as a way of achieving
womanhood.

Yet Willa Cather, among other emerging writers of her
time, challenges this definition of womanhood in her female
characters. Cather creates women that form their identities
outside of the traditional sphere of the home, choosing
instead the land to reflect their ambitions and desires. She
creates characters who struggle to evolve outside of the
conventional identity of woman as wife and mother, dependent
on men for their existence. When Cather does place a woman in a
conventional role, she portrays her situation as insecure,
dependent, and frustrating. Yet Cather's conception of these
characters did not grow out of a serene and certain background
of belief in the inherent strength of women. She struggled
with her identity both as a woman and a writer and these
struggles are often reflected in her characters.

Willa Cather was born in 1873 in Back Creek, Virginia, and
eventually moved with her parents and six younger brothers and
sisters to the plains of Nebraska in 1883 and finally to the
nearby town of Red Cloud in 1884. Her father, Charles Cather,
was a gentle and well-read man who was quite pleased with his
daughter and encouraged her intellectual ambitions. His
soft-spoken, aesthetic character eventually provided the
model for several of her characters, such as Mr. Shimerda and
Carl Linstrum, alternatives to the powerful, domineering,
masculine stereotype of the time (O'Brien, Willa Cather 14).
Both of Willa's grandmothers, Caroline Cather and Rachel
Silbert Boak, and one great-aunt, Sidney Cather Gore, were
strong women who found ways to express and assert themselves

*Title of work
included since
list of works
cited contains
two works
by this author*

while still remaining within the boundaries set for nineteenth-century women. Willa's mother was a complex personality and may have contributed to Cather's ambiguities about her own femininity.

In her biography of Cather (Willa Cather 39-41), Sharon O'Brien presents Mary Virginia Boak Cather as a beautiful, impeccably dressed product of a boarding-school education. She was well-versed in society's codes and her efforts at socializing Willa into these codes met with a great deal of resistance. On the one hand she was a strong-willed disciplinarian and overshadowed her husband in the home. Yet, O'Brien points out, she didn't seem to exercise much control over her own life. She was often sick, a victim of the classic nineteenth-century woman's disease, hysteria, and relied passively on the care of doctors during these periods. Often her illness followed the birth of a child and one can't help but wonder whether she really wanted seven children. She also allowed Charles to move the family to Nebraska despite her strong objections, and once there sank into even more frequent bouts of illness.

O'Brien suggests that these contradictions within Cather's mother's character contributed to Cather's own ambivalence toward the female role in general (42-46). Cather struggled with her desire for identification and connection with her mother, yet feared losing her own sense of self when faced with her mother's domineering, powerful nature. She also recognized the futility of her mother's strength when she succumbed to her bouts of illness and to the decisions of her husband.

Cather's view of women in this early period of her life was complex to say the least. As an adolescent she declared

Welsh 8

herself William Cather and took on a male persona in both
public and private life. According to O'Brien, socialization
into the role of the passive woman was repulsive to Cather and
the only way to accommodate her ambitions as an artist was to
reject the female identity categorically. By doing so she
placed herself at the other end of a socially constructed
dichotomy, not resolving the conflict, simply perpetuating it
(100-101). Cather dropped her male persona after her first two
years at the University of Nebraska but she still saw herself
as deviant because of her intimate relationships with other
women.

Author's name repeated to acknowledge source of specific information

Intimate female relationships were socially condoned
during most of the nineteenth century and often known as Boston
Marriages. This acceptance was due to the belief that women
had no sexual nature and therefore no ability to have sexual
relations between themselves (Smith-Rosenberg 8). But with
the advent of new psychosexual theories came the tendency to
label these relationships deviant by the turn of the century.
Cather identifies herself as lesbian, despite the fact that
the word didn't exist at the time, by admitting to the
"unfortunately deviant" nature of her friendship with Louise
Pound (O'Brien, "The Thing Not Named" 580-585). Cather
continued to have relationships with other women throughout
her life. Phyllis Robinson says of her attachment to Edith
Lewis, "Their life together was undoubtedly a marriage in
every sense. But Willa was too conscious of her ties to home
and family, and too much a conservative Midwesterner herself,
to live openly with Edith" (208).

Period placed after parenthesis

In her analysis of Willa Cather's female characters,
Susan Rosowski suggests that each woman must struggle to
synthesize two selves. The first is the worldy, interactive

self exposed to family and friends, while the second is the imaginative and creative inner self. The struggle is against imposed social roles that can trap the woman in one self or the other (261-62). Cather denied seeing herself as a woman for some time in order to see herself as an artist, and she openly scorned women who tried to be both.

One of the factors in Cather's upbringing that contributed to this rejection of female creativity was the body of literature that Cather read as a child. The literature she was exposed to and drawn toward during these crucial formative years of her life had a major impact on her future perception of herself and of the creative process. Not surprisingly, nearly all the authors she encountered were male and she strongly identified with the male adventurer-hero, similar to Lewis' American Adam, of classics such as Treasure Island, Tom Sawyer, Huckleberry Finn, Robinson Crusoe, The Count of Monte Cristo, The Iliad, The Odyssey, and even Pilgrim's Progress and Emerson's writings (O'Brien, Willa Cather 82-84). In her university days in Lincoln, Nebraska, and later, Cather saw creativity as an exclusively male property and publicly scorned women's writing. As Phyllis Robinson states in her biography, "About her own sex Willa was inclined to be uncharitable. . . . 'Sometimes I wonder why God ever trusts talent in the hands of women, they usually make such an infernal mess of it,' she wrote. She thought women were sentimental and horribly subjective" (56).

Sharon O'Brien suggests that Cather's acquaintance with Sarah Orne Jewett provided the key to her resolution of herself as woman and writer. By encouraging Cather to express women's feelings and intimacy in her writing, and through the example of her own work, Jewett fostered a respect for the female voice

Single quotation marks indicate words quoted in original source

(O'Brien, <u>Willa Cather</u> 334-350). The development of Cather's
female characters often centers around their struggle to
emerge as women and creators, to synthesize their two selves,
and they often succeed. Yet it is difficult to argue that her
characters' successes mark a definite resolution of Cather's
own conflicts. Both Alexandra and Thea in <u>O Pioneers!</u> and <u>The
Song of the Lark</u> are creators and women, yet <u>My Antonia</u> and
<u>A Lost Lady</u>, both written after the previous two books, use a
male narrator who is introduced as the creator writing of his
muse, the female protagonist. Cather's use of this male
narrator seems a step back into the schism between woman and
artist.

    Cather led an unconventional life for her time period and
it was perhaps the individuality and independence that she
developed while struggling with the various conflicts
encountered in her own life that allowed her to create such
strong and unconventional characters in her literature.
Alexandra and Thea are strong, positive alternatives to the
limited options offered by the male writers of the period, and
Antonia and Marian Forrester portray the struggle and
sacrifices that women had to undergo to establish their
identities in the face of the limitations society put on them.

    In <u>O Pioneers!</u>, Cather relates the history of Alexandra
Bergson's struggle to define herself in her own terms and to
accomplish her goals in her own way. From the beginning Cather
presents Alexandra as a character who challenges female
stereotypes. She walks "rapidly and resolutely as if she knew
exactly where she was going and what she was going to do next"
(6). She carries herself not as a woman trying to market
herself in a male world but as someone whose body reflects her
inner strength: "her body was in an attitude of perfect

Short quotations subordinated to Welsh's main point and used to support general point

repose, such as it was apt to take when she was thinking earnestly" (61). When a traveling man exclaims at her "shining mass of hair" (7) she shoots him "a glance of Amazonian fierceness" that makes him feel "cheap and ill-used" (8). This is a definite reversal of the traditional concept of woman as object. Alexandra shows not only "resourcefulness and good judgment" (23), but she has intelligence to mix with it and these qualities encourage her father to pass the responsibility for the farm over to her rather than to her brothers.

Her identity is reflected most strongly in her connection to the land. Unlike her father, who saw the land as a resistant

As long as the source of quotations is obvious, not necessary to repeat source in citations

force, an "enigma . . . a horse that no one knows how to harness" (22), Alexandra sees the land as a vast opportunity: "For the first time, perhaps, since that land emerged from the waters of geologic ages, a human face was set toward it with love and yearning. It seemed beautiful to her, rich and strong, and glorious" (65). Yet the ability to take advantage of this opportunity requires not only strength and intelligence but creativity as well: "A pioneer should have imagination, should be able to enjoy the idea of things rather than the things themselves" (48). This ability to create makes Alexandra the active agent of her life. She does not base the quality of her life on the achievements and direction of a husband, or of her brothers. She takes the initiative to form her own wellspring of vitality that both feeds her and is nurtured by her.

Citation placed within sentence to indicate that ideas in first part of the sentence only belong to Rosowski

This creativity can also be seen as the resolution of Alexandra's second self, to use Rosowski's terms. By putting all her energies into developing the land, Alexandra is nurturing and fulfilling the "the otherworldly, imaginative" aspect of herself (Rosowski 263) and only when this has been

Welsh 12

achieved does she feel ready to turn to her relationship with
Carl.

This couple appears as a nearly inverted cultural
stereotype. Carl is "a thin, frail boy with brooding eyes,
very quiet in all his movements. There was a delicate pallor
in his thin face, and his mouth was too sensitive for a boy's"
(O Pioneers! 10). Alexandra, on the other hand, is tall,
strong, and brusque. Cather extends this inversion even
further in describing their perspectives: "The eyes of the
girl, . . . [looked] with such anguished perplexity into the
future; . . . [while] the sombre eyes of the boy . . . seemed
already to be looking into the past" (14). The sentimentalism
and passivity of "looking into the past" fit the
stereotypical image of a woman's preoccupation, while
Alexandra is the active, forward thinker of the two. When Carl
returns from the East, Alexandra again defies the expectations
of her gender by not handing the farm over to her brothers and
not accepting a passive role in her relationship with Carl.
She instead offers to share what she has with Carl, supporting
him through her own means: "Well, suppose I want to take care
of him? Whose business is it but my own?" (167). Ironically,
it is Carl's inability to accept Alexandra's offer that keeps
him from staying on. Pressured by the voices of society,
expressed by the Bergson brothers, Carl hasn't the strength to
defy convention as Alexandra does. He apologizes to her: "To
take what you would give me, I would have to be either a very
large man or a very small one, and I am only in the middle
class" (182).

This inverted love story is presented against the
background of the conventional and tragic story of Emil and
Marie. In Marie, Cather presents us with a more traditional

Welsh repeats title of novel to indicate that she is switching sources, from Rosowski to Cather. Context of paper makes it clear that Cather wrote O Pioneers!, *so most meaningful citation is to novel title and page*

female character faced with a traditional temptation. Before
their fateful meeting, both Marie and Emil experience an
epiphany about their love. Marie discovers that she can bear
living the pain as long as no one else is hurt. This is the
selfless woman of the nineteenth century, always taking on the
burdens of others; she becomes angelic through her sacrifices.
Emil resolves to love Marie chastely and maintain his honor
and goodness. He will ask nothing of her and leave without the
stain of sin. But the imagery Cather uses seems to be working
against the two lovers: "Everywhere the grain stood ripe and
the hot afternoon was full of the smell of the ripe wheat"
(257). The ripe grain, as a symbol of fertility, is the
all-pervasive force of nature, and overcomes the lovers'
resolutions. The result is the consummation of their love and
their violent death at the hands of Frank Shabata.

The contrast between this tragic subplot and the
harmonious joining of Carl and Alexandra is striking. While
Marie is self-sacrificing, Alexandra is openly generous and
giving but still acknowledges her need for Carl as himself.
Carl comes to the realization that he too, unlike Emil, will
accept Alexandra's offer of himself. They challenge the rules
of society yet Cather gives them happiness and success in
comparison with the tragedy of Marie and Emil. As Alexandra
states, "I think when friends marry they're safe" (308).

In the end Alexandra has fulfilled both the creative and
personal aspects of her self in ways that challenge social
convention. She is not an accessory to another's life; she is
the active agent of her own successful existence. And it is
not her value as an object, or ornament, that fulfills her
relationship with Carl, but rather her strength and vision in
combination with their mutual need for each other.

The character of Thea in <u>The Song of the Lark</u> evolves in an entirely different way than Alexandra does, and yet she shares many of Alexandra's characteristics. Her piano teacher compares her to "a thin glass full of sweet-smelling, sparkling Moselle wine" (38). The wellspring of life for Thea is not the Nebraska plains but her own inner power. Her story most closely parallels Cather's own realization of her creative power. Thea's struggle is to find the ultimate expression of her inner voice. To achieve this she passes through the hands of a series of mentors only to find that the key to unlocking her power lies ultimately within herself.

Each of the influential characters that interact with Thea during her childhood aid her in developing as a singer. Her mother furnishes her with her own attic room: "The acquisition of this room was the beginning of a new era in Thea's life . . . the clamour about her drowned the voice within herself," but here "She thought things out more clearly" (73). Dr. Archie, Ray Kennedy, and Spanish Johnny instill a sense of uniqueness in Thea. Through them she learns of and yearns for the world. They encourage her special abilities, and Dr. Archie in particular helps to shelter her from conventional expectations of girls by asserting that, because of her talent, she deserves better things. Each of her teachers as well presents her with tools and paths to fulfilling herself but each is painfully aware of his inability to bring her secret out into full bloom.

Early on she has a strong sense of her own inherent power, yet she doesn't see this as truly part of herself for some time: "She knew, of course, that there was something about her that was different. But it was more like a friendly spirit than like anything that was part of herself" (100). She never doubts her potential or her ability and is fully confident that she is equipped for whatever events shall arise: "She lacked nothing. She even felt more compact and confident than usual. She was all there, and something else was there, too-- . . . that warm sureness, that sturdy little companion with whom she shared a secret" (199).

Her first real grasp of her own power occurs during her visit to Panther Canyon. This portion of the novel is highly autobiographical and in her biography Sharon O'Brien parallels Thea's experience with the struggle of contradictory forces in Cather's own life. According to O'Brien Cather's perception of creativity for most of her youth was tied exclusively to male violence and virility, making it impossible to synthesize the feminine identity with the creative process (<u>Willa Cather</u> 171). This association of "sword/penis/pen/male/artist" shifts when Cather discovers the pottery left by the ancient Indians in the caves of the canyon. She begins to formulate a new conception of creativity based on the image of the vase that associates "vessel/womb/throat/voice/artist" (171) and therefore makes creativity a female process. Thea experiences this association in a very physical sense. In climbing the trails of Panther Canyon she begins to identify with the ancient women who used those same paths: "It seemed to Thea that . . . certain feelings were transmitted to her. . . . They were not expressible in words, but seemed rather to translate themselves into attitudes of body" (<u>Song of the Lark</u> 376). As she identifies with these ancient artisans she begins to make the connection between the pot that holds the precious but elusive water, and the body that holds the voice: "what was any art but an effort to make a sheath, a mould in which to imprison

Welsh 16

for a moment that shining, elusive element which is life itself" (378). It is at this point that Thea begins to realize that her power to create lies solely within herself; her own body is the wellspring of her voice. The belief that women can create by their own power and be self-sufficient contradicts the image of the nineteenth-century woman as passive and dependent. It challenges the belief that women's energies must be funneled through husband, child, or church to be valid.

Thea's discovery of her power is also linked to her flowering relationship to Fred Ottenburg. The dynamics of the two are similar to those of Alexandra and Carl. Although Fred is an extremely virile character, Thea's new-found strength surpasses his endurance in their walks. Her relationship to him is strengthened by her own sense of independence and self-sufficiency; as Thea sees it, "It's waking up every morning with the feeling that your life is your own; that you're all there and there's no sag in you" (394).

As Thea's career explodes she is drawn farther and farther into the professional world but as we meet her again with Dr. Archie and Fred she still has not achieved the final fulfilling expression of herself. She finds this ultimately in the end, when she sings the challenging role of Sieglinde. O'Brien suggests that the opera character herself provides the means for Thea's final fulfillment (Willa Cather 108). Sieglinde is separated at birth from her twin Siegmund and Cather uses their scene of reunion as lovers and siblings for Thea's performance. For Cather, the joining of the male and female sibling could signify the ultimate resolution of the male and female sides of her personality. For Thea, it means the final realization that the "sturdy little companion with whom she shares her secret" (Song of the Lark 199) is an inalienable

Welsh 17

aspect of herself: "That afternoon nothing new came to Thea Kronborg, no enlightenment, no inspiration. She merely came into full possession of things she had been refining and perfecting for so long" (571).

In My Antonia, the female protagonist is seen through the eyes of Jim Burden, an orphan sent out to his grandparents' farm in Nebraska after the death of his parents. In a sense, Antonia is Jim's creation, as reflected in the title and introduction of the book, which sets the story up as his memories of her. Not only does Jim give the male view of a female character, he also embodies society's own views and expectations at the same time. Susan Rosowski suggests that Jim is the embodiment of the creative self, while Antonia is the passive muse (265). Yet the vital element of the novel lies in Antonia's actions, which work against this structure. Throughout the book, Antonia challenges Jim's perceptions and expectations of her, refusing to be categorized or molded to fit into society's limitations.

Jim's impressions of Antonia when he first meets her are striking. She is darkly beautiful, foreign, mysterious. She is drawn and connected to the land from the beginning, sleeping in a hole dug into the wall of her family's sod house. Despite Jim's wishes that she conform to social standards she works as an equal with the men on the farms, developing strong arms and a sunburned face. She is strong-willed and opinionated and as soon as she is able to speak English she openly expresses her thoughts. This leads to Jim's first resentment of her as a superior, controlling figure. Despite the fact that she is four years older than he, Jim feels that he "was a boy and she was a girl and he resented her protecting manner" (My Antonia 43). This pattern continues in her protection and proud

Welsh summarizes aspects of the plot relevant to her main point; direct quotation kept to a minimum

Welsh 18

attitude toward him in the town. She actively tries to keep
Lena Lindgrad from him and tells him often that "you're not
going to sit around here and whittle store-boxes and tell
stories all your life. You are going away to school and make
something of yourself. I'm just awful proud of you" (224).
Jim's perception of Antonia carries overtones of Fryer's Great
Mother archetype, who continually tries to dominate men
through controlling them. Yet Antonia cannot be described as
striving for power over Jim. She protects him as a mother
might, nurturing his abilities and encouraging him, but she
does not see herself as superior to him. When he kills the
rattlesnake, as well as when he makes the graduation speech,
she openly expresses her admiration of his skills.

When Antonia comes to town to work as a housekeeper she
starts going to dances with the other hired girls, discovering
her emerging sexuality and independence. Jim and others
begin to accuse her of transgressing the boundaries of purity
and modesty so essential to the nineteenth-century definition
of women. Her sexuality definitely holds an allure for Jim,
a temptation to sneak out and attend the fireman's balls. Yet
she doesn't use it in a manipulative way. One gets the
distinct impression that she is simply enjoying herself. When
asked by Mrs. Harling what has come over her, she replies, "I
don't know . . . something has. . . . A girl like me has got to
take her good times when she can. Maybe there won't be any tent
next year" (208). She doesn't use her sexuality to tempt Jim,
either, and even reprimands him for kissing her with any sort
of passion. Her actions are not manipulative, or done for
effect; she is simply asserting her right to enjoy the few
years of leisure she may have.

While Jim is away at school she falls in love with Larry

Ellipses within quotation indicate material has been omitted

Donovan. Jim is angry and believes that she is lowering
herself by associating with a simple passenger conductor, "a
cheap sort of fellow" (304). His expectations of her marrying
a "respectable" man and raising a conventional family are
simply projections of society's values onto her. Antonia's
intentions are honest and open: "I thought if he saw how well
I could do for him, he'd want to stay with me" (313). She shows
independence, control, and pride in her own life when she
refuses to capitulate to society and hide away the child of the
man that deserted her. She continues her life with
characteristic strength and perseverance and pledges to raise
her child to have a better chance than she ever had.

Antonia's final situation fulfills each side of her life
on her own terms. She is no longer the passive inspiration of
Jim's work. She has become a creator in her own right, of her
children and her orchard. Jim wants her in a specific role,
defined in relation to men: "a sweetheart, a wife, or my mother
or sister--anything that a woman can be to a man" (321). But
she rejects being placed in any one of these categories,
creating her own definition of womanhood that stands
independent of any role defined by men. In the end she becomes
a combination of her greatest talents: a mother and friend to
her children, a ruler of her own household and orchard, an
equal companion to her husband, and a friend to Jim, "the
closest, the realest face, under all the shadows of women's
faces" (322).

In A Lost Lady, Cather presents us with a different type
of character. Marian Forrester is, as Susan Rosowski states,
"a wife, and as such, a woman defined in terms of society"
(268). Here the story does not revolve around a woman's
process of creating her identity, but rather around the

*Welsh signals
that she is
moving on to
discussion of
another novel
by giving the ti-
tle of the new
novel in the be-
ginning of the
sentence*

Welsh 20

effects of imposing an identity created by society onto a
woman. Marian is seen through the eyes of Neil, a young orphan
who is drawn to her and worships her as he is growing up. Neil
not only presents a male view of Marian but represents also the
viewpoint of conventional society.

Susan Rosowski presents a useful interpretation of Marian
Forrester. She argues that Marian is an object, the valued
possession of her husband (268). Capt. Forrester brought her
from California to complete his idyllic house. As his guests
drive up the lawn they are able to admire all his property: his
poplars, his wide meadows, his stream, and there on the porch,
his wife. She is the incarnation of the order, happiness, and
success of his own life. This is the role she must fulfill to
maintain her position. In Neil's eyes what is essential is not
only her value as a beautiful possession, but her ability to
transform the world around her to conform to Neil's idealized
and romantic illusion (Rosowski 269). He sees her as an
angelic figure: "Her skin had always the fragrant,
crystalline whiteness of white lilacs. . . . There could be no
negative encounter, however slight, with Mrs. Forrester. . . .
One became acutely conscious of her fragility and grace" (A
Lost Lady 31). She is an oasis of vitality and aesthetic beauty
in a world that threatens Neil's romantic ideals.

Yet just as Antonia challenges Jim's expectations, Marian
disillusions Neil. She maintains the facade of the
effervescent wife for some time at least, yet Cather shows us
flashes of the life she would prefer to live. She loves high
society, the dancing, and the parties. She yearns to have an
outlet for her explosive energy and tells Neil, "I feel such a
power to live in me" (125). As her husband becomes
increasingly ill their trips to Denver become impossible and,

Welsh 21

shut up in the house all winter, she begins to fade. Marian's
options are limited. As Jennifer Bailey states in her article
"The Dangers of Femininity in Willa Cather's Fiction," "The
only method by which Marian can assert her identity and refuse
to decline as a symbol of a passing age is to use her powerful
sexuality" (402). This is her sole means of power and in using
it she destroys the idealistic image Neil has of her and in
doing so she destroys his romantic view of the world.

The scene in which Neil overhears Marian and Frank
Ellinger in her bedroom is filled with images of burgeoning
sexuality: "thickets of wild roses, with flaming buds, just
beginning to open. . . . burning rose-color . . . made of
sunlight and morning and moisture, so intense that it cannot
possibly last . . . must fade, like ecstasy" (A Lost Lady 82).
Neil cuts these roses for Marian, symbolizing his own sexual
awakening. At this point the idealistic Marian is still
intact in his mind; his sexual awareness of her does not
necessarily endanger that ideal. Yet when he realizes that
she is with Frank in the bedroom, that she has asserted her own
sexuality, the ideal is shattered: "It was not a moral
scruple that she had outraged but an aesthetic ideal" (84).
This aesthetic ideal is the role set up by society that denies
women the power over their own sexuality. They are accepted as
sexual objects but not as sexual beings. As Barbara Welter
argues in her "Cult of True Womanhood," the only action
nineteenth-century women were to take with their sexuality was
to keep it hidden until the night when they handed it over to
their husbands (24). In presenting Marian in a situation where
her only way to assert her own identity is by exercising her
own sexual power, Cather exposes the dilemma of the
conventional role of wife.

Commas always placed inside quotation marks

Welsh 22

When her husband dies, Marian no longer makes any effort
to maintain the facade. She creates her own society in the
house by inviting young men over for dinner: "they call me the
Merry Widow--I rather like it" (A Lost Lady 158). She
exchanges her sexuality for Ivy Peters' protection in order to
survive. She leaves eventually for California, and our last
image of her is as the wife of a "rich, cranky old Englishman"
(174), but she is laughing and living the high life once again.
As Neil states, "she preferred life on any terms" (172),
meaning that she chose to use the power of her sexuality, the
one option that lets her live the life she desires. Cather
makes the cost of this choice quite apparent, for she is once
again the property of another man, attempting to measure up to
the expectations of a socially defined role.

Willa Cather grew up in a period dominated by the
literature of the male canon. She began to write
professionally just after the turn of the century, as ideas
were changing but old stereotypes still maintained their hold
on society. Yet she, among other writers such as Jewett and
Chopin, drew on her experience of these stereotypes and the
struggle she went through to resolve her perception of herself
with that projected onto her by society. Judith Fryer's
"American Eve" defines herself solely in relation to Adam,
whereas Cather's women define themselves through their
experience and their achievements. The idealized woman of the
"Cult of True Womanhood" finds her ultimate fulfillment in a
happy home and a happy husband, whereas Cather shows the
idealized domestic scene as dangerous and costly for a woman.
In challenging the social conventions Cather chips away at
their validity and authority. She opens a path toward a new
conception of women, creating a precedent for a long line of

strong female writers and characters to follow. Contemporary
feminist literary critics are part of this line and therefore
must maintain the tradition of challenging stereotypical
conventions of society through their work. Only by chipping
away at the validity of the male canon will it lose its
exclusive authority. "Re-vision" is the only means to bring
such writers as Cather into this canon to correct and balance
the expression of American experience.

Welsh 23

Works Cited

Bailey, Jennifer. "The Dangers of Femininity in Willa
    Cather's Fiction." Journal of American Studies 16
    (1982): 391-406.

Baym, Nina. "Melodramas of Beset Manhood: How Theories of
    American Literature Exclude Women Authors." American
    Quarterly 33 (1981): 123-139.

Cather, Willa. A Lost Lady. 1923. New York: Knopf, 1973.

---. My Antonia. Boston: Houghton, 1918.

---. O Pioneers! Boston: Houghton, 1913.

---. The Song of the Lark. 1915. Boston: Houghton, 1983.

Fryer, Judith. The Faces of Eve: Women in the Nineteenth-
    Century American Novel. Oxford: Oxford UP, 1976.

Lewis, R.W.B. The American Adam: Innocence, Tragedy, and
    Tradition in the Nineteenth Century. Chicago: U of
    Chicago P, 1955.

O'Brien, Sharon. "The Thing Not Named: Willa Cather as a
    Lesbian Writer." Signs 9 (Summer 1984): 576-599.

---. Willa Cather: The Emerging Voice. New York: Oxford UP,
    1987.

Rich, Adrienne. "When We Dead Awaken: Writing as Re-Vision."
    College English 34 (1972): 18-30.

Robinson, Phyllis C. Willa: The Life of Willa Cather. Garden
    City: New York: Doubleday, 1983.

Rosowski, Susan. "Willa Cather's Women." Studies in
    American Fiction 9 (Autumn 1981): 261-275.

Smith-Rosenberg, Carol. "The Female World of Love and Ritual:
    Relations between Women in Nineteenth-Century America."
    Signs 1.1 (1975): 1-29.

Welter, Barbara. Dimity Convictions: The American Woman in
    the Nineteenth Century. Athens: Ohio UP, 1976.

Works Cited always begins on new page. Heading centered 1 inch from top of page. All lines double-spaced.

Sample journal entry

Second and subsequent lines in entries indented 5 spaces

Two works by same author

Sample book entry

Both volume and issue numbers given

The Effectiveness of Lithium Carbonate

and Imipramine in the

Treatment of

Bipolar Affective Disorders

*Author's name
and informa-
tion about
course*

Sarah Jo Chaplen

Psychology 218

Professor Schoeneman

April 30, 1985

Chaplen 1

Abstract

I selected ten articles that analyzed the effects of lithium carbonate and imipramine on bipolar affective disorders (manic depression). Seven of the articles looked at lithium carbonate versus placebo treatment; the other three articles studied the effectiveness of imipramine in the treatment of bipolar affective disorders. The study was accomplished by comparing the results of four different patient treatments: lithium carbonate by itself; imipramine by itself; a combination of both lithium carbonate and imipramine; and a placebo treatment. The consensus in these articles was that lithium carbonate is an effective treatment for bipolar affective disorders, although it controls manic episodes better than depressive episodes. Imipramine, on the other hand, is effective in dealing with depression, but in patients prone to mania and in some women it increases the frequency of manic episodes. The combination of lithium carbonate and imipramine is less effective than lithium carbonate alone, and more people suffered side effects from it.

Abstract typed on separate page following title page; main points of paper summarized in one paragraph

Chaplen 2

Appropriate use of first person

In this paper I examine the effectiveness of certain drugs in treating bipolar affective disorders. To be considered truly effective, the drugs have to be able to control both the manic and the depressive episodes which occur in this disorder. Specifically, the three drug treatments examined are lithium carbonate, imipramine, and a combination of both.

Names of all authors of a work, followed by date, given the first time a work is cited. Citations to different works separated by semicolons. Works listed alphabetically according to last name of first author

In the first half of my paper I shall examine the seven articles comparing lithium carbonate and a placebo treatment (Dunner, Stallone, & Fieve, 1976; Fieve, Kumbaraci, & Dunner, 1976; Goodwin, Murphy, Dunner, & Bunney, 1972; Peselow, Dunner, Fieve, & Lautin, 1982; Prien, Caffey, & Klett, 1973; Prien, Caffey, & Klett, 1974; Stallone, Shelley, Mendlewicz, & Fieve, 1973). In the following half, I evaluate three articles on imipramine's effectiveness in comparison with lithium carbonate and in combination with it (Prien, Klett, & Caffey, 1973; Prien et al., 1984; Quitkin, Kane, Rifkin, Ramos-Lorenzi, & Nayak, 1981).

Within these articles the working definition of bipolar affective disorders varies. It ranges from the definition of the bipolar affective disorders as one or more manic episodes with or without depression, which is the one used by Prien et al. (1974), to the division of the bipolar affective disorder into three categories: bipolar I, bipolar II, and bipolar

After a work by 3 or more authors cited once, subsequent citations use name of first author followed by et al. and date

other (Peselow et al., 1982). Patients with bipolar I are those patients whose mania is severe enough to have warranted hospitalization. Bipolar II patients, on the other hand, suffer from hypomania (a mild form of mania) and have been hospitalized for depression. Bipolar other, or cyclothymic, patients are those who have had episodes of both depression and hypomania, but never severe enough to warrant being hospitalized. One other division which is worth mentioning is

Chaplen 3

that of Rapid Cycling, which is defined as four or more
affective episodes per year (Dunner et al., 1976).

   To select patients for their studies, the authors of these
articles used two main diagnostic instruments to classify the
bipolar affective disorder. In three of the lithium carbonate
and placebo experiments the criteria used were the Research
Diagnostic Criteria for use in psychiatric research developed
by Feigher and his associates (Dunner et al., 1976; Fieve et
al., 1976; Peselow et al., 1982). Similarly, two of the
combination drug studies as well as one of the lithium studies
utilized Spitzer's Research Diagnostic Criteria for a
selected group of Functional Disorders (Peselow et al., 1982;
Prien et al., 1984; Quitkin et al., 1981). The other studies
followed the hospital's or clinic's classifications and thus
did not carry out as thorough checks as the others.

   In this paper I will be carefully examining the methods of
treatment, the subjects, and the definitions of failure used
in these studies; I will be paying special attention to the
controls set up by the experimenters. In addition, I will be
comparing and contrasting not only the effectiveness of the
drugs during the manic and depressive episodes but also within
the different divisions of bipolar affective disorders. To
conclude, I will discuss several factors which affect the
results: for example, the dropout rate of subjects and what
implications the results have for treatment.

Effectiveness of Lithium in Bipolar Affective Disorder

   To begin with, studies were carried out on the
effectiveness of lithium in both manic and depressive
episodes. Several studies in the 1960s suggested that lithium

A series of citations listed alphabetically according to last name of first author; citations separated by semicolons

Form for first-level headings

was an effective antimanic agent. However, trying to prove it
was effective in the treatment of depressive episodes was more
difficult, as was clearly shown by Stallone et al. (1973).
First, their sample of 52 patients had histories of severe
mania. Moreover, they had a large dropout rate in the study:
31 out of the 52. Of the patients who dropped out, 22 were in
the placebo group, which had an adverse effect on the validity

*Brackets indi-
cate words have
been added or
changed in
quoted material*

of the control group. Furthermore, "18 of [the dropouts] were
directly attributable to the disruptive effects of an acute
episode, usually manic" (Stallone et al., 1973, p. 1009).
This meant that, with no effective control group, it was
difficult to evaluate lithium's prophylactic effect on
depression. The experimenters failed to find a statistically
significant difference in the severity of depression suffered
by the lithium-treated group and the placebo group, which
could be attributed to the sample bias produced by the high
dropout rate. Prien, Caffey, and Klett's study (1973) also
ran into difficulties because their sample of 205 patients did
not have many "depressive relapses"; the experimenters found

*Ellipses indicate
words omitted
in quoted
material*

that "lithium carbonate [patients] . . . had a lower incidence
of depressive relapses than placebo patients but the
difference was not statistically significant" (p. 340).

   Dunner et al. (1976) decided to deal with the bias
introduced by the bipolar patients suffering from acute
mania--that is, patients who suffered from hypomanic episodes
(a milder manic state) and had been hospitalized for
depression. They found no reduction in the frequency of
depressive attacks in the patients receiving lithium
carbonate. Surprisingly enough they discovered that "the
mean number of episodes of depression per patient year was
slightly greater for the lithium carbonate group as compared

Chaplen 5

with the placebo patients" (Dunner et al., 1976, p. 119).
However, the experimenters did find that the severity of the
depressive episodes was lessened if the patients were
receiving lithium. This was fully demonstrated by the fact
that fewer of them were actually hospitalized for depression.
As an explanation for their results Dunner et al. (1976)
suggested that "prophylaxis of mania and hypomania may be
demonstrated prior to prophylaxis of depression" (p. 120). In
fact, later on in a letter in the Archives of Psychiatry they
wrote that there had been a mistake in the computer program
they had utilized and, on recalculation of the data, lithium's
prophylaxis of depression was proved statistically
significant, especially after the extra months the patients
had been studied (Dunner, Stallone, & Fieve, 1982). The
question of lithium's effectiveness still had to be studied
further and that is what the following studies attempted to do.

When material is quoted, page number included in citation

When no words quoted, citation is made to work as a whole

Treatment Administration

Most of the follow-up lithium studies used the same
general research design with only a few variations. In the
first phase the studies fell into two camps: those that
incorporated a stabilizing period utilizing lithium (Dunner
et al., 1976; Peselow et al., 1982; Prien, Caffey, & Klett,
1973; Prien et al., 1974); and those that did not (Fieve et al.,
1976; Goodwin et al., 1972; Stallone et al., 1973). Those
studies which used a stabilizing period stabilized patients in
one of two ways. One way was to stabilize the patients with
maintenance doses of lithium carbonate following remission of
the manic episode and prior to their discharge from the
hospital. This would mean that the patients would be free of

Chaplen 6

When authors
given in text,
only date is
put in paren-
theses (directly
after authors'
names) When
authors and
date already
provided, quo-
tations fol-
lowed by page
number only

manic episodes when they were released. The other method,
used by Peselow et al. (1982), was to define the patients'
"starting point . . . of prophylaxis" as a month after the
patient had reached a point of stability (p. 748). After this
stabilizing period, the tests began. The patients came in
every four weeks to have their serum lithium levels monitored.
Consequently, the physician could ascertain if the patient
had been taking his/her medicine regularly and whether the
dosage needed to be lowered or raised. The clinical raters,
usually the nurses, rated the patients on a number of scales
and tests in order to check the severity of their depression
and mania. The most common tests they used were the Hamilton
Depression Rating Scale, or a modified version of it; the
Global Affective Scale, an interview for evaluating
symptoms and functional impairment; and the Self-Report Mood
Scale.

*Form for
second-level
headings. These
headings indi-
cate how
Chaplen has
broken down
her analysis of
these 10 articles*

Subjects

Some of the factors which influenced the choice of
subjects have already been discussed. The experimenters
interested in studying the effectiveness of lithium on
depression chose bipolar II subjects (Dunner et al., 1976;
Peselow et al., 1982). Two of the studies compared both
bipolar I and bipolar II patients (Fieve et al., 1976; Goodwin
et al., 1972). Likewise, Dunner et al. (1976) wanted to find
out specifically if there was a "relationship between lithium
carbonate prophylaxis and frequency of affective episodes
prior to the double-blind trial" so they picked a sample which
contained "rapid cyclers" who would have had four or more
affective episodes in the previous year (p. 117).

Chaplen 7

Definition of Failure

The definition of what constituted a failure in the
treatment also depended on what the experimenters were looking
for. If they were looking at the effectiveness of lithium on
depression, then failure would be classified as a failure to
remain free of depression (Peselow et al., 1982; Quitkin et
al., 1981). In the other studies either an episode of mania or
depression was regarded as a failure, especially if extra
medication had to be given or hospitalization occurred.

Controls

The issue of controls is very important in studies like
these where the full potential of the drugs being tested is not
known. It is essential that there be adequate controls to
prevent biasing of the results and thus expensive replication
of the studies. All the studies randomly assigned patients to   *Text of paper*
the separate categories being tested. Despite that, not all   *double-spaced*
the people who came into contact with the patients were blind
as to whether the patient was receiving lithium or a placebo.
The fact that the physician who gave the medication to the
patients knew what the patients were taking could have had a
biasing effect on the whole study (Prien et al., 1974). Prien,
Caffey, and Klett (1973) controlled for this possible
physician bias by using additional methods and people in
making the decisions as to whether to hospitalize the patients
or not. Tests made on the patients were filled out by nurses,
social workers, and the patients themselves. The test results
showed that the committed patient was indeed ill and not
committed as a result of physician bias (p. 340).   *Bottom margin*
                                                                   1 inch

Chaplen 8

Another effective control which was used in three of the
seven lithium and placebo studies and one of the three lithium
and imipramine studies was to have the subjects diagnosed
separately by two psychiatrists before the subjects could be
admitted to the study (Fieve et al., 1976; Peselow et al.,
1982; Prien et al., 1984; Stallone et al., 1973). Goodwin et
al.(1972) took the issue of controls one step further by using
both treatments on the same patient, first of all withdrawing
the lithium hoping to see a relapse, and then administering it
and hoping to see an improvement.

Results

Effectiveness of Lithium Treatment

*Main point of
this section
summarized in
first sentence*

The results on the effectiveness of lithium carbonate as a
treatment for bipolar affective disorder depended on the
severity and type of the disorder. The initial category of
manic depressive was found to be too encompassing. Stallone
et al. (1973) discovered that their criteria for labeling a
subject manic depressive were too broad, due to the fact that
there were several possible subgroupings reacting differently
to the lithium. They found that lithium was effective in
treating mania and that those who responded best to its
treatment were those who had a family history of mania. Prien
et al. (1974) came to similar conclusions; they demonstrated
that those patients being treated with lithium were less
likely to have severe relapses. Their research also suggested
that patients who have failed with lithium once responded only
slightly better than the placebo group for the rest of the
treatment. In neither Prien et al.'s 1974 study nor in

Chaplen 9

Stallone et al.'s 1973 study were the data on lithium's effectiveness with depression significant.

As for the results of the other studies, the studies of bipolar II patients show they can be effectively treated with lithium: the duration of the depression is shorter and the severity of it is lessened (Dunner et al., 1976; Fieve et al., 1976; Peselow et al., 1982). However, the cyclothymic or bipolar other patients did not respond as well as the bipolar II patients did, although some improvement could be seen (Peselow et al., 1982). Lithium prophylaxis also occurred in bipolar I patients (Fieve et al., 1976). But the situation was different for the "rapid cyclers," who evinced a very poor prophylactic response to lithium (Dunner et al., 1976).

Effectiveness of Imipramine and Its Combination with Lithium

The three "combination" studies I looked at used several different combinations of treatments, but they followed the same experimental format as the lithium studies did: the check-ups, the controls, and the standards for failure were the same. Prien, Klett, and Caffey's 1973 study divided bipolar patients into lithium, imipramine, and placebo groups. For the bipolar patients the lithium treatment was more effective than the imipramine and placebo. Those who took imipramine had a "relatively high incidence of manic episodes" (p. 423). In the previous lithium experiments I have reviewed lithium has been shown to be more effective than placebo. Quitkin et al. (1981) looked at treatment for bipolar I patients. Their subjects were divided into patients treated with lithium plus imipramine hydrochlorine, and lithium plus placebo. The results suggested that some women

Chaplen 10

and mania-prone patients would be likely to suffer a manic
relapse if treated with imipramine (p. 906). The lithium
treatment was as successful as it had been in the Prien studies
(Prien, Caffey, & Klett, 1973; Prien et al., 1974; Prien et
al., 1984; Prien, Klett, & Caffey, 1973).

In their 1984 study, Prien and his associates placed
bipolar patients into three treatment categories: lithium,
imipramine, and a combination of both. Again, this study
reached the same conclusion: lithium was more effective than
imipramine in protecting against manic recurrences. Although
earlier work in this area had suggested that imipramine was
more effective in dealing with depression, Prien and his
associates (1984) argued that lithium was just as effective as
imipramine when it came to dealing with depression and that
even when the two were combined they were no more effective
than lithium was by itself. Although this was the argument
they made, they also said that lithium was "more effective
with patients whose last episode was manic than with patients
whose last episode was depressive" (Prien et al., 1984, p.
1102).

Short quotations placed in quotation marks. Period after parenthetical citation

Discussion

A reading of all 10 articles raises three issues about
lithium carbonate and experimentation examining its
effectiveness: experimental design, ethics, and problems with
lithium usage.

Problems have arisen with the validity of the basic
experimental design utilized by the experimenters. First, the
majority of the subjects used were patients who had been
hospitalized due to the severity of their bipolar affective

Chaplen 11

disorders: subjects have been placed in the hospital because
they cannot deal with life outside. The question arises, how
applicable is the information gained about lithium and
imipramine to a much milder bipolar disorder? It is possible
that lithium would be effective with the milder disorders even
if it does not work with severe bipolar disorders.

*Chaplen
critiques the
research she's
described*

    The second problem faced in the experimental design is
deciding when to start administration of the lithium. It is
believed by many experimenters that bipolar affective
disorders come in cycles. So if an experimenter is faced with
a relapse at the beginning of the experiment, is the patient
merely suffering from the last stages of the episode for which
he/she was hospitalized, or is he/she beginning a new cycle
(Prien, Caffey, & Klett, 1973, p. 340)? How long a period does
an experimenter have to wait before he/she can guarantee the
patient is beginning a new episode? This issue really raises
the question as to what degree the results in the studies were
actually beyond the control of the experimenters.

*In rare cases,
when reference
is made to a
specific point in
a source, page
number in-
cluded in cita-
tion*

    The last problem with the study of lithium carbonate and
its effectiveness is that sufficient control groups are often
hard to maintain. There was a large dropout rate in the
placebo group. The untreated subjects dropped out of the
study during severe manic or depressive episodes which, since
the experimenters were studying acute cases of bipolar
affective disorders, occurred frequently. By dropping out of
the experiment the placebo subjects biased the results.
However, dropout was also a problem amongst the lithium
subjects: some of them had bad side effects from the lithium
and imipramine, and others, feeling cured, did not want to
continue taking drugs.

    In addition to the experimental design problems I feel

Chaplen 12

there was an ethical problem. Since lithium seems to be an
effective treatment, how ethical is it to continue to have
placebo groups in attempts to define the precise lithium
dosage? How ethical is it to let someone suffer a severe manic
or depressive episode when it is known that lithium works,
especially when two of the placebo patients in the experiments
committed suicide (Prien, Caffey, & Klett, 1973; Prien,
Klett, & Caffey, 1973)?

Since lithium is an effective treatment, its usage raises
several problems. The treatment is expensive due to the
regular blood checks needed to prevent lithium blood
poisoning. A patient has to be conscientious about taking the
prescribed amount of lithium at the right time since it is
essential for its effectiveness; however, manic depressives
are not reliable when they are in the middle of an episode.
Furthermore, side effects in the use of lithium and imipramine
are both prevalent and acute; Prien and his associates (1984)
noted that side effects "were reported by 94% of patients
receiving combination treatment, 81% of the patients treated
with imipramine" (p. 1100).

But despite all lithium's drawbacks I would treat bipolar
affective disorders with it. It might not be as effective with
depressive episodes as it is with manic; nevertheless it does
not precipitate mania to the degree that imipramine does. I
feel lithium is a valuable treatment but there should be no
Chaplen's sug- more placebo experiments. In the future what needs to be
gestions for
future research concentrated on is refining dosage techniques and working to
see if lithium carbonate can deal more effectively with the
depressive episodes as well as decreasing its side effects.

Chaplen 13

References

Dunner D.L.,Stallone,F., & Fieve, R.R. (1976). Lithium carbonate and affective disorders V: A double-blind study of prophylaxis of depression in bipolar illness. <u>Archives of General Psychiatry</u>, <u>33</u>, 117-120.

Dunner, D.L., Stallone, F., & Fieve, R.R. (1982). Prophylaxis with lithium carbonate: An update [letter to editor]. <u>Archives of General Psychiatry</u>, <u>39</u>, 1344-1345.

Fieve, R.R., Kumbaraci, T., & Dunner, D.L. (1976). Lithium prophylaxis of depression in bipolar I, bipolar II, and unipolar patients. <u>American Journal of Psychiatry</u>, <u>133</u>, 925-929.

Goodwin, F.K., Murphy, D.L., Dunner, D.L., & Bunney, W.E. (1972). Lithium response in unipolar versus bipolar depression. <u>American Journal of Psychiatry</u>, <u>129</u>, 76-79.

Peselow, E.D., Dunner, D.L., Fieve, R.R., & Lautin, A. (1982). Lithium prophylaxis of depression in unipolar, bipolar II and cyclothymic patients. <u>American Journal of Psychiatry</u>, <u>139</u>, 747-752.

Prien, R.F., Caffey, E.M., & Klett, C.J. (1973). Prophylactic efficacy of lithium carbonate in manic-depressive illness: Report of the Veterans Administration and National Institute of Mental Health Collaborative Study Group. <u>Archives of General Psychiatry</u>, <u>28</u>, 337-341.

Prien, R.F.,Caffey, E.M., & Klett, C.J. (1974). Factors associated with treatment success in lithium carbonate prophylaxis: Report of the Veterans Administration and National Institute of Mental Health Collaborative Study Group. <u>Archives of General Psychiatry</u>, <u>31</u>, 189-192.

Prien, R.F., Klett, C.J., & Caffey, E.M. (1973). Lithium carbonate and imipramine in prevention of affective episodes: A comparison in recurrent affective illness. <u>Archives of General Psychiatry</u>, <u>29</u>, 420-425.

Reference list starts on new page; center heading

Works by same authors ordered by date from older to more recent

Works listed alphabetically by (1) name of first author, (2) name of subsequent authors in order in which they were given on title page of source

Chaplen 14

Sample journal
entries

Prien, R.F., Kupfer, D.J., Mansky, P.A., Small, J.G., Tuason,
    V.B., Voss, C.B., & Johnson, W.E. (1984). Drug therapy
    in the prevention of recurrences in unipolar and bipolar
    affective disorders: Report of the NIMH Collaborative
    Study Group comparing lithium carbonate, imipramine, and a
    lithium carbonate-imipramine combination. Archives of
    General Psychiatry, 41, 1096-1104.

Quitkin, F.M., Kane, J., Rifkin, A., Ramos-Lorenzi, J.R., &
    Nayak, D.V. (1981). Prophylactic lithium carbonate with
    and without imipramine for bipolar I patients: A double-
    blind study. Archives of General Psychiatry, 38, 902-907.

Stallone, F., Shelley, E., Medlewicz, J., & Fieve, R.R.
    (1973). The use of lithium in affective disorders, III:
    A double-blind study of prophylaxis in bipolar illness.
    American Journal of Psychiatry, 130, 1006-1010.

Second and
subsequent
lines in entries
indented 3
spaces

The Study of Fossil Flowers

by

Karen McCracken

Biology 241

Plant Systematics

Dr. Steven Seavey

Spring, 1984

Title centered between margins, ⅓ of the way down page; information about author and course given in an aesthetically pleasing manner

Abstract

The discovery of the earliest fossil angiosperm will be able to tell paleobotanists much about the evolution of flowers. The earliest accepted traces of angiosperms tell us that they existed about 120 million years ago. As paleobotanists pursue their search for fossil flowers, they encounter technical difficulties as well as difficulties with the current Linnean system of classification.

Running heads with author's name and page number ½ inch from top of page

Abstract typed on separate page following title page; main points of paper summarized in one paragraph

McCracken 2

For hundreds of years, scientists have been fascinated with the seemingly sudden rise and diversification of angiosperms, or flowering plants, during the late Mesozoic era. So far the earliest accepted traces of flowering plants have been found about 120 million years ago in the Lower Cretaceous period of the geologic time scale (see Appendix). Before this time, it was the gymnosperms--plants that have no true flowers, such as pines--that were abundant, but in increasing numbers and complexity fossil angiosperms can be found in later Cretaceous rocks. Most of the early angiosperm record consists of pollen, seeds, fruits, and leaf parts of the angiosperm. Fossil flowers are not as common because the delicate structures were less likely to be preserved. Still, paleobotanists continue to search for the most ancient flower. This paper will look at the importance of studying fossil flowers, what has been found, and what difficulties have been encountered while studying fossil flowers.

Fossil flowers can reveal extremely important information about the time, place, and biological origin of angiosperms. Also, fossil flowers are of particular interest to paleobotanists since modern-day classification of angiosperms is based primarily on floral morphology; seeds, pollen, and leaf morphology are of only secondary importance. With what we learn from each newly discovered fossil flower we can test the many hypotheses about primitive flowers that are made based on living angiosperms.

Paleobotanists ultimately want to reveal the origin of the angiosperm, but there are several questions surrounding this general search for the origin of flowering plants. First of all, paleobotanists wish to know where and when angiosperms arose (Hughes 1976b). This can be answered by where flowers

Body of paper begins 1 inch from top of page.

Reference to an appendix that will be found on a separate sheet following the body of the paper

Bottom margin 1 inch

are found in geologic strata and what other types of fossils
are found with them. Also of significance to scientists is
finding the family to which the primitive flower belongs, or,
in other words, which family of modern-day angiosperms is the
most primitive; recent literature indicates that this is the

A series of works cited in alphabetical order according to last name of first author; semicolons separate works

most immediate question to be resolved (Basinger and Dilcher
1984; Dilcher et al. 1976; Friis and Skarby 1982; Hughes 1976b;
Tiffney 1977). In 1915, Charles Bessey suggested that the most
ancient flower resembled flowers like the magnolias that are
large, bisexual, and insect pollinated, but others thought
that the first angiosperms were small, unisexual, and wind-
pollinated (Dilcher and Crane 1984). Although most botanists
side with Bessey, this debate has yet to be resolved by what can
be found in fossil flowers (Dilcher and Crane 1984). One
question that is raised by this argument is whether the most
primitive flowers were pollinated by insects or wind. Since
gymnosperms are primarily pollinated by wind and 85% of
angiosperms are pollinated by insects, the answer could reveal
information about the genetic lines along which angiosperms
originated. Whether the first angiosperms were wind or insect
pollinated can be answered by the morphology of fossil
flowers. Another question pertaining to the evolution of
angiosperms that could be resolved by further evidence is
whether the flowering plants arose monophyletically or

Author and date given in parenthetical citation

otherwise (Beck 1976). Finally, botanists are confronted with
the difficulty of finding fossils to confirm their own
speculations about the origin of angiosperms (Dilcher et al.
1976). To answer these many questions paleobotanists continue
their search for the most primitive fossil flower.

In view of the fact that few fossil flowers have been found
as yet, the ultimate goal to find enough evidence to explain

McCracken 4

the evolution of angiosperms seems unattainable. The most
major fossil finds have been made in the past decade. Three
various flower types are represented by mid-Cretaceous fossil
flowers. The fossils have been dated as far back as Cenomanian
age. Pollen and leaf fossils are the only evidence that
angiosperms existed before this time. This evidence will be
briefly discussed later. The diversity of the early fossil
flowers appearing in the same age indicates that divergence
occurred early in the history of angiosperms.

The most complete fossil flower was found in Nebraska in
the locality of Rose Creek (Basinger and Dilcher 1984; Dilcher
and Crane 1984). This flower is symmetrical with five sepals
and five petals. The sepals are joined at the base and form
a stiff shallow cup. The showy petals are about half an inch
long and spread out, alternating with the sepals. There are
also five stamens and five carpels. The stamens have stout
filaments and massive anthers which spread out, lying against
the petals. The pollen grains found with these fossil
flowers are extremely small (8 to 12 microns in diameter) with
three sculpturing furrows. Between the base of the stamens
and carpels is a ring of swollen tissue that is believed to have
produced nectar, indicating insect pollination. These
fossil flowers are most closely related to three living orders
of angiosperms--Saxifragales (Rosidae), Rosales (Rosidae),
and Rhamnales (Rosidae). Although similar to these orders,
the fossil flower could not be placed in any one of these orders
since none have the same floral features.

Another fossil flower, most like flowers of the order
Magnoliales, has been found in Kansas and is of similar age to
the previously described fossil flower (Dilcher and Crane
1984). This is a large, solitary flower borne at the end of a

*Text of paper
double-spaced*

leafy shoot. The diameter of the flower is five to six inches
with three outer sepals and six to nine petals. The fossil
shows scars where the stamens were once attached. There are
believed to be 150 carpels which each contain about 100 ovules,
but only 20 to 40 developed into seeds. Botanists believe that
this flower was insect pollinated because it was large and
radially symmetrical. The leaf structure suggests that this
fossil flower belongs to an extinct species because the leaf
resembles no leaf of any living angiosperm.

The third fossil flower is most widespread (Dilcher and
Crane 1984). Many small, apparently unisexual flowers make up
a spheroidal head about one-quarter of an inch in diameter.
About thirty-six heads are arranged in regular intervals on a
long axis. If there are any sepals or petals, they are too
small to be seen in the fossil. The flowers have anywhere from
four to seven carpels. Most fossils show no sign of stamens;
however, similar flowers found in the USSR appear to have
produced pollen. The morphology suggests wind pollination.
This fossil flower is most similar to the genus _Platanus_ or
the sycamores.

Fossils of secondary structures such as stems and leaves
are more abundant than the flower parts since they are more
easily preserved in the geologic strata. The earliest
evidence indicating that angiosperms existed before
Cenomanian time are miospore fossils, which are found in
Berriasian and Valanginian ages (Hughes 1976b). These are
fossils of spores or pollen of unknown function. These
miospore fossils provide no conclusive evidence of the
existence of angiosperms at the time. A small fruit, _Onoana_
californica, found in marine strata of Barremian age, is one of
the most important discoveries to paleobotanists (Hughes

When letter added after date in reference list, that letter always used in citations in text

McCracken 6

1976b). The genus was newly formed and placed in the family
Icacinaceae. This family is not regarded as primitive but
fossils of this family have been found in Eocene deposits. A
smaller species, O. nicanica, has also been found in Aptian age
strata in the USSR (Hughes 1976b). Fossil leaves and woody
structures have been found with increasing abundance in later
geological periods.

Paleobotanists confront several difficulties in their
search for the earliest angiosperms. One of the major
problems in solving the angiosperm mystery through fossil
flowers is the scarcity of the fossils themselves. The more
abundant, widely disseminated and robust the plant part, the
more likely it is to be preserved (Dilcher and Crane 1984).
Because the cutin-covered surfaces of the secondary
structures (stems, leaves, seeds, and the walls of the spores
and pollen grain) are designed to keep water out, these parts
are more easily preserved than the reproductive parts of the
flower. Consequently the majority of the fossil information
is found in the secondary structures, which reveal little
information (Hughes 1976b). Fossils of early Cretaceous show
only single organs or fragments and the numbers increase
steadily until whole plants can be found in Turonian age
(Hughes 1976a). Aside from the difficulty in preservation,
another explanation for the lack of fossil flowers may be the
location of origin of the first angiosperm. If flowers first
originated in upland areas where there are no soil deposits, as
opposed to aggradational areas such as deltas, then the
preservation of flowers would be very rare.

Some general problems of data handling must be resolved
before many of the questions about angiosperm origin can be
answered. Most of the work with fossil flowers goes directly

McCracken 7

into comparative morphology of living angiosperms (Basinger
and Dilcher 1984; Cronquist 1968; Dilcher et al. 1976; Hughes
1976b). Although this is an important aspect in the study of
fossil flowers, the tendency is often to overlook evolutionary
elements. The scientific belief that the "present is the key
to the past" allows botanists to assume many things about
primitive flowers and their evolution. This belief can lead
to many obstacles when parallels between extinct and living
species of angiosperms are drawn too closely (Hughes 1976a).
The current system for handling fossil data is the Linnean

When author's
name given
in text, only
date put in
parentheses

system, which is the classification system used for modern-day
flowering plants. Norman Hughes (1976b) suggests that this
system is inadequate for paleontological material. He
believes that a system needs to be designed where fossils can
be conveniently analyzed and compared. Otherwise, as the
system is now, retrieval is too difficult. Hughes' proposed
paleontological system would provide time-correlation,
geographic limits of the rock from which the specimen is taken,
and the nomenclature for the specimen. This system could be
helpful in comparison of fossils and would allow for easy data
retrieval. Placing fossil flowers in the Linnean system
forces botanists to find the family to which the fossil
belongs. Often a fossil cannot be affiliated to one family
because it is a representative of an extinct family. Another
problem that hinders the study of fossil flowers is
categorizing the actual structure of the flower as primitive
or advanced. First of all, there may be differing views on
what is primitive (Beck 1976). As mentioned earlier, most
botanists believe a magnolia-type flower is most primitive but
some also believe that a much smaller, unisexual flower is more
primitive. For the most part, however, the analysis of a

McCracken 8

fossil flower as primitive or advanced has been helpful in separating fossil flowers from extant flowers (Hughes 1976b).

The fossil flowers have been useful in confirming most morphologists' belief of what is a primitive angiosperm (Dilcher et al. 1976), but still there are some questions. Both insect and wind pollination existed in the earliest fossil flowers, as seen earlier in the description of the fossils. Further evidence of earlier ages needs to be found to confirm which form of pollination is most primitive. Fossils of later years can reveal much about the coevolution of insects and flowers which brings up another interesting area of study in fossil flowers (Crepet 1984). Paleobotanists have been able to determine that angiosperms first occurred at low latitudes in tropical areas. But the most important question about the time of origin still remains unanswered, although evolution must have taken place before mid-Cretaceous as suggested by the diversity in the fossils found in Cenomanian age and other fossil finds before that age (Crepet 1984; Cronquist 1968; Dilcher et al. 1976; Hughes 1976a). Finally, as far as the biological origin of angiosperms is concerned, there is still much speculation. Perhaps angiosperms have arisen from an undiscovered extinct seed plant, or from gymnosperms, but little evidence supports these hypotheses. Further study of the morphology of fossil flowers can reveal more supporting evidence for these speculations and new information for other hypotheses. By continued concentration on the fossil record, in particular fossil flowers, the mystery of the origin and evolution of angiosperms can ultimately be resolved.

Works by 3 or more authors cited by using last name of first author followed by et al. and date

Appendix

Table showing sequence of ages of the Cretaceous period
(Hughes 1976b, fig. 7.1).

Appendix con-
tains informa-
tion helpful to
the reader but
not central to
the develop-
ment of the
argument of the
paper; typed on
a separate sheet
following the
body of the
paper

Era	Period	Age	Million years
Mesozoic	Cretaceous	Maestrichtian	65 ± 2
		Campanian	
		Santonian	
		Coniacian	
		Turonian	
		Cenomanian	(100)
		Albian	
		Aptian	
		Barremian	
		Hauterivian	
		Valanginian	
		Berriasian	135 ± 5

McCracken 10

References

Basinger, J.F., and D.L. Dilcher. 1984. Ancient bisexual
flowers. <u>Science</u> 224:511-13.

Beck, C.B. 1976. Origin and early evolution of angiosperms:
A perspective. In <u>Origin and early evolution in
angiosperms</u>, ed. C.B. Beck, 1-10. New York: Columbia
University Press.

Crepet, W.L. 1984. Ancient flowers for the faithful.
<u>Natural History</u>, April, 39-44.

Cronquist, A. 1968. <u>The evolution and classification of
flowering plants</u>. Riverside Studies in Biology.
Boston: Houghton Mifflin Company.

Dilcher, D.L., and P.R. Crane. 1984. In pursuit of the first-
flower. <u>Natural History</u>, March, 57-60.

Dilcher, D.L., W.L. Crepet, C.D. Beeker, and H.C. Reynolds.
1976. Reproductive and vegetative morphology of a
Cretaceous angiosperm. <u>Science</u> 191:854-6.

Friis, E.M., and A. Skarby. 1982. <u>Scandianthus</u> gen. nov.,
angiosperm flowers of saxifragalean affinity from the
Upper Cretaceous of southern Sweden. <u>Annals of Botany</u>
50:569-583.

Hughes, N.F. 1976a. Cretaceous paleobotanic problems. In
<u>Origin and early evolution of angiosperms</u>, ed. C.B. Beck,
11-22. New York: Columbia University Press.

---. 1976b. <u>Palaeobiology of angiosperm origins: Problems of
Mesozoic seed-plant evolution</u>. Cambridge Earth Science
Series. London: Cambridge University Press.

Tiffney, B.H. 1977. Dicotyledonous angiosperm flower
from the Upper Cretaceous of Martha's Vineyard,
Massachusetts. <u>Nature</u> 265:136-7.

*Reference list
starts on new
page; center
heading*

*Sample work in
a collection*

*Sample maga-
zine article*

*Listing of 2
works by same
author pub-
lished in same
year*

*Sample journal
article*

Index